OTHER BOOKS BY JOHN SCARNE

SCARNE'S NEW COMPLETE GUIDE TO GAMBLING
SCARNE'S ENCYCLOPEDIA OF GAMES
SCARNEY DICE—40 NEW KINDS OF DICE GAMES
THE WOMAN'S GUIDE TO GAMBLING
THE ODDS AGAINST ME
SCARNEY—25 NEW KINDS OF SKILL GAMES
THE AMAZING WORLD OF JOHN SCARNE
SKARNEY—30 NEW CARD GAMES
SCARNE ON TEEKO
SCARNE ON MAGIC TRICKS
SCARNE ON CARD TRICKS
SCARNE ON CARDS
SCARNE ON DICE

SCARNE'S
CASINO

GUIDE TO GAMBLING

by JOHN SCARNE

SIMON AND SCHUSTER • NEW YORK

Some of the material in *Scarne's Guide to Casino Gambling* is taken from *Scarne's New Complete Guide to Gambling,* Copyright © 1961, 1974 by John Scarne

DESIGNED BY EVE METZ
MANUFACTURED IN THE UNITED STATES OF AMERICA

1 2 3 4 5 6 7 8 9 10

LIBRARY OF CONGRESS CATALOGING IN PUBLICATION DATA

SCARNE, JOHN.
  SCARNE'S GUIDE TO CASINO GAMBLING.

  INCLUDES INDEX.
  1. GAMBLING. 2. PROBABILITIES. I. TITLE.
II. TITLE: GUIDE TO CASINO GAMBLING.
GV1301.s36   795'.01   78-57543

ISBN 0-671-24219-9

The design and name of Scarney Baccarat are trademarks of John Scarne Games, Inc.; no part of the game can be reproduced in any form without written permission from its owner and distributor: John Scarne Games, Inc., 4319 Meadowview Avenue, North Bergen, New Jersey 07047

THIS BOOK IS DEDICATED TO

MY WIFE, STEFFI,
AND MY SON, JOHN TEEKO

CONTENTS

INTRODUCTION

Millions of casino gamblers, present and future, in all parts of the world, will ever be grateful to John Scarne for his years of untiring effort in making this book available to them. This is the most complete, most authoritative and most up-to-date book on casinos, casino games and casino gamblers ever written.

Because of the recent legalization of casino gambling in Atlantic City, New Jersey, America's legal casino gambling scene has changed considerably and its growth has skyrocketed. Incidentally, John Scarne played a major role in the legalization of casino gambling in Atlantic City. (See "The History of Atlantic City Casino Gambling," pages 42 to 48.)

The book's main purpose is to give the casino gambler the most scientifically reliable information and the best possible playing strategy for each of the major casino gambling games. Thus we present here many highly guarded casino secrets that have never been published in book form before; these, if used correctly, will make the average casino gambler as gambling-wise as the top professional gamblers in Las Vegas and Atlantic City. And, who knows? Perhaps by making use of the Scarne playing strategy, and with a little luck, you'll become such a consistent winner that you'll be barred from playing at the casinos' gambling tables.

Included in this never before published casino material are Scarne's improved basic Black Jack strategy; a revised percentage-strategy Black Jack table; a synthesis of the misleading gambling information found in today's literature; the truth about gambling junkets; Scarne's winning Black Jack system—which barred him from playing in Las Vegas; an analysis of Professor Edward O. Thorp's highly publicized winning Black Jack system; Scarne's $100,000 Puerto Rico Black Jack Challenge; the average house percentage at Las Vegas Craps, New York Craps, Scarney Craps and Money (or Open) Craps—and which style of Craps is best for the player and where it is found; how to spot a short payoff at Roulette; how to spot a rigged slot machine, and more.

In addition, you will find a detailed history of Black Jack, Craps, Roulette, Baccarat-Chemin de Fer, Scarney Baccarat, Slot Machines and Keno. Also, up-to-date rules of play, the exact house percentage advantage at each of these casino games, plus the player's best bets, best playing strategy, sucker bets to avoid, and how to protect yourself against casino cheating methods, both new and old—all this and much more will be discussed in the following pages.

Mr. Scarne is the author of many successful books on games, magic, and gambling, including the classic best seller *Scarne's New Complete Guide to Gambling,* and the standard reference books on card and dice games, *Scarne on Cards* and *Scarne on Dice.* He has also written the most definitive up-to-date reference book on modern games, *Scarne's Encyclopedia of Games.*

But Scarne is not only a writer of game rules—he invents them! John Scarne has invented more than 200 games; among them *Teeko,* the fantastic board game which rivals checkers in skill and entertainment, *Scarney,* the first true solitaire all-skill board game ever invented, *Skarney,* acclaimed by millions of players as the world's most fascinating four-handed partnership card game, and *Scarney 3000,* an entirely new dice game of skill and chance that surpasses all present-day family and club dice games in action and fun. Scarne has his own game company (John Scarne Games, Inc., North Bergen, N.J. 07047) to market them. *Scarne's Encyclopedia of Games* contains the rules of play for these games and countless other Scarne games.

John Scarne is recognized as the world's foremost authority on games and gambling. The once universal "According to Hoyle" has been replaced among smart-money players throughout the world with the phrase "According to Scarne." Among these knowledgeable players, "According to Scarne" means "correctly played" or "played according to the universally accepted rules." Recognition as the world's top authority could only be achieved by a man like Scarne, who has spent a lifetime in constant study and research into every phase of games and gambling.

How does one get to be the world's foremost authority on games and gambling? The answer is simple: You need to be a magician. It helps even more, of course, if you are also a magician's magician—a reputation John Scarne acquired when he first appeared on the magic scene at the age of seventeen. Nate Leipzig, who was starred for many years in vaudeville as the International King of Cards, saw an exhibition of the young Scarne's skill and said, "He is the most expert exponent of wonderful card effects and table work that I have ever seen in my life." John Northern Hilliard, the author of *Greater Magic,* a classic treatise on conjuring, and manager of Thurston the Magician wrote the following when John was only nineteen: "To those who do not know magic, John Scarne's card effects must seem to be little short of true sorcery. To those who do magic, his card tricks and table effects are equally bewildering. I have seen all kinds and conditions of magicians in all parts of the world, but I have yet to see anyone who surpasses him in originality and sheer skill of hand; his skill is unbelievable."

By the age of twenty-one, Scarne had baffled all of America's top magicians, including such immortals as Houdini, Blackstone, and Thurston—

as well as the infamous racket bosses of the prohibition era, which included Al Capone, Arnold Rothstein, Lucky Luciano and Dutch Schultz; he amazed them all with his fantastic ability with a deck of cards. Fooling magicians and professional gamblers with his dazzling card dexterity today is still Scarne's hobby. In addition, as a magician and card manipulator, he performs and/or lectures on gambling at colleges and for special functions. His fees range from a low of $1,000 to a high of $5,000.

But proficiency in sleight of hand is not the whole answer. Scarne is also a natural mathematical genius, and since all games of chance have a mathematical basis, this helps. Early in his career, not knowing that mathematicians Daniel Bernoulli, Laplace, Gauss and others had worked out the probability formulas that are used to figure odds and percentages—about a hundred and fifty years earlier—Scarne started from scratch, worked out his own methods and, in effect, redid the work for himself.

Guesses never satisfy Scarne (his name incidentally is pronounced Scarney); he is a perfectionist. This quality explains why he is acknowledged as the world's foremost game and gambling authority. His worldwide fame as a gambling authority dates from World War II when he acted as gambling adviser to the United States Armed Forces. During the war he gave hundreds of gambling demonstrations before thousands of members of the Armed Forces to show them how to avoid being cheated by crooked gamblers. He also has been called into consultation as an expert on casino games and gambling by the United States Senate, the Federal Bureau of Investigation, the British Home Office, the Puerto Rican government, the government of Panama, the government of the Netherlands Antilles, the Hilton International hotel chain and numerous other governmental and hotel agencies throughout the world. He is also game consultant to the Encyclopaedia Britannica and the World Book Encyclopedia. In addition to the books already mentioned, he has authored hundreds of magazine articles and more than 20 books on magic, games and gambling. Scarne has appeared on more than 600 national television shows and has made numerous television commercials that display his magical dexterity. He has appeared as a magician at the White House numerous times for Presidents Franklin D. Roosevelt, Harry S. Truman and Dwight D. Eisenhower. On April 15, 1978, the Society of American Magicians honored John Scarne by naming him the Magician of the Year.

Casino games are never static; they continually evolve and change. Most other gambling books continue to print out-of-date rules and give the incorrect house percentages on Black Jack, Craps, Baccarat-Chemin de Fer and Roulette. Scarne, unlike other writers on gambling, is and always has been on the inside of the gambling business. Therefore both casino operators and gamblers the world over rely on Scarne for the most accurate and up-to-the-minute gambling information. In the professional casino world he is considered to be the greatest authority on rules, odds, percentages and the mathematical structure of every type of gambling game.

Scarne's books are the only ones that leading makers of professional gaming equipment, Ewing Manufacturing Company of Las Vegas, B. C. Wills & Company of Reno, and others, list in their catalogues; this says, in essence, that no casino employee or operator should be without any of Scarne's books.

Making certain that everyone gets an honest deal is John Scarne's main business. The casinos hire him for this purpose, and he carries on the work in his books, magazine articles, lectures, and nationwide television demonstrations that expose crooked gambling and explain how to detect crooks at work. Law-enforcement agencies, gambling operators, players and gamblers have praised him—and countless cheats and purveyors of phony winning Black Jack systems have damned him—for having done more to combat dishonesty in private and casino gambling than all the other efforts made toward this end combined.

Since 1949, Scarne has been retained by the Hilton International hotel chain to oversee their global casino operations. In this capacity he screens prospective casino administrators, helps install new casino operations, selects and buys the proper gaming equipment, helps set up and supervises training programs and croupier schools to teach new employees, and makes frequent inspections of these casinos to insure that both management and patrons continue to get an honest deal.

No card or dice cheat anywhere can perform as many different cheating moves as can John Scarne. There's a reason. A skilled card mechanic or bust-out man can make a good living if he is expert at one method of executing a smooth and undetectable second deal or dice switch. That's all he needs to know and all he bothers with. But there are many different methods, and every time Scarne spots a new one, he isn't satisfied merely to know how it is done. He doesn't sleep until he has practiced it so that he can do the move as well as or better than the cheat he caught using it. This comprehensive knowledge enables him to detect cheaters quickly and surely.

Scarne's knowledge of playing strategy equals his skill at detecting cheats. In fact, he knows so much that he is barred from playing in casinos throughout the world. He was first barred from playing Black Jack in 1947 by the management of four Las Vegas casinos: the Flamingo, the El Rancho Vegas, the Last Frontier and the Golden Nugget.

John Scarne is also on the alert to expose the many so-called "surefire" winning systems on Black Jack, Roulette, Craps and other casino games that constantly keep popping up in books, magazines, and newspapers, due to the fact that each year thousands of unsuspecting casino players fall for these systems. In addition to the purchase price of the book or pamphlet, these players lose their hard-earned cash at the casino tables before they realize the system is worthless. Scarne claims it is his duty as the world's foremost game and gambling authority to expose every one of these ridiculous get-rich-quick casino gambling systems as they appear.

Over the years John Scarne has been instrumental in having the rules of casino games changed, including those for Black Jack. In 1967 he developed a new dice layout known as the Scarney Craps layout, which has since been installed in many casinos in Curaçao, Aruba, Haiti and throughout the world. Scarne's latest casino game invention is Scarney Baccarat, the first really new casino banking game in the past century. It combines the principles of Baccarat, Chemin de Fer and Black Jack. This fantastic new banking card game is featured in many casinos the world over and is destined to become a rival to Black Jack as the number one casino banking game in the near future. Scarne follows the changes and variations of all kinds of casino games; he revises his official rules regularly and incorporates new variations; and he often recommends new rules of his own which protect both the player and the casino against casino cheats; such rules as Scarne's Casino Black Jack rules and Scarne's Four-deck Black Jack Shuffle have become standard in casinos in Las Vegas, Atlantic City, Reno, Puerto Rico, Bahamas, Aruba, Curaçao and casinos the world over.

In order to make *Scarne's Guide to Casino Gambling* the definitive work in this field, John Scarne has spared neither expense nor effort. Each phase of each casino game is treated separately, technical terms are fully defined, and official rules for each casino game are given in full. The background of the times and the reason for various changes have been ascertained, and the rules of casino play are in strict accord with today's needs.

In addition to his extraordinary dexterity as a magician and his unparalleled knowledge of casino gambling, Scarne has the unique ability to explain clearly and simply the fundamentals required for the making of an expert casino gambler. The famed magazine writer and editor, Sidney Carroll, aptly wrote about John Scarne, "To call Scarne an outstanding expert on games of skill and chance is to praise him with a faint damn. He is by all odds the world's greatest." And the late John Lardner wrote, "Scarne is to games what Einstein is to physics."

Scarne's Guide to Casino Gambling is the most all-inclusive, up-to-date and authoritative book on casino gambling ever published. It is a book that only John Scarne could have written.

SIMON AND SCHUSTER

1

MISLEADING INFORMATION FROM THE NATIONAL GAMBLING COMMISSION, THE NEWS MEDIA AND OTHERS

ADVICE FROM CASINO EMPLOYEES

In the past twenty-five years in my capacity as gambling consultant to the Hilton International hotels and other Las Vegas and Puerto Rican hotel casinos, as well as foreign governments, I have met and talked to thousands of casino employees such as casino managers and their assistants, pit bosses, supervisors, dealers and croupiers and found that although they consider themselves gambling experts by virtue of working in a casino, with very few exceptions they know little about the actual mathematics and science of casino gambling.

The majority of the casino employees that I've met over the years gamble at other casinos. (As a rule casino employees are not permitted to gamble in casinos where they work.) Of the casino employees that gamble, few have a nest egg set aside.

If you ask them for advice on how to win at Black Jack, Craps, Roulette or other casino games, as casino patrons often do, the advice received may be honest, but it is usually inaccurate. These men, like millions of casino gamblers, for the most part are losers over a period of time. They think that they can beat the casino, but the fact they are still working for a salary proves they know very little about the games they deal. And when they give advice to women gamblers, they usually are boasting.

Probably the best example of a losing casino boss is my friend Tommy Renzoni, the former capable Baccarat boss at the Sands Hotel Casino in Las Vegas. As boss of the Sands Baccarat game for fifteen years, Renzoni not only received a fabulous yearly salary but a substantial piece (share) of the Baccarat action. In spite of the millions he earned at the Baccarat table, Renzoni, who liked to call himself a professional gambler, was broke more often than not, due to his Baccarat gambling at casinos other than the

Sands. Why? Because he, like thousands of other casino employees, believed he could beat the odds at the game he knew best.

HOW AMERICA'S NEWS MEDIA MISLEAD THE PUBLIC

It has become obvious to me that America's news media have been conned into believing that the casino game of Black Jack is soon to become a thing of the past. That's what prestigious national periodicals such as *The New York Times, Newsweek, Time, Reader's Digest, Sports Illustrated, Life* (now defunct) and others have been telling their readers for the past thirteen years. One would think these magazine editors would have smartened up when they noticed that the number of Black Jack tables in Las Vegas casinos and the Caribbean have tripled in the past thirteen years. But, no—they just keep on publishing their phony stories about some so-called Black Jack expert and how he keeps beating the Black Jack tables in Las Vegas.

This Black Jack hokum in the news media all began the week of March 27, 1964. This was the week *Life* magazine ran a nine-page story by Paul O'Neil titled, "The Professor Who Breaks the Bank." The story concerned Edward O. Thorp, a thirty-one-year-old mathematician and a faculty member at New Mexico State University. The main theme of the *Life* article concerned the game of Black Jack and stated that Thorp, by making use of an IBM 704 computer as a partner, came up with a system at Black Jack that was certain to beat the house.

Quote from *Life* magazine:

Humans have been betting on games of chance since the dawn of history, but Thorp—a faculty member at New Mexico State University—must be considered the greatest system player of all time. . . .

Thorp calculates he could average $300,000 a month if he could play the casinos head on (alone against a dealer) for eight hours a day and if he could make the $500 maximum Nevada bet on suitable occasion without stirring up a hornet's nest. He is certain, in fact, that under these conditions he could win the earth and everything in it in 80 days. In reality, he can realize but a tiny fraction of his system's potential. Still, he feels that he can visit Las Vegas or Reno perhaps four or five times a year and, by using false names and disguises, betting small and moving from casino to casino, that he can "pump out" $2,000 or $3,000 each time before attracting attention.

Prior to the publication of the *Life* article, an editor of *Life* (who had previously written two *Life* stories about me) showed me the galleys of Paul O'Neil's story on Edward O. Thorp. I informed the editor that the entire story was pure fiction dreamed up by Thorp, and that his Black Jack system, which I had previously analyzed from his book *Beat the Dealer* (1962), was based on a false mathematical premise and would not work even if Thorp could obtain all the favorable conditions he sought.

Several days later the same editor phoned me and said, "John, *Life*'s printing the O'Neil story on Thorp. I gave my boss your views on the story but he just shrugged his shoulders and muttered, 'Sour grapes.'" He told me that *Life*'s research team had contacted a dozen or more mathematicians and computer specialists from the IBM Corporation, Aberdeen Proving Ground, Los Alamos, General Dynamics, and Sperry Rand and in essence each said that Thorp's Black Jack gambling system had been proved accurate and workable by their computer study. Thorp's winning Black Jack system and countless other such systems that have sprung up in recent years are based on mathematical fallacies, and rather than help the player beat the dealer, they do just the opposite. (For proof, see pages 115 to 119.)

As soon as *Life* magazine hit the streets, several hundred Thorp system players armed with Thorp's printed strategy system cards (courtesy of Thorp's book publisher) descended upon Las Vegas. Because of these two incidents, the Las Vegas casino operators became so alarmed that they changed the playing rules of Black Jack. In a highly publicized press conference, the Las Vegas Resort Hotel Association, on April 1, 1964, announced that doubling down was now restricted to a two-card 11 only, and that a pair of aces could no longer be split.

The reason Professor Thorp gives for these changes in the Black Jack rules is that gamblers who learned his Black Jack winning system from *Beat the Dealer* were consistently beating the Las Vegas Black Jack tables. This is not true because Thorp's system is pure hokum; it could not possibly have worked then and it doesn't work now.

Several days after the Black Jack rules changes went into effect, I received a phone call from a Sands Casino executive, Aaron Weisberg, requesting me to come to Las Vegas to discuss the *Life* article and the rules changes. I arrived in Las Vegas April 14, and met with Jack Entratter, president of the Sands Hotel, with Sands casino manager Carl Cohen, and his trusted aides, Sanford Waterman, Charles Kandel, and Aaron Weisberg. At the close of the meeting, the rules changes at the Sands Casino were quietly rescinded and within a couple of days all Las Vegas casinos were dealing Black Jack as before.

Then on April 28, 1964, with the approval of Governor Grant Sawyer, Edward A. Olson, head of the Nevada Gaming Control Board, and the Sands Hotel Casino executives, I challenged Professor Thorp to a $100,000 Black Jack contest to be held at the Sands Casino in Las Vegas. This match was designed to test the merit of Thorp's winning Black Jack system. When I issued the challenge I was dead sure it would never be accepted for the obvious reason that Professor Thorp's so-called Black Jack system for beating the dealer is strictly humbug. Thorp's reply to my $100,000 challenge was, as expected, a big NO.

The Las Vegas *Sun* of Friday, May 1, 1964, carried a five-column headline which told the story:

NIXES $100,000 CHALLENGE
Gambling Professor Won't Accept Offer
A gambling New Mexico mathematics professor declared yesterday he would not accept a challenge to play a $100,000 game of 21 in a Nevada casino with cardmaster John Scarne . . .

That same *Life* article pulled another major hoax by stating that Thorp also had developed a computer-tested system for beating Baccarat's side bets of 8 and 9. The Nevada casino owners became alarmed by this alleged computer-tested winning system so they doubled their house percentage by replacing the 8 and 9 side bets with a side bet marked "Ties Pay 9 for 1." This Baccarat rule change was never rescinded, and today's Nevada Baccarat tables no longer possess 8 and 9 side bets on their layouts.

The most recent Black Jack publicity-seeking gimmick used in Nevada casinos by several self-styled card counters in order to get national publicity to help sell their phony betting systems is to purposely get themselves barred from a number of casinos by objecting to the casino's single-deck Black Jack rule that permits a pit boss to order the dealer to reshuffle the entire 52-card deck any time during play. Several of these windbags, having achieved their intended goal of being barred from a number of casinos due to their disruptive behavior, hired lawyers to start court actions against these casinos for violating their civil rights, and each asks enormous damages for his alleged sufferings. The reason each of these windbags gave for being barred from the Black Jack tables was that he won too consistently. Rubbish. Need I say more?

I believe these frivolous lawsuits will eventually be dismissed by our federal judges on the grounds that there is no constitutional law that gives a person the right to gamble at cards. Furthermore, there is nothing in the Nevada constitution that guarantees Black Jack players the right to violate the house rules while supposedly counting cards.

If these Nevada-barred windbags really want action, they can get it in Puerto Rico because the casinos are run under government supervision, and no legitimate gambler can be barred from playing in any Puerto Rican casino.

If the reader wants to be barred from playing Black Jack in Las Vegas, do as I say and it's a good bet you will be. Find a Las Vegas casino that deals single-deck Black Jack; there are many that do. Then seek a vacant Black Jack table. After you're seated, try to appear suspicious by staring behind and around as if you were looking for someone. Next, bet the minimum for the first five or six dealt hands. Then look around suspiciously and plunk down $1,000 on the next hand. The pit boss, who believes in systems (most of them do), will order the dealer to reshuffle the entire deck. During the shuffle, feign anger, say "No bet," pick up your $1,000 while mumbling angrily and walk away. Try this in the same casino several times and you are sure to be told to take your business elsewhere. Any person who acts as you did would be considered a nuisance and would be barred.

For more than a decade, many other national periodicals such as *Time, Newsweek, Sports Illustrated* and *The New York Times Magazine* have been jumping on the bandwagon and have published their own phony stories concerning some character and his surefire winning Black Jack system. The national television networks have done the same. From 1964 to the present day the three major television networks, NBC, CBS and ABC, have featured dozens of individuals who claim to have invented their own surefire winning Black Jack systems. Naturally, these characters were plugging their books on how an amateur can get rich beating the Las Vegas Black Jack tables. Often casino operators seeking publicity for their casinos work in cahoots with these so-called Black Jack experts, as was demonstrated many times during the past 15 years on national television. This exposure helps casino business by bringing more suckers to the tables. Therefore, over the past 15 years, the news media have been directly responsible for the making of thousands of new Black Jack suckers and for earning billions of dollars more for casino operators here and abroad by publicizing the inventors and their phony systems.

Based on what I have witnessed at the casino Black Jack tables during the past 15 years, plus the enormous quantity of Black Jack information that I have gathered from casino personnel in Nevada, the Caribbean and Europe, I am convinced beyond a doubt that Professor Edward O. Thorp's highly publicized system has cost tens of thousands of Thorp system players a minimum loss of $500 million at the casinos' Black Jack tables. I personally know a half dozen high rollers who in the past decade have lost over $3 million by making use of Professor Edward O. Thorp's winning Black Jack system before they became convinced that the system was a player's losing proposition rather than a computer-proven winning one.

SCARNE VERSUS THE NATIONAL GAMBLING COMMISSION

In 1974, the National Gambling Commission was delegated by Congress to investigate gambling in the United States and to report its findings and recommendations to Congress by late 1976. The reason for the formation of the National Gambling Commission was to help our Federal Government reshape its gambling policy in the United States.

The commission held a number of hearings with many supposedly knowledgeable gambling experts as witnesses, and it hired the Survey Research Center of the University of Michigan to conduct a gambling survey in the United States. In late 1976 its findings and recommendations were submitted to the National Gambling Commission. The survey team presented a 500-page report, prepared at a cost of $500,000 of the taxpayers' money, which in my opinion isn't worth the piece of the paper it's printed on. The report arrives at the Disneyland conclusion that legal betting in the United States is three times more than illegal betting.

The National Gambling Commission survey team's final report states that the yearly betting of all illegal gambling in America totals about $5 billion, compared with $17.3 billion wagered legally at racetracks, casinos, Bingo, lotteries and other forms of legal gambling.

To top this nonsense, the report further states that football wagering is one of the least exciting forms of gambling. It becomes obvious to me that among the 1,736 adult respondents to the survey, not one bigtime or even average sports bettor or sports bookie was included. If he had been, the survey takers could not possibly have concluded that only $2.3 billion was bet each year with illegal bookies on sports events such as football, baseball, hockey, etc. It listed the national illegal horse wagers at $1.3 billion, the numbers game at $1 billion, sports pools at $191 million and illegal casino banking games at $110 million.

In contrast, racetrack records show that the parimutuel race-betting handle at all thoroughbred and harness tracks in the United States for the year 1974 totaled a $7.5 billion parimutuel race-betting handle, and an additional $814 million betting handle in legal race wagers was handled by the OTB (off-track betting shops in New York) during the same period.

After reading the survey report, it is apparent to me that the National Gambling Commission and the Survey Research Center of the University of Michigan do not know the difference between the terms "betting handle" and "gross revenue" and treat both the same, thereby creating havoc in the gambling world.

As an example, the survey report lists the legal $7.5 billion race handle and the legal gross revenue of Bingo, lotteries, casinos and other forms of legal gambling in the same manner and merely states that these were amounts bet during 1974. The $7.5 billion parimutuel race handle includes money won and lost by the millions of racetrack-goers whereas the money wagered legally at Bingo, lotteries, casino games, etc., is the gross revenue figure.

To understand the difference between a betting handle and a gross revenue, let's take the official figures on legalized casino gambling in Nevada in 1974. The 100-odd Nevada gambling establishments reported to the State Tax Commission a combined gross revenue of some $1 billion.

To calculate the casino betting handle in Nevada, I made use of the following formula. After clocking the five most popular casino games a great many times, I found that on an average 4 cents out of each dollar bet is retained by the house. If this seems low because some casino games have a house percentage greater than 4%, remember that there are several bets in Bank Craps, the game that receives the most money action, on which the house percentage is considerably less. This is also true of Baccarat-Chemin de Fer.

If this $1 billion gross revenue is 4% of the betting handle, then the betting handle for all legalized casino gambling in Nevada in 1974 comes to $25 billion. If this seems high, remember that more than 18 million tourists visited the state, most of whom placed bets ranging from 5 cents to $10,000 and more, gambling in more than 100 casinos which were open for business 24 hours a day. Also bear in mind that the same dollars in any betting handle figure are counted a good many times before they are won or lost and eventually become the gross revenue for the casino operators.

My 1974 Scarne Gambling Survey, based on interviews with 500 of America's top sports offices and bookies, revealed that sports betting has an annual gross betting handle of some $30 billion. Of this $30 billion yearly figure, $15 billion was bet on college and professional football. Baseball, basketball, hockey and other sports contests accounted for the remaining $15 billion. My survey listed the numbers game with a $10 billion yearly betting handle, rather than the $1 billion listed in the National Commission's report—and my numbers game figures have been accepted by most of U.S. law enforcement agencies.

In order to get an approximate figure for money wagered off-track with the tens of thousands of illegal bookies in this country, I questioned 3,000 horse players at and away from the tracks in different parts of the country —every kind of player from the $2 bettor to the high-rolling bettor who bets $100 to $20,000 on a race with a horse office (a combination of three or more horse bookies who are grouped together so they can handle the big-time bookies' layoff action). The answers I collected revealed that $7 is wagered away from the track with illegal horse bookies in America for every $1 wagered legally at the track. Multiplying the legal $7.5 billion 1974 parimutuel race handle in the United States by 7 gives us a total of approximately $52.5 billion wagered illegally by millions of horse players with tens of thousands of illegal bookies in America. This $52.5 billion is quite different from the ridiculous figure of $1.3 billion in the report made by the Survey Research Center of the University of Michigan.

In order to get an approximate figure as to the yearly betting handle of the illegal casinos in the United States, I interviewed some 200 operators and employees of illegal gambling houses, large and small in various sections of the country. I found that for every dollar wagered in the 100-odd legal casinos in Nevada, $4 was wagered in the thousands of illegal casinos in the country. When we take into consideration Nevada's $25 billion legal betting handle, this 4-to-1 ratio means that the illegal yearly casino betting handle in 1974 was $100 billion, of which the illegal gross revenue based on a 4% win average totals a gross revenue of $4 billion—quite a difference from that National Gambling Commission's report of a yearly betting handle of $110 million.

A most perplexing single statement in the survey report concerns the effect of legal off-track betting on attendance at New York racetracks. "What can be asserted," the study claims, "is that the data provides no support for the hypothesis that legal off-track betting detracts from track attendance or the track's parimutuel betting windows."

Attendance figures for the three thoroughbred tracks operated by the New York Racing Association (N.Y.R.A.)—Aqueduct, Belmont Park and Saratoga—reveal just the opposite. During 1970, the year before the opening of the off-track betting shops in New York, daily average attendance at the three racetracks operated by the New York Racing Association was approximately 20,000. Of all things, the study states that the off-track findings were based on interviews with only 28 OTB patrons. It is apparent that the survey takers failed to question officials of the N.Y.R.A.

A spokesman for New York's Yonkers Raceway remarked to this author that the Survey Research Center's report for the National Gambling Commission must have been made up by a bunch of kids who don't know what gambling is all about.

My OTB survey revealed that the OTB made thousands of new horse bettors in New York and adjoining states. And many of these new horse bettors have left the OTB shops and are now betting with illegal horse bookies who in time of need will give them credit and a better percentage break by not having to pay OTB's additional 5% tax.

A reading of the 73-page summary of the survey discloses that a "heavy illegal bettor is defined as one who wagered more than $50 for the entire calendar year of 1974." A recent survey of mine taken in northern New Jersey revealed that among 500 football sports bettors interviewed, not one wagered less than $500 on professional football during the 1974 season. Furthermore, according to the findings of the Survey Research Center of the University of Michigan, the biggest bettor in their survey reportedly wagered $32,000 during 1974 on all forms of gambling. Obviously the survey takers didn't meet up with any one of the tens of thousands of high rollers in the United States whose weekly betting action totals $100,000 or more in one gambling session in Las Vegas or on a single professional football weekend.

Other so-called major findings in the survey report list the following: Six of every ten Americans, or 61% of our adult population, participated in some form of gambling during 1974. Only 11% of the adult population did any illegal gambling during 1974. Gamblers and nongamblers regard horse racing at the track by far the most exciting form of gambling, while sports betting, even in the opinions of loyal customers, fails to reach even the midpoint rating on excitement. It's obvious that the survey takers never visited a Las Vegas sports betting office during a Super Bowl game or a baseball World Series game and caught up with some really big betting excitement.

The biggest bettor on football games in 1973 was a Texas oil man who is also well known for his big casino betting in Nevada. His bets during the college and professional football season averaged $2 million each week. He usually bet between $50,000 and $100,000 with a single bookie office, and spread his week's business among about 20-odd bookies operating in widely separated cities. During the closing week of the college football season this big-time bettor wagered $1,100,000 on 23 different football games. He won $50,000 on the week's play. This same bettor wagered $500,000 on the Minnesota Vikings to beat the Miami Dolphins in the 1973 Super Bowl game. Three sports offices booked this $500,000 losing wager.

Organized and private gambling in the United States, despite all the Federal and state restrictions against it, is the leading industry in the country, both in the number of participants and the amount of money involved. Its betting handle surpasses the combined total money volume of the 100 largest industrial organizations in the country, including such giant corporations as U.S. Steel, General Motors, General Electric, Metropolitan Life, Ford Motor Company and any others you care to name. Today about 90 million adult Americans—of whom 43 million are men and 47 million are women—are gambling the astronomical sum of $500 billion annually.

Almost 90%, or $450 billion, of this huge betting handle is wagered illegally; only $50 billion legally. Note that this $500 billion betting handle does not represent the gambling industry's yearly gross revenue—it is the annual betting handle. It is all the money handled, money that is bet and rebet many times during the year—it is the total amount wagered. Many of the dollars in this yearly betting handle are duplications because they are bet and rebet back and forth many times between players and between players and gambling operators before they are finally won or lost.

Of the $500 billion betting handle, the actual cost to the betting public for their yearly gambling pleasure—the annual gambling revenue from all forms of organized and private gambling—amounts to about 10% of the $500 billion for a gross revenue of $50 billion. As proof of the reliability of my survey figures my 1961 survey results were accepted by the U.S. Senate Subcommittee on Gambling Investigations headed by Senator McClellan, the Department of Justice and the Internal Revenue Service.

This $50 billion is divided as follows: $45 billion is paid to the illegal gambling industry and $5 billion to the legal gambling industry. This is a far cry from the figures issued by the National Gambling Commission which state that the amount bet legally in the United States is three times greater than the amount bet illegally.

2

GAMBLING CASINOS LEGAL AND ILLEGAL, YESTERDAY AND TODAY

LEGAL CASINOS

Casino gambling is legal in only two places—Nevada and Atlantic City, New Jersey—and yet the sum of money earned by its casino operators is exceeded only by the earnings of state and track betting on the horses at the tracks' parimutuel windows. Today 33 million American casino gamblers, of whom 20 million are men and 13 million women, be it for pleasure or for gain, contribute more than $2 billion yearly to legal casino operators in Nevada, Atlantic City, Puerto Rico, Bahamas, Aruba, Curaçao, the Dominican Republic and Haiti.

The major casino games in American and Caribbean casinos that get the most player action (number of players) listed in order of their popularity, are Black Jack, Slot Machines, Craps, Roulette, Baccarat-Chemin de Fer and its variant Scarney Baccarat. Next in player popularity are Keno, the wheels of chance—Big Six, Money Wheel, Racehorse Wheel—and casino side games such as the dice games Chuck-a-Luck, Hazard, Beat the Shaker, Under and Over Seven and Barbouth; also played are Monte, Trente et Quarante and Bingo Casino Style.

The results of my many Nevada casino surveys over the past ten years show that ever since the late sixties, when big business conglomerates took control of Nevada's major hotel casino industry, stealing from casinos has been constantly on the rise, so much so, in fact, that for the past ten years Nevada casino ripoffs have reached the staggering yearly total of $100 million.

I could write a book about the 100-odd different types of new and old casino ripoffs in use in Nevada today by crooked casino personnel, from the lowly dealer to the casino bosses, and by teams of amateur and professional player cheats working independently or in collusion with casino employees. This book, however, has not been written to protect casino owners, so most of these ripoffs shall not be exposed here. Besides, I head Scarne's Casino Consultants, Inc., a firm that specializes in casino protection. A number of these major casino ripoffs, however, including the $7 Million Casino Slot Machine Ripoff, are exposed in the following pages.

A casino ripoff, if not detected immediately, is seldom solved later because, unlike situations in other big business enterprises, the casino's chip inventory usually remains the same. There seems to be an unwritten law with casino personnel not to inform on their brother worker cheats, and for that reason, when a casino owner suspects a big money ripoff, he usually fires not only the suspected employee but other personnel working close by.

This $100 million yearly Nevada casino ripoff has been taking place for the past several years in spite of all the anti-stealing and anti-cheating precautions taken by the casino owners, state gaming investigators, city and sheriff investigators, hotel and casino guards, and security personnel hired from various private detective agencies such as Griffin and Intertel, all of whom are supposedly trained in the art of detecting casino cheats. In addition, casino employees and players are watched by hidden television cameras in the ceiling which are capable of zooming in on any gaming table and are viewed on screens in the bosses' offices; they are also watched by skilled casino-cheating-detection employees stationed in the "eyes in the sky," a maze of walkways running above the gaming tables, where the action is observed through one-way mirrors in the floors of these walkways. There are dozens of other casino protective schemes designed to prevent thievery.

Crooked casino managers often work in collusion with player cheats and outside crooks in ripping off their own casinos. I know of some 20 hotel casinos in Nevada, Puerto Rico, Curaçao and elsewhere that were forced into bankruptcy by crooked casino managers working in cahoots with outside casino cheats.

The main reason for this gigantic increase in Nevada casino cheating in the past ten years is due to the fact that casino crooks do not fear big business conglomerate owners as they did Nevada's former private casino owners.

One of the best-protected casinos in Nevada is the prestigious Caesars Palace situated on the Las Vegas Strip. Here we find my friend Al (Mokey) Faccinto, Caesars Palace casino manager, showing a $76,400,000 gross win for 1977. As the casino boss at Caesars, Mokey supervises 39 Black Jack tables, nine Craps tables, six Roulette wheels, two big Money Wheels, four Baccarat tables, 520 slot machines, a Keno lounge that seats 100 persons, and a large Poker and Pan room. Since Caesars Palace casino, like other Nevada casinos, operates three eight-hour shifts around the clock 365 days a year, Mokey requires a staff of 615, including 360 dealers, to oversee this gigantic casino operation. Caesars Palace actually possesses two casinos, the Caesars Forum casino situated off the main entrance and the Forum of the Twelve Caesars located on the second floor directly above the main casino.

Most casinos situated in the Caribbean that are owned by big business conglomerates are also being victimized by ripoffs, and I expect these casino ripoffs to occur in Atantic City as well as in other places that legalize casinos. Casino owners may very well reduce the number of these ripoffs, but they can't possibly eliminate them completely.

EIGHT TYPES OF CASINO GAMBLERS

There are eight different kinds of men and women casino gamblers. Which category are you in?

1. The occasional casino gambler who visits a gambling casino only during a vacation or business trip and who knows little or nothing about the hard mathematical facts of the casino games on which he now and then wagers some money. The vast majority of America's tourist gamblers fall into this class, and it is their losses at the slot machines and tables that contribute more than 50% of the casino revenues.

2. The degenerate or habitual casino gambler who visits a casino to gamble at any opportunity he gets. He knows considerably more about casino games than those in the first category, but is not smart enough to know that he can't beat adverse odds. He craves action, any kind of action, and he lives in a dream world in which he hopes someday to break the casino bank and then quit gambling forever. When he does win a bit, he almost always gambles it all back, and, like most casino players, winds up broke.

3. The skilled casino hustler who knows a lot more about casino gambling than the occasional or the habitual gambler, knows the rules and odds of casino games better than the game dealers. He usually knows which are best percentage bets in Craps. He plays the Don't Pass line at Craps and takes the free odds. He doesn't lose as much as the degenerate gambler in the short run—he lasts much longer—but in the end he winds up a loser.

4. The casino cheat or crook who makes money by cheating at Black Jack, Craps, Roulette, Slot Machines, Baccarat-Chemin de Fer and various other casino games. Also included in this category are casino owners of crooked gambling houses and their employees, whether or not they do the actual cheating themselves. The casino cheat's gamble is not so much in winning or losing as in whether or not he will get away with it.

5. The woman casino hustler who really is only a sneak thief. She knows that the only sure way to get money in a casino is to get herself a male sponsor to finance her play. She gets it by inducing her male escort to give or loan her money with which to gamble at the tables. She usually bets only part of the money and pockets the rest. If she wins, she conceals all or part of the winnings. This is the favorite racket of many women casino hangers-on such as showgirls and party girls.

6. The casino system gambler who lives in a dream world all his own, believing it is only a question of time until he finds an infallible casino

betting system he can use to amass a fortune. He is a perfect mark (sucker) for winning systems for Black Jack, Roulette and Craps. He buys most of the advertised systems, and although they fail, one after another, he buys more, always hoping to find the one that is perfect. The system casino player spends as much money on worthless tips and systems as he bets at the casino tables, and he wastes hours, days and months rolling dice, spinning a Roulette wheel, or dealing out Black Jack hands at home trying to figure out if the system he just bought works.

7. The professional gambler or casino operator who earns his living by his involvement in casinos: casino owners, managers, pit bosses and other casino executives fall into this category. He is called a gambler because he runs or helps run a casino operation, but he doesn't really gamble. He is a businessman (or woman), an owner or an employee who runs or helps run a casino. The casino operator or professional gambler, like the legitimate banker and insurance operator, acts as a middleman in the risks the players take at each game; he charges a commission (hidden percentage or a direct charge) on each bet made at a casino game or gambling device in his casino. He is not betting against the player. The player is actually betting against adverse odds.

8. The junketeer and his nongambling players. The casino gambling junketeer who fails to live up to the rules laid down by the casino operator with respect to signing up only qualified gamblers on a junket is nothing but an out-and-out crook since he is taking money under false pretenses. He swears on a stack of Bibles that all the players on his junket have been carefully screened and all are qualified gamblers who will pay their markers on leaving, and that he, the junketeer, guarantees any losses by his junket players. Most of these promises prove to be lies. This character purposely loads up his junket with whoever wishes to join because he usually receives $75 to $100 for each supposed gambler, plus his commission on airline tickets. He and his wife or mistress also get a free vacation paid for by the casino. This junketeer then has the nerve to give thousands of reasons why his stiffs did not gamble: "They were sick, the tables were too crowded, the hotel service was bad, etc.," ad nauseam.

The nongambler who joins a junket with no intention of gambling is just as big a crook as the junketeer who brings him because they are both misrepresenting themselves to the casino operators who are footing all the bills.

CARPET JOINTS

Casinos are divided by the inveterate gambler into two groups. The plush luxury casinos, like those on the Las Vegas Strip and Atlantic City, are known as *carpet joints* or *rug joints*. Unpretentious casinos without all the fancy decoration, such as those found on Fremont Street in downtown Las Vegas, are called *sawdust joints*.

A carpet joint is usually an annex to a hotel or night club. It contains flashy modern casino equipment, brocade drapes, wall-to-wall carpeting and other expensive décor, and it caters to a mink-stole-and-dinner-jacket clientele. The carpet joint's casino and credit managers dress formally and are as suave and sleek as their most distinguished guests, soft-spoken and apparently full of good will. A small carpet joint may have four to six gaming tables; a large one, legal or illegal, may have 60 or more.

Most of the larger rug joints here and in the Caribbean, except those in Puerto Rico, were once operated by gambling syndicates of former illegal gambling operators. These gamblers seldom appear in the limelight as the owners and, in the case of legal casinos, not even on the gambling licenses issued by the state or Federal Government. The apparent owner or front man is usually an *easy-money guy* (a wealthy speculator) without a police record. He may be a lawyer, politician, businessman, or anybody.

Before big business bought out most of the Las Vegas Strip casinos, the front man formed a corporation issuing 100 shares of stock, called points, which sold, depending on the size and potential of the casino, for $25,000 to $50,000 per point, or even more. A few years back, a one-point interest in the plush Sands Hotel casino, of which my friend Frank Sinatra owned nine points, was selling for $92,000. Shares in Caesar's Palace once sold for only $50,000. The professional gambling operators, under various fronts, usually took the controlling interest and sold the other points to friends, some of whom were legitimate business-men. The floorwalkers and pit bosses usually purchased one or two points (known as working points) on the understanding that they were to be employed at the customary weekly salary, and casino managers and shift bosses usually found it difficult to get jobs without buying in.

SAWDUST JOINTS

Most of the legal gambling establishments are rug joints, and most illegal ones, because they must move around in order to evade the law, are *sawdust joints*. The latter cater only to men and usually favor dice games such as Money or Bank Craps, or both; and the operators are usually a *combination* (syndicate) of neighborhood toughs, one of whose members is the racket boss of the area. The sawdust joint is also a meeting place and gambling rendezvous for the racket guys.

In a big city, a sawdust joint which has five or six dice tables often grosses more money annually for its operators than do some of the carpet joints of Nevada, but it pays much more in protection money than the Nevada operators have to pay in license fees and taxes. The ice demanded of a sawdust joint in and around New York City once ran as high as $7,500 per week, in the Chicago and Los Angeles areas $5,000, and in the St. Louis area $3,000. Compare these weekly payments with the annual $30,000, plus 1% of gross revenue, Puerto Rican casino tax which such plush rug joints as the Caribe Hilton Hotel casino and the El San Juan Hotel casino pay, and you see why the professional casino operator prefers to run a legal casino—and why some politicians and police officials get rich.

Big-city sawdust joints usually rent two or three locations at once so they can make quick overnight moves when the protection man tips them off that law-enforcement agents not in on the graft have learned the location and intend to make a raid. The sawdust joint is usually a floating Craps game or floating gambling joint which moves from place to place and is often located in a warehouse or large garage.

THE $800,000 PLAYER WIN AT OPEN CRAPS

The most successful of all sawdust joints, one which played a prominent part in the Senate crime probe in the fifties, was located in Bergen County, New Jersey, and was called the Barn. It started in 1937 about eight blocks from my home in Fairview, in the cellar of a local gambler. It housed one Money Craps game, and the gambler booking the game was known as the Baron. The game grew in size so fast that the Bergen County racket boys pushed the Baron out and took control. The joint moved from Fairview to Cliffside Park, back to Fairview, to Little Ferry, to Fort Lee and to Lodi, where it was when it folded as a result of the Kefauver probe.

Lodi is only a few miles from where I live, but when I visited the Barn there in 1945 I first had to go to New York City; local patronage was discouraged. A Cadillac limousine picked me up outside the swank Sherry-Netherland Hotel (a service that extended to all the first-rate New York hotels) and took me to a used-car lot in Little Ferry, New Jersey, where I met other men with the same destination. Another car took us to the Barn.

We entered a large rectangular building, formerly a taxi-repair garage, and found ourselves in a small anteroom just about big enough to contain four men. A sliding panel in an inner door moved aside and a pair of eyes gave us the once-over through the small glass window. Then this opened and we passed into another small room, where we were searched for weapons. This was not just a formality; I saw that several pistols and revolvers had already been checked in the "frisk room" by their carriers. It was done to minimize the possibility of the casino's being held up by gunmen.

Leaving the frisk room, we entered the Barn itself. There were six dice tables, four Black Jack tables and a Shimmy (Chemin de Fer) table. It was in this sawdust joint that I saw the biggest dice gambling of my career. Seven of the biggest gamblers and casino owners in the country were present: Bugsy Siegel, New York and West Coast gambler and racketeer; Willie Moretti, then racket boss of Bergen County; his brother, Sally Moretti; a wealthy shirt manufacturer named Herbert J. Freezer; a celebrated New York lawyer; movie star George Raft; and a Chicago department-store owner. The wagers made that night were all in the thousands of dollars and few bets were made with the bank. The biggest single bet was on the point 4. Willie Moretti took $120,000 to $60,000 from the other big-time gamblers. P.S.: Willie missed the 4. At the end of the evening Herbert J. Freezer, now long retired, had won $800,000— in cash, not chips or IOUs.

The Barn's annual gross during its 15 years of operation was greater than that of any casino in the world. Its monthly gross profits averaged more than the annual gross profit of Monaco's Monte Carlo Casino during its best years. The largest single night's take by the Barn's operators was that of September 1, 1946, when the 11 gaming tables showed a gross profit of $1,250,251.

The largest number of illegal gaming tables in a single casino at one time in America were in operation during the early forties at the Devon Club, a sawdust joint in Toledo, Ohio. It catered largely to Detroit horse bettors who were transported the intervening 50-odd miles in Greyhound buses at the club's expense. The Devon Club had 20 Bank Craps tables, 25 Black Jack tables and eight casino side games—53 gaming tables in all.

THE RACKET BOYS MOVE IN

Casino operations in America prior to 1932 were on a small scale. Every city and town had its back-alley dice games and smoke-filled card rooms, run usually by well-known local political figures or sportsmen. Most towns were wide open for gambling but, except for a few of the larger sawdust joints and a few elegant rug joints with a well-to-do clientele, the gambling was not really organized. Each operator was on his own, and the cops and politicians had little or no idea of the earning power of casino gambling. If you ran a Craps game, paying the cop on the beat a few bucks would buy all the protection you needed.

Racketeers paid little attention to the business; the big racket money was all in bootlegging. In fact, it was the bootlegging crowd who were the sawdust joints' biggest suckers; they wagered their bootlegging profits with abandon. They were the sawdust-joint operator's delight. Then the repeal of Prohibition left the racket boys without their customary source of revenue, and they turned their attention to gambling operations.

Little by little the bootleg mobs began to move in on the casino business and other forms of gambling such as the Numbers game; former owners, like the Barn's original owner, the Baron, were pushed out. By 1934 the mobs had control and the business was organized. The politicians with their icemen were put on the *pad* (payroll) and the cops, at the request of the local mob, began raiding all the small dice and poker games. Organization to a mob means monopoly. The politicians were put on the payroll, and one of their duties was to see that the cops raided all the small private dice and card games and put the competition out of business. By 1935 the country was divided into geographical sectors ruled by different mobs.

It was also during this period, from 1933 to 1935, that rug and sawdust joints sprouted everywhere like mushrooms. It was the biggest casino boom America had ever known. Every major nightclub had its back-room casino. The Miami area of Florida had more than 50 rug and saw-dust joints; Saratoga Springs in New York State had 8. Every resort area and large city had at least a couple.

The racket boys had their own ideas about how gambling should be operated. I visited a great many rug joints during that period and I doubt if more than 30% were operated on the up and up. There was nearly always a *dice mechanic* (a cheat skilled at switching) around, ready to go into action if any big money showed. The Roulette wheels were rigged and the Chuck-a-Luck cages wired.

But there was usually at least one game in town that was honest—a sawdust joint that operated honestly not because of any integrity on the part of the operator but because this was the joint patronized by a very discriminating clientele: the racket boys themselves, and all the dice and card cheats, professional crooks, pimps, easy-money guys and some legiti-mate businessmen.

Dice mechanics were at a premium. Con Baker, the greatest of them all, could switch phony dice into a game with either his right or his left hand. His fees, 10% of the winnings, netted him over a million dollars in his best year. He didn't retire wealthy, however, he died at the age of 37, dead broke.

EARLY CASINOS

There was gambling in this country long before the American continent was discovered by Europeans; the American Indians were inveterate gam-blers. European games of chance arrived with the English, French and Spanish explorers. There were apparently a few sawdust joints in opera-tion among the American colonists very soon after the landing of the Mayflower, because only four years later, in 1624, the Virginia Assembly passed a law stating that "Mynisters shall not give themselves to excess in drinking or yette spend their tyme idelie by day or by night playing at dice, cards or any unlawful game."

Charles Cotton in his *Complete Gamester,* published in 1674, says that the most popular casino game at that time in England was Hazard, the ancestor of modern Craps. Hazard, Faro, Macao, Quinze, Trente et Quarante and Rouge et Noir were the major English casino games of the seventeenth, eighteenth and nineteenth centuries. French casinos of the same periods featured Roulette and Trente et Un.

The members of the famous English gambling clubs, White's and Brooks in the eighteenth century and Crockford's in the nineteenth, were the titled nobility; accounts of their enormous losses are numerous. The Crockford rug joint (1827–44), with a nightly bankroll of £5,000, is said to have netted about £300,000 in its first two seasons. The first issue of the *Gentleman's Magazine* in 1731 printed the following list of gambling-house employees and their functions; many of these jobs still exist, under other names, in present-day casinos.

A Commissioner, always a Proprietor, who lookes in of a Night, and the Week's Accompt is audited by him, and two others of the Proprietors.

A Director, who superintends the Room.

An Operator, who deals the Cards at a cheating Game, called Faro.

Two Crowpees, who watch the Cards and gather the Money for the Bank.

Two Puffs, who have Money given them to decoy others to play.

A Clerk, who is a check upon the Puffs, to see that they sink none of the Money that is given them to play with.

A Squib, is a Puff of lower Rank, who serves at half Salary, while he is learning to deal.

A Flasher, to swear how often the Bank has been stript.

A Dunner, who goes about to recover Money lost at Play.

A Waiter, to fill out Wine, snuff Candles, and attend in the Gaming Room.

An Attorney, a Newgate Solicitor.

A Captain, who is to fight a Gentleman that is peevish about losing his money.

An Usher, who lights Gentlemen up and down Stairs, and gives the word to the Porter.

A Porter, who is, generally, a Soldier of the Foot Guards.

An Orderly Man, who walks up and down the outside of the Door, to give Notice to the Porter, and alarm the House, at the approach of the Constables.

A Runner, who is to get Intelligence of the Justices meeting.

Linkboys, Coachmen, Chairmen, Drawers, or others, who bring the first Intelligence of the Justices meetings, or, of the Constables being out, at Half a Guinea Reward.

Common Bail, Affidavits, Ruffians, Bravoes, Assassins, and many others.

The first casino operator in America to endow a sawdust joint with elegance and make it a rug joint was John Davis of New Orleans, owner of the Theatre d'Orleans and of the famous Orleans Ballroom. In 1827 he built the first lavishly decorated casino in this country. Its furnishings and gaming tables, and Mr. Davis's wines and liquors, were imported from England and France. The buffet suppers he served his customers have become standard practice in many American carpet joints. But the luxury casinos of today not only serve free drinks and sandwiches to patrons but often spend considerable amounts to get high rollers into the casinos.

John Davis' first American carpet joint, like the Nevada casinos, was open for business 24 hours a day, and his Roulette and Hazard tables were well patronized by the wealthy plantation owners of Louisiana. Eight years later, in 1835, when the Louisiana Legislature enacted a law making the operation of a gambling house a felony, Davis quit the casino business and returned to theater management.

In the meantime other operators had noted the success of the Davis casino and established other rug joints in the principal cities of the country. The most famous was the one which Edward Pendleton opened in 1832 on Pennsylvania Avenue not far from the Capitol in Washington, D.C. He called it the Palace of Fortune, but after a year of operation so many players had lost so much at its Roulette, Faro and Hazard tables that Washingtonians referred to it as "the Bleeding Heart." Cabinet members, Senators, Congressmen and other Federal officials were attracted by its gaming tables and its free expensive wines and liquors. President James Buchanan, it was rumored, occasionally visited the private gaming room for a fling at Faro. The Palace of Fortune operated without interruption until Pendleton's death in 1858; President Buchanan attended his funeral, and several Congressmen were pallbearers.

FARO

By 1850 there were carpet and sawdust joints throughout the country, and Faro was the big game. Plantations and slaves in the South, and many a poke of gold in the West, were won and lost at the Faro bank. The Western sawdust joints advertised that Faro was available with a sign outside bearing the likeness of a tiger, and playing against the Faro bank came to be known as *bucking the tiger.* The legendary stories of the crooked gamblers of the Mississippi River boats and the Western mining-town saloons mostly concerned individual card cheats and confidence men who traveled from place to place hunting suckers. In one respect they were no different from the gambling cheats of today who usually go broke trying to beat a banking game in a *square* (honest) joint: The old-timers did the same bucking the tiger in some sawdust joint.

Many of the Faro banks of that day were crookedly run, but this was not because Faro is a dead-even game which cannot be dealt honestly and still make money, as some writers have stated. The Faro bank has a 16⅔% edge on the *last turn,* approximately 2% on *splits,* and is dead even on *cases.* The bank requires that a player must make at least one split bet before he can bet on cases.

Many people believe that the game has now disappeared, but at the time of writing there is a game in operation in Nevada.

MONTE CARLO

The year 1858, which saw the closing of the Palace of Fortune, also saw the opening of a European casino that was destined to become the most famous in the world. Some 15 years earlier a young Parisian, François Blanc, along with his brother Charles, began speculating on the Paris Bourse. They displayed such an uncanny foreknowledge of the rise and fall of stocks that the brokers became suspicious and hired detectives to investigate. They found that the brothers had set up a system of signaling by semaphore which brought them news of closing prices elsewhere before they were known on the Bourse. The brokers demanded that they be sentenced to penal servitude but the fraud was so novel that the French Criminal Code had no penalty for it and the judge had to stretch a point to give the Blanc brothers seven months' imprisonment. Although they had returned large sums to some victims so that they would not appear as witnesses, they still had 100,000 francs left. With this stake, François obtained a gambling concession in Homburg, Bavaria, in 1842, and in a few years transformed the town into such a world-renowned resort that Lord Brougham, high chancellor of England, called him the most brilliant financier of his time.

Since the oftener you play, the more likely you are to lose, any gambling casino that allows local residents to patronize its tables will eventually absorb so much of the local capital that the town may be pauperized. This began to happen in Homburg, and by 1863 Blanc saw that a mounting wave of adverse public opinion would eventually force him to leave. So he prepared a line of retreat. Prince Charles, of the royal family of Grimaldi, desperately in need of funds to run his principality of Monaco, had in 1858 sold a gambling concession to a French combine which had erected a small imitation of Blanc's Homburg casino. After passing through several hands, it was about to fail when Blanc appeared and purchased the concession for 1,700,000 francs.

He spent more millions rebuilding the casino into a showplace which began to attract thousands of visitors from Nice. Residents of Monte Carlo were not allowed to play. It operated for seven years as a branch office of his Homburg casino on a touch-and-go basis. When the latter closed, in 1870, Blanc transferred his headquarters to Monte Carlo and by 1872 had sunk the whole of his capital, plus large amounts borrowed from Paris bankers, into the operation. Under his personal management the casino prospered so greatly that on his death in 1877 he left a fortune of 200 million francs.

Under the management of the Blanc family and especially François' son Camille, Monte Carlo became, as it still is, the world's most famed casino, although its annual betting handle today is small compared to that of a top Nevada casino.

Of the many stories about Monte Carlo, the one which brought the operators their greatest publicity bonanza began on a July day in 1891 when an English thief and con man, Charles Wells, sat down to play with a £4,000 bankroll of swindled money. He faced exposure and imprisonment if he lost, but after 11 hours of play he had won 250,000 francs (about $50,000). Two days later he broke the bank a dozen times. This is not as profitable as it sounds because it was not the casino bank, but merely the 100,000-franc bank at the Roulette table. Wells claimed his success was due to an infallible system, and he became famous overnight. His phenomenal luck persisted, and at the season's end he returned to England a winner, although grossly exaggerating the profits, which he soon spent. His fame and his ability as a con man enabled him to acquire another bankroll from backers who swallowed his system story, and he returned to Monte Carlo in 1892. He again broke the bank six times before his luck deserted him and he lost everything. On his way back to England he was arrested on charges of fraud, was tried in Old Bailey and sentenced to an eight-year prison term. Later swindles got him another three-year stretch in England and one of five years in France.

Even if the casino had never regained in 1892 any of the money he had won the season before, the operators would still have profited enormously, because Charles Wells became the hero of an international song hit that advertised the casino throughout the world: "The Man Who Broke the Bank at Monte Carlo." Shortly before his death in 1922 he admitted that he had played strictly according to a system only during the second season, when he had lost.

CANFIELD AND BRADLEY

The best-known casino operator in any period of American history was Richard Canfield. He operated rug joints in New York City and Saratoga, New York, from 1890 to 1905, and had the most distinguished clientele in the country. His three best-known casinos were the Madison Square Club and the gambling house at 5 East 44th Street next to Delmonico's in New York City, and the Saratoga Club House which ran during the racing season in Saratoga. To minimize the possibility of police raids, many casinos of this period were incorporated as private clubs and issued membership cards. But Canfield still had the iceman to deal with; he paid $100,000 a year as protection money in order to be able to run his two New York City rug joints without police interference.

In 1898 a soft-spoken thirty-nine-year-old man, Edward Riley Bradley, later famous as Colonel Bradley, opened the Beach Club in Palm Beach, Florida. In strange contrast to Canfield's expensively decorated casinos the Beach Club was in an ordinary frame house costing perhaps $4,000 to build. It housed four Roulette tables and one Hazard game. No women or Floridians were admitted, or men not wearing evening clothes, or anyone under the influence of liquor. The no-women rule was rescinded in later years. A new building containing an octagonal gaming room was built in 1912. This, too, was an unpretentious frame house, distinguished from its neighbors only by the initials B.C. lettered in white on the wide lawn in front.

I visited the Beach Club in 1932, had a pleasant chat with the colonel, who was then about seventy-three years of age, and did card tricks for him. At this time the club had nine Roulette tables and one game of Hazard. The Roulette limits were $25 on a straight number and $1,000 on an even-money payoff such as red, black, odd or even.

I asked what the house percentage was at Roulette (the tables had both the 0 and 00). "Young man," Colonel Bradley said, "it's $5\frac{5}{19}\%$, no matter how you bet."

This surprised me a bit. "Colonel," I said, "are you saying that every wager made at your Roulette table has the same $5\frac{5}{19}\%$ house percentage?"

"That's correct, young man. I've been watching these wheels for about fifty years and I ought to know."

The colonel wasn't far wrong. The house percentage on all bets at Roulette is $5\frac{5}{19}\%$—except for one. I walked over to an unoccupied table and put a stack of chips on a five-number bet.

"Colonel," I said, "that bet has a percentage of $7\frac{17}{19}\%$ against the player."

He didn't take my word for it; I had to prove it, but after I had explained the mathematics, he said, "How do you like that? A kid walks into my casino and tells the old colonel something about a wheel he never knew before." The gracious old gentleman treated me to a wonderful dinner at the Beach Club restaurant.

Colonel Bradley's Beach Club had the longest run of any illegally operated casino in America—from 1898 until he died in 1941. And that is ample proof that he ran a percentage game, not a crooked one.

NEW CASINO GAMES

About 1915 the sawdust joints began banking two new games: Fading Craps and Black Jack. These were both popular private games and they met with immediate favor among casino players. About 1917 a version of Fading Craps called Black Craps entered the picture, although some gamblers objected at first, not liking the rule that all bets at Bank Craps must be made against the bank. In Fading Craps (today called Money Craps or Open Craps) players could also wager among themselves and bet with the bank. But this resistance vanished, and in a few short years Bank Craps could be found in most of America's sawdust and carpet joints. By 1918 the Faro bank had been replaced by Bank Craps as the number one banking game. Colonel Bradley didn't go along with this trend. His answer when I asked him in 1932 why he had no Craps tables was, "Can you imagine the Vanderbilts and Astors playing a back-alley game?" The colonel at this point was seventy-three, a millionaire several times over, and was thinking of retiring.

More new banking games made their appearance in the early twentieth century than at any other period in American gambling history; among them Bank Craps, Money Craps, Black Jack, Slot Machines, Chuck-a-Luck, Klondike, Keno and Under and Over Seven. Since the casino's favorable percentage in each of these games was considerably greater than in Faro, their introduction marked the beginning of the casino boom and of gambling as an organized, big-time national business.

THE HISTORY OF THE LAS VEGAS STRIP

In 1931 the Nevada Legislature passed a bill making gambling legal in the state. Actually, it merely put the stamp of approval on the gambling which was already there. In the rest of the country a good many sermons were preached on the pitfalls of gambling, and most of the nation's press called the bill an experiment that was doomed to fail, as did the legalized gambling experiment in Louisiana in the nineteenth century.

The growth of Nevada's gambling industry for the first 15 years was slow. The gambling houses were all sawdust joints patronized mostly by Western gamblers and the gambling there was small time compared with the gambling that took place in the illegal luxury casinos and the larger sawdust joints in Florida, Illinois, New Jersey, New York, and elsewhere. In 1946 things began to happen that were destined very soon to make Nevada the gambling mecca of the world.

The Las Vegas sawdust joints were on downtown Fremont Street, and the now famed Strip on the road leading to Los Angeles had only two casinos: the Last Frontier and El Rancho Vegas, both designed in Western style and not in the carpet-joint class. Then, on December 26, 1946, Benjamin (Bugsy) Siegel opened the Flamingo Casino, the first of Nevada's plush rug joints.

I visited it two weeks after its opening, staying at El Rancho Vegas because the Flamingo hotel accommodations were not yet completed. The Flamingo opened with six Bank Craps tables, six Black Jack tables, three Roulette tables and one Hazard game. I didn't meet Siegel on this trip, but shortly after I checked in again, a couple of months later, an assistant manager phoned and said that Benny wanted to see me. No one called him Bugsy if he was likely to overhear it; it was a nickname he hated. I went to his suite and found him playing Gin Rummy with Monk Schaefer, the casino manager, and several other men.

"I've seen your *Scarne on Dice* book and your magazine publicity and I'd like to see some of your card tricks," Bugsy said. "Would you show me and the boys a few?" Gamblers are always a good audience for card magic, and I did tricks for an hour or so, getting quite a laugh out of Bugsy's baffled reaction.

The next afternoon I looked for Bugsy in the casino and found him talking to Monk near one of the dice tables. "Thanks for the tricks," he said. "They're the best I ever saw; they have all the boys dizzy."

"Glad you liked them," I told him. "Maybe you'll do something for me? Tell me: Why did you put up a five-million-dollar casino and hotel in the middle of the desert?"

He grinned. "I had a little trouble with Governor Earl Warren. I owned a piece of all those gambling ships that were getting plenty of action three miles off the coast of southern California. Business was so good we had plans to add a dozen more boats. And just when I thought I had it made, Governor Warren came along and closed gambling up tight as a drum, not only in the state but on the boats too. Overnight my dream of a Monte Carlo in the ocean is killed.

"So I'm thinking about where I can find another spot away from any other casinos—a place like the ocean so that when people come to gamble they can't go anyplace else but have to stick with me. There were too many sawdust joints in Vegas, Reno and other Nevada towns, but I figured it this way. If people will take a trip out into the ocean to gamble, they'll go to a desert, too—especially if it's legal and they don't have to worry about being pinched. So one day I drive into Nevada looking for a nice desert spot and I picked this one because the price was right and it's on the main road to L.A. Then I took a trip around the country and tried to interest some of the boys in the proposition. Some of them thought I was nuts. But I dug up the dough, and here I am with a five-million-dollar hotel and a casino full of customers."

And then Bugsy made a prediction. "Scarne, what you see here today is nothing. More and more people are moving to California every day, and they love to gamble. Since it's legal here in the desert, and not very far away, they'll come here. In ten years this'll be the biggest gambling center in the world."

Bugsy was wrong on only one count: it didn't take ten years. One reason, I believe, was that his murder at the home of a friend, Virginia Hill, in Beverly Hills, California, several months after I saw him, gave his Flamingo so much nationwide publicity that everybody heard about it. Even in death Bugsy Siegel helped turn a chunk of Nevada desert into the now famous Las Vegas Strip, with its blaze of multicolored neon lights, its plush hotels, its carpet gambling joints with their mink-stole clientele, and its live entertainment that is unmatched anywhere in the world.

By 1950, only three years after Bugsy's assassination, the Strip was well on its way to fulfilling his prophecy. Gambling combines from New Jersey, New York, Michigan, Texas and Ohio had already located on the Strip or were planning to do so. Three additional multimillion-dollar casino hotels had been built, and three others were being constructed. There were 25 large gambling houses in Nevada and scores of smaller ones. Their revenue for 1949 was about $41 million.

In November 1950, the U.S. Senate Crime Committee made an on-the-spot study of gambling in Las Vegas to find out whether nationwide legalized gambling would be a deterrent to organized crime. The committee reported that "Nevada's system of licensed gambling casinos has not resulted in excluding undesirables from the state, but rather served to give gambling a cloak of respectability." They concluded that "as a case history of legalized gambling, Nevada speaks eloquently in the negative."

This opinion came as no surprise to me nor to anyone sophisticated in the ways of casino gambling. As one Strip operator said, "Who did the Senate Committee expect to find running the games here in Vegas? Father Flanagan?" Only an experienced casino operator who has learned his trade in the illegally operated joints can protect a casino bankroll of hundreds of thousands of dollars. It's a sure bet that he was arrested a time or two while getting this experience. Anyone who tries to run a casino without such experience would be quickly driven into bankruptcy by predatory casino employees, larcenous players, dice and card cheats and *agents* (player cheats working in collusion with house dealers).

Even an experienced operator with a half dozen or more trusted and skilled pit bosses must be constantly on his guard against cheating. Some Nevada casinos have hired ex-card and dice cheats as pit bosses or house spotters in order to help protect the casino bankroll. Some of the larger Nevada casinos have observation posts concealed behind one-way glass in the walls and in the ceilings above each gaming table, known as "eyes in the sky."

One would think that the unfavorable publicity from the Senate Committee would have cut down the Nevada gambling handle, but, like the publicity from Siegel's murder, it brought more tourists to the state and the gambling handle increased. The Kefauver probe had another result. Most state and county officials in states visited by the committee clamped down the lid on most of their illegal big-time casinos, particularly in Florida, New York, New Jersey, and Ohio—and the operators began moving to Nevada. One of the most successful told me, "Scarne, I love that man Kefauver. When he drove me out of an illegal casino operation in Florida and into a legalized operation in Nevada, he made me a respectable law-abiding citizen and a millionaire." Other Nevada operators have told me the same.

THE HISTORY OF ATLANTIC CITY CASINO GAMBLING

On November 8, 1976, New Jersey voters by a 3 to 2 majority approved a proposal to legalize casino gambling in Atlantic City, home of Miss America, thereby joining Nevada as the second state in the nation to permit privately operated casino gambling.

For whatever it's worth, I take responsibility for playing a major role in passage of the Atlantic City casino referendum. For the full story, let us backtrack to early 1974, several weeks after Brendan Byrne had taken over the governorship of the state of New Jersey. I received a phone call from my lawyer at the time, Charles C. Carella (Governor Byrne's most trusted aide, whom the Governor later appointed Chairman of New Jersey's Racing Commission), requesting that my wife and I come to his office to sign some corporation tax papers he had prepared. It was at this meeting that I first told Carella that if state-run casinos were permitted to operate in Atlantic City, the state would not require a state income tax to solve its fiscal problems, and state-run casinos would remake dilapidated Atlantic City into America's number one Eastern resort city. When Governor Byrne received my message, he requested and received an autographed copy of each of my books, including, *Scarne's Complete Guide to Gambling, Scarne on Cards* and *Scarne on Dice*.

Thereafter I attended several meetings with Carella in which I informed him that state-run casinos in Atlantic City would in due time yield the state a yearly minimum gross revenue of $500 million, but if the casinos were privately owned and operated, casino taxes then would gross the state only about $60 million yearly.

To bolster my position I informed Carella that in 1960 I was hired by the President of Panama, Roberto Chiari, to install a government-run casino in the Panama Hilton Hotel in Panama City, for which the government was to pay the Panama Hilton Hotel 20% of its yearly net casino profits. The same 20% deal was paid to privately owned motels, which harbored the government-owned slot machines. At that time I wrote a set of casino rules and regulations, installed an internal control system against all types of casino cheating, and trained some 60-odd croupiers, including several casino managers and assistant managers. Some three months later I opened the government-run casino at the Panama Hilton Hotel. Today Panama boasts of seven large government-run casinos situated in Panama's major privately owned hotels, each of which receives 20% of the casino's net profits for allowing the government-run casino to operate in it.

In 1974, the 45,000-odd slot machines working around the clock in the state of Nevada grossed more than $450,000,000. State-run casinos in Atlantic City which has a 65,000,000 nearby population to draw from compared to Nevada's 20,000,000, would easily double Nevada's $450 million yearly slot take. When we consider the potential profits to be derived from table games such as Bank Craps, Black Jack, Roulette, and Baccarat and its variants, my projected yearly state gross profit of $500 million from Atlantic City's state-run casinos appears to be understated. In 1978 Nevada harbored 65,000 working slot machines.

It soon became apparent to me that I had sold the administration on state-run casinos in Atlantic City when the Governor began speaking out in favor of them. During one of Governor Byrne's press conferences he stated, "The administration had been discussing how to operate state-run casinos with John Scarne, national gambling expert who advises casinos in Las Vegas and Puerto Rico."

The public question (referendum) voted on by the New Jersey Legislature and later destined to appear on the ballot was broader than the Governor's recommendations and took in cities all over the state, whereas the Governor's recommendations were concerned with Atlantic City only. The broadened bill angered Governor Byrne and he said he would not support it and threatened to veto the bill if passed. Without the Governor's support, the casino-gambling referendum was defeated on November 5, 1974, by a 3 to 2 majority.

Most of the State senators and assemblymen who voted for the proposal, with the exception of State Senator William Musto and Assemblyman Christopher Jackman, did little or nothing to help the passage of the state-run casino referendum in November 1974. Why should they? The state-run casinos would benefit the state to a tune of $500 million yearly but would bring no riches to themselves. Most of the politicians I spoke to later said they would have campaigned for the casino referendum if the proposal had stated casinos would be privately owned and operated. Sure, because this way the politicians and their cronies could cut themselves in on that yearly $500 million casino take—not forgetting legal fees, real estate ripoffs, and hidden casino partnership deals.

By early 1976, the defeat of the state-run casino referendum of 1974 was no longer discussed—that is, until March 1976, when the current issue of *John Scarne's Newsletter* carried a feature article titled "New Jersey's $500,000,000 Casino Ripoff." The article stated exactly what was lost by the state of New Jersey and its residents by the defeat of the state-run casino referendum. The article contained all the tidbits explained above and ended up, "What the State of New Jersey and its residents lost by the 1974 defeat of New Jersey's casino referendum is a real damn shame—$500 million in yearly state revenues, a $1 billion construction and building project for Atlantic City and year-round work for more than 100,000 state residents."

With the appearance of this article, New Jersey State legislators, politicians and out-of-state casino operators began discussing Scarne's $500 million yearly gross projection for Atlantic City casinos and began scheming how they could personally benefit by—what else but—*privately owned and operated Atlantic City casinos.*

Several weeks after my newsletter appeared, the proposal for privately owned casino gambling in Atlantic City was well on its way to legalization. Soon large billboards were seen all over the state in red, white, and blue colors telling the passers-by to vote "Yes" on casino gambling. The money for this campaign was supplied by out-of-state casino interests, Atlantic City's bankers, realtors, lawyers, businessmen and their politician friends —all hoping to grab as much as they can of the yearly $500 million Atlantic City casino pie. As mentioned earlier, on November 8, 1976, New Jersey voters by a 3-to-2 majority approved a proposal to legalize privately owned casino gambling in Atlantic City.

The major obstacle that is slowing down Atlantic City's hotel casino expansion is the politically motivated state casino law that requires a casino-license applicant to possess a hotel with a minimum of 500 rooms, each comprised of at least 325 square feet, a 25,000-square-feet meeting hall and a 40,000-square-feet indoor entertainment and sports center. If the hotel complex meets the 500-rooms requirement, the state law allows for a maximum 30,000-square-feet casino. A 1,000-room hotel is allowed a maximum 50,000-square-feet casino, and a 2,000-room hotel a maximum 100,000-square-feet casino. This drastic politically motivated law eliminated all but one existing Atlantic City hotel. That means building entirely new hotel casino complexes at tremendous costs.

It would take a minimum of $50 million to build a hotel casino complex that would meet the state's requirements, and few individuals or corporations have that kind of money to gamble on a new casino project. At the time of writing, banks and investment firms are reluctant to lend millions on a proposed hotel casino complex in Atlantic City.

The Casino Control Commission can charge casino-license applicants whatever it costs to investigate their qualifications to hold a license. The costs of the investigation must be paid by an applicant in advance and may run as high as $750,000 or more. Resorts International Hotel, the first to apply for a casino license in Atlantic City, paid the commission a nonredeemable $543,000 to be investigated by the State's Division of Gambling Enforcement. While the Resorts International Hotel Casino license investigation was taking place, the New Jersey State Legislature, at the behest of Governor Brendan Byrne, backed away from its original strict investigative casino applicants law and passed a casino law that permits the granting of temporary casino licenses prior to investigation of the applicants. Resorts International Hotel, Atlantic City's only existing hotel to meet the state's real estate requirements, took advantage of the new state casino law and opened its casino on May 26, 1978, thereby becoming the first legal gambling casino in the nation outside the state of Nevada.

Once a hotel casino complex has been built and a casino license granted, the big gamble is whether or not the original owners will make a go of it. To begin with, the first year's casino operating license costs $200,000, and $100,000 for each succeeding year. A yearly Federal tax of $200 for each casino slot machine must also be paid. But the major headaches Atlantic City casino owners must face are the annual 8% state tax on gross revenues (casino winnings less payouts), enormous mortgage and interest payments, exorbitant casino personnel salaries, huge entertainment costs, player gratuities, advertising costs, local real estate taxes, money-losing junkets, the nonpayment of gamblers' debts and the loss of millions of casino dollars to professional casino cheats and crooked casino employees. For further information concerning casino operations, see "Casino Owners and Their Problems," pages 327 to 329.

In answer to my question as to why he didn't build a hotel casino complex in Atlantic City, a major Las Vegas hotel casino owner had this to say: "Scarne, I'm in no hurry. I'll just wait and then buy the first hotel casino complex that goes broke—and I'll buy it at my price. You just wait and see."

It took Las Vegas 47 years to get 50-odd hotel casinos in operation (casino gambling was legalized in Nevada in 1931), and during that time many of these same casinos went bankrupt not once but two or more times. Some were sold at a loss and some took in new partners to try and make a go of it. These occurrences took place because of casino ripoffs and bad managements. I expect the same to occur in Atlantic City.

Most major Las Vegas Strip hotel casinos whose yearly gross casino revenue totals $40 million or more are content with a net profit of 20% of the casino's gross revenue. A major Las Vegas Strip casino recently reported a yearly gross casino win of approximately $43 million and a casino operating expense of $35 million, for a casino net profit of slightly more than $8 million. The same year this hotel casino complex reported a net profit of slightly more than $1 million for the entire hotel casino operation.

The day the Atlantic City casino referendum was approved by the voters of New Jersey, I had great hopes that Atlantic City would some day rival Las Vegas as the casino mecca of the nation. Governor Byrne and the state's legislators blew that golden opportunity by their enactment of the most unrealistic and ludicrous state casino laws.

The biggest drawback to Atlantic City's future growth as a major casino center is the casino laws that demand the Casino Control Commission standardize the game layouts, rules of play, payoff odds and betting limits of the legislature's previously authorized casino games of Baccarat, Craps, Black Jack, Roulette, Slot Machines, and Big Six.

On May 26, 1978, the New Jersey Casino Control Commission issued their revised casino games rules. And what an amateurish and unfavorable-to-player rules some of them turned out to be! The commission doesn't appear to know the difference between a Big Six and the Money Wheel because the games rules describe the Money Wheel payouts under the section headed "Big Six Wheel."

The Commission really takes the cake, however, with its Black Jack rules. It copied part of my casino Black Jack rules, including my indicator stop card ruling, from *Scarne's New Complete Guide to Gambling,* then made a shambles of the Black Jack rules by adding the unfavorable-to-the-player "Surrender Bet" with its monstrous 22½% house advantage. The surrender bet is an Asian importation which is the biggest Black Jack sucker bet (see pages 98 and 99). If that wasn't enough, the Commission further reduced the player's chances by ruling that he could only split pairs, not ten-count cards, and only be permitted to play a maximum of three hands at each round of play. These rulings may be tolerated by players in

England and the Caribbean, but I doubt that America's sophisticated Black Jack fraternity will take kindly to rules that, from a player's viewpoint, turn Black Jack into a game of chance instead of the game of skill and chance combined that have made it the most popular casino game.

I could write a book on the countless other games rules errors and rules omissions committed by the Commission in their rules presentation, but I won't because I head Scarne's Casino Consultants, Inc., a firm which specializes in casino protection of all sorts and, in addition, supplies expert casino games rules for governments and casinos alike.

Even when the Atlantic City casino games rules are corrected, this standardized casino policy eliminates competition among casino owners and makes Atlantic City a dull and unexciting gambling town. In Nevada, casino operators are permitted to install their own type of casino games and game layouts and to set their own games rules, payoff odds and maximum betting limits. This casino policy leads to competition among casino operators. Therefore the best possible games rules, best payoff odds and highest betting limits arc to bc found in Nevada.

Atlantic City casino gambling when compared to Las Vegas gambling, becomes uninteresting and unattractive to high rollers because of the boring fact that regardless of which Atlantic City casino he may patronize, he will find the same casino games, same layouts, same rules of play, same payoff odds and same betting limits.

Nevada casino gambling never becomes boring because a gambler can shop from casino to casino until he finds the game, rules of play, payoff odds and betting limits that suit him best. Examples: Some Nevada casinos deal single-deck Black Jack, some double-deck, and some four, five, six, and even eight decks. Some casinos offer double free odds on the front and back lines at the Craps table. Some deal single-zero Roulette, some deal single- and double-zero Roulette. Some casinos increase their maximum betting limits for special high rollers to $5,000, $10,000 or more at the Baccarat tables. Some casinos offer a 97.4% payback at the one-dollar slot machines. And the same competitive casino policy prevails for all other casino gambling games found in Nevada, and not in Atlantic City, such as Keno, Faro, Poker, Pan, Bingo and casino race and sports books.

However, in time, these unrealistic and ludicrous casino laws will be changed and Atlantic City gambling will grow bigger and bigger and the city will prosper at the expense of thc out-of-town gamblers. In the near future, I expect to see casino gambling legalized in New Jersey's other resort areas. In time legalized casinos will appear in many of the nation's resort areas that find themselves in financial distress from Maine to Miami Beach and from Atlantic City to Las Vegas.

At the time of writing, I have met with Richard Corbisieri, Jr., Chairman of New York State's Racing and Wagering Board concerning possible casino legalization for the state of New York. Other states that are presently thinking about legalized casinos are Florida, Pennsylvania, Washington, Louisiana and Massachusetts.

GOVERNMENT SUPERVISION OF PUERTO RICAN CASINOS

Other than Nevada and Atlantic City, Puerto Rico is the only place under the Stars and Stripes where casino gambling is permitted by law. Many U.S. legislators and foreign officials who are considering legalized gambling for their own states or countries credit the big American tourist boom in Puerto Rico to its government-supervised casinos. Only 8% of the patrons of the island's casinos are residents of Puerto Rico; the other 92% are tourists. Here, for these legislators and the reader, is a report on how that supervision operates.

The casino rules and regulations of Puerto Rico which, as gambling consultant to the Puerto Rican government, I helped write, were formulated with several objectives in mind. The principal aim, to attract tourists to the island, has met with more success than anyone dreamed.

Another objective was to discourage visits from professional and big-time bettors; the government wanted casino gambling on a small scale so that the tourists would not be hurt too badly at the gaming tables. This aim was partly achieved by setting a low maximum betting limit of $100 and keeping the casinos open only seven hours a day. Today the maximum betting limit is $200 and the casinos are open fifteen hours a day.

Here is a summary of the important Puerto Rican casino regulations. Before gambling was legalized on the island in 1949, authority for regulating games of chance was vested in the Economic Administration, an agency of the Commonwealth government. Within this administration, gambling regulations are specifically handled by the Office of Tourism and an appointed advisory committee. The Office of Tourism insists on painstaking investigations to show that applicants for casino licenses are bonafide businessmen who will comply with the gambling laws. The laws require that there be other hotel facilities in conjunction with the casino, and an unblemished character and reputation on the part of all owners, stockholders, operators and employees. Croupiers, dealers, and floormen must be licensed, and only after careful inquiry as to their desirability. Equipment such as Craps, Roulette and Black Jack layouts must be of a standard and approved type and quality. All Puerto Rican casinos must adhere to standardized approved procedures, rules of play, maximum and minimum betting limits, and payoff odds. Only the banking games of Bank Craps, Black Jack, Roulette, Baccarat, Chemin de Fer and Slot Machines are permitted in the island's casinos.

Trained government inspectors on the administration payroll must be on duty in the casinos from opening until closing time. They test the equipment used before each night's play, and also during the play, if this action seems warranted. The casinos are not considered to be public rooms; admittance is at the discretion of the management, and the casino manager or the government inspector may ask a disorderly or otherwise undesirable person to leave. Today, the casinos open in the afternoon at 1 P.M. and close at 4 A.M. Soft drinks, coffee and sandwiches are served in the casinos, but no alcoholic beverages. The rules for each game are prominently posted on the walls in English and Spanish. Only chips may be wagered—coins and bills may not.

In 1973 the Commonwealth government became a slot-machine operator. Puerto Rico followed pre-Castro Cuba and Panama with government-owned slot machines. The Puerto Rican government takes 60% of the profits and the hotel casinos receive 40%. And believe it or not, the slot machine hold percentage is a whopping 20%, giving the player little or no chance to win or have any pleasure. Casinos situated in the state of Nevada have a hold percentage of from 3% to 17%. It's my opinion that the Puerto Rican government should get out of the slot-machine business or cut down that monstrous 20% slot take.

CASINO OPERATION

Most of the bigtime illegal gambling establishments in the United States are controlled by gambling combines. In Nevada, although formerly illegal operators are responsible for opening most of the casinos on the Vegas Strip, many law-abiding businessmen have bought in. Few of the old-time professional gamblers who helped make Nevada the gambling mecca of the world are in the state today. Most have passed away or retired.

It is a tribute to Nevada's law-enforcement agencies that in spite of some underworld infiltration in the casinos, and despite the fact that gambling draws thousands of undesirables to the state each year, there is little crime in Las Vegas and Reno, and no gangland violence has occurred in Nevada for several years. Even when you add the 18 million tourists who visit Nevada annually to the state's population, it still has one of the lowest percentage crime rates in the United States.

You can find among Nevada casino employees a good many veteran dealers and croupiers who learned their trade in illegal joints and have police records to prove it, but this picture is changing. Dealer and croupier schools are turning out hundreds of formally trained dealers who are *clean* (without police records). It is probable that the next generation of casino employees will be indistinguishable from an equal number of bookkeepers or salesmen. It is also probable that the great majority of the owners and operators will eventually be businessmen without police records like those in Monaco, France, Italy and other countries where legalized casinos have been in operation for half a century or more.

Most of the carpet joints on the Strip have no windows in their gaming rooms to remind a player whether it is day or night, and there are no clocks to indicate the hour. From the casino point of view, day or night means nothing—it is all gambling time. The wheels never stop, the cards are always being dealt and the dice continue to roll. Spectators have no place to sit, except at the Black Jack and Roulette tables, and anyone who sits there becomes a player because the chairs are reserved for that purpose.

The average Strip casino has eight Bank Craps tables, 20 Black Jack tables, four Roulette tables and one side game such as the Money Wheel. Around the walls are hundreds of one-armed bandits ranging from nickel to dollar machines. Maximum betting limits at the tables run from $200 to $1,000, although the casino will raise this for high rollers.

A Strip rug joint has the following employees, who, except for the dealers, croupiers and a few others, work a total of six hours of each eight-hour shift—each hour is divided into 40 minutes on and 20 minutes off.

Casino manager: He is in charge of the operation and supervises the shift bosses on the three working shifts. Salary: $70,000 to $125,000 per year, plus bonus.

Casino host: He acts as a good-will ambassador to outstanding high rollers and their wives; he takes them to dinners, shows, makes their hotel and plane reservations and generally keeps them happy. He sends the women orchids and candy and even gives them money to play the slots when their husbands are high-rolling at the tables. Salary: $30,000 to $50,000 per year.

Credit manager: The next most important employee. He screens your credit cards and has the authority, if they prove satisfactory, to extend whatever credit you require—$500, $1,000, $5,000 or more. Salary: about $30,000 to $50,000 per year.

Since few people carry thousands of dollars in cash around with them, high rollers pay big losses by check. But don't just walk into a Nevada casino and ask to have a check cashed. None of them will do it unless you have filled out a casino credit form and have been issued a casino credit card. The credit manager, whose responsibility this is, checks on you by telephoning your bank; don't expect him to okay you for credit unless you ask during banking hours. If you already have a credit card from another casino it's simpler; the manager makes a phone check with them, and casinos are always open. Ordinary credit cards, to most credit managers, don't even rate $50 in credit.

Old-time casino operators have considerable patience with broke credit players. They will make a deal with a loser who has lost more than his checking account holds, allowing him to pay off on the installment plan. But they don't like welshers. If, after returning home, you put a stop on checks signed in Nevada because you remember that gambling debts are by law uncollectible in your state, you will first get a firm letter demanding payment, then a phone call, and finally a couple of tough-looking visitors. At this point or shortly thereafter, the would-be welsher pays up. One casino manager told me: "We had a character here last year who took $5,000 worth of credit, won $10,000 at Craps the last night, walked out without picking up his 'hold checks,' and later when we put the checks through he stopped them. Some character, eh? But he changed his mind later."

Big corporations, which now own most of Nevada's major hotel casinos, resort to legal methods rather than strong-arm tactics to collect long-time unpaid gambling debts. A New Jersey Superior Court judge recently ruled that a Las Vegas gambling casino cannot collect a gambling debt in New Jersey through a civil suit because Nevada laws specify that gambling debts may not be collected in that state. If other states adopt this ruling, Nevada casinos are in real trouble. As I see it, this Nevada law will soon be changed.

Shift boss: He acts as casino manager during his working shift. Salary: $40,000 to $50,000 a year.

Cashier: He counts the casino bankroll and makes a chip inventory before and after each work shift. He supplies each gaming table with the necessary number of chips at the beginning of the game and more when required. Some casinos allow players to cash their chips at the main cashier's cage. In others, the pit boss pays off winners at the table where the money was won, and in this case the pit boss makes three copies of a cash-out slip. A runner takes two of these to the cashier, who initials the slips and exchanges one of them for the cash amount. The cashier is the employee who does all the casino's bookkeeping. Larger casinos have a main cashier's office and a pit cashier at a small desk in the ring formed by the circle of Roulette and Black Jack tables. There are usually three cashiers to each working shift. Salary: $350 per week each.

Pit boss: He acts as a floorman or inspector over a Black Jack or Roulette table, makes out and signs cash-out and fill slips, and watches constantly for any errors the dealer or croupiers may make and for any cheating on players' or dealer's part. Salary: $80 to $125 per day.

Spotter or lookout: An employee who observes the play secretly when the house wants to check on the honesty of the dealer. He does this either from behind a one-way mirror, usually located in the ceiling, or by acting as a player at the table. Salary: $60 per day.

Black Jack dealer: He deals at the Black Jack table, collects losing bets and pays off winning bets. Salary: $36 per day plus *tokens* (tips) which may total considerably more than his salary.

Croupier: He deals the game of Roulette, collects losing bets and pays off winning bets. Salary: $36 per day, plus tokens.

Craps dealer: He collects and pays off bets at the Craps tables, and alternates with other Craps dealers as a *stickman* (one who calls the numbers thrown). Salary: $36 per day plus tokens.

Shill: A male or female employee who poses as a player in order to stimulate the action. Salary: $20 to $35 per day.

Runner: He runs errands between the cashier's cage and the pit bosses or box men, carrying cash-out and fill slips and money. Salary: $17.50 per day.

Boxman: He has charge of a dice table and handles all cash and chip transactions between the table and the cashier's office. Salary: $60 to $80 per day. When a player gives the Craps dealer money in exchange for chips, the dealer passes the paper money to the boxman seated at the center of the table. He is called a boxman because, using a paddle, he pushes the paper money into a slot in the table and it falls into a locked *drop box* underneath. *Cash-out slips* and *fill slips* which he writes and signs go into the same box. Fill slips indicate how many additional chips have been brought to the table from the cashier's cage.

At Black Jack and Roulette tables, money and duplicate slips are pushed into the drop box by the dealer, but the slips must be written out by the cashier or pit boss and signed by the pit boss and the dealer and a copy returned to the cashier. At the end of each eight-hour shift, the locked boxes are taken from each table to the *count room,* where they are unlocked and the contents counted by three or four casino part owners or their representatives.

Ladderman: He sits on a high stand overlooking the dice table just above the dealers and boxman, corrects any mistakes the dealers may make that go unobserved by the boxman, and watches for dice cheats. He usually alternates as a boxman. Salary: $60 to $80 per day.

Side game dealer: He deals Big Six, Money Wheel, Race Horse Wheel, Hazard, Chuck-a-Luck or sometimes others. Salary: $36 per day plus tokens.

In addition to the above employees there are also floorwalkers, house spotters, slot machine attendants and mechanics, waitresses, Keno runners, busboys, bartenders, porters, doormen, bouncers, publicity agents, lawyers, tax experts and accountants. The busy swing shift requires about 100 employees to keep the action rolling and about half that number during the slower day and graveyard shifts.

The casino payroll is small compared to the tens of thousands of dollars spent weekly for the live entertainment in the casino's nightclub as a lure to bring in the customers. These shows have made Las Vegas a capital of live entertainment. More television, motion-picture and night-club stars perform there nightly than in Hollywood and New York City combined. The top-notch casino nightclub shows cost hundreds of thousands of dollars to produce and feature stars sometimes receive as much as $250,000 per week. All this is paid by the casino management, and when you add in state taxes, employees' salaries, rent, free drinks for customers and other incidental expenses, the annual cost runs into the millions.

THE TRUTH ABOUT GAMBLING JUNKETS

A group of gamblers solicited to travel to a gambling casino for the sole purpose of gambling is called a *gambling junket*. The organizer of such a group is known as the *junket leader* or *junketeer* and a gambler on a junket is called a *junketor*. (To avoid confusion I have coined the word "junketor" to replace the redundant "junketeer.") Thousands of junketors, including thousands of "stiffs" (nongamblers), are junket-bound weekly for Las Vegas, Atlantic City, Puerto Rico, Bahamas, Haiti and places as far away as Monte Carlo.

Before the legalization of gambling in Nevada in 1931, junketeers were called "luggers" and they made use of either cars or buses to transport gamblers free of charge to illegally operated horse rooms and gambling casinos throughout the United States. The Barn, the most successful of all illegal gambling casinos, made use of some 50 luggers with their Cadillac limousines to pick up gamblers in New York City and vicinity and drive them to the Barn.

The Devon Club in Toledo, Ohio, the largest illegal horse room and gambling joint in operation during the forties made use of luggers driving buses to pick up horse players and casino gamblers from Detroit, who were transported the intervening 40-odd miles to the Devon Club. At the time, most luggers throughout the country were usually paid at the rate of $25 per gambler. Some were on a weekly salary.

The first Nevada-bound gambling junket came from Hollywood to Benjamin (Bugsy) Siegel's Flamingo Hotel Casino in Las Vegas in early 1947. It was comprised mainly of movie moguls and their wives. The gambling junkets for the next decade or so were, as a rule, put together by the casinos. They involved a host of certified gamblers who loved to gamble and had the cash to do so. In return for their gambling action, these invited guests received everything free—room, food, drinks, night-club shows and plane transportation. The only charges were tips and phone calls. It can be said that Bugsy Siegel was not only the "father of the Las Vegas Strip," but also of the Las Vegas gambling junket.

The gambling-junket business shifted into high gear during the year 1958, not only in Las Vegas but in Havana as well. Las Vegas at the time boasted of ten major hotel casinos, which included the Sands, Wilbur Clark's Desert Inn, Sahara, Thunderbird, Tropicana, Stardust, Flamingo, Dunes, Riviera and the Freemont. The biggest moneymaking hotel casinos on the Las Vegas strip were the Sands, Wilbur Clark's Desert Inn, and the Stardust, simply because they catered to most of the country's high rollers, who visited their casinos on a "comp" basis (everything paid by the house except tips and phone calls). These hotels shied away from organized junkets—they had their own invited high rollers. However, other Strip casino operators, never having been in the illegal gambling business, had no high rollers, so, in an attempt to bolster their casino business they began accepting junkets to their hotels.

Today's Las Vegas junketeers receive $75 to $100 for each junketor. However, the junketeer makes an additional 5% or 10% commission on the purchase of plane tickets, and some junket operators charge a registration fee from $50 to $100 for each person on the junket; also, the junketeer and his wife or mistress have a free all-expenses-paid vacation with each of his monthly junkets.

Soon junkets became a way of life with Las Vegas casinos. Weekly plane loads of so-called high rollers and their wives were arriving in Las Vegas as guests of the hotel casino, all in the hope that the casino would earn back its expenses plus a profit from the action the junketors would give the casino during their stay.

Some of these junkets were moneymakers for the casinos. Others were losers. For several years so went the junket business as new hotels were being built in Las Vegas. As examples I cite the two following incidents.

On November 16, 1960, the Flamingo Casino in Las Vegas flew in a jet-plane load of more than 100 Miami Beach high rollers, wealthy hotel and restaurant owners, real-estate operators, brokers and garment manu-facturers. This party cost the casino $46,000, but since the guests lost more than $200,000 at the tables, it was a highly profitable operation. It doesn't always work out that way, as the pre-Castro Habana Hilton Hotel Casino operators in Havana discovered when they spent $65,000 bring-ing in and entertaining a plane load of New York City high rollers who went home with $250,000 of the casino's cash and a free vacation in Havana.

During the sixties and early seventies, many a Las Vegas casino and Caribbean casino were fleeced by mob-controlled junketeers. The opera-tors of these ripped-off casinos, never having been in the illegal gambling business and having no mob protection, were easy victims for mob-controlled junketeers who often worked in cahoots with crooked casino managers. I will cite just one of the many casinos that were taken to the cleaners by such junketeers.

I was in Las Vegas at the time when a mob-controlled junket from Boston arrived at the Bonanza Hotel Casino, formerly situated at the present site of the M-G-M Grand Hotel. I learned that the credit-card ratings of each of the hundred-odd Boston junketors ran from a low $5,000 line to an "open line" (no limit to credit rating) of $50,000 or more. The action given the Bonanza casino by these Boston junketors was fantastic. In all its history Las Vegas had never witnessed so many junketors betting the then $500 house limit, and I doubt if it ever will again. Most of the credit-card ratings were in fictitious names used by the mob guys who were on the junket and who had no thought of paying their losses. At the end of the junket, the Bonanza Casino had some $500,000 or more in markers (record of moneys owed the casino) and had paid out some $300,000 or more to the winners. The $300,000 paid out to the junketor winners plus plane fares and hotel accommodations for the entire junket paid by the casino totaled some $70,000 for a total cash outlay of $370,000 to the casino. The $300,000 collected for chips won (or collected from other junketors) by the mob members on the junket, either from the Bonanza cashier's cage or from various other strip casinos, was given to the mob bosses back home to disperse as they wished. At the time, chips from one casino could be cashed in all other Strip casinos. And, since the mob's junketeer was given possession of the markers for collection, the moneys collected from legitimate losing junketors also went into the mob's coffers.

The reason given the Bonanza Casino bosses by the mob junketeer why the $500,000 in markers had not been collected was, "Someone broke into my place of business and stole the markers." No markers—no collections. But the mob junketeer assured the Bonanza Casino bosses that he himself would make good the markers in due time, providing he was permitted to continue sending junkets to the Bonanza.

After entertaining a couple more of these Boston mob cheating junkets, the Bonanza Hotel Casino went into bankruptcy. At the time, several other Strip casinos, including the Riviera, were also forced into bankruptcy by mob-controlled junkets.

Mob-controlled cheating junkets are responsible for the bankruptcy of many casinos in the Caribbean and Europe. These junkets caused the British government to ban not only American junkets to casinos in England but to expel all American casino operators as well.

Soon thereafter several Las Vegas and Caribbean casinos began hiring junket coordinators and opened their own junket offices in cities such as New York, Chicago, Los Angeles, etc. With the Federal Bureau of Investigation keeping a watchful eye on the junket operators, the mob-operating junketeers either quit the business or hired front men to head their junket operations.

By the middle sixties, with the demise of mob-controlled junkets, countless small-time travel agents and gamblers who were once on junkets became junketeers. They know little or nothing about the casino business and most of the people they put on junkets as gamblers had never been in a casino before. By 1969 there were over 2,000 junketeers in the United States, and most of the so-called gamblers on their junkets were "stiffs" (freeloaders and vacation seekers) who had never before played a casino game. These stiffs failed to realize that the casinos pay all the bills to bring junketors to their casinos because they hope to make their profits from gambling losses at the gaming tables. These stiffs were out to get a free vacation without gambling, or just gambling some small amount for a short period of time. They bought chips in large amounts and then cashed them in at the next-door casino without playing a chip's worth, making it appear that they lost thousands of dollars when they paid off their markers at the end of the junket, or, after they had bought in $500 or $1000 worth of chips, they gave them to their wives or sweethearts to cash in. Some even had the gall not to show up in the casino at all. Like the mob-controlled gambling junkets, these thousands of stiffs caused many a casino to close its door or carry on under new management. The latest victim of this junket scam was the Americana Hotel Casino in San Juan, Puerto Rico. American Airlines, owners of the hotel, closed its doors after losing $500,000 during the busiest winter season Puerto Rico ever had.

Today, to avoid such skullduggery, most casinos in Las Vegas, Atlantic City and the Caribbean, insist the junketeer put up $3,000 to $5,000 in cash for each junketor and his wife, and all junketors must pay their markers on leaving. This helps a bit, but does not completely eliminate stiffs.

My Nevada and Caribbean casino junket survey reveals that about 50% of the markers (moneys) owed by junketors after their casino departures are never collected by the casinos. In comparison, uncollected gambling debts owed by non-junket casino high rollers average only 5%. Most junketeers rarely, if ever, collect all the moneys due the casino, and if they do, they hold out a considerable sum and swear on a stack of Bibles that the players never paid them. In all my casino experiences, I have still to meet one junketeer who does not owe one or more casinos thousands of dollars. And for this reason most junketeers are constantly shopping around for new hotel casinos in which to ply their tricks.

When a casino fails to collect its junket gambling debts, it loses not only the money owed it, but money the casino advanced on plane fares and hotel accommodations, plus the cash crooked junketors stole from the casino. This stolen cash comes from the redeemed unplayed chips these junketors give their wives, mistresses or partners to cash in at the host casino or some other casino in town. It is my educated guess that for each junketor's $10,000 unpaid gambling losses, the casinos are ripped off for an additional $5,000 in actual cash.

Several casino operators in the Caribbean islands remarked to me that they do not know if a junket they have okayed will be loaded with stiffs or not, but since they have little business otherwise, they have to take that chance. "Our only hope is to beat one or two high rollers on the junket real big—that will pay our hotel expenses, plane fares, junket commission and so on, and all the small amounts lost by the stiffs will be profit. If we don't beat one or more gamblers big, we are sure to have a losing junket."

Recently one gambling operator returning from Europe said, "Scarne, you know we ran dozens of junkets to blank-blank and we cheated every person on the junket—and you know what? We still couldn't meet our expenses. We went broke simply because most of these junkets carried too many nongamblers and freeloaders."

Or, having learned their junket lessons the hard way, some Las Vegas Strip casinos have installed an alternate junket protection system that also helps to eliminate many welshers and nongambling junketors. But this system, too, has many weak spots that sophisticated stiffs take advantage of. The casino insists that any new junketors must deposit with the casino $5,000 in cash, money order or certified check. All other credits extended the junketor must be guaranteed by the junketeer. In addition, Strip casinos have abolished the policy of cashing each other's chips. These preventive measures help some. But there are dozens of other junketor scams that these so-called knowledgeable casino managers who work for big business conglomerates and whose annual salaries run to $100,000 or more fail to prevent. If they do know these scams, why don't they stop them? And how can they explain the fact that a hotel casino with an 80% year-round occupancy and a casino filled with junketors loses money yearly?

Since I'm not writing this book for big business conglomerates and casino managers, I'm not exposing these junketor scams, and these self-styled gambling geniuses will have to find out the hard way.

However, I'm going to let these gambling greats in on a mathematical formula that will permit them to compute each gamblers's action on the junket. My clocking over the past 30 years has proven that on the average, four cents out of each dollar wagered by a casino player is retained by the house. If this figure seems low because many bets at Bank Craps, Black Jack and Roulette have a house edge greater than 4%, remember that in Bank Craps there are several bets such as the pass and don't pass line and the come and don't come with their free take and lay bets where the house percentage is less than 1%. I shall use this 4% figure to calculate what kind of action a junketor must give the house to pay for his so-called free vacation.

Let's suppose that it cost the casino $1,000 to bring a junketor and his wife there to gamble, and let's make use of the 4% earned figure on each dollar wagered. The junketor must give the house $25,000 worth of action for the casino to retrieve its $1,000 junketor's expense. After the junketor gives the house $25,000 worth of action (back-and-forth action), the house begins to earn a profit of four cents on each additional dollar wagered—wins and losses notwithstanding.

A junketor who places $25 bets at random over the Craps layout, and these bets give the house a 4% edge, must on the average make 1,000 $25 bets for the casino to earn its $1,000 junketor cost. If the junketor bets $50 on the pass line and takes $50 worth of free odds on the thrown point number, and we accept a 1% figure as the house's percentage, this same junketor must make 1,000 such $100 bets for a total of $100,000 worth of action for the house to earn its $1,000 junketor cost.

If the Las Vegas casinos did not have thousands of daily walk-in customers and relied only on junkets, they would go broke before you could say Las Vegas. Today a junketor with a $3,000 credit line is not as welcome in casinos as he was years ago. Why, you may ask? Merely because for years everything has been increasing in cost—casino rentals, taxes, salaries, entertainment, drinks, food, hotel accommodations and air travel. Strangely enough, the only thing that has not gone up (except betting limits) is the house's percentage at casino tables. Believe me, junkets are not the bonanza that "big business" casino owners are misled into believing.

I predict that privately run junkets will be a thing of the past in the top casinos. Individual high rollers, of course, will always be welcomed by the casino and will receive everything free except for tips and phone calls. However, I doubt that there are enough high rollers around to satisfy the countless number of casinos springing up throughout the world. Thus, then, a toast: "To the millions of small-time gamblers who keep the casinos in business."

NEVADA GAMBLING AND BIG BUSINESS

The old-time gamblers and mobsters who built and operated most of the luxury casinos in Las Vegas and Reno have either gone public or sold their interests to big corporations. Today, the fathers of the Las Vegas Strip, experienced gamblers who made Las Vegas the entertainment capital of the world, have little or no say in the internal operations of any of the luxury casinos on the Las Vegas Strip. Gone with these operators are their friends—the big-time gamblers, the boys who could lose or win $20,000 to $250,000 in one session of play. As I have stated, the high rollers, although not quite dead, are fast becoming extinct. Absent from Las Vegas Strip casinos are most of the illegal race bookies who operated in every hamlet and city in our country and made up the bulk of Las Vegas's high rollers. Due to recently enacted Federal and state anti-gambling laws, most of the country's top illegal race bookies are either in jail, indicted, retired, laying low or on the lam. And most who are still operating avoid Las Vegas as if it were a plague since it is rumored that Nevada is infested with more FBI and Internal Revenue agents than any other state in the union. When experienced gamblers ran the Strip's casinos, high rollers seldom welshed on paying gambling losses. Today, one casino group has more noncollectible outstanding debts than all the combined casinos on the Strip during the regime of the old-timers.

Big business practices, in fact, are making Las Vegas a prissy, penny-pinching old lady. Gone is big-time gambling excitement, the glamour ignited by high rollers and the fantastic round-the-clock cocktail lounges with their star-studded entertainment. Cocktail lounges in most of the Strip's luxury casinos are a thing of the past. In their place are Keno lounges. I predict it won't be long before the $100,000 and $200,000 weekly salaries of headline acts will also be a thing of the past.

In short, big business is changing the gambling character of Nevada— it plans to cater to the average tourist who visits Nevada. In fact, the businessmen have already eliminated the high roller in their plans and cater to the new breed of gamblers: the average man and woman. It's a big gamble on the part of big business. In my opinion, take the glamour and big-time gambling out of Las Vegas and it will become just another tourist town. Then why should anyone from the East Coast patronize Nevada? And with the recent legalization of casinos in Atlantic City, New Jersey, and the possible legalization of casino gambling in the state of New York in the near future, big business in Nevada better take a second look at their casino operations. At the time of writing, I have been requested to formulate a series of casino and gaming rules for several Eastern states.

HONEST CASINOS VS STEER JOINTS

The millions of people who gamble today are much less likely to be cheated than they were 35 years ago, and I think I can claim that this is due in great part to my efforts. I began writing early during World War II about the cheats who were clipping the GIs, and from then until the end of the war I served as gambling adviser to the United States Armed Forces and gave hundreds of lectures and demonstrations to military personnel here and abroad. I wrote a series of articles exposing cheating methods and explaining how to detect and guard against them for *Yank: The Army Weekly*—articles which were highly praised by such military leaders as Admiral Ernest J. King, chief of naval operations, and General Hap Arnold, commanding general of the Army Air Force.

Articles about my crusade against cheating in the Armed Forces giving the general public my anti-cheating information appeared in most of our national magazines: *Life, Saturday Evening Post, The New Yorker, Time, Newsweek, American Magazine, The New York Times Magazine, Parade,*

Science Digest and others. Syndicated feature services carried my articles to newspapers throughout this country and they were published in Canadian, Australian, Indian and South American magazines and newspapers.

Then, in two big, definitive books, *Scarne on Dice* (1945) and *Scarne on Cards* (1949), which are still selling today, and in *Scarne's Encyclopedia of Games* (1973), I included thorough exposés of the cheating methods in use. Gambling cheats, knowing that so much of this previously secret information was available to the public, became more and more hesitant about using the exposed methods.

Curiously enough, these exposures of cheating have been a blessing to some crooked casino operators. As the players wise up, the operators find that they have to run their games honestly, and when they do that they discover something that should be obvious: an honest percentage game makes more money for its operators than a crooked game. For one thing, honest casinos get more customers with less trouble. A *steer joint* (crooked casino) has to hire dice and card mechanics and sometimes install rigged gaming tables. It isn't long before the casino help are telling their friends not to patronize the joint, and they in turn tell their friends, and in a very short time hundreds of people know all about it. At this point, the only way to get action is to hire a flock of *steerers* or *agents* to locate and bring the suckers in to be fleeced. A steerer may be anyone: a show girl, an entertainer, a cab driver, a bartender, a business associate, a friend. And steerers are expensive; they sometimes have to be cut in for as much as 50% of the amount lost by the victim or victims brought in. The crooked casino is pretty empty most of the time until a sucker is steered in, and then all the shills and steerers have to put on an act and make it look as if there was a lot of action going on.

Steer joints are mostly located in resort areas, usually have a short season, and are seldom in the same spot the next season. The operators have to depend on taking big sums from a few victims to make a profit; after giving the steerer 50% and paying the mechanic, the shills and all the other people involved, the *touch* or *score* (money won dishonestly) must be real big to make the remaining sum amount to much.

An honestly run casino gets action from everyone: the owners themselves, dealers, croupiers' friends, local townspeople, even rival casino owners. Everyone takes a shot at an honest game even when he knows he can't beat the percentage in the long run. The honest casino has continuous action, and the crooked casino, when the steerers don't have a mark in the place, looks like a morgue.

The casino at Monte Carlo is proof that honest operation is more profitable than dishonest operation. This casino has always been known for its honest operation, and it not only makes a handsome profit for its owners but pays a tax that supplies the government of Monaco with its only source of revenue. It has been in continuous operation since 1858;

the largest crooked gambling house known to the author lasted only eight months before folding.

TIPS ON HOW TO SPOT A CROOKED CASINO

Is there any simple, surfire method by which you can be certain your favorite casino is on the level? No, it's not that easy. But it can be done. Your best protection is to have in your head the information on cheating at casino games which you will find in this book. In addition, ask yourself the following questions:

1. How long has the casino been operating? The fact that a casino is crooked leaks out faster than you think, and only the honest ones stay in business year after year.

2. Is the casino lavishly decorated or is it a makeshift affair? The bigger the casino's investment in its quarters and furnishings, the more likely it is to be honest. Crooked dice, Roulette and card games are usually found in small casinos, hotel rooms, private homes, at charity balls and conventions behind closed doors.

3. Is the casino well patronized and doing good business, like the legal casinos in Nevada and Puerto Rico? If so, you can almost be sure the operators aren't out to take you for every nickel they can get. A crowded casino is the best proof that it is honest. Don't be the only player or one of a few players in a nearly empty casino whose operators have worried faces!

If you are a high roller and are betting as if you are trying to win the casino—pardner, you're on your own!

As in many other things, your best protection lies in knowing what you are doing. If you know the cheating methods explained in these pages, you have a chance of spotting crooked work. And then, give yourself the best possible chance of winning by sticking to those casino bets which have the smallest house percentage against you. You'll find all that information here, too.

CASINO GAMES AND THEIR EARNING POWER

As a gambling consultant, casino figures are very important to me. When I visit a casino where I'm employed, my first duty is to check the hold (win) percentages at each table. A table's hold percentage is the percentage expected to be earned by each table. This is the difference between the cash and credit slips dropped into the cashbox under each table minus the payout slips (money paid to winning players). The cashbox has a slot opening on top where the dealer pushes the player's money for chips purchased. If the actual win percentage equals or exceeds the expected hold percentage, I have had an easy visit—if it falls far below, I have to check out the reason. If the payouts to winners are greater than the money and credit slips in the box, the table is a loser. If the money and credit slips total a greater amount than the winner's payouts, the table has won money.

There is no mathematical formula that can be used to compute the overall earning power for a given period at any casino game. This is especially true for Bank Craps Nevada and Puerto Rico style, simply because there are dozens of different Craps bets made at the dice table, each having a different favorable house percentage. Also, players are very unpredictable as to the type of bets they prefer. However, I have standardized a percentage that each Bank Craps table is expected to earn in a month. This earned percentage, based on my study of daily, weekly, monthly and yearly financial records of Bank Craps tables in a number of major casinos in Nevada and Puerto Rico for over 25 years, is about 20%. This means that when a player hands a boxman at a Bank Craps table $100 to purchase chips, the house is expected to earn $20 of the $100, on the average. Even though some players win, some lose and some break even, the table will not depart much from this average in a month.

At times, for days and even for weeks, a Bank Craps table may lose. At other times, the table may win heavily and hold a much higher percentage, but in the long run, the 20 percent figure is the approximate hold percentage of each and every Craps table that is run honestly both from the inside and the outside.

The casino's monthly hold percentage at Scarney Craps as played in Aruba, Curaçao, Haiti, and elsewhere is about 24%. The casino's monthly hold percentage at New York Craps as played in the Bahamas is about 28%.

My study of casino records at Black Jack over the past 25 years in Nevada and other casino locations where the player is permitted to double down on any two cards amounts to a monthly hold percentage of about 21%. Casinos situated in Puerto Rico, Aruba, Curaçao and other spots where the casino only permits a double down on a count of 11 or 9, 10 and 11, the monthly hold percentage is about 23%.

American Roulette with its zero (0) and double zero (00) has a monthly hold percentage of about 26%. European Roulette with its single zero (0) and its imprisonment of Red, Black, Odd, Even, 1–18 and 19–36 has a monthly hold percentage of about 19%.

Nevada style Baccarat's monthly hold percentage amounts to about 19%. Slot machines which possess a house advantage of 10% or thereabouts possess a monthly hold percentage of about 80%. Slot machines that possess a house advantage of 15% to 20% have a monthly hold percentage of about 90%. The casino side games such as Keno, Big Six, or the Money Wheel, where the house's edge is 20% to 25%, have a monthly hold percentage of about 90%. The monthly hold percentage figures listed above should convince the reader that the casino's overall percentage take will break even the best casino gamblers in the long run.

3

BLACK JACK: AMERICA'S MOST POPULAR CASINO GAME

Black Jack, or Twenty-one, is the most widely played casino game in the world today. My latest casino survey shows that more American casino patrons gamble at the intriguing and often perplexing form of casino Black Jack than at Bank Craps, Roulette or Baccarat. This makes casino-style Black Jack as played in Nevada, Atlantic City, Puerto Rico, the Bahamas, Curaçao, Aruba, St. Maarten, Dominican Republic, Haiti and elsewhere first in player popularity and second only to Bank and New York Craps in the volume of money wagered.

Today, casino-style Black Jack boasts of approximately 24 million players, of whom 8 million are women. Although men still outnumber women Black Jack players by 2 to 1, many more men and women play the game each year. And, because of the recent legalization of casino gambling in Atlantic City, I predict that more than 3 million nongamblers will become addicted to Black Jack within the next five years.

Black Jack today is played in every gambling casino in the country, in most private clubs and in about five out of every ten illegally run cardrooms. Today, it is a sure bet that in any big-time Las Vegas or Atlantic City gambling casino you will find at least 30 Black Jack tables, two cards in front of each player, and the dealer trying to look as poker-faced as possible, with the players calling "Hit me," "Stand," "That's enough" and "Oh, damn! I busted," or indicating these calls by hand motions.

During the past decade, the popularity of casino-style Black Jack grew by leaps and bounds. If it continues to increase at the same rate, another ten years will probably see Black Jack replacing Craps as the foremost casino banking game in the volume of money wagers. At the time of writing the M-G-M Grand Hotel Casino on the Las Vegas Strip harbors 61 Black Jack tables—the greatest number found in any casino throughout the globe. This great upsurge in the play of Black Jack stemmed from *Scarne's Complete Guide to Gambling* because there, in 1961, for the first time appeared in print the scientific analysis of Black Jack with its optimum strategy. But, more important, the book for the first time ever scientifically broke down the dealer or house advantage at 5.9% against the Black Jack player. Without this information any mathematical analysis of Black Jack would have been impossible.

After *Scarne's Complete Guide to Gambling* was published, my techniques were parroted by hundreds of so-called Black Jack experts and writers on gambling.

CASINO BETTING LIMITS

One proof of this vast increase in the popularity of Black Jack is a comparison of the maximum betting limits of a few years ago with those of today. A decade ago, most Nevada casinos had a $50 and $100 maximum, and the top limit at casinos in Puerto Rico was $100. Today most casinos in Nevada, Atlantic City, the Bahamas, etc., have a $1,000 limit, and many casinos will raise this to $2,500 or more for a big-time gambler or high roller.

Most casinos in the Caribbean advertise a $200 or $300 limit but this isn't adhered to for the big bettors. The majority, except the Puerto Rico casinos, which keep to $200 limits, will raise stakes to $1,000, $1,500 or even $2,000, and if you think this isn't big-time gambling, think again, brother. Recently, at the Curaçao Hilton Hotel casino in the Netherlands Antilles, I saw a woman delegate to the United Nations who had been given a limit of $1,000 lose $80,000 at Black Jack in a couple of hours. The casino manager then offered her a $5,000 limit on each hand. She refused, apparently feeling than an 80-grand loss was enough for one evening. Incidentally, the largest single loss on record by a Black Jack player was $500,000 over a period of a week's play at the Paradise Isle Casino in the Bahamas a couple of years ago.

The gambler who suffered the $500,000 loss was making use of Professor Edward O. Thorp's highly publicized winning Black Jack system. At the time of this incident, the Black Jack card counter was on Captain John's junket, which originated in Baltimore, Maryland.

EXPERT LOSES 51 CONSECUTIVE HANDS AT CAESARS PALACE

A few years ago a card counter who prefers to be known as "Robbie" sat at a vacant four-deck Black Jack table in Caesars Palace, Las Vegas. Robbie asked the pit boss for a maximum $1,000 limit (at the time $500 was Caesars top limit), which he received after the pit boss got the okay from Ash Resnick, the casino manager, who came over to greet him. The dealer pushed several stacks of $100 chips in his direction.

The four decks were thoroughly shuffled by the dealer and cut by Robbie by inserting an indicator card at the desired cut spot. The dealer cut the deck at that position, inserted the indicator card some 52 cards from the bottom of the card packet indicating that the deal would end at that position and a new shuffle and deal would take place. The four-deck packet was inserted into the dealing shoe and the game was ready to start.

At this time two of Robbie's friends joined him at the table to observe his play. One was Billy Weinberger, the president of Caesars Palace, and the other was Joe Louis, the former heavyweight champion of the world, who officiates at Caesars as a casino greeter.

Robbie placed a $1,000 bet on a single betting space. This was the beginning of what later turned out to be the longest losing Black Jack session ever encountered by an expert card caser and locater, or for that matter by anyone in the history of Las Vegas.

Robbie's first two dealt cards were two paints (two picture cards), a count of 20. The dealer showed a 10-count card, turned up his hole card and revealed a 6 spot, a total count of 16, an automatic hit for the dealer. The dealer drew a 5 spot making 21, beating Robbie's 20 count.

His second play was comprised of a $1,000 bet on two different spaces which later showed a count of 17 and 19. Dealer's upcard was a 7 spot. He faced his hole card—it was an 8 spot for a 15 count, another automatic hit for the dealer. He pulled a card and it was a 5 spot for the dealer for a count of 20. Robbie was down $3,000 at this period of play.

Robbie next played three hands at $1,000 each and busted the three hands. He was now a $6,000 loser.

The dealer was preparing to push Robbie several more stacks of $100 chips when Robbie turned to Ash Resnick and said, "Forget the chips, it's too much work. I'll bet $1,000 on each hand. Just give me six chips to identify the number of hands I want to play."

Resnick said, "Okay, $1,000 for each played hand. And keep track of the amount he wins or loses," he instructed the pit boss.

Robbie, the expert card caser and locater, played on and on without winning a single hand. His style of play was scientific in purpose. Sometimes his card count strategy called for playing of one hand per deal, other times two, three, four, or five hands per deal, and occasionally the maximum six hands permitted at the Black Jack table. But whatever style of game or strategy Robbie employed, he failed to win a single Black Jack hand.

During a dealer shuffle Robbie turned to Resnick and said, "Ash, this losing streak could not even take place in a bust-out joint [crooked gambling joint]."

Louis, Weinberger and Resnick agreed that this was the longest losing streak they ever witnessed at Caesars—certainly not a bust-out joint. After losing two consecutive deals, each comprised of six losing hands, Robbie asked Resnick to give him a count of his losing hands. Resnick scanned the pit boss's tally sheet and said, "Robbie, you owe us $51,000.

You lost 51 consecutive hands. I am sure you broke the record for Black Jack losing hands in Las Vegas."

Robbie's retort was a classic. "Gentlemen," he said, "that's all for now. I do not wish to tie or break Joe Di Maggio's 56 consecutive baseball games' hitting streak."

An hour later I ran into Robbie in Caesars coffee shop. He was seated at a table with Larry Snow, Caesars Baccarat boss, and Jimmy Grippo, Caesars magician entertainer. It was there that Robbie related the details concerning his record-breaking 51 consecutive losing Black Jack hands.

The first question I asked Robbie was, "How come such a great card counter and caser as you lost 51 consecutive Black Jack hands?"

He eyed me quizzically and replied, "Scarne, if you're unlucky, all the card casing and locating won't help you a bit. Card casing and locating cuts down the house's edge a bit, but it doesn't guarantee you'll beat the game because, more often than not, the cards you're expecting to show will never come into play. And that's because of that Puerto Rican Black Jack rule of yours of having the dealer cut off about 52 cards from the bottom of the four-deck card packet."

Larry Snow then turned to me and said, "Scarne, what the hell are the odds against Robbie losing those 51 straight hands?"

"The odds must be in the millions," remarked Jimmy Grippo.

I asked the waitress for a sheet of paper and pencil, which she promptly produced, and after several minutes of arithmetic, I said, "Gentlemen, assuming that Robbie's Black Jack strategy gave him a fifty-fifty chance of beating the dealer, the odds against his losing 51 consecutive hands are approximately 2,252 trillion to 1 or exactly 1 chance in 2,251,799,813,-685,248."

THE $250,000 WIN IN CUBA

Black Jack happens to be a very tricky game, and raising the limit to $2,000 may not be so smart if the players are card hustlers who know much more about the game than the casino operator suspects. This is especially true when deviations from the usual rules, such as accepting *proposition bets* (wagers that are not standard), are allowed.

As an instance, let's take the biggest Black Jack winning play of pre-Castro Cuba. Three men proved to the Cuban casinos that they knew more about the subtleties and chicaneries of Black Jack than the operators by winning a cool $250,000. Let me start with this excerpt from an article written by my good friend Edward Scott, "Going for Broke at the 23rd Parallel." It appeared in the October 16, 1958, issue of the *Havana Post:*

There's a lot more to this gambling business than meets the eye, as the losers are perfectly willing to admit after they have dropped a packet. But sometimes a man can devote a lifetime to the profession, as has been done by Lefty Clark, and still, along the way, he can pick up important pieces of new information. Sometimes this additional knowledge costs more than a trifling sum of money.

A few weeks ago, a couple of Americans went to the gambling casino then being well and efficiently operated by Mr. Clark in Marianao (he is no longer associated with that establishment) and entered with him into ye gayme and playe of blackjack. At the request of the patrons, a higher limit than usual was fixed for the wagers.

The players were consistent winners. Mr. Clark knew that they were "on the level," but he could not figure out how they could enjoy such amazing luck. Not for one second (and it was he who told me this) did he imagine that they could keep count of the face cards that had fallen, because the dealer's box contained four packs of cards.

That, however, is precisely what they were doing. Mr. Clark then resorted to the practice of shuffling the cards [all four decks] when only a third of them were left in the dealer's box. Nevertheless, the visitors continued to win and cashed in for a substantial sum of money.

The following night, or several nights later, the Americans went to play at another legal establishment in Old Havana, where they have no limits on bets. [He means that limits are raised for special players—J.S.] After about two hours of play, they cashed in for $59,700. After the pay-off, there was a misunderstanding, but the Americans were able to prove their bona fides. One is a wealthy, highly respected New York business-man, and the other is an atomic scientist.

During the course of the discussion resulting from the misunderstand-ing, the two Americans offered to play the house for half a million dollars —and the New York businessman established that he had that kind of money, and plenty to spare. At first it looked like a good thing to the house, but wiser counsel prevailed. The Americans went away, but they were back in town on Tuesday and I saw them in operation.

These two Americans are a phenomenal couple, and the first one to admit it is Lefty Clark. They memorize the number of face cards, includ-ing aces, which have fallen, and when they get down to about one third of the pack, they know exactly how many face cards have yet to fall and what the possibilities are of making a good hand by opening a pair of tens, jacks, queens, kings, or aces.

On the night of the $59,700 coup, I saw them split a pair of kings on which they had wagered $1,000. The house permitted them to bet $2,000 on each king and they won on both hands.

When I first read Mr. Scott's article I knew that the people he had interviewed didn't really know just what had happened. I was in Havana at the time, so I'll add a few firsthand details and observations. The Marianao casino mentioned is the one at the famed Tropicana nightclub. The old Havana establishment is the casino in the Sevilla Biltmore Hotel. No mention is made of a third casino which these boys took for $50,000— the Casino de Capri. I like to think that these men didn't show up to play at the Habana Hilton Casino because I was there as gambling overseer for the Hilton Hotel chain.

The wealthy New York businessman and the atomic scientist were just that, but they were also smart American card hustlers. Actually, there were three of them. I ran into the trio in the lobby of the Habana Hilton just after they had left the Sevilla Biltmore with $59,700 in winnings. A moment later Señor Analito Batisti rushed in, accompanied by several police officers. Batisti at that time operated the casino in the Sevilla Biltmore and was Cuba's top gambler. He was also a former representative of Dictator Fulgencio Batista's Congress. Batisti hurried over to the three Americans and accused them excitedly, "You cheat me! You cheat me!"

The Americans were promptly hauled off to the hoosegow at gunpoint. Batisti's beef was that they had cheated him by marking the cards. He said that after the trio left his casino he checked the deck and found that several cards were *crimped* (bent). This is a typical casino operator's reaction when he loses a bundle; they are nearly all bad losers. Batisti was not only a bad loser but he had to squeal to the cops, too. He used to claim proudly that his casino would deal a high roller the biggest limit in Cuba. After this incident his claim wasn't taken very seriously.

THE $1 MILLION FREEZE-OUT

The hustlers denied the charge that they had marked the cards and insisted they had merely used honest mathematical strategy. They also claimed they could beat any casino bank in the same way and challenged Batisti to a $500,000 "Black Jack freeze-out." They would put up $500,-000 to Batisti's $500,000 and play Black Jack until one or the other went for broke. They said that they would not touch any of the cards, and all their cards could be dealt face up. They insisted, however, that the same casino rules be adhered to as on the night they had won the $59,700. They wanted the $1,000 limit, the right to split a count of 20, and to double down on each split hand.

Batisti accepted the challenge. He and the hustlers each posted with the police captain $30,000 in cash as a forfeit, in the event that either backed out. Batisti then withdrew his complaint, and the three Americans were released. During the ten hours they had been locked up, Batisti had been severely criticized by the other casino operators in Havana for having the big-money winners arrested. It might, they objected, scare off high rollers from gambling in Cuba. Forty-eight hours later, an agent of the hustlers arrived from the United States with half a million in U.S. currency. Batisti stated that he had an equal amount tucked away in the casino safe waiting to be wagered.

The news of this million-dollar freeze-out spread like wildfire. Casino, bar, nightclub, restaurant and barbershop patrons talked about little else. As a sample, my barber asked me this:

"Mr. John, I hear one of the Americanos is a memory expert and can remember all the cards in four decks. Another Americano is a scientist and has the brain of an adding machine, only faster, and the other is one of the greatest card players in the United States. So, I think Batisti will lose his half million dollars."

Others wondered whether it was possible to beat Black Jack honestly, as the three winners maintained. People talked about it as excitedly and as often as they talk about baseball in this country during a World Series.

The excitement grew still greater when another $600,000 was added to the money at stake on the day before the freeze-out. A pool of American casino operators, including those who had lost such large sums, asked Batisti if he would accept this 600 grand as an additional wager that the Americanos would win. (Who says gamblers don't gamble?) Batisti accepted and told them to bring the money with them to the big game.

I arrived at the Sevilla Biltmore an hour before the game was scheduled. The casino was packed with big- and smalltime gamblers. The three Americans and Batisti were in one corner of the room talking in low tones. An excited air of expectancy filled the place. And why not? This would be the biggest single gamble between player and bank in the history of gambling. The total sum involved was $2,200,000.

But the big gamble fizzled. At the hour it was to begin the principals left the casino and an attendant announced that the freeze-out had been called off.

The three Americans were staying at the Habana Hilton and I talked to them later in their suite. They said that ten minutes before zero hour Batisti had chilled and called all bets off. "But," they added, "he did apologize for the humiliation and inconvenience he had caused us by the arrest." Batisti's reign as Cuba's top gambler ended suddenly on New Year's Day, 1959, when Fidel Castro overthrew Batista's government.

Some years later, many casino gamblers are still trying to figure out how these three hustlers managed to buck the Black Jack percentage over a period of time and win a quarter of a million dollars. They don't like the idea that some players may be able to beat the bank by splitting a pair of tens, jacks, queens and kings, and they worry even more over the possibility that there may be some hidden gimmick they know nothing about.

In order to bring the reader up to date on the further activities of these three American card hustlers, let's turn to Edward O. Thorp's book, *Beat the Dealer* (1962) in which he states that he and two of his New York multimillionaire gambling backers, whom he dubs Mr. X and Mr. Y, had beaten the Black Jack tables in Reno and Lake Tahoe for $11,000 in five days' play.

My investigation of this gambling spree revealed that Thorp's Mr. X and Mr. Y were not the two innocent gambling backers that he claimed them to be, but instead were two of the three American Black Jack hustlers who had beaten the Seville Biltmore Casino in Havana for $59,700 a few years earlier. To get the real lowdown on this big $11,000 win of

Thorp and Co., I looked up Mr. X, who at the time was vacationing at the Caribe Hilton Hotel in Puerto Rico. Mr. X, in answer to my question why he and his partner teamed up with Thorp, had this to say: "I read several magazine stories about Thorp and his unbeatable Black Jack system, and being that he is a mathematics professor, I though there might be something to these stories, so we called him on the phone and inquired if he would like to team up with me and my partner to beat the Nevada Black Jack tables by making use of his unbeatable system. Thorp agreed and after the first three days of play in Reno, Nevada, we realized that Thorp knew nothing about the science of Black Jack play, and his count-down system never seemed to work. We were getting our brains knocked out. We finally decided to resort to the old-time gambler's ten-card count system, and recouped a few bucks. It was then that we decided to give Thorp the air. Thorp later admitted to us that he never really gambled, but took this gambling trip with us for material he might gather for the book he was in the process of writing."

My next question to Mr. X was in reference to Thorp's statement that the trio was cheated on a number of occasions in Reno and Lake Tahoe. Mr. X replied, "Scarne, you know better than that—if there was any cheating taking place, we'd be doing the cheating."

Mr. X and I then discussed his caper with Mr. Y at the Seville Biltmore Casino in Havana. I told him that in my opinion he and Mr. Y had the dealer fixed by having him tip off his hole card to them. He replied, "What else? The B.J. proposition bets were made to throw Batisti off the track that we had his dealer in our pocket."

Several years later Mr. Y was caught red-handed at Caesars Palace in Las Vegas trying to bribe a Black Jack dealer to tip off the value of his hole card whenever the dealer was dealt an ace or ten as his upcard.

SCARNE SEEKS A JOB AS A CROOKED BLACK JACK DEALER

I made a thorough survey of gambling establishments near Army camps at the request of the Army's General Staff during World War II in order to find out if the GIs were being fleeced. I found at that time that a number of the smaller joints only hired dealers who were card *mechanics* (a mechanic is the card sharp who does the sleight of hand). The first question asked of an applicant for the job of Black Jack dealer was "Can you deal a good second?" I know this because one of the best ways to find out if a casino is using a dealer who cheats is to apply for the job. In 1944, on one special Army assignment, I went into a casino whose name I won't mention because it is still in operation and is now being run honestly under new management.

I approached the casino boss and asked if he could use a good Black Jack dealer.

He half-smiled. "Who recommended you?"

"No one," I told him. "But I need a job and thought you might be looking for a good number two man." A "number two man" is gambler's slang for a second dealer, who can deal the second card from the top and make it look as though he were dealing the top card.

The half-smile was replaced by an icy look. "So you're a mechanic. Okay, come into the office and give me a gander at what you can do."

There he told me his name was Bucky. I gave him an alias, John Orlando, and said I was from New Jersey.

"Okay, John," he said. "Here's a deck. Let me see you work."

I shuffled the cards and dealt myself the same Black Jack hand three times in a row. Bucky's sales resistance vanished.

"You've got a job starting tonight. I'll give you twenty-five bucks a night and ten percent of the table's winnings over and above our normal day's business." Then, as an explanation of why the casino was cheating, he added, "You know our season here at the Lake is pretty short. We have to get the money in only three months."

"Yeah," I told him, "I understand."

John Orlando, however, did not report for work that night, there or anywhere else, although I had accepted two other dealing jobs in this town that same day. Each time I had to prove my ability at ripping seconds. These casinos were no exception to the general rule. The country was flooded with card mechanics, and they didn't worry about whom they clipped, or where. GIs were fair game, like anybody else.

Today, gambling casinos of established reputation in Nevada and elsewhere fight the crooked casino operators as a menace to business. When the players eventually get wise that casinos are cheating, business drops off. Your best protection against the crooked Black Jack dealer is to know the game and to be informed on cheats and their methods. For the last, see pages 107–110.

BLACK JACK'S HISTORY

Black Jack as a private rather than a casino banking game was the most popular card game, even more popular than Poker, among the doughboys of World War I. The GIs of World War II played the banking version of Black Jack more than any other card game. The biggest sum of money won by a Black Jack banker in the Armed Forces during that war was $137,500, won by an Army corporal in the Pacific theater. P.S. His occupation in Chicago before the war: Black Jack dealer.

There is almost as murky a scholarly dispute over the origin of Black Jack as there is over Poker and Gin Rummy. Italy, France and Spain have claimed it. The French allege a blood relationship with Vingt-Un and Trente et Quarante. The Spanish say it is an adaption of their One and Thirty. The Italians insist that it is a slightly modified form of either

Baccara or Seven and a Half. These last two have the closest similarity to Black Jack.

The basic object of the three games is the same: to reach a count of 21 in Black Jack, 9 in Baccara and 7½ in Seven and a Half. The Seven and a Half deck contains only 40 cards, the eights, nines and tens being absent. Court cards each count ½, the others count their numerical value. The king of diamonds is wild and may have any value. When a player, trying to get as close to a count of 7½ as possible, draws cards totaling 8 or more, he busts, as he does when going over 21 in Black Jack. Since this is the feature that has made casino-style Black Jack so popular and since it first appeared in Seven and a Half, I believe that this game, more than the others, is the direct forerunner of Black Jack.

The basic principle of Black Jack is the simple adding of card values in an attempt to reach a total of 21; there have been many similar games. In Crockford's, the celebrated London carpet joint (1827–44), such elite sporting bloods as the Duke of Wellington, Charles, Marquess of Queensberry, Talleyrand, Prince Esterhazy, Disraeli and Bulwer-Lytton played at Quinze, in which the object was to reach a count of 15. In order to conceal their emotions from the scrutinizing eyes of the dealer they sometimes wore masks.

The earliest known printed reference to the Spanish game of One and Thirty appears in *The Comical History of Rinconete and Cortadillo,* published in 1570.

The *American Hoyle* of 1875 calls Black Jack Vingt-Un, and *Foster's Hoyle,* 30 years later, calls it Vingt-et-Un. The English corrupted this to Van John; the Austrialians' French pronunciation was even wider of the mark—they called it Pontoon—but the basic principle, a desired count of 21, was the same.

Through most of its history, Black Jack, or Twenty-One, its earlier name, was a private game, and it wasn't until 1915 that it began to make its appearance as a banking game in the top casinos of this country. I queried many old-time gambling-house operators and Black Jack dealers in an effort to pin down the exact date of the first Twenty-One banking table. None had seen one prior to those which were introduced in horse rooms in and around Evansville, Indiana, in the early part of 1910.

HOW BLACK JACK GOT ITS NAME

The betting limits at these first Twenty-One tables ranged from a low of 25¢ to a high of $1, but they received little action, and the tables disappeared only a few months later. Then, late in 1912, a new form of Twenty-One appeared in the Evansville horse rooms. Players were paid off at 3 to 2 odds when they made a count of 21 with the first two cards, and if the two-card 21 was made up of the ace of spades and the jack of either spades or clubs, the holder received a $5 bonus for each 50¢ he had wagered. This induced the horse bettors to take a whirl at the game, and it began to receive more action. Before long, the players began to distinguish the two-card count of 21 from a three-or-more-card count of 21 by calling it "Black Jack."

In 1917, printed signs began appearing above the Twenty-One tables reading: "Black Jack pays odds of 3 to 2." Early in 1919 a Chicago manufacturer of gambling equipment began selling tables with this announcement printed in bold black letters on the green baize playing surface. Since then the game itself has been called Black Jack.

At that time, gamblers in the eastern states paid little attention to Black Jack; they devoted their time to Indian and Take-off Craps, which were faster and could be played in back alleys, open lots and cellars, as they required no table. But the game spread, and early in 1920 Black Jack tables began to appear in horse rooms and sawdust joints throughout the country.

From 1920 to 1930 its growth was gradual. Each year various casinos added new rules and dropped old ones. Then, in 1931, Black Jack tables were introduced in most of Nevada's legalized gambling establishments, and visiting players from other parts of the country spread its popularity across the nation. Prior to this it was a man's game because it had been played only in sawdust joints and horse rooms, dives which women did not frequent. Now women began to play Black Jack.

The most popular banking card games at this time were still Banker and Broker, Red Dog, Stuss and Skin, to name a few; but when thousands of servicemen who had learned Black Jack in the Armed Forces during World War II returned home, Black Jack rapidly became America's most popular banking card game. By 1948 it was second only to Craps in the casinos.

Before the appearance of my gambling articles in *Yank: The Army Weekly* during World War II, which contained the most comprehensive treatise on Black Jack up to that time, the gambling-house operators and Black Jack dealers had almost no idea of what the bank's favorable percentage at Black Jack was. The game-book writers had even less. (This is especially true of those Bridge experts who stray from their subject and write books and articles on other gambling games. Some state that no one knows what the bank's P.C. is except the casino managers, who aren't telling. In spite of this, they proceed to outline a strategy or system which, they claim, will beat the game. Any system or strategy for winning that is cooked up by someone who admits he doesn't know what odds he is bucking has to be sheer nonsense. Some of these Bridge experts seem to know less about gambling than the average casino sucker, and the editors who buy their "authoritative" articles obviously know even less.)

My articles in *Yank* did not contain an exact mathematical breakdown on the bank's favorable edge, but it did give the first approximate percentage breakdown. It would have been foolish at that time for me to undertake the complex calculations required because the rules governing the dealer's play often varied from casino to casino. In some the dealer's count of 16 was optional; he could either draw or hit. Other casinos specified that the dealer's count of 16 was an automatic hit; still others ruled that a dealer's soft 17 had to be hit.

To add to the general confusion, some casinos paid a bonus on a 21 count with two nines and three aces; some paid bonuses on a 21 count with the six, seven and eight of one suit, or a count of 21 with seven cards; others paid a bonus to the holder of the ace and jack of spades. The bonus amounts also varied from a low $5 on the ace and jack of spades to a high $25 on a seven-card count of 21. These bonuses were paid off on any bet larger than the minimum bet permitted.

CASINO RULE VARIATIONS

The basic rules of Black Jack as played in legal casinos the world over are the same except for some dealing and "doubling down" variations. Some casinos deal Black Jack with single or double decks from the hand. Others use two, three, four, five, six or eight decks dealt out of a miniature Chemin de Fer box called a shoe. Some European and Caribbean casinos, in order to prevent the Black Jack dealer from tipping off (signaling) his hole card to agents (player cheats), do not permit the dealer to look at his facedown card when his upcard is an ace or a ten. This rule was devised by me for Cuban casinos back in late 1957. Some casinos have gone one step further: they rule that the Black Jack dealer is to be dealt only one card face up: the dealer's second card is dealt face up after all the players have played out their hands.

Some Nevada casinos deal the player's first two cards face down and permit a double down on any two cards. Some Caribbean and European casinos permit doubling down on counts of 9, 10, 11; others on counts of 10 and 11; and others permit doubling down on 11 only.

As far back as 1949, while acting as gaming consultant to the Puerto Rican government, I developed the two- and four-deck Black Jack dealing box and ruled that all cards be dealt face up except the dealer's hole card and the player's double-down card. In 1963 I devised the ruling that 50 or more bottom cards of the four-deck packet should never come into actual play. This was achieved by having the dealer insert an indicator card 50 or more cards from the bottom of the 208-card packet and end the hand when the indicator card made its appearance. These innovations accomplish the following: (1) The card box eliminates 95% of the cheating methods employed by crooked house dealers. (2) When the player's cards are dealt face up, it helps the dealer to correct any errors that the player may have made when totaling the numbered value of the playing hand. In addition, it prevents any card-cheat player from switching one or both of his face-down cards that he may have secretly palmed, and at the same time, owing to the fact that the dealer(house) does not have any discretionary powers on when to hit or stand, it doesn't matter whether the dealer sees the player's cards or not. (3) The purpose of inserting the indicator card toward the bottom of the 208-card packet is to prevent the cut-off cards from coming into actual play, which in turn prevents "card counters" or "countdown" players from memorizing or clocking the cards as they are being dealt and by so doing learn the identity of the last 50 undealt cards, and thereby gain an advantage over the house. (4) The only other method of cheating that the house could resort to would be to use marked cards and deal seconds. When the dealer recognized a valuable card by the hidden markings on the back, he would deal a second (the card below the top card of the packet). This method is commonly used by dealer cheats when Black Jack is dealt from the hand. To eliminate this house-cheating possibility, I recommend that the four-deck packet be comprised of two red- and two blue-backed decks—because if a valuable red-backed card is on top the dealer would not dare to deal the card below, because he has no way of knowing if the card below is a red- or a blue-backed card. Imagine six players at a Black Jack table seeing a red-backed card about to be dealt and a blue-backed card turns up.

I have selected for analysis the Black Jack rules I formulated, which are now in use in countless casinos the world over. They have been chosen because they are the best of all casino rules—not only for the player's protection, but for the casino's as well. I predict that within a few years Scarne's Black Jack casino rules will be adopted by most casino operators throughout the world.

SCARNE'S CASINO BLACK JACK RULES:
KNOWN AS "THE SCARNE DEAL"

REQUIREMENTS

1. A regulation Black Jack table with six or seven betting spaces on its layout.

2. A check rack filled with betting chips and silver dollars.

3. A card-dealing box called a shoe.

4. Four standard decks of 52 cards each (two red-backed decks and two blue-backed decks) shuffled together and used as one, a total of 208 cards dealt as a single packet.

5. Two indicator cards—one is used by players to cut the packet, the other is used to determine the end of the deal.

6. A shill, a house employee (male or female) who poses as a player to stimulate business.

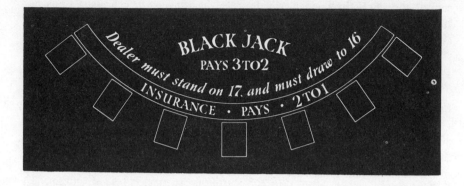

Black Jack layout.

7. A pit boss who is a casino inspector and who stands alongside the dealer, observing every action of play. He sees to it that no mistakes are made by the dealer or players. He is in complete charge; he rules on all disagreements and his decisions are final. All players and the dealer must abide by them, provided they are within the laws set down by the casino and in conformity with the regulations set down by the particular state or country.

NUMBER OF PLAYERS

1. The houseman who is the steady dealer and the banker. He never surrenders the deal or bank.

2. One to six or seven active players, each of whom may bet on several hands depending on the betting space available.

3. Any number of outsiders, kibitzers, who may wager on each player's hand. They must not advise the player how to play his hand.

VALUE OF CARDS

The cards have the following value:

1. Aces count either 1 or 11 at the discretion of the player holder. However, the dealer must value the ace as set down by the casino rules.

2. Kings, queens, and jacks each have a count of 10.

3. All other cards are counted at their face value.

THE OBJECT OF THE GAME

A player tries to obtain a higher total card count than the dealer by reaching 21 or as close to 21 as possible without exceeding that count. If the player's total count exceeds 21, he has *busted* and must turn his cards face up at once. He has lost his bet, and the dealer immediately scoops it up. The player, at his proper turn of play and at his own discretion, may stand or draw one or more cards in an attempt to better his count.

THE BETTING LIMITS

The casino sets its own limit, but the minimum and maximum bet must be announced to the players.

The minimum bet limit in the Las Vegas Strip casinos is always one silver dollar. The maximum limit is $100 in some; in others it is $200, $300 or $1,000. The operators will often raise the maximum to $2,500 or more at the sight of a high roller.

If you like your Las Vegas Black Jack action small and can't stand the silver-dollar minimum, you can go to the downtown Las Vegas tables, where the minimum may be as little as 10¢. This also holds true in Reno and other Nevada towns.

THE SHUFFLE AND CUT

The cards are shuffled by the dealer, who then hands a player an indicator card and says, "Cut, please." The player inserts the indicator card into the packet to show where he wants the cards cut. The dealer cuts the cards at this position, putting the indicator and all the cards above it on the bottom. The indicator goes to the bottom of the packet. The dealer then inserts the second indicator card 50 cards or thereabouts from the bottom of the deck, and places all the cards into the dealing box face down. The shoe is now ready to be dealt by the dealer. When the indicator card inserted by the dealer makes its appearance and enough cards have been dealt to complete the hand in progress, the deal ends—and the dealer must begin a new shuffle and again repeat the above-described procedure.

BETTING

Before the deal begins, each player must place his bet in cash or chips in the betting space—which may be indicated as a circle, rectangle or some other symbol—painted on the playing surface directly before him in full view of the dealer.

Nevada casinos permit players, especially high rollers, to bet as many hands as there are available *holes* (betting spaces). Most Black Jack tables bear six or seven betting spaces. When a player plays more than one hand at a time, he must play the hand farthest to his right to completion before being permitted to look at his next hand or hands.

The dealer may check the amount of the player's bet to see that it is not greater than the maximum limit. If a player desires a higher limit, he may ask the pit boss, who will either grant or refuse it.

THE DEAL

After all players' bets are down, the dealer removes the first card from the dealing box and places it face down without showing its face value in the discard receiver. This is known as burning a card or a "burnt card." All cards used to make a hand are discarded in the same manner. After the first dealt card has been burnt, starting with the player on his extreme left, the dealer begins dealing clockwise, giving one card face up to each player and one face up to himself. He next deals each player, starting with the player on his extreme left, a second face-up card, and one down to himself.

THE PLAY

If the dealer's face-up card is a 10 count or an ace, he must look at his *hole* (face-down) card. If he has a natural 21 (a count of 21 with two cards) he must face it and announce "Twenty-One" or "Black Jack."

Any player with a natural 21 also announces it, and the dealer declares this to be a *standoff* or *push*. There is no action on his hand, and no payoff is made.

The dealer wins and collects bets from players not having a natural 21.

When the dealer does not hold a natural 21, the player at his extreme left plays first. If the player holds a natural 21, he announces it and faces his cards so the dealer can verify the count. The dealer pays off the winning natural at 3 to 2 odds. This means that if the player has bet $2 he collects $5—his own $2 plus an additional $3. The dealer then burns the two played-out cards.

If the player's two cards total less than 21 he may elect:

1. To stay. Either he is satisfied with his count or he fears that a third card may make his count go above 21. He says, "Good," "I have enough" or "I stand"; or he signifies that he is staying simply by sliding his cards under the chips he has bet.

2. To draw a card or cards. When the player is not satisfied with his count, he says, "Hit me," or makes a beckoning motion by closing and opening his hand, or a come-on motion with a finger. The dealer then deals another card off the top of the deck face up before the player and next to his original two cards. Although the cards are dealt one at a time, the player may continue to draw as many as he likes. When he believes his count is as good as he can do, he stays. If he draws a card which puts his count above 21, he must announce a bust. The dealer scoops up the player's bet and cards and burns the cards in the discard pile.

The play moves to the player's left, clockwise around the table until all players have played out their hands.

THE DEALER'S TURN AT PLAY

If all players have busted, the dealer merely places his own cards in the discard pile and deals a new hand. If any active player or players are left, the dealer plays his hand.

1. He turns up his hole card so that all his cards are exposed.

2. If his count is 17, 18, 19 or 20, the dealer must stay.

3. If his count is 16 or less, he must draw a card and continue to draw until his count reaches 17 or more—at which point he must stay. If the dealer holds a *soft 17,* i.e., a 17 count which includes an ace, he must also stay. This also applies to a soft 18, 19 or 20.

It is important to note here that the Black Jack dealer has no choice of whether to stay or draw. His decisions are predetermined and known to the players. Since all the dealer's cards are exposed at his turn of play, he has no opportunity for any departure from these rules.

The rule requiring the dealer to hit on 16 or less and stay on 17, 18, 19, 20 and 21 is standard today in all major casinos here and abroad.

Additional rule: If a dealer errs and deals a player a card which the player did not call for, and the card is refused by the player, the card is considered a "dead" card and must be burnt and placed in the discard receiver. The B.J. pit boss has the last word in deciding whether the player called or did not call for a card.

FINAL SETTLEMENT

At the end of his play the dealer starts with the first active player on his extreme right and moves around the table counterclockwise, paying off players who have a higher count than his with an amount equal to the bet they placed, and collecting the placed bets from players showing a lesser count. If player and dealer have the same count, it is a *standoff,* or tie, and no one collects or loses. If the dealer busts, he pays off each surviving active player an amount equal to his bet.

SPLITTING PAIRS

Any two cards that are identical except for suit may be treated as a pair. Also, any two cards each having a value of 10 may be treated as pairs, such as a ten and jack, jack and queen or queen and king.

A player who receives two cards forming a pair or considered to be a pair on the initial round may, if he chooses, separate the two cards and treat each card as the first card dealt in two separate hands. This is called *splitting pairs.* When pairs are split, the player's original bet is placed on one of these cards and an equal amount must be bet on the other.

The player is then dealt one face-up card on the face-up card on his right, and he must play his hand out. If, in drawing to the first face-up card, he forms a pair again, he may again split pairs, betting an amount equal to his first card on this third hand. He may continue to split any further pairs.

The first hand on the player's extreme right must be played to completion before the adjacent split hand is dealt a second card. Each split hand must be played out in its proper order from the player's right to his left.

When a player splits a pair of aces, he is only permitted to draw one card to each split ace, giving him two cards in all.

If a *paint* (picture card) or ten or ace is part of a split hand and the player makes a two-card count of 21, it is not a natural and the player is paid off at even money.

THE DOUBLE DOWN

A player, after being dealt his first two cards (which may be any two cards), may elect to double his bet and draw one additional card only. This is known as a double down, or down for double. A player, before calling "Double down" or "Down for double," must double his original bet. He is then dealt a third and final face-down card on his two face-up cards. Player is not permitted to look at the face-down card until the dealer turns it face up after the deal has been completed. Some Nevada casinos allow a second double down on a count of 9 if the player draws a deuce as his first double-down card. Many Caribbean casinos permit doubling down on an 11 count only. Others permit a double down on counts of 9, 10 and 11.

INSURANCE BETTING

In many casinos, when the dealer's face-up card is an ace, players may make an insurance bet against losing to the banker's possible natural. The dealer, before looking at his down card, inquiries if any player wants insurance. A player who desires insurance places an amount equal to half his present wager on his own hand.

When this bet is made, the dealer looks at his down card. If it is a 10 count, he turns it face up and announces a nautral. The insurance bettor is paid off at the rate of 2 to 1 for every unit wagered. If the dealer's down card is not a 10-count card, the player loses his insurance bet.

SCARNE'S CASINO FOUR-DECK SHUFFLE

Scarne's Casino Black Jack Rules and Scarne's Casino Four-Deck Shuffle were first introduced in Puerto Rico and soon spread to Aruba, Curaçao and to casinos the world over. The Sands Hotel Casino in Las Vegas was the first casino in Nevada to deal Black Jack from a shoe (card box) with four decks, making use of my casino Black Jack rules. The first night the new system went into effect, my friend Carl Cohen, then casino manager of the Sands, and now casino director of M-G-M's Grand Hotel, requested me to study each dealer as he shuffled the four decks prior to placing them into the shoe. Later that evening I informed Carl Cohen that the shuffling method employed by his dealers made the Sands a real setup for top notch card casers.

Basically, the shuffle that dealers were using at the time was as follows: They would divide the 208-card deck into three piles and shuffle each pile individually. I explained to Carl that although the cards were being shuffled, few cards left each of the three piles. For example, let's say that 12 aces fell in the bottom 70 cards of the 208-card packet. Should the dealer follow this procedure of shuffling, the 12 aces would remain in the same 70-card pile regardless of the shuffle. Right then and there, the Scarne Casino Four-Deck Shuffle was introduced at the Sands. Soon after, casinos throughout Nevada followed.

The Scarne Casino Four-Deck Shuffle, which you may have seen, is executed as follows: The dealer separates the 208-card packet into two piles. Then he removes about 35 cards from the top of each pile and shuffles them together. He repeats the same procedure twice more with the remaining cards. The dealer then squares the packet and gives it several running cuts. This being done, the dealer pushes the packet to the player to be cut.

Then the player inserts an indicator card into the packet to show where he wants the cards cut. The dealer obliges, the indicator card going to the bottom of the packet. Next, the dealer inserts a second indicator card 50 or more cards from the bottom of the packet. The 208-card packet is now placed into the dealing box face up, ready to be dealt.

THE BLACK JACK DEALER'S EXACT PERCENTAGE TAKE

Why do you lose at Black Jack? What is your chance to win? What odds are you bucking? What is the bank's favorable advantage, and where does it exist?

Before I calculated the bank's advantage at 5.90% when the player adheres to the dealer's fixed strategy, no one, including mathematicians, bridge experts, game-book authors, players and casino employees, knew the right answers. Without this information, any mathematical analysis of Black Jack would be meaningless.

Bridge experts Ely Culbertson, Albert Morehead and Geoffrey Mott-Smith admitted they didn't know either. In *Culbertson's Card Games, Complete with Official Rules,* they say: "In no game that has been played for high stakes has there been less analysis of the science of playing than in Black Jack. The only available guide to strategy is empirical; no one has more than his opinion on which to estimate the advantage of the dealer."

I want to go on record here and now that *Scarne on Cards* (1949) published the first scientific and comprehensive analysis of the dealer's advantage caused by the player playing first and busting first. This player-and dealer-busts analysis revealed that the player who mimicked the dealer was bucking a house advantage of 4%. At that stage of Black Jack, player bonuses were in vogue, such as a $5 bonus for each dollar bet on holding the ace and jack of spades, 6-7-8 of the same suit, plus many more bonuses. I based this 4% figure on my clocking the action and bust results of ten different Black Jack tables for a one-month period. The following is reprinted from *Scarne on Cards*.

Let's get the bust percentage straight first. You don't have to use my clocking if you don't like it; clock a few hundred games yourself, and then use your own figures. But it works out as follows:

There are four players and a dealer. Now, don't make the mistake of basing your calculation on what happens in a single hand. Take at least four hands. And let's say that each player averages to bust once each four hands, a total of four busts in sixteen player-hand units. So the house has collected four bust bets.

But something like the same average of busts will hold for the dealer, regardless of his wisdom and piety. The dealer will bust just as often as the players if he and they follow the same rules as to drawing or staying. It's true that players are not bound by the rules and, tempted by bonuses, tend to draw when they shouldn't, whereas the dealer follows the safe rules. On the other hand, some players are extra cautious and stay when they shouldn't. While the dealer gets the benefit of this foolishness by winning the majority of such hands, this factor does tend to balance off to some extent the rash drawing of the Iron Dukes. For the sake of the figures, however, let's say players and dealer follow the same rules. Then the dealer also busts one out of four.

And when he goes over 21, he must pay the three players still in the game.

So, on the sixteen player-hand units the dealer has collected four busts and paid out three busts, and the percentage in his favor on this count is 6⅔ per cent.

But, out of 6⅔ per cent collected in busts, the dealer has to pay off bonuses, and this is percentage in favor of the player. The largest percentage that the player receives from bonuses is three to two, which the bank pays the player who holds a "natural." This occurs approximately once in twenty-one deals. Therefore the bank pays the player one additional unit as a bonus on approximately every forty-two deals. This amounts to 2⁸⁄₂₁ per cent paid to the player. (The stand-off which occurs when both the dealer and the player each hold a natural [21] and occurs in approximately 441 deals does not affect this figure.)

Taking into consideration additional bonuses, which vary in amount with different houses—such as a $5 bonus for a $1 bet on holding the ace and jack of spades, or the 6, 7, and 8 of the same suit plus some minor additional bonuses—we can safely estimate that the bank pays back 3⅔ per cent to the players out of this 6⅔ per cent that it enjoys in busts. But we must also give the bank at least another 1 per cent break in its favor earned with splits, insurance bets, etc., bringing the percentage in the bank's favor to approximately 4 per cent.

Before we dive into a mathematical analysis of the game as it is played today, I should tell you just what part of the game gives the bank an advantage. If you ask a dealer what happens to your bet when he and you tie with the same count, his stock answer is: "All ties are a standoff; no one wins and no one loses." This implies that the dealer doesn't take your bet if you tie. This isn't quite right; in fact it's dead wrong.

True, the dealer doesn't take your bet when you tie on a count of 21 or less, but if his statement that all ties are standoffs is true, then he should keep his hands off your dough when you tie at 22, 23 or anything above 21. Does he? No, that's not the way Black Jack is played. When a player busts, the dealer doesn't wait to see whether he will also bust and tie at a count above 21. He rakes in the bet and closes that transaction. The player has lost, even though his count may later tie the dealer's.

This is the crux of the hidden P.C. in the bank's favor. This is the real reason why casino operators like Black Jack and why most players lose at the game.

The bank has an advantage in the unspoken and largely unnoticed provision that ties stand off, or push, *provided the count is 21 or less*. Want to prove it? That's easy. Just ask your dealer to play his hand out after you have busted and ask him if he also busts and goes over your count to pay you off. You'll get a fast answer telling you exactly where to go and when.

It is, of course, not feasible to figure the exact percentage against individual players because their play differs so much. Some players will stay on 12, 13 and 14; some will draw on 15 and 16; others stay on 15 or more; and there's always the dub who will draw to an ace and nine.

However, since the dealer has no choice whether to stay or draw, because the rules predetermine this, we can calculate the exact percentage working in his favor. It isn't easy, but it can be done. We know first that the banker's hidden advantage lies in the fact that the player must play first, and if dealer and player both bust at a count above 21 the player loses his bet. If it were not for this (and if, when the dealer's face-up card was dealt face down the bank paid off a natural at even-money odds, and a player could not split pairs or double down) the game would be an even-up proposition.

There is also another complication. Unlike the bank's P.C. at Craps and Roulette, which doesn't vary, the bank's P.C. at Black Jack changes considerably during the play. It goes up or down as each card is dealt. The following analysis, therefore, must be based on a full-deck composition. We assume, for purposes of analysis, that all 52 cards are present, none having yet been dealt.

Next, we find out how many dealer busts may be expected in the long run. We make use of the standard permutation and combination formulas, plus some straight thinking and simple arithmetic. We calculate how many different ways (using a 52-card deck) the dealer's initial two face-down cards can produce all the possible counts. Like this:

BLACK JACK TABLE I

THE 1326 TWO-CARD COUNTS IN BLACK JACK

Count	Number of Ways It Can Be Made
21	64
20	136
19	80
18	86
17	96
16	86
15	96
14	102
13	112
12	118
11	64
10	54
9	48
8	38
7	32
6	38
5	32
4	22
3	16
2	6
Total Number of Ways	1,326

We find that the dealer's first two cards can produce the counts from 2 through 21 in 1,326 different ways. Note that the player can count an ace as either 1 or 11, but the dealer must count the ace as 11 in all soft hands with a count of 17 or more; the above table is figured on that premise. We don't try to calculate how many hands out of these 1,326 the dealer will bust, because we'll run into too many fractions. We'll discover what we need to know, however, and avoid most of the fractions, if we multiply 1,326 × 169 to get a common multiple of 224,094. Now suppose your favorite dealer dealt this many hands and suppose each combination of two cards appeared exactly as often as probability theory predicts it will in the long run.

Two-card counts of 17, 18, 19, 20 and 21 will show up 462 times out of 1,326, which is 462/1326 × 224,094 = 78,078 times. The Black Jack rules demand that the dealer must stay on all these hands, so he cannot bust on any of them.

Two-card counts of 12, 13, 14, 15 and 16 will be held by the dealer

514 times out of 1,326 or $514/1,326 \times 224,094 = 86,866$ times. Since the rules demand that the dealer must draw to a count of 16 or less, he will bust 47,456 times and reach 17 to 21 counts 39,410 times out of the initial 86,866 dealt hands.

Two-card counts of 2, 3, 4, 5, 6, 7, 8, 9, 10 and 11 will appear 350 times or $350/1,326 \times 224,094 = 59,150$ times. When the dealer gets any of these counts he must, according to the rules, draw one or more additional cards; he will bust 17,018 times and reach a 17 to 21 count 42,132 times out of the initial 59,150 dealt hands.

Now, adding the busts gives a total of 64,474, and adding the nonbust hands gives a total of 159,620. Divide the 64,474 busts into the total 224,094 hands and we find that the dealer will bust on an average once out of every 3.47 dealt hands, or about 28 out of every 100 dealt hands.

Since the rules of play give the player more freedom in his decisions and since players don't conform to any single strategy (many aren't even consistent, playing one way at one time, another way a few minutes later) how do we arrive at a figure for the number of busts the player may expect? First we must consider a hypothetical player who is consistent in his play and who follows the same rules as does the dealer. He stays on a count of 17 or over, draws to count of 16 or less, and cannot split pairs or double down. If we assume this, we can calculate an exact percentage by finding out how many times probability theory says that dealer and player will bust on the same round.

Since we calculated above that the dealer can expect to bust 64,474 times out of 224,094, and since our hypothetical player is playing according to the rules governing the dealer, he will bust the same number of times. We multiply their chances, expressed as fractions like this: $64,474/224,094 \times 64,474/224,094$, for an answer of $4,156,896,676/50,218,120,836$. Now divide the top figure by the bottom one, and there's the answer: The bank or dealer has a favorable bust percentage of 8.27%.

Out of this 8.27% that the bank collects in hidden percentage, it has to pay off players holding a natural 21 count on their initial two cards at odds of 3 to 2. This occurs, in the long run, once in 21 deals. The bank, therefore, pays out one additional unit as a bonus once every 42 deals, or 2.37%. (The standoff, which occurs when both dealer and player hold a natural 21, happens once in 441 deals; it affects the P.C. figure so very little that we can forget it.)

When you deduct the 2.37% player's advantage from the 8.27% bank advantage, the final favorable percentage for the bank comes to 5.90%. Make a note of that 5.90%. Better yet, memorize it: you now know something about Black Jack that your dealer doesn't know—at least, not until he reads this.

Any questions? Yes, I can hear someone saying, "Wait a minute, Scarne. If the only advantage the bank has is the one it gains when player and dealer both bust, why can't the player turn this bust factor to his advantage?

He merely doesn't draw to a count of 12, 13, 14, 15, 16 or more, thus avoiding all bust hands, while the dealer, who must draw on a count of 16 or less, will still bust once out of every 3.47 hands. Brother, I'm heading right now for the nearest Black Jack table!"

Don't be in such a hurry, Dick. The casino operators won't argue the matter with you, because it's the players with the wrong answers who give them a handsome profit. But take it from me, the answer to your question is a big NO in capital letters.

Why? Remember that the bank's advantage is based on two factors, not one: the double-bust factor and the fact that the player must play his hand out first. If your strategy consists in avoiding bust hands by not drawing on counts of 12, 13, 14, 15, 16 or more, you'll be fighting an even greater percentage than if you followed the dealer's rule of hitting on 16 or less and standing on 17 or more.

You want proof? Okay, here it is. Let's assume the game is two-handed—playing are the dealer (who must abide by the casino rules) and one player whose fixed strategy is never to draw to a possible bust hand. The dealer's 224,094 completed hands will be made up of 64,474 bust hands and 159,620 hands with counts of 17, 18, 19, 20 and 21.

The player is also dealt 224,094 hands, but since he refuses to draw on counts of 12, 13, 14, 15, 16 or more, he doesn't bust a single hand. He will, however, get 106,133 hands with counts of 17, 18, 19, 20 and 21, and 117,961 hands with counts of 12, 13, 14, 15 and 16. Since the dealer's lowest count of a completed hand is 17, the player never wins except when the dealer busts by exceeding 21. The dealer's 64,474 bust hands appear as follows: 33,939 (117,961/224,094 × 64,474) occur when the player holds a count of 12 to 16, and 30,535 (106,133/224,094 × 64,474) occur when the player holds a count of 17 to 21. Subtracting the 33,939 dealer busts from the player's 117,961 12-to-16-count hands, we find that the player will lose 84,022 such hands. Subtracting the 64,474 dealer bust hands from the 84,022 player's losing hands, we note that the player loses 19,548 more hands than the dealer. In percentage that is 19,548 divided by 224,094, or an edge for the bank of 8.72%.

Again we deduct the 2.37% which the bank pays to holders of a natural 21 and get a final favorable percentage for the bank of 6.35%. I am sure you don't want to buck 6.35% instead of the 5.90% we were talking about before you got this bright idea of standing on a 12-to-16 count hand.

4

BLACK JACK STRATEGY

THE SCIENCE OF BLACK JACK

The player can cut down the dealer's advantage of 5.90% to about 2% in Nevada and Atlantic City casinos if he follows the Scarne strategy for hitting, standing, splitting, doubling down and taking insurance. Contrary to what most present-day Black Jack winning-system authors state, the employment of their basic strategies at their best only cuts down the dealer's 5.90% edge to about 3½%.

Following are the percentage cut-down figures that can be achieved by the player if he follows the Scarne Black Jack strategy.

1. About 1½% for proper hitting or standing on both "hard" and "soft" hands.
2. About 2% for proper doubling down when the casino permits a double down on any two cards. About ¼% for proper doubling down when the casino permits a double down on a count of 9, 10 or 11—it holds about the same for proper doubling down when the casino only permits a double down on 11.
3. About ½% for proper splitting of pairs.

The percentage figures shown above apply only when the Scarne strategy is used intelligently. The mathematical analysis of the Scarne strategy that follows is based on a single-deck composition of 52 cards. However, the Scarne strategy also applies to four-deck Black Jack as proven by "Scarne's 30,000 Black Jack Hands Experiment" (see pages 100 to 101).

Various other Black Jack hands experiments show that the Scarne strategy and the percentages figures shown above are equally applicable to a two, three, five, six, seven, and an eight-deck game. There is, however, a slight percentage variance in each of these multideck games, but the above percentage figures are affected so very little that we can forget about them.

To use the Scarne strategy successfully demands an unusual combination of skills on the part of the player in Black Jack.

1. The player must have a vast knowledge of the game's mathematics so that he knows when it is to his advantage to hit or stay, when to double down and when to split pairs.

2. He must be able to judge the approximate number of ten-count cards remaining in the undealt portion of the deck so as to evaluate if it is to his advantage to take insurance should the occasion arise.

3. He must know money management—when to bet big and when to bet small.

Plenty of vital information (much more than you'll find in any other book) is given and, if properly used, will reward the average Black Jack player with a surefire formula for cutting down his losses. And, if you happen to have a flair for the game, you'll find enough valuable hints here to give the bosses of your favorite casino a headache because of your above-average winnings.

I must begin by re-emphasizing one fact you should not forget: that the only positive advantage in favor of the bank is the edge it gains through double busts and having the players play first. And keep that 5.90% favorable percentage to the bank in mind, remembering also that it is calculated on a full-deck composition of 52 cards before the deal begins, and assumes that the player follows the draw and stand rules that govern the dealer.

There are several situations which, played properly, give the player an opportunity to cut down this house percentage. Most players handle these situations so inexpertly that instead of reducing the percentage they are bucking, they add to it. Here are the playing factors which can be utilized to the player's advantage:

1. The player actually knows a little more than the dealer because one of the dealer's two initial cards is dealt face up; this gives the player important information about his possible card count. The rules governing the dealer's play prevent him from making use of similar information about the player's hand, even if the latter's first two cards were dealt face up.

2. Unlike the dealer, the player can stay or draw on any count provided it does not exceed 21. At one turn of play he may draw to a count of 12 or more and at other times may stand on the same count. In some situations the player can gain an advantage from this.

3. The player can decide to double down or split pairs, a strategy denied to the dealer.

4. The player is paid off at odds of 3 to 2 when he holds a natural, but when the dealer holds a natural he only receives even money.

5. The player may play as many hands as there are available betting spaces; the dealer can only play one hand.

6. The player is the one who decides the amount of the bet and can raise or lower it at will within the prescribed betting limits.

A player who can take full advantage of all six of these factors can join the select few who are considered experts at Black Jack.

STRATEGY FOR DRAWING AND STANDING

The most important decision the Black Jack player has to make is whether to hit or stand on a count of 12, 13, 14, 15 or 16. The question arises in the long run a little more than once every two hands (to be exact, 698 times in every 1,326 hands). In practice it can occur three or more times during a single hand. Players who do not understand the reasoning that should determine such a vital decision have little or no chance of beating the Black Jack bank in a long session.

The only cut-and-dried procedure of hit-or-stand play that is sound for the player is to hit a count of 11 or less and stand on a count of 17 or more. This will keep most players out of trouble. But the player who doesn't know how to answer the question of whether to hit or stand on a count of 12, 13, 14, 15 or 16 is sure to run into double trouble.

The player who goes against the bank's favorable edge of 6.35% by refusing to draw a card when he has one of these counts for fear of busting his hand is a member in good standing of the Black Jack Chump Society. The lure of Black Jack is its fast action. Wagers are won and lost with the dealing of each new hand, and the pace is so fast and furious that the bank's favorable 6.35% will eat up the amount of the chump player's wager in about 16 dealt hands. Let me illustrate how this works out in dollars and cents. Assume that you are the chump and have played the dealer single-handed and made a $10 bet on each of 300 dealt hands for a total betting handle of $3,000. The bank collects, in hidden percentages, .0635 × $3,000 or $190.50. This is what you pay to sit at Black Jack table for two or three hours of play if you stubbornly refuse to hit a count of 12, 13, 14, 15 or 16.

Suppose you adhere to the dealer's fixed strategy of hitting a count of 16 or less and standing on 17 or more. Here the bank's favorable edge is 5.90%, and on $3,000 worth of your action it would cost you $177.

These figures should make it obvious that both of these hit-or-stand procedures add up to a big percentage charge to the player in the long run.

Since a player's position is weakest when he holds a count of 12 to 16, he should use some strategy that will cut down his losses by helping him to win or draw as many of these hands as possible. He must find a way to cut down the bank's 5.90% edge over the player who adheres to the dealer's fixed strategy. The player can do this by varying his hit-and-stand strategy to fit specific situations. The following three factors, when considered together, will enable him to do that.

1. The knowledge of the dealer's fixed strategy (hit 16 or less; stand on 17 or more) and its influence on the dealer's completed hand.

2. The sight of the dealer's upcard and its mathematical bearing on the dealer's possible two-card count.

3. The knowledge of the mathematical possibilities of the player's own count of 12, 13, 14, 15 or 16.

The hit-or-stand strategy that follows is based on these three factors. Before we suggest any hit-or-stand rules, the player must know what his chances are of busting a count of 12, 13, 14, 15 or 16, or bettering it by reaching a count of 17 to 21. These chances, some exact, others approximate, are shown in the following table:

BLACK JACK TABLE II

Player's Count with Two or More Cards	Total Chances of Bettering the Count by Reaching a Count of 17 to 21	Total Chances of Busting when Trying to Reach a Count of 16 to 21	Chances of Busting with a One-Card Draw
16	20 in 52	32 in 52	32 in 52
15	22 in 52	30 in 52	28 in 52
14	23 in 52	29 in 52	24 in 52
13	25 in 52	27 in 52	20 in 52
12	27 in 52	25 in 52	16 in 52

This table can be very helpful to the player even if he only retains a general idea of his chances of busting on each of these counts. Probability theory says that, in the long run, when the player and dealer are both holding a count of 17 to 21 they are expected to win, lose or draw an equal number of hands. Therefore, the only losses suffered by the player in the long run under similar conditions will be on the bust hands.

The information in the table becomes very important when combined with a knowledge of the strength of the dealer's upcard. We have no sure way (short of cheating) to know the value of the dealer's hole card. But knowing the value of his upcard enables us to calculate how many completed hands he will bust and in how many he will reach a count of 17 to 21 in the long run. Then, by considering these results in relation to the possible results of the player's completed hands when holding a count of 12, 13, 14, 15 or 16, we can decide whether it is more advantageous to hit or stand in certain situations.

I am always amused by the Black Jack strategy recommended by computer experts. Since they all seem to copy from one another, they usually end up with the same wrong answers. For instance, they all state that when the dealer's upcard is an ace or ten the player should hit a count of 16 because, they say, the dealer's hand is best when he shows an ace or ten spot. This may seem like good common sense at first glance but what seems like common sense is noted for supplying wrong answers. This is one of them.

Let's analyze it. Assume that the dealer's upcard is an ace and the player's first two dealt cards total 16. Should he draw a card, as the computer experts recommend, or should he stand?

Whenever the dealer's upcard is an ace, he must peek at his face-down hole card to see if it is a 10 count. If it is, he turns it up, and there is no problem; the player has lost the bet then and there. If, however, the dealer fails to turn up a natural (21), we know that he doesn't have a 10 count in the hole, and that his highest possible two-card count is 20 and his lowest 12. We can now calculate the exact number of hands the dealer will bust and the exact number of completed 17-to-21-count hands he will hold in the long run.

Since most of our Black Jack calculations are based on a full-deck composition, with the dealer's upcard and the player's considered mathematically in the full-deck composition, we will do the same here. To simplify the mathematics, suppose that dealer and player are each dealt 52 hands, that each of the dealer's 52 upcards is an ace, and each of the player's 52 hands has a 16 count. Also suppose that each of the player's hole cards and all the remaining cards dealt to both dealer and player fall exactly as probability theory predicts.

Out of 52 hands, the dealer will turn up a natural Black Jack 16 times, bust 11 hands, and reach a count of 17 to 21 on the remaining 25 completed hands.

Because the player holding a 16 count immediately loses the bet each of the 16 times (out of 52 hands) that the dealer holds a natural, these 16 hands cannot be considered. Therefore, a player who stands on a 16 count when the dealer's upcard is an ace will collect 11 dealer busts and lose 25 dealer completed hands out of every 36 dealt hands—a net loss to the player of 14 hands.

If the player hits the 16 count in each of his 36 dealt hands, then he will bust 22 hands and reach a count of 17 to 21 in the remaining 14 hands. From this player loss of 22 bust hands we must subtract the dealer's busts.

We calculate the number of dealer busts in the player's and dealer's 14 competing hands by multiplying the dealer's bust probability by 14. In this case $11/36 \times 14 = 4\ 5/18$ dealer busts. Since the dealer will hold 1½ twenty-one counts less than the player, he will lose 1½ completed hands out of his remaining 9 13/18 completed hands. We subtract the 4 5/18 dealer-bust hands and this 1½ completed hand loss from the player's 22 bust hands and find that the player hitting a count of 16 when the dealer shows an ace will suffer a net loss of 16 4/18 hands out of each 36 hands. And the player who stands on the 16 count will suffer a loss of only 14 hands.

This proves that, in spite of the advice to the contrary given by the computer experts, it is to the player's advantage to stand rather than hit on a count of 16 when the dealer shows an ace as his upcard.

BLACK JACK TABLE III

Dealer's Upcard Count for 52 Hands	Completed Hands with a Count of 17 to 21 in 52 Hands	Number of Dealer's Busts in 52 Hands
11 (ace)	41	11
10	40	12
9	39	13
8	39	13
7	38	14
x 6	29	23
5	30	22
4	32	20
3	33	19
2	34	18

This example should make it clear to the reader why Black Jack experts attach so much importance to the dealer's upcard. It should also indicate why the following table based on the strength of the dealer's upcard is of the utmost importance, especially when it is used in conjunction with Black Jack Table II. Remember that the table is based on 52 hands, each possessing the same-valued upcard, with the hole card and all other dealt cards falling exactly as probability theory predicts they will fall in the long run.

The table does not take the natural 21-count hands the dealer receives into consideration because if he turns up a natural when his upcard is a 10 or 11 count, there can be no hit or stand action for the player.

Taken together, Black Jack Tables II and III are the most valuable information a Black Jack player can possess.

Note that, since he will bust about 23 hands out of 52 in the long run, the dealer is in his weakest position when his upcard is a six spot.

Since our analysis shows that the player should stand on a 16 count when the dealer's upcard is an ace, common sense would seem to indicate that the player should also stand on a 16 count when the dealer's upcard is a seven spot. Again, common sense isn't to be trusted; this is another wrong answer.

Here's the proof. When a player stands on a 16 count and the dealer shows a seven spot, the dealer will bust 14 hands and complete 38 hands with a count of 17 to 21. Since the player will lose the 38 completed hands and win the 14 dealer busts, he will have a net loss of 24 hands out of 52 hands.

If the player hits his 16 count for each of his 52 hands, he will bust 32 hands and make 20 completed hands equally divided among the counts of 17, 18, 19, 20 and 21. The dealer's 20 opposing hands will be comprised of approximately 5 busts ($14/52 \times 20 = 5\ 5/13$) and about 15 hands comprised of a count of 17 to 21, about 7 of which possess a count of 17. The dealer loses about 4 and a fraction of his 15 completed hands for a total loss of about 10 of the 20 dealer hands. Subtracting the 10 dealer losses from the player's 32 busts, we find that the player who hits a count of 16 against a dealer's seven spot upcard will have a net loss of 22 hands, 2 hands less than the player who stands on 16.

Therefore it is to a player's advantage to hit 16 when the dealer shows a seven spot as his upcard.

Let us analyze another believe-it-or-not factor of Black Jack. The dealer's upcard for 52 hands is a 10 count (ten, jack, queen or king) and the player's count is 16 for the same number of hands. When the dealer's upcard is a 10 count the dealer must peek at his hole card to see if it is an ace. If it is, he immediately turns up his natural and collects the player's bet. Since the dealer's hole card will be an ace 4 hands out of 52, that leaves us with 48 hit or stand hands. If on these 48 hands the player stands on his 16 count, the dealer will bust 11 times and reach a 17, 18, 19, 20 or 21 count 37 times—a net loss of 26 hands to the player. If the player hits his 16 count in each of his 48 dealt hands, he will bust 30 hands and reach a 17-to-21 count 18 times. Of the dealer's 18 opposing hands the dealer will bust about 4 hands. Subtracting the 4 dealer busts from the 30 player busts, the player has a net loss of 26 busts or hands out of 48. In this case it would seem to make little difference if the player hits or stands on the 16 count, since each action shows a loss of 26 player hands.

But it does make a difference because the player's 18 hands are equally divided among the counts 17, 18, 19, 20 or 21, while 7 of the dealer's completed 14 hands carry a high count of 20 and the remaining 7 are divided among counts of 17, 18, 19 and 21. This means that the dealer will win 3 more completed hands than the player. Adding these 3 additional player losses to the 26 losses he suffered previously, we find that the player who hits 16 against the dealer's 10-count upcard will suffer a net loss of 29 hands in 48 hands compared to the 26 lost hands suffered by the player who refuses to hit.

Therefore it is to the player's advantage to stand on 16 when the dealer shows a 10 count as his upcard.

It should now be clear that for each possible upcard the dealer shows, there is a certain player's card count on which the player should stand, and up to which he should continue to draw, in order to cut down the bank's favorable percentage.

The hit-and-stand rules which I recommend below will shave the bank's 5.90% edge down about 4⅖% against the player who follows the same hit-and-stand rules as does the dealer.

1. *When the dealer's upcard is a five or six spot, the player should stand on a count of 12 or more.*

2. *When the dealer's upcard is a two, three or four spot, the player should stand on a count of 13 or more.*

3. *When the dealer's upcard is an ace or 10 count, the player should stand on a count of 16 or more.*

4. *When the dealer's upcard is a seven, eight or nine spot, the player should hit a count of 16 or less.*

I have not given the mathematical proof for all these contingencies, in order to save space. The reader who wants to work it out can do so by using the figures in Black Jack Tables II and III and following the same procedure I used when calculating the strength of the dealer's hand when his upcard is an ace, 7 or 10 count, in relation to the strength of the player's hand.

PLAYER'S SOFT HAND, OR TWO-WAY COUNT

When a player holds a hand that contains an ace, there are sometimes two possible counts, neither of which exceeds 21. A hand containing an ace and a six may have a count or value of either 7 or 17 because an ace can be valued as either 1 or 11. This ambiguous type of hand is known to Black Jack dealers as a *soft count* or a *two-way* hand. Playing it correctly requires special strategic considerations, as follows:

1. *When the dealer's upcard is an eight, nine, ten or ace, the player should stand only on a soft 19 or higher.*

2. *When the dealer's upcard is a two, three, four, five, six or seven, the player should stand only on a soft 18 or higher.*

Note that the holder of a soft hand should never stand until his total count is at least 18. He should continue to draw to his soft count and stand as indicated above. If, when the player draws one or more cards, his soft count exceeds 21 (this occurs often, since a high soft count is being hit), the player should revert to the standard hit-or-stand strategy, because he no longer holds a soft hand.

Example: The dealer's upcard is a six spot, the player hits a soft 14 and draws a nine spot. If he counted the ace as 11, he would have a count of 23. The hand is no longer soft, so the player reverts to his standard strategy and stands on 13.

Soft hands are advantageous to the player because if he uses the right strategy he gets two chances: he first tries for a high count by hitting a soft count, and if that fails he reverts to the standard hit-and-draw strategy.

SPLITTING PAIRS

Splitting pairs of any two 10-count cards allows the player to make two hands out of his initial two cards. If this situation is handled properly the player can cut down the bank's advantage by about ½%. As before, the important factors that tell the smart player whether or not to split are the value of the dealer's upcard and the strength of the player's initial two-card count.

The decision is made this way: Add the values of the two cards of the pair to get the total count and compare this with the total count of each single card. If the single-card count has a better mathematical chance of winning than the two-card count, split them. If the two-card count has the best chance, don't split. The chances are shown in Black Jack Tables II and III on pages 90 and 92.

Here is a specific example showing how the tables are used for this purpose. Suppose the player is dealt a 16 count composed of two eights, and the dealer's upcard is a six. First refer to Table II in which a 16 count shows 20 completed hands and 32 busts. Then turn to Table III which tells you that when the dealer's upcard is a six there are 29 completed hands and 23 busts.

Mentally split the 16 count into two eights. Table III shows that when the dealer's upcard is an eight there are 39 completed hands and only 13 busts. Since this holds true for each of the player's split eights, it is obvious that he should split them.

Another bit of strategy when splitting pairs is one I use which I have named the *overlay*. The rule is that it is to the player's advantage to split when his single card has a greater count value than the dealer's upcard.

If, after splitting a pair and drawing one or more cards, the player finds either or both hands have a count of 12, 13, 14, 15 or 16, he should resort to the original hit-and-draw strategy.

Here are my rules for splitting pairs or two 10-valued cards:

1. *Never split fours, fives, sixes or tens.*
2. *Always split eights unless the dealer's upcard is a nine, ten or ace.*
3. *Split sevens when the dealer's card is a five, six or seven.*
4. *Always split aces even when the casino rules permit only a one-card draw to a split ace.*
5. *Split nines unless the dealer's upcard is a ten or ace.*
6. *Split twos and threes when the dealer's upcard is a two, three, four, five, six or seven.*

As a matter of fact, I often split 10-valued cards when the dealer's upcard is a 19 count. Under most conditions this will replace the house's advantage of 5.90% with a player advantage of 1.71%.

Here again, remember that these splitting recommendations are based on a full-deck composition of 52 cards.

DOUBLING DOWN

The technique of doubling down deserves closer study than either the hit-and-stand strategy or the splitting of pairs because when properly handled it can cut down the bank's advantage about 2%. And, because it can be made on each dealt hand, it becomes the most potent weapon the Black Jack player possesses. A general memorization of previously dealt cards is a great aid to the player. As in the hit-and-stand strategy, there are many times when the initial two-card count indicates that it is to the player's advantage to double his bet.

This is the only single play at Black Jack which permits him to bet an amount that exceeds the casino's maximum limit. The double-down rules give the player a chance to increase his bet to twice the amount of the bank's maximum limit.

Because most Black Jack players know little or nothing about the mathematics of a double down, their lack of any suitable strategy for using it actually increases the bank's favorable percentage instead of cutting it. Most players double down merely because the dealer asks, "Do you want to double down?"

The art of doubling down at the proper time is an integral part of the best Black Jack strategy and a powerful tool in the hands of an expert.

Since the standard Black Jack rules permit a player to draw only one card to double down a hand, the player should have some good reason to back up his decision as to whether or not to double down. In deciding this question we again have to consider the possible strength of our double-down hand and the value of the dealer's upcard. Assume that the player was dealt 52 hands, each of which has a double-down count totaling 11. Then assume that each card dealt to the 11 count falls just as probability predicts. There will be 20 hands with a count of 12 to 16, and 32 hands with a count of 17 to 21. Note that 16 of these 32 hands are made up of a 21 count. If the dealer shows a 10 count as his upcard, turn to Black Jack Table III and note that the predicted value of the dealer's exposed 10 count is 40 hands with a count of 17 to 21, and 12 bust hands.

This shows that the player will gain an advantage of approximately 2 hands in 52 by doubling down on an 11 count when the dealer's upcard shows a 10 count. Since the dealer, showing a 10 count, is in his strongest position, the player will gain a still greater advantage doubling down on an 11 count when the dealer's upcard is an ace, nine, eight, etc.

This is the best strategy for doubling down:

1. *Always double down on a count of 11 no matter what the value of the dealer's upcard is.*

2. *Double down on a count of 10 when the dealer's upcard is anything but a 10 count.*

3. *Double down on a count of 9 when the dealer's upcard is a two, three, four, five or six.*

4. *Double down on a count of 8 when the dealer's upcard is a four, five or six.*

5. *Double down on a soft 13, 14, 15, or 16 when the dealer's upcard is a four, five or six.*

6. *Double down on a soft 17 or 18 when the dealer's upcard is a three, four, five or six.*

7. *Double down on a soft 19 when the dealer's upcard is a five or six.*

The player is in the most advantageous position for a double down when the dealer's upcard shows weakness, i.e., any card with a count of 2 through 6. Proof of this weakness is shown in Black Jack Table III.

The strategy rules given above take into consideration all the Black Jack bets permitted in any casino the world over. However, only in Nevada will you find a casino in which you can put into play all strategy rules described above. For example, casinos in Puerto Rico permit a double down on 11 only. Casinos in Curaçao, Aruba and St. Maarten permit a double down on 10 and 11 only. Most casinos in Nevada permit a double down on *any* two cards. And so it goes, from country to country. However, the hit-and-stand strategy rules on both the hard and soft counts are usable in all casinos, and will be of great help in cutting down the house's advantage. So, memorize them first.

INSURANCE BETTING

Whenever the dealer shows an ace as his upcard, players may elect to make a so-called insurance bet against losing to a dealer's Black Jack. Since the insurance bet pays off at 2 to 1 odds, the player should win one-third of the time to get a dead-even proposition. If the dealer's upcard is an ace, and you have no knowledge of any other cards, then the dealer's down card may be considered drawn at random from 51 cards that remain unseen. But under such conditions the 51-card deck contains 16 10-count cards, and the player can win this bet only when the dealer has a 10-count card in the hole. In the long run he will win only 16 of his bets, losing 35. Since insurance bets are paid off at 2 to 1, or 32 to 16 against an expectation of 35 to 16, the player is shorted $3/51$, or approximately 6%, or to be exact, $5\frac{15}{17}\%$.

Most players insist on buying insurance whenever they hold Black Jack on the grounds that they want to be sure of a win. The odds are 34 to 15 the dealer doesn't have a natural, and you will not receive the 2 to 1 insurance odds. Your expectation is minus $4/49$ for a house edge of about 8%.

The casual card caser (counter) can use the insurance bet advantageously if he has kept track of the 10-count cards dealt in previous hands. For example, suppose half the deck (26 cards) has been dealt and the card caser recalls that only three 10-count cards have been dealt. If an insurance bet could be made on the next deal, if would be wise to take out insurance. For the above reason, insurance bettors are only permitted to bet half of their initial bets.

SURRENDER

Recently several Nevada casinos have added the option of Surrender to their Black Jack rules. Surrender first appeared in casinos in the Far East, particularly those found in the Philippine Islands and in Macao, a small Portuguese colony just a short hop by hydrofoil from Hong Kong.

I first learned of Surrender in London many years ago. I was in that city at the request of the British Home Office to help the government formulate a new set of gaming rules for their legalized private clubs (casinos). When the question of Surrender came up and I informed the British officials that the Surrender rule carried a monstrous 22½% favorable house advantage whenever the player surrendered a possible two-card bust hand, the Surrender rule was immediately discarded.

The Surrender rule works as follows: A player, after being dealt his first two cards, may surrender (throw in) his hand, retaining one-half the amount of his bet and losing the other half to the dealer.

LONDON DEAL

In 1957 there were dozens of Cuban player cheats ripping off American casino owners in pre-Castro Cuba by bribing Cuban dealers to signal the value of their hole (face-down) card to them. To combat this dealer/player collusion, I recommended the ruling to the management of the Habana Hilton Hotel Casino that the Black Jack dealer was not permitted to look at his face-down (hole) card until all players had played out their hands. After two weeks of Black Jack player complaints, and because of the results of my mathematical analysis which showed the skilled player lost a possible 1½% to the house, the new dealing method was rescinded and the old deal reinstated.

In the middle sixties, several American casino operators in London took my discarded Cuban Black Jack rule a step further and ruled that the Black Jack dealer was to be dealt only one card face up, and the dealer's second card (former hole card), like the dealer's other possible hit cards, was to be dealt face up after all the players had played out their hands. However, should the dealer hit a natural 21 with his second dealt card, players who have split or doubled down lose only their original bets. All splits and double-down bets are returned to the players.

The London Deal eliminated one possible casino ripoff by dealer and player cheat working together. But it replaced it with several possible major opportunities for the house to cheat the player, including marked cards and stacked decks with a house cheat acting as a player seated at the anchor seat of the Black Jack table.

This unfavorable-to-the-player Black Jack dealing method has since become known in casino circles as the 'London Deal" because of England's 1970 revised gambling laws that demand its usage in all licensed private gambling clubs (casinos) in London and the rest of England.

The London Deal makes for a slower, duller, more confusing and considerably less scientific game. The London Deal automatically eliminates 38.50% of the player's optimum strategy, thereby giving the basic strategy player considerably fewer opportunities to reduce the house's average favorable advantage of 5.90%. When the London Deal is used with Scarne's Casino Black Jack Rules, the house's favorable advantage jumps from 2% to 3½%. In other words, the London Deal causes the player to fight an additional 1½% house advantage. When the London Deal is in use and the casino rules permit a double down only on 11, or 9, 10, and 11, the house's advantage of 5.90% can only be reduced by .90%. In other words, the most skilled Black Jack player must buck a big 5% house advantage.

ADDITIONAL BLACK JACK STRATEGY

Here I would like to submit an additional bit of mathematical proof that the bank percentage at Black Jack not only varies with the dealing of each card but may, at times, even be in favor of the player.

Since the bank pays off a holder of a natural Black Jack at odds of 3 to 2, the bank's advantage (based on a full-deck composition) is sliced down by $2\frac{8}{21}\%$. Because this percentage goes up and down during the deal it can easily be used to the player's advantage.

Suppose, for example, that an experienced Black Jack player has remembered that in the first 26 cards dealt there were no aces, and only half (8) of the 10-count cards were dealt. He now knows that in the remaining 26 undealt cards there are four aces and eight 10-count cards. The partial card casing tells him that the bank's edge has been cut down considerably more than $2\frac{8}{21}\%$, and that this is the time to increase the size of his bets.

However, if all the aces have made their appearance in the first 26 dealt cards, the player has no natural percentage in his favor and the bank's advantage cannot be sliced down by the dealing of a natural.

The average Black Jack player who fights the usual house percentage has almost no chance of winning in the long run. I am sure that the reader will feel that the price he paid for this book has been well spent when he realizes that a study of and proper use of the Black Jack strategy recommendations I have given will cut the bank's advantage of 5.9% to about 2%—and with just a little luck the player will have many more winning Black Jack sessions than he would have had otherwise.

SCARNE'S 30,000 BLACK JACK HANDS EXPERIMENT

Today, casinos in Nevada, Atlantic City, Puerto Rico, Bahamas, Aruba, Curaçao, Dominican Republic, Haiti and the world over accept as standard my casino Black Jack rules which call for four decks dealt from a shoe, plus an indicator card, and which use my Puerto Rican ruling that 50 or more bottom cards of the four-deck packet may never come into actual play. This is done by having the dealer insert the indicator card 50 or more cards from the bottom of the 208-card packet and end the deal when the indicator card makes its appearance.

My four-deck 208-card packet deal, in which only about 156 cards (three decks) come into actual play, throws a monkey wrench into the game's mathematics because of the billions of different possible Black Jack hands that rule out all mathematical formulas. The reason for this is that each new three-deck packet that comes into actual play is never comprised of the same identically valued cards. This situation makes it impossible to ascertain mathematically how much the bank's favorable edge of 5.90% would be cut down by making use of my strategy for hit, stand, split pairs, double down and insurance taking (I refer to this as my basic strategy).

With the above thought in mind I decided to conduct a Las Vegas style Black Jack cardplaying experiment to determine to what extent my basic strategy would cut down the bank's 5.90% edge and to ascertain the specific percentage reduction for hit, stand, splits and double down in four-deck play. The experiment consisted of a record 30,000 played hands and spanned a six-month period. It is most important to describe how and under what conditions these 30,000 Black Jack hands were played. The experiment was conducted in my experimental laboratory in North Bergen, New Jersey. My laboratory is fitted with a regulation casino Black Jack table and all its requirements—four-deck dealing shoe, cards, casino-type chips, small counters to keep track of the number of tied, winning, and losing hands as they were dealt, pads and pencil to record the results. My son, John Teeko, and several casino dealer friends dealt this huge 30,000 Black Jack hands experiment. I was the lone player and I employed my basic strategy rules for hitting, standing, splitting and doubling down. My betting was constant, a one-chip bet on each of the 30,000 dealt hands. Furthermore, when a split or double down took place, each was recorded as an additional dealt hand.

And now, for the first time in print, as a result of my huge Black Jack experiment, I have attained an approximate strategy percentage figure against the player at four-deck casino Black Jack.

At the end of the experiment I tied 2,664 hands, lost 13,970 and won 13,366, for a loss of 604, which, divided by 30,000, gave me an overall loss of 2%. In casino Black Jack this amounts to a player disadvantage of 2%, or a player loss of 2¢ on every dollar wagered. Subtracting this 2%

from the average dealer advantage of 5.90%, we learn that my strategy had cut down the dealer edge about 3.90%.

Further experiments revealed that a player, by making use of my strategy in casinos which permit doubling down only on a count of 11, or 9, 10 and 11, will achieve a player disadvantage of about 3.50%.

THE GAMBLER'S TEN-CARD COUNT STRATEGY

Ever since the day Black Jack tables first made their appearance in illegal gambling joints in 1910, Black Jack hustlers have been trying to beat the game without resorting to outright cheating. Most seasoned Nevada Black Jack gamblers of that era made use of the Gambler's Ten-Card Count Strategy described below. However, when "breaking the deck" (reshuffling of the dealt and undealt cards) became a rule in legalized Nevada casinos, this Black Jack strategy was termed worthless by most gamblers and discarded as unworkable. During World War II, while acting as gambling advisor to *Yank: The Army Weekly,* I wrote a pamphlet on the subject titled "Beware of the Ten-Card Count Black Jack Strategy," which the Army distributed to millions of GIs. Following is a partial reprint from the pamphlet:

The most valuable natural aptitude a Black Jack player can possess is the fairly rare faculty of remembering the previously played "tens" (tens, jacks, queens, kings). The player who cannot do this decreases his chances of winning considerably no matter how well he plays otherwise. Since the bank's favorable percentage goes up or down with the dealing of a ten, the expert player will not use cut-and-dried standard strategy near the end of the deal. The more dealt tens the player can mentally count and remember, the greater chance he has of making an advantageous play when 20 or less cards remain in the undealt portion of the deck.

You can't possibly remember all tens dealt in a five- or six-handed Black Jack game. A couple of reasons are that each player's first two cards are dealt face down, and many players do not show their hands after a bust —they merely throw them to the dealer face down. Also, the professional dealer (former casino Black Jack dealer now in the service) scoops up the completed player hands so fast that there is hardly enough time to spot the tens let alone keep a mental running ten count. The expert card counter who is out to take your Army pay tries to minimize these factors by asking the dealer for change during the deal, and whenever possible by playing with only two or three players. In addition, the card counter prefers third base, the seat at the dealer's extreme right, as a base of operations, because this is the best vantage point for keeping track of the exposed ten cards.

There are hundreds of former professional Black Jack gamblers and casino dealers in the Army whose talents for clocking an approximate number of dealt tens is remarkable. I know a gambler who operates a gambling dive on the outskirts of Fort Benning, Georgia, who can keep a running conversation and still spell out the correct number of previously dealt tens at any time during a deal. The card counter who keeps track of tens alters his hit and stand strategy near the end of the deal to suit the situation. Suppose 36 cards have been dealt and 8 of the remaining 16 undealt cards are tens—the Army Black Jack card hustler does not risk a hit on a count of 12, 13, 14, 15, or 16 even though you think his hand calls for a hit. Since a full deck has four cards in each of 13 ranks (four aces, four deuces, four threes, etc.) the proportion in each rank is 4 in 52 or $\frac{1}{13}$. As the tens are dealt, the proportion of tens in the undealt portion of the deck keeps changing. This means that the dealer's favorable percentage before the start of the deal also changes, increasing and decreasing with every dealt go-around. At times, the composition of the remaining tens to be dealt may favor the player and other times the dealer. However, the Army Black Jack hustler will only be able to take advantage of these favorable situations when 20 or less cards remain in the undealt portion of the deck—when he will usually increase the size of his previous bets tenfold.

To protect yourself as dealer against a ten-count Black Jack hustler is easy if you follow *Scarne's G.I. Gambling Tip of the Month,* which follows: When you are the dealer during the play of Black Jack and you notice that a certain player usually makes the same-size bet during the early and middle part of the deal, then when 20 or less cards remain in the undealt portion of the deck he makes a big-sized bet, and this type end-game betting occurs often during a Black Jack session, Brother, beware; It's a sure bet you are up against a vicious ten-card counter who is out to steal every G.I.'s monthly pay he possibly can. To guard against such chicanery, whenever the suspected ten-card counter increases the size of his bet near the end of the deck, simply reshuffle the dealt and the remaining undealt cards together and continue play in the same manner as if the deck had run out. This is a sure way to stop any ten-count card hustler in the Army because it ruins his strategy count.

Soon after the Army had distributed these pamphlets, most illegal casino operators here and abroad joined the vast number of servicemen Black Jack dealers in the art of breaking the deck. However, it wasn't until two years after the end of World War II that Las Vegas and Reno casino operators smartened up and began breaking the deck. In 1947 Benjamin "Bugsy" Siegel, owner of the Las Vegas Flamingo Casino, heeded my advice and became the first casino operator in Nevada to rule that when half the deck or more had been dealt and a player has increased his upcoming bet or bets to double or more the size of his previous bet or bets, the Black Jack pit boss must order the dealer to break the deck. However, strange as it may seem, most of today's Black Jack system authors do not know, or if they do know, fail to inform their readers, that the breaking of a 52-card deck has been a casino house rule in Nevada for the past 30 years or more.

BEATING THE BLACK JACK TABLES IN THE PAST

The most valuable natural aptitude a Black Jack player can possess is the fairly rare faculty of remembering most of the previously exposed cards.

The player who cannot do this has little or no chance of beating the bank in the long run, no matter how well he plays otherwise. Since the bank's favorable percentage goes up or down with the dealing of each card, the expert player will not use any cut-and-dried strategy. The more dealt cards the player can remember, the greater chance he has of making the correct play on future hands in that deck.

One can't remember all the exposed cards dealt to a full table of players in either a single-deck or multiple-deck Black Jack play. One reason is that in single-deck Black Jack the first two cards to each player are dealt face down. Also, the dealer scoops up the completed hands so fast that there is hardly enough time to spot their values, let alone memorize them. However, before Scarne's Casino Black Jack rules became standard in casinos, and before "breaking the deck" in single-deck Black Jack became a rule, the card counter minimized these factors by playing, whenever possible, at a table that had only a few players, or better yet, at one where he was the only player. He preferred third base, the seat at the dealer's extreme right, as his base of operations, because this is the best vantage point for keeping track of the exposed cards. Even under these conditions, an expert job of counting the dealt cards required unusual natural ability and considerable practice at the casino table. Although remembering the cards at Black Jack is much harder than at Contract Bridge, there were a number of Black Jack players in the late forties whose talent for card counting made them a living.

The player who could clock the deck was better able to evaluate his chances of winning after about two-thirds the deck had been dealt. Since a full deck has four cards in each of 13 ranks (four aces, four twos, four threes, etc.), the proportion in each rank is 4 in 52, or $\frac{1}{13}$. As the cards were dealt, the proportion in the undealt portion of the deck kept changing. This means that the dealer's favorable percentage (5.9% before the deal starts) also changed, increasing and decreasing. At times the composition of the ten or fewer remaining undealt cards of the deck gave the player a favorable percentage rather than the bank. When the card counter knew the odds were in his favor he increased the size of his bets; if the odds figure was against him, he decreased his bets, or even backed away from the table and stopped playing.

I have seen counters who had been betting $2 on each hand suddenly bet the $300 or $500 limit on the next hand and win. I have also seen some of the best counters in the United States increase their $50 bets to $500 on seven hands (a full table) and lose $3,500 on the play.

Never in the history of Las Vegas has any one countdown artist won any sizable sum playing the count by himself. All the recorded big money count winners in Nevada and elsewhere always worked as a team of three. A description of their scheme follows: Confederate number 1 scouts the casino for the least experienced Black Jack dealer. Having made his selection, he sits down to play at this dealer's table. Minutes later one of his confederates sits at the same table. Soon after, the third confederate joins his buddies at the same table. The trio act as strangers to each other. Their running count is arrived at as follows: Confederate 1 counts the ten-valued cards and the aces; confederate number 2 counts the sevens, eights and nines; confederate number 3 counts the number of cards dealt plus the twos, threes, fours, fives and sixes. As soon as confederate 3's count has reached 32 cards, he signals his two confederates for their count information. Upon receiving said information, he analyzes the strength of the undealt cards. Are they favorable to the dealer or to the trio? Should his bets be small, big, or the maximum house limit? Having decided his course of action, he places his bets accordingly. His confederates, seeing the size of his bet, place identical bets.

The most successful of all countdown teams in the history of Nevada was headed by that legendary Las Vegas gambler Joe Bernstein. His Black Jack winnings during the forties and fifties surpassed the $2 million mark. I was in Las Vegas when he and his team of counters beat the Sahara Hotel Casino for $75,000. I must add, however, that Joe Bernstein and his card mob, like most present-day card mobs, were caught cheating on many an occasion.

SCARNE'S WINNING BLACK JACK SYSTEM

During my many years in gambling, I have known of only six Black Jack players who beat the game playing alone by putting the percentage in their favor through endgame strategy and card counting, or as it is more commonly known, "counting down the deck." And the sums won by these counters were small, a couple of thousand dollars at the most. In fact, I was the first person playing alone to beat the game in Las Vegas with a countdown. I was also the first player barred from playing Black Jack there.

In 1947, I was barred from playing Black Jack because I told four casino owners in Las Vegas that I could beat their games with a countdown. The four casino owners challenged me to prove my statement, and when I beat the Flamingo, the El Rancho Vegas, the Last Frontier and the Golden Nugget, I was barred from the Black Jack tables throughout Nevada.

In my autobiography, *The Odds Against Me* (1966), I included a simplified version of the system I used back in 1947 to beat the Las Vegas casinos. At the time I wrote, "When you get to be as good as I am working several stacks of different-valued chips, you'll be able to know the identity of the last ten to twenty undealt cards." This simplified version of my system also appeared in *Scarne's New Complete Guide to Gambling* (1974). However, in both instances, for personal reasons, I purposely omitted the part the stacks of different-valued chips played in my Black Jack winning system.

Here, for the first time in print, is a complete description of my Black

Jack winning system, which I made use of from 1936 to 1947 to beat many a mob-controlled gambling joint here and abroad.

My countdown system puts all past and present-day card-count systems to shame. Actually the winning strategy in my system is based on the fact that the composition of the last 20 or fewer undealt cards changes during play, and because of this, the advantage in Black Jack shifts either to the player or to the dealer. When using my counting or checking gimmick, I bet small until about two thirds of the cards are dealt. Then I consult my count gimmick to know exactly how many aces, ten-count cards, sevens, eights, nines, and twos, threes, fours, fives, and sixes remain in the undealt portion of the deck. With this information I can decide if it is wise to draw a card, double down, split a pair, and what the chances are of busting my hand. You must remember that Black Jack is the only banking game where the odds fluctuate and where sometimes the deck favors the dealer and other times favors the player. However, the only time this information can be ascertained by the player is when only a few undealt cards remain. My scheme is to find out if the remaining undealt cards near the end of the deal favor the player or the dealer. If they favor the player, I increase my bets and play more hands than before. My hit-and-stand strategy as detailed in this book was not put to use when using my countdown system because, knowing the value of the undealt cards, I simply used common sense as to when to stand, draw, split pairs and double down.

My Black Jack system involves three basic requirements for playing alone—to be a fast card reader, to possess a remarkable memory, and to be a convincing actor so the dealer will believe you are the nervous type by the way you handle your chips.

Now for the secret of my Scarne Countdown System. First thing I did when I sat down at a vacant Black Jack table was to buy three stacks of chips—two $5 stacks and one $25 stack. As you know, each stack contains 20 chips. I would place the three stacks in a row in front of me—the $25 stack to my right and the two $5 stacks to the left of the $25 stack. Before the deal began, I would remove four chips from the $25 stack and place them to the right of the stack. The $25 16-chip stack now represented the ten-count cards, the $25 4-chip stack represented the four aces. The first $5 20-chip represented the twos, threes, fours, fives and sixes (all favorable dealer cards). Next I would remove eight chips from the second $5 20-chip stack, leaving a $5 stack of 12 chips, which represented the sevens, eights and nines. The eight $5 chips were used to make my bets and they were placed in front of the four stacks of 4, 16, 20 and 12 chips, a total of 52 chips, one for each card in the deck. The $5 and $25-chip stacks indicated the values of the undealt cards. The chip handling gave me stalling time, but it appeared to the dealer that I was nervous and trying to make up my mind what sum I wanted to wager on the next go-around.

Let's suppose that three tens and an ace were dealt on the first round;

I removed three chips from my 16-chip $25 stack and one chip from my four-chip $25 stack. These chips were placed in the front of my four clocking stacks and were used to place my bets. Suppose in the next round of play my completed hand was made up of ace, two and six. I removed one chip from my three-chip $25 ace stack, and two chips from my 20-chip $5 stack. The dealer busted and his cards revealed two sevens and an eight. I removed three chips from the 12-chip $5 stack. This left two chips in the $25 ace chip stack, 13 chips in the 10-chip $25 stack, 18 chips in the $5 two-, three-, four-, five-, six-chip stack, and nine chips in the $5 seven-, eight-, nine-chip stack. I followed this procedure with each dealt hand, and whenever I wished to know exactly how many cards still remained to be dealt and their values, I would simply consult my four stacks of chips. The number of chips remaining in each of the stacks gave me the answer. This information decided my strategy and the size of my next bet or bets.

Back in the early fifties, I gave the just-mentioned system to only four men. Three of them got together and formed a team and won about $250,000 each before they were barred from playing single-deck Black Jack in Nevada. Today, of course, Nevada pit bosses keep a sharp eye out for single-deck card counters. If a pit boss suspects a player of counting the deck, he instructs the dealer to reshuffle the complete deck when only half of it has been dealt. Known card counters are either barred from playing or not permitted to play alone at a table. If a card counter is the only player at the table, the management sends in a shill who gives the card counter little or no opportunity to see his cards so that counting the deck becomes impossible. And the ruling that I devised that 50 or more bottom cards of a four-deck packet should never come into actual play makes it virtually impossible to count down four decks.

Today card casing, or counting down the deck, is a lost art. However, now and then you spot a Johnny-come-lately trying it on some casino boss. If the boss doesn't know his business, the card counter may get away with it.

The machinations of a modern-day single-deck card counter stand out like a bright light in a moonless night. First he seeks a vacant Black Jack table for himself. Then his confederate, who is usually a woman, and a partial card counter, takes a position beside him. Sometimes he makes use of two confederates. At the beginning of each deal, his bets are usually the house minimum on one or more of the six or seven betting spaces. This type of betting continues until near the end of each deal, when a whispered consultation takes place between the card counter and his confederates. If they agree that the remaining undealt cards appear disadvantageous to the house, they increase the size of their bets to the maximum house limit. A smart houseman counters this Black Jack chicanery by reshuffling the entire deck, including the undealt cards. The card counter complains a bit, calls off his bets, exits from the casino and shops around seeking a casino whose bosses are stupid enough to stand for such nonsense. That's the life of a professional card counter. Most card counters haven't got a dime and are always seeking some sucker to bankroll their play. Therefore my advice is: Don't try to be a card counter, and don't bankroll one if you meet him.

CHEATING AT BLACK JACK

Because most private Black Jack games and illegally operated gambling joints, as well as a number of major casinos in Nevada, still insist on dealing single- or double-deck Black Jack from the hand, this section is of vital importance. Casinos which insist on dealing Black Jack from the hand reshuffle the entire deck when half or more of the deck has been played out or whenever a player substantially increases the size of his bet or bets. Therefore, all reasons given by the casino management that it's to a player's advantage to deal Black Jack from the hand are pure rubbish.

More cheating takes place at the Black Jack tables when the cards are dealt from the hand than when they are dealt from a card box because Black Jack dealt from the hand offers more opportunities for cheating. Most complaints made to me about cheating in Nevada casinos concern Black Jack dealt from the hand. A recent complaint brought to my attention by a high roller went like this: "I was a $30,000 Black Jack winner at————[name purposely omitted] in Las Vegas where the cards were dealt from a card box. Then around 4:00 A.M. I was informed that the table I was playing at was being closed and I was asked to move over to the open Black Jack section, which I did. At this table, the cards were dealt from the hand. Two hours later, I had not only lost my $30,000 in winnings but $20,000 of my own money besides. Scarne, was I cheated?"

I shrugged my shoulders and said, "I don't know. I didn't see the play, but since it's so easy to cheat at Black Jack when the cards are dealt from the hand, my advice is to seek a table where Black Jack is dealt from a card box."

The latest alleged cheating scandal to surface from a major Las Vegas Strip hotel casino involves a sum of $450,000. The gambler states that he was cheated out of $450,000 over a period of several days playing single-deck Black Jack dealt from the hand at a major Strip hotel casino. The casino management claims the gambler lost only $250,000.

The cheating charge was made by the gambler because he spotted two fives of spades dealt during Black Jack play. The casino management does not deny the fact that the gambler found two fives of spades during play. However, it claims that the gambler lost his money honestly and that this particular deck of cards was a freak deck and the fault of the card manufacturer.

The Nevada Gaming Control Board agreed with the casino management and stated from now on all decks of cards must be examined before being put into play. What the Nevada Gaming Control Board ruling indicates is that prior to this alleged cheating incident in this major Strip casino, it was not required that cards be examined before being put into play.

Sometimes it is the casino operators who complain that they have been cheated by hand-muckers or cross-roaders (card sharps). This occurs when a player's two cards are dealt face down and are switched for two palmed cards, or a cold deck is switched into play.

Nevada casinos are fleeced out of millions of dollars yearly by agents (cheats acting as players) in collusion with crooked Black Jack dealers and pit bosses. This happens in spite of their so-called ironclad security controls, which include the hiring of ex-card cheats as pit bosses and the use of one-way mirrors in casino ceilings. In fact, casinos the world over are fleeced out of untold millions of dollars annually by crooked dealers tipping their hole card when an ace or ten shows as their upcard, and by dealers overpaying bets or paying off losing bets as winning bets. I doubt that there is a casino anywhere operating Black Jack tables that is not taken for a bundle each year by outside and inside cheats.

Some agents pose as card casers or countdown artists when in fact they are working with a Black Jack dealer who is tipping off his hole card. This gimmick is used to avoid suspicion of collusion. Caesars Palace on the Las Vegas Strip recently caught one of the country's best-known so-called card casers trying to bribe one of their Black Jack dealers. So much cheating of this type took place in England's casinos that the government passed a ruling that the Black Jack dealer is to receive his hole card after all players have completed playing out their hands. See pages 98–99 for further information.

Most gambling casinos of established reputation fight both the casino and player cheat as a menace to the business, but some of their unscrupulous competitors hire card sharps to deal the game and instruct them to play honestly with the smaller players but to *go for the money* (cheat) when a high roller makes his appearance. Black Jack is the card cheat's paradise, whether it is a casino or private game, because a new hand is dealt every minute or so, because the action is fast, because the players are occupied in studying their own hands rather than the dealer's hand and because only a few cards, all of them crucial, are dealt each hand. These circumstances all combine to make cheating downright easy and steadily profitable.

Marked cards and a mastery of their use are for obvious reasons a tremendous advantage in a game in which a knowledge of the next card to be dealt is so important.

There are a few crooked tricks which are peculiarly suited to Black Jack. *Peeking* is an example. The dealer gets a peek at the top card of the deck. He usually does this while pretending to examine his hole card, but the fact that the deck is held in the left hand, which is often in motion, gives him many other opportunities to obtain a secret glimpse. He also uses misdirection; he makes a gesture or some other move with his right hand which takes attention away from his left hand. At that precise instant the deck is turned slightly and the left thumb pushes the top card forward against the index finger, causing the card to buckle just enough so that the dealer gets a quick glimpse of the index. Because of the position of the indexes, this sleight is easier for left-handed dealers; instead of having to buckle the card they can merely move the top card so that it projects slightly over the side of the deck, far enough for part of the index to show.

When the top card is known, the second deal comes into play, a feat made easier by the tradition in Black Jack that the cards are usually held in the left hand and dealt with an overhand motion. When the second dealer peeks and sees a card he could use himself, he simply deals seconds until his own turn comes and then goes honest for a split second.

Dealers who cannot deal seconds—it's not an easy move—use an *anchor man,* who sits in the playing position farthest to the dealer's right. Assume the dealer has a 16 and a peek at the top card shows it to be a six spot or more, which would make him bust. The dealer signals the anchor man to ask for cards and continues to deal to him until a card he wants comes to the top. Then he signals the anchor man to stand and deals the useful card to himself.

The most common stacking method, the ancient business of arranging cards as they are picked up, is easy at Black Jack and very effective because certain cards and their sequences are so important. The dealer cheat reaches out with the left hand, which holds the deck, turns the deck over and gathers up some of the face-up discards with this hand. This maneuver places these cards on the top of the deck instead of the bottom where they should go. It is made quickly and smoothly, and most players never see anything wrong with the action. The right hand helps misdirect because it is also in action at the same time, picking up the remaining discards which, when the deck has been turned right side up again, are then slowly burned on the bottom in the usual manner.

Usually a 20 or a natural is stacked in this fashion. When the dealer sees a 10 count and an ace, and the game is three-handed, he arranges the cards during the pickup in such a way that ace is third and the 10 count sixth. When this sequence is returned to the top rather than the bottom of the deck, the next deal will give the dealer a natural; he'll get the ace as his face-down card and the 10-count as his upcard. Beware of the dealer who constantly keeps turning the deck over while picking up discards. And if you ever see a card dealt which was dealt in a previous hand when only one deck of cards is being used, take your business elsewhere.

The most common cheating method used in crooked casinos when making use of four decks (208 cards) is to remove a number of 10-count cards and to replace them with 5-count cards. Because the dealer must hit a count of 16, the substitution of fives for tens avoids many a normal dealer bust and supplants these with additional dealer twenty-ones. To protect yourself against such cheating subterfuges, count the 5-counts and

10-counts as the hands are played. If you count less than 64 10-count cards or more than 16 5-count cards—seek the nearest exit. For your own safety, don't make a scene. A thief caught red-handed is always a dangerous thief.

For information on crooked dealing boxes (shoes), see "Cheating at Baccarat and Chemin de Fer," pages 268 to 270.

The best assurance you can have that the game is honest is to see the cards dealt out of a card box as is done in most casinos. I predict that before long *all* Nevada casinos will deal Black Jack from a card-dealing box rather than from the hand.

5

BLACK JACK
WINNING SYSTEMS
AND THEIR FALLACIES

MATHEMATICIANS AND THEIR NUMBERS GAME

It is a well-established fact that millions of present-day casino Black Jack players here and abroad make use of my basic strategy to help them improve their chances of winning. It is also a fact that there are hundreds of thousands of Black Jack players trying to make their fortune at the casino tables by using a so-called winning Black Jack system that was highly touted by the news media, and that, instead of making a fortune, they are losing their bankrolls.

Ever since 1961, when *Scarne's Complete Guide to Gambling* first hit the stores, more than 500 books and pamphlets have been published on the subject "How to Beat the Casino Game of Black Jack." Each author tells how he was barred from playing in Las Vegas because his system was sure to beat the house. Notable among these authors are Professor Edward O. Thorp, author of *Beat the Dealer* (1962), Dr. Allan N. Wilson, author of *The Casino Gambler's Guide* (1965), Lawrence Revere, author of *Playing Blackjack as a Business* (1969), and Julian Braun, an instructor in computer programming at the IBM Customer Education Center in Chicago. Mr. Braun has written many articles on winning at Black Jack. In addition, Mr. Braun is credited by Thorp, Wilson and Revere with supplying them with his 7044 computer analysis of Black Jack.

The following copy is reprinted from the dust jacket of *Beat the Dealer* by Professor Thorp, currently teaching at the University of California at Irvine and formerly Associate Professor of Mathematics at New Mexico State University.

Ever since the time of Cardano and Pascal, mathematicians have been delving into the theory of games of chance. Like many predecessors, Edward O. Thorp has often spent hours theorizing about the game of Blackjack; unlike his precursors, he has devised and tested a system for consistently winning this game as it is played in casinos today.

Dr. Wilson, leader of the analysis group in the Analog Computer Laboratory at General Dynamics/Astronautics in San Diego, in his book *The Casino Gambler's Guide* states:

Blackjack (or "21") is the only casino game in which an amateur can learn to win consistently over the long run. In fact, it is surprisingly easy to learn, but in order to discourage you from trying to learn, the blackjack dealers and casino operators will undoubtedly tell you that you have to be an Einstein or a Boston lawyer to succeed. Don't you believe what they say. Go ahead and read this and the subsequent four chapters, and you'll be amazed at what you can win!

Lawrence Revere, a mathematics major, in his book *Playing Blackjack as a Business,* states:

Blackjack is the only casino game an amateur can learn to play and at which he can definitely win. My purpose is to show you the strategies which will make a winner of you just as they made a winner of me. I am a professional gambler—my single purpose is to beat the house at one of its own games. If winning is your goal, this book is written for you.

I am writing this chapter because it sickens me to see men and women lose their hard-earned cash, which many of them can ill afford, at the casino tables just because they believe some professional mathematician who has stated in print that a computer study proves his Black Jack strategy is sure to beat the house. It is my duty as a gambling expert to expose this humbug.

The most highly publicized system player in all gambling history is Professor Edward O. Thorp. Thorp, unlike Charles Wells, who broke the Monte Carlo Roulette bank about 15 consecutive times, did not achieve his fame at the gambling tables, but rather by writing a Black Jack book, *Beat the Dealer* (1962), in which he described the workings of his "infallible" winning system, which follows. Thorp, however, doesn't seem to think too highly of his own system, because the only two gambling experiences that are documented in his book involved him and two other gamblers, who not only played at the same Black Jack table with him but also financed the trip and supplied the gambling bankroll. In other words, Thorp wasn't risking his own money.

Thorp's first of these two trips took place in 1961 and consisted of a week's play in several Reno and Las Vegas casinos. Thorp was accompanied by two old-time gambling hustlers whom he referred to as Mr. X and Mr. Y. Thorp claims that the trio won $11,000 for one week's play. Mr. X told me later that after three days' play they stopped using Thorp's system because it never seemed to work. Several years later Mr. Y was caught cheating at Caesars Palace.

Thorp's second gambling trip took place in 1964 and consisted of a week's gambling at a $50-limit Black Jack table at the La Concha Hotel Casino in San Juan, Puerto Rico. The La Concha Casino at the time dealt two-deck Black Jack out of a Faro-type dealing box. All the players' cards (except a double-down card) were dealt face-up and the two-deck card packet was dealt to the last card. This, according to Thorp, made an ideal situation for his Black Jack system. This trip was financed by a New York television station to the tune of $2,000, and the gambling bankroll was supplied by two young men, Messrs. M and N (as Thorp prefers to call them), who played with Thorp at the same Black Jack table. After a week's play, the three great system players lost several thousand dollars. The trio's style of play convinced me that I was watching three mixed-up amateur gamblers playing Black Jack for the first time. As official gambling consultant to the Las Concha Casino, I watched their play from various sections of the casino.

In the past 15 years, a numbers game has developed among several non-gambling mathematicians and computer experts to try and outdo each other by further reducing the dealer's favorable edge at the game of Black Jack by the use of various basic strategies. And do you know what? They are succeeding—not that it's visible in actual casino play, but it does make an interesting paper to submit to the American Mathematical Society at one of their annual meetings. If this numbers game continues, I expect one of these mathematicians to someday state that the 5.90% dealer's edge favors the player instead of the house. Example: Roger R. Baldwin, Herbert Maisel, Wilbert E. Cantey and James P. McDermott, authors of *Playing Black Jack to Win* (1957), list the dealer's edge at 0.62%. In 1962, Thorp's *Beat the Dealer* reduced that figure to 0.21%. Then came Allan N. Wilson's book, *The Casino Gambler's Guide* (1965), which listed the figure at 0.00%. In the middle sixties, Julian Braun stated that he could not only cut the dealer's edge but could give the player an advantage of 0.10%. In 1969, Lawrence Revere, in *Playing Black Jack as a Business,* further increased the player's favorable advantage to 0.12%.

Over the past 15 years, I have clocked several hundred of Thorp's Basic Strategy players at the Caribe Hilton Hotel Casino in Puerto Rico. Thorp's strategy players are easy to spot because while playing they refer to small strategy cards supplied by Thorp's book publisher. My Caribe Hilton Hotel Casino clocking experiment revealed that the average Thorp strategy player lost about 4.5 cents or 4½% on each $1 bet (casinos in Puerto Rico only permit a double down on a two-card 11 count). My Las Vegas clocking experiment (Nevada casinos permit a double down on any two-card count) on Thorp's strategy players revealed a house edge of 3.50% rather than the 0.21% noted in Thorp's *Beat the Dealer*. Similar experiments of mine using each of the basic strategies recommended by Wilson, Braun, Revere and the Baldwin group showed a favorable house advantage of approximately 4.50% making use of Puerto Rican rules, and 3.70% using Nevada rules.

As gambling consultant to the Caribe Hilton Hotel Casino since its opening in 1949, I receive a monthly casino operation report which lists the previous month's gross play, credits, paid outs, cancel credits, and net win at the three casino table games of Black Jack, Craps and Roulette. A study of these reports over the past 15 years reveals that for each $250 million gross Black Jack play, the casino's favorable advantage on each dollar wagered amounted to about five cents, or 5%. Strange as it may seem, of the countless big-money Black Jack card-hustler mobs who have gambled at the Caribe Hilton Hotel Casino, I don't recall one mob that beat the casino for a sizable amount. However, I can recall dozens of Black Jack card-count mobs who lost $50,000 or more in several sessions of play. Many of these mobs were making use of Thorp's ten-card count system. All Black Jack countdown artists, like all other gamblers, are welcome to play at the Caribe Hilton Hotel Casino.

Before we analyze Thorp's Black Jack system, it is necessary for us to learn to what extent Thorp's basic system is supposed to reduce the dealer's edge of 5.90%. This 5.90% figure first appeared in print in *Scarne's Complete Guide to Gambling* and a year later in Thorp's *Beat the Dealer*.

The main basis in determining expert Black Jack strategy is to decide when and why the player should hit, stand, split and double down on various two-card totals as permitted by casino rules. These decisions are decided upon from the player's dealt cards and the dealer's exposed up-card. The results of the correct player decisions are mathematically analyzed, totaled and then transposed into a percentage figure. This figure is then subtracted from the initial dealer's advantage figure of 5.90%. Thorp informs us that he made use of an IBM 704 computer to achieve his goal, and that the result, as stated earlier, turned out to be a dealer's advantage of 0.21%. However, the way I see it, since Roger Baldwin and his co-authors of *Playing Black Jack to Win* furnished Thorp with their computational details in their work on Black Jack, Thorp took their house advantage figure of 0.62% at face value, then simply proceeded to reduce it to 0.21%. If he hadn't done so, there would have been no reason for him to write his book. Thorp offers no mathematical proof for this 0.21% figure.

Thorp states that his basic strategy "is better than any other published Black Jack strategy and that it is also better than any published strategy for any other gambling games." This statement might make some sense if the table shown in Thorp's book had listed the correct percentage figures for these other gambling games. To understand the inaccuracy of Thorp's percentage table, compare the percentages in Thorp's Table 1 with Scarne's Correct Best Plays percentage figures shown in Table 2. Scarne's correct percentage figures and their analyses for each of these five casino games are found in this book under their corresponding chapter headings.

TABLE 1—THORP'S BASIC STRATEGY COMPARED WITH BEST PLAY IN OTHER CASINO GAMES

Game	Player's advantage (best play) (in percent)
Black Jack, basic strategy	—0.21 is typical
Craps	—1.40
Roulette (Europe)	—1.35
Roulette (United States)	—2.70 to —5.26
Baccarat and Chemin de Fer	—1.11 to —5.00

TABLE 2—SCARNE'S CORRECT BEST PLAYS IN OTHER CASINO GAMES

Game	Player's advantage (best play) (in percent)
Black Jack, Thorp's basic strategy	—3.50
Craps	—0.591
Roulette (Europe)	—1.35 and —2.70
Roulette (United States)	—5.26 and —7.89
Baccarat and Chemin de Fer	—1.19 and —1.34

A comparison of the above tables should prove to the reader that Thorp's Black Jack percentage figures as shown in *Beat the Dealer* should be taken with a grain of salt.

EDWARD O. THORP'S FAMOUS BLACK JACK SYSTEM

Following is my mathematical analysis of Edward O. Thorp's Black Jack system, which, due to the gambling ignorance of the news media, made Thorp world famous. Thorp calls his system *A Winning Strategy on Counting Tens*. It should be noted that Thorp bases his system on a 52-card deck dealt to the last card. *Beat the Dealer* (1962) entirely ignores the Nevada casino Black Jack ruling that should a player substantially increase the size of his bet or bets after 26 cards or more have been dealt, the pit boss orders the dealer to reshuffle the entire deck.

Thorp's so-called winning system requires the use of a different basic strategy. As an explanation of this new strategy, *Beat the Dealer* employs four large bewildering charts loaded with misinformation and mathematical errors not worthy of inclusion in these pages. To what extent this new basic strategy reduces the dealer's advantage, Thorp fails to mention. He entirely ignores the dealer's 5.90% advantage and handles his system mathematics as if Black Jack were a dead-even game for both the player and dealer. If this is mathematical cricket, my name is not John Scarne.

Thorp's winning system is based on an erroneous theory that the richer the undealt cards are in "tens" (tens, jacks, queens, kings), the better off the player is. The richer the undealt cards are in "others" (aces, twos, threes, fours, fives, sixes, sevens, eights, nines) the better off the dealer is.

We shall now think of the 52-card deck as divided into two groups, 16 tens and 36 others.

Thorp's system demands that the player keeps a mental running count of tens and others as each card is dealt. The result of this mental count will determine the amount of money to be wagered by the player on his next hand or hands.

Thorp informs us that the underlying principle of his winning system is that the player's advantage is measured by the ratio of tens to others. For a 52-card deck, it is 36/16 or 2.25. When the ratio is below 2.25, the player has the advantage and must increase the size of his bet. When the ratio is above 2.25, the dealer has the advantage and the player must decrease the size of his bet.

In a later edition of *Beat the Dealer* (1966) Thorp states that the undealt cards give the player the advantage half of the time and this advantage ranges from 10 to 15%. However, in Table 3 (page 117), Thorp again contradicts himself and lists the player's maximum advantage at 9% rather than the 15% maximum figure stated above. As I see it, 6% one way or the other makes little difference when applied to Thorp's unworkable system. Thorp says the dealer has the advantage half of the time in the undealt cards, but this advantage only ranges up to about 3%. The farther the ratio gets above the 2.25 mark, the more the player's disadvantage grows. The farther the ratio gets below the 2.25 mark, the more the player's advantage grows.

Thorp's system requires the player to count backwards as each card is dealt and seen. Example: The first count before the deal begins is 36–16. Now suppose the player is playing the dealer head on (alone), and on the first dealt hand the player sees four exposed others: The count reads as follows (36–16); nine of spades (35–16); eight of spades (34–16); seven of diamonds (33–16); eight of hearts (32–16). The player divides the 16 (ten figure) into the 32 (others figure) and gets a corresponding ratio of 2.00. The chances of an average player performing this single-deck running count flawlessly at a fast seven-player casino Black Jack table I estimate to be one in a million. However, Thorp has taken care of this one-in-a-million situation by telling the reader to take into account only the cards that he sees. In short, if the system player sees only half the deck, the system still works. Statements such as these make me wonder where Thorp got the gall to write *Beat the Dealer*.

As an example of the many misleading and contradictory card-counting examples found in *Beat the Dealer,* we reprint the following:

Here is one very special example of a favorable situation that would be uncovered by a careful count of the cards that are played. Suppose you are playing the dealer "head on"; this means you are the only player at the table. Suppose also that you know that the unplayed cards, from which the next round will be dealt, consist precisely of two Sevens and four Eights. How much should you bet? Answer: place the maximum bet the casino will allow. Even borrow money if you have to, for you are certain to win if you simply stand on the two cards you will be dealt.

Here is the analysis. If you stand on your two cards, you do not bust and are temporarily safe. When the dealer picks up his hand, he finds either (7, 7), (7, 8), or (8, 8). Since his total is below 17, he must draw. If he holds (7, 7) there are no sevens left so he will draw an eight and bust. If he holds (7, 8) or (8, 8) he will bust if he draws either a seven or an eight— the only choices. Thus the dealer busts and you win.

The above example is not only misleading but untrue as well. There is no possible way that Thorp or any other player that is using the others and tens count system could possibly know that the last six undealt cards were two sevens and four eights. What Thorp's ten-count system does reveal is that the last six undealt cards are a combination of *others,* which, according to his system's rules, calls for a minimum casino bet rather than the maximum as cited in the above example.

To emphasize—Thorp states that the underlying principle of his winning system is measured by the ratio of tens to others. When the ratio is below 2.25, the player has the advantage and must increase the size of his bet. When the ratio is above 2.25, the dealer has the advantage and the player must decrease the size of his bet.

Tables 3 and 4, which follow, have been reprinted from *Beat the Dealer.* Table 3 depicts various values of the ratio Others/Tens in terms of percentages. Table 4 depicts various values of the ratio Others/Tens in terms of betting units.

Tables 3 and 4 are incorrect in their entirety as I shall now go on to prove.

Believe it or not, Professor Edward O. Thorp's unbeatable winning Black Jack system—which made him world famous because of the ignorance

TABLE 3—APPROXIMATE PLAYER ADVANTAGE IN THE TEN-COUNT STRATEGY

Others/Tens	Normal approximate advantage (in per cent)
3.00	−2.2
2.25	−0.2
2.00	1.0
1.75	2.0
1.63	3.0
1.50	4.0
1.35	5.0
1.25	6.0
1.16	7.0
1.08	8.0
1.00	9.0

TABLE 4—A CONSERVATIVE BETTING SCHEME FOR THE TEN-COUNT STRATEGY

Ratio	Bet, in units
above 2.00	1 (minimum)
2.00–1.75	2
1.75–1.65	4
1.65–1.50	6
1.50–1.40	8
below 1.40	10

about gambling of the national communications media and various mathematicians—is really not a system at all. It is simply the old-time gamblers' ten-card count strategy in disguise—a strategy almost all seasoned players have been using since Black Jack was first invented. The only difference between Thorp's unworkable system and the gamblers' old ten-card count strategy is that Thorp made it more difficult, if not unworkable, by adding that ridiculous ratio to "Tens and Others" to the original old-time gamblers' ten-count strategy.

"The Gambler's Ten-Card Count Strategy" is discussed on pages 101 to 102. The best this strategy can possibly do for the player is to cut down the house's favorable 5.90% to about 3.90%. And the same can be said of the Thorp system, providing the player keeps a correct card count—which, as I stated earlier, is one in a million of doing in a fast seven-player casino Black Jack game.

Actually, all Thorp's system does (same as the Gamblers' 10-Card Count Strategy) is inform the player how many ten-count cards remain in the undealt cards. And if you were to call this an unbeatable Black Jack winning system in the presence of seasoned gamblers, they would immediately say, "Okay, let's go. We'll book your Black Jack action." The knowledge that there are six ten-count cards in the remaining 17 undealt cards may help you calculate a favorable insurance bet, but that's about all—unless you happen to know the correct values of the other 11 cards. Lumping aces, deuces, threes, fours, fives, sixes, sevens, eights, and nines together in the same breath, and giving each of these cards the same point value, is strictly nonsense. Thorp should receive some national honor for achievement in pulling the wool over the eyes of the communications media and many of the country's top mathematicians with his Black Jack hoax. Imagine giving the lowly two spot the same importance as an ace. The ace can be used either as a one or 11—it can be used in a soft count—and when matched up with a ten count, this gives a player a natural 21 and a 3-to-2 payoff. In addition, Thorp makes the mistake of ranking sixes, sevens, eights and nines with twos, threes, fours and fives.

To prove mathematically the inaccuracy of Thorp's ratio system and each of the figures shown in Tables 3 and 4 would clutter up these pages with calculations that serve no useful purpose. Instead I have selected two easy-to-understand ratios from Table 4 for analysis. However, both Tables 3 and 4 will be consulted. The results achieved by these analytical calculations will be conclusive proof that Thorp's system is based on a false theory—Others/Tens—and all the facts and figures (including those in Tables 3 and 4) pertaining to this system, as shown in *Beat the Dealer,* are incorrect.

The ratio figure to be discussed is "below 1.40" as shown in Table 4. In this instance, I'll make use of the lower ratio of 1.00. By consulting Tables 3 and 4, we learn that ratio 1.00 possesses a 9% player advantage and calls for a maximum bet of ten units. Let's examine this 1.00 ratio figure closely. To do so, we'll suppose the deck has been dealt toward the end. We stop and record our count of Others/Tens and learn that our count reads five others and five tens (5–5) for a corresponding ratio of 1.00. After the ten remaining cards have been dealt and played, we learn that the five "others" are made up of one eight and four nines. These ten dealt cards make up five two-card hands that do not call for a "hit" by either the player or the dealer, and therefore this 1.00 ratio rather than possessing a 9% player advantage, as shown in Table 3, becomes a dead-even game. Neither the player nor the dealer has any advantage.

Let's further suppose that the last six cards in the deck are five others and one ten (5–1) for a corresponding ratio of 5.00. This 5.00 ratio, according to Thorp, would give the dealer about a 4% advantage and it calls for a player's minimum bet of 1 unit. After the six cards have been dealt out and played, we learn that the five others are made up of one eight and four nines. Again, as before, these possible three two-card hands do not call for a "hit" by either the player or the dealer. Therefore, this 5.00 ratio, rather than possessing a 4% dealer advantage, becomes a dead-even game for the player and the dealer.

Countless situations similar to the two described above pop up in various disguises during the play of Black Jack. Very often a ratio which is listed in Tables 3 and 4 as favorable to the player is found to favor the dealer, and a ratio listed as favorable to the dealer is found to favor the player.

THE WILSON PLUS-MINUS WINNING SYSTEM

In 1965, Dr. Allan N. Wilson, in his book *The Casino Gambler's Guide,* described his plus-minus count system, which he calls the Wilson Point-Count System. This plus-minus system is strictly an amended version of the Thorp's ten-count system simply because his running count total involves others. Wilson claims that his plus-minus system is far superior to Edward Thorp's ten-count system simply because his running count total involves only one number whereas Thorp's card-count technique requires a player to keep track of two numbers and then mentally compute a ratio. The chances of the average player's performing Wilson's running plus-minus count flawlessly from the beginning of the deck to the end at a fast seven-player casino single-deck Black Jack Table I estimate to be one in 500,000.

Wilson, like Thorp, informs us that the undealt portion of the deck is either "rich" (tens and aces) or "poor" (others) in some varying degree. And in view of this theory, he advises the player to keep track of his running plus-minus count as follows: Deduct four points for each ace that has been dealt, deduct one point for each ten-count card, and add one for each "other" card. In theory, the plus-minus count could go as high as +32 or as low as −32. But in practice it rarely ranges in value beyond +10—or −10.

Wilson states that his winning system is based on the fact that the most favorable cards for the player are aces and tens. He continues that if the deck from which hands remain yet to be dealt contains an excess of aces and tens, then in general the player has a positive expectation; if it contains a deficiency of aces and tens, in general the player has a negative expectation.

Wilson's count system is based on the false premise that when the dealt cards have a plus value (+1, +2, +3, etc.) the count favors the player and he should increase the size of his next bet accordingly, and when the count has a minus value (−1, −2, −3, etc.) the player should decrease the size of his next bet accordingly.

The technique for Wilson's running plus-minus count is as follows: With the dealer starting from a freshly shuffled 52-card deck, the "prior" count is zero. Suppose the first six cards dealt are "others"; the count is +6. The next card happens to be an ace and the count becomes +2. The next six dealt cards turn out to be six ten-count cards; the count is now −4—and so it goes. The player is advised to use this count along with Wilson's basic strategy. Wilson pulls another goof when he advises his readers to make use of his basic strategy in endgame situations. All top Black Jack countdown artists vary their endgame strategy as dictated by the value of the remaining undealt cards.

Wilson, like all other authors of these so-called winning systems, totally ignores the house's favorable advantage of 5.90% and treats Black Jack as a dead-even game. To prove how misleading Wilson's plus-minus count is, I have selected one easy-to-understand situation from among hundreds to prove the point. Example: Take the case when the endgame count is +8 and according to the system requires a big bet of seven units and an expected player advantage of 4½%. After the cards have been dealt and played, we find that the endgame consists of eight cards, and they are all ten-count cards. Actually all the player can do in this case is to push with his 20-count hand against the dealer's 20-count. Here we find that the player's advantage of 4½% is exactly zero.

What does Dr. Wilson think of his own system? For the answer we reprint the following from his book.

The moral of the story is that the Wilson point-count system is not perfect. I do not claim that it is. Nonetheless, it is a good practical scheme for keeping rough track of the cards and for making bet changes that will in general be advantageous. There is nothing to prevent you from noting how far into the deck you are, and then allowing extra weight for cases near the end of the deck. You merely look at the dealer's undealt stack, and guess roughly what fraction of the deck remains.

THE REVERE PLUS-MINUS WINNING SYSTEM

Lawrence Revere, in his book *Playing Blackjack as a Business,* also makes use of the plus-minus system but assigns different values to the dealt cards: twos and sevens count +1; threes, fours, fives and sixes count +2; eights and nines count 0 (zero); and aces and ten-count cards count −2.

Revere, like Thorp and Wilson, treats the game of Black Jack as a fifty-fifty proposition for both the player and dealer. Thorp, Wilson and Revere, in their winning system, may ignore the 5.90% house advantage arrived at by the player busting first, but the Black Jack dealer doesn't—he immediately scoops in the player's bet after a bust hand.

All three of the above mentioned mathematicians assign different point values to the same cards. This alone is proof that their Black Jack systems are worthless. Revere, of all things, assigns a 0 (zero) count to eights and nines, which simply means eights and nines are treated as if they did not exist in a 52-card deck. Thorp's, Wilson's and Revere's books list a combined total of some 18 surefire winning Black Jack systems. If any one of these systems was sure to beat the dealer as claimed, who would need the other 17?

A review of the results of my mathematical analyses of Thorp's, Wilson's and Revere's systems as described earlier leads me to believe that these so-called winning systems were not developed by a modern-day electronic computer as claimed, but were invented at home by the use of a little number-puzzle imagination and some simple arithmetic. And I might add that the number-puzzle imagination was sadly misplaced. The only reason I can see for Thorp, Wilson and Revere to invent these phony Black Jack systems was to include them in their forthcoming books in order to help their book sales. Furthermore, I believe that each invented his system during the time he was writing his book.

Countless variations of card-counting systems are being sold to the gullible public today, and like Thorp's, Wilson's and Revere's, they are all based on a false mathematical foundation, making all of them worthless.

We must bear in mind that in only a few Nevada casinos will one find single-deck Black Jack being dealt from the hand, and the number of such tables is negligible compared to the number of four-deck tables. Example: Caesars Palace Casino in Las Vegas harbors 39 Black Jack tables but only two of these deal single-deck Black Jack. The authors of these worthless systems fail to tell their readers that when single-deck Black Jack is dealt from the hand in Nevada, whenever 26 or more cards have been dealt and a player has substantially increased the size of his bet, the pit boss orders the dealer to "break the deck," which means to reshuffle together the previously dealt and the undealt cards. This casino policy of breaking the deck has been in effect since the day after John Scarne beat four Las Vegas casinos with his chip count-down system back in early 1947. For further information, see pages 104 to 107.

I predict that in the very near future casino single-deck Black Jack dealt from the hand will become a thing of the past. Today, casinos in Nevada, Atlantic City, Puerto Rico, Aruba, Curaçao, Bahamas, Haiti and the world over have adopted as standard Scarne's Casino Black Jack Rules and Scarne's Casino Four-Deck Shuffle (pages 75 to 81). The reasons for so doing are as follows:

1. The inserting of the indicator card toward the bottom of the 208-card deck prevents the cutoff cards from coming into play and prevents count-down players from clocking the cards to learn the identity of the remaining undealt cards, and at the same time rids the casino of the Johnny-come-lately card-counting nuisances.

2. The card-dealing box eliminates 95% of the cheating methods employed by crooked casinos.

3. Dealing the player's cards face up helps the dealer to correct any errors in totaling the value of the player's hand and prevents card cheats acting as players from switching one or both of their hole cards for cards they had previously palmed out of the deck.

If the Scarne Casino Black Jack rules are followed faithfully by the casino pit bosses and the dealers, I will go on record to say, "Black Jack cannot be beaten by the most skilled Black Jack count mob comprised of two, three or more card hustlers at the same table."

SCARNE'S $100,000 BLACK JACK CHALLENGE

In the May 1976 issue of *John Scarne's Newsletter,* in an effort to alert America's Black Jack fraternity and the communications media to the fact that all the highly publicized computer-tested systems were strictly humbug, I challenged Professor Thorp, Dr. Wilson, Julian Braun and Lawrence Revere to a big, simultaneous $100,000 Black Jack Freeze-out Match to be held at the Caribe Hilton Hotel Casino in San Juan, Puerto Rico, in November 1976. This I did with the approval of the Puerto Rican Gaming Commission and the management of the Caribe Hilton Hotel Casino.

To fulfill my part of the challenge, I would put up $100,000 as a casino bankroll with the casino management, and I insisted that Thorp, Wilson, Braun and Revere do the same as a guarantee against the possible $100,000 loss they might suffer.

Thorp, Wilson, Braun and Revere would sit and gamble at the same Black Jack table and make use of their surefire systems to win my $100,000 bankroll. In brief, I would permit the four Black Jack wizards to gamble together at the same table.

The freeze-out contest would involve, if necessary, a week's play of eight hours a day—and if, at the end of the seven days' play, neither side had won the other's $100,000, the side that was out front (winner) at that time would receive the remainder of the loser's $100,000.

To prevent any stalling by a member or members of the quartet, a maximum time limit of one minute would be allowed for the play of each single hand. Should a player fail to complete the play of a hand within a minute's play, the hand would be considered a "bust" by the timekeeper and the player would lose the bet. This rule would prevent the quartet's deliberate slowdown in play, should they be winners at a given period of play, so as to effectively halt the contest, as in a sit-down strike, and demand the remainder of my $100,000.

The Black Jack contest rules of play in the Caribe Hilton Hotel Casino must be the government's official Black Jack rules, which are posted on the wall of each Puerto Rican casino. (It should be noted here that Puerto Rico's casino gambling rules can only be amended by the legislature.)

The government's regulated minimum and maximum betting limits at Black Jack are $5 to $200 respectively. However, with the Puerto Rican Gaming Commission's approval, I was agreeable to raising the minimum and maximum betting limits to $25 and $1,000 respectively (same as in Las Vegas casinos).

In Puerto Rico the player's cards are dealt face up (except the double-down card) from four decks. The cards are dealt from a miniature Chemin de Fer shoe, and 50 or more bottom cards of the card packet are cut off and do not come into play. There are seven places (betting spaces) to play on the table, and each of the four wizards would have to play a minimum of one hand and a maximum of four hands, if available, on each dealt go-around.

Dealing cards face up is ideal for their card-counting systems, much more so than when the players' cards are dealt face down.

Thorp, Wilson, Braun and Revere would be permitted to discuss each other's card count during the game. Imagine those four wizards at the same table casing the aces, tens, fives and low cards as they were dealt, then holding a discussion before the play of each hand. How could they possibly lose?

A Puerto Rican government supervisor would be on hand to observe the play—and the dealer or dealers for the contest match and the supervisor, or pit boss and timekeeper, would be designated by the Puerto Rican Gaming Commission.

All I asked for myself is that I be permitted to stand in the Black Jack pit to observe the play and have the authority to complain to the government supervisor of any irregularity committed by the dealer, Thorp, Wilson,

Braun or Revere—and naturally, his decision would be final. The same privilege would be granted to the observer selected by Thorp, Wilson, Braun and Revere.

The expenses incurred by the quartet's week stay in Puerto Rico would be paid for by me or by the Caribe Hilton Hotel.

John Luckman, owner of the Las Vegas Gambler's Book Club, was acceptable to act as intermediary for Thorp, Wilson, Braun and Revere, and to contact my intermediary, Richard Kane, President of Marden-Kane, Inc., publishers of *John Scarne's Newsletter*. However, before any discussion would take place, Luckman was required to present a notarized letter signed by Thorp, Wilson, Braun and Revere to the effect that each was willing to accept my $100,000 freeze-out challenge. This offer would expire on October 15, 1976. Thorp's, Wilson's, Braun's and Revere's refusal to accept my challenge would prove to the gambling world that each of their surefire winning systems was simply a gimmick to rip off the country's gullible Black Jack players through the sale of their betting systems!

On July 1, 1976, I received a telephone call from John Luckman informing me that the four had accepted my challenge. I thanked Luckman and said I would make arrangements with the Puerto Rican government officials to sanction the contest. Luckman suggested we move the challenge contest to Las Vegas as the contestants preferred that location. I then informed Luckman to contact Richard Kane by sending him a notarized letter of acceptance from Thorp, Wilson, Braun and Revere.

When Kane received the Luckman letter of July 1, 1976, it turned out to be a horse of a different color. Luckman's letter contained only Revere's so-called acceptance letter accompanied by a short note by Luckman which read in part, "I'm enclosing the original letter I received from Lawrence Revere who has apparently contacted the other principals, e.g., Dr. Allan N. Wilson, Julian Braun and Dr. Edward O. Thorp and they unanimously agree to accept the subject challenge match."

Revere's letter to Luckman stated that he had contacted Thorp, Wilson and Braun, and the four had accepted my $100,000 challenge provided the challenge contest rules were changed to include some five rules of his own making. As I suspected at the time, and later learned was true, the statement by Revere that all had accepted turned out to be a deliberate falsehood on his part. Following are the five rules changes Revere demanded.

1. We will play Puerto Rico rules. Four decks, double on any two card eleven, deck to be dealt to the level they generally deal. (Please specify the exact amount of cards to be dealt.) Deck will be thoroughly shuffled . . . to our satisfaction.
2. We suggest the money be deposited with John Luckman: $100,000 by Scarne and $100,000 by the four of us as soon as the date is agreed on. The money to be paid to the winner or winners as soon as they return to the United States.

3. We will play eight hours a day—three, three and two hours a day for seven days. Whoever is ahead at the end of seven days will take the money.
4. In the event the game cannot be played in Puerto Rico it will be played in Las Vegas using Puerto Rico rules.
5. In the event one or more of us is unable to play, the remaining player or players will put up the $100,000 and play the four hands.

For Revere to suggest rule #2 to the Caribe Hilton Hotel Casino management and to the Puerto Rican Gaming Commission—that they grant permission to hold a $100,000 Black Jack challenge contest in their hotel casino in Puerto Rico while the $200,000 challenge moneys were placed with John Luckman in Las Vegas, Nevada—was a tip-off that Revere was looking for an excuse not to accept the challenge. When I showed Revere's letter to a member of Puerto Rico's Gaming Commission, he said, "Scarne, Mr. Revere's #2 rule is a deliberate insult to all Puerto Ricans." Later, during a phone conversation, Luckman confirmed the insult when he said, "Scarne, we don't trust those Puerto Ricans."

However, going along with Luckman's suggestion, and in order to accommodate Revere on rule #4, I wrote a letter to Philip P. Hannifin, Chairman of the State Gaming Control Board, Carson City, Nevada, requesting permission to hold the challenge match in a Las Vegas casino. Hannifin's reply was: "The Black Jack Challenge you have described would no doubt require licensing of the individuals involved if the event were to be conducted in Nevada. Such a procedure would pose problems for your challenge, and accordingly I would suggest that your Puerto Rico place may be the best."

Upon receipt of the letter I phoned Luckman and spoke to him about the contents of the letter and my dealings with the Nevada Gaming Control Board. I then asked him if he would try to get Caesars Palace, the Sands, or any other large Strip hotel to sponsor the match and possibly use their influence with the State Gaming Control Board. His answer was short and sweet: "Scarne, I don't know any casino owners in Las Vegas."

On July 9, 1976, in order to force the Black Jack wizards out into the open, Dick Kane requested that Thorp, Wilson, Braun and Revere each submit a certified letter stating his acceptance of the match as stipulated in my *Newsletter*.

After a few weeks passed by without hearing from them, I called Luckman several times. He was finally forced to admit that Revere had lied in his letter when he stated he had contacted Thorp, Wilson and Braun and they had agreed to the $100,000 match. Luckman informed me that he had not heard from Thorp or Wilson and that Braun was not a Black Jack player—therefore we should count him out.

On July 20, 1976, Julian Braun, the non-Black Jack player who we were told to count out, sent a notarized letter accepting my challenge but at the same time proposed that the following additions be made to Lawrence Revere's suggested conditions. They were as follows:

1. At least 156 cards shall be dealt from a four deck shoe. When all the hands have been played, if less than 156 cards have been dealt, the deck cannot be shuffled without the consent of the players. The decks will only be shuffled upon completion of the hands in play and at least 156 cards having been dealt with the possible exceptions being a required shuffle in case the shoe having been exhausted of cards, or some irregularity which makes a shuffle desirable, the players assenting.
3b. Insert after paragraph 3:
3b. To preclude dealer stalling or the possibility of a player's hand being considered a bust by one minute delay of the dealer, as could happen on shuffling, the time limit specified in paragraph 3 shall apply only to an individual's playing time and shall not include dealer time. The dealer shall be expected to perform without undue delay with due allowance for necessary shuffling, which, when it does take place, shall be performed to the player's mutual satisfaction.

I did not hear further from any of the Black Jack wizards until August 10, 1976, when a notarized letter was received from Allan Wilson. Wilson added five more rules of his own as a condition of his acceptance, which are as follows:

I accept the Blackjack challenge of John Scarne, depending on his acceptance of both the playing conditions suggested in Lawrence Revere's letter of July 14, AND five further conditions stipulated below:

1. Add the following sentence to condition #6 of Revere's referenced letter: Anyone who is unable to play, for any reason whatever, shall not be subject to any penalty.
2. Each player shall be guaranteed a room which is reasonably quiet and comfortable at all hours (e.g., not next to noisy elevator, not bothered by adjacent late-hour celebrants, no loud TV-playing neighbors, etc.). The players shall be given adjacent rooms if requested.
3. The cards shall be shuffled thoroughly to the satisfaction of the players. Any reasonable request for additional shuffling shall be honored, except that the players shall not use this as a stalling device.
4. There shall be TV monitoring of the shuffle, the deal, the play, and the pick-up of the cards; it shall have zoom capability, so that all hand motions are clearly discernible. This monitor capability may be worked into the "network" coverage, so as to be inconspicuous, provided that it fulfills the purpose of providing the players with subsequent re-play viewing in slow motion. The expense associated with TV monitoring shall be borne by the challenger (Scarne) and/or the host hotel and/or the TV network.
5. If any intermediary is to hold monies or negotiable checks for the contesting parties, that person shall be appropriately bonded.

If Wilson's rule #1 were to be incorporated in the official challenge rules, it would permit Wilson, Thorp, Braun and Revere to quit the contest game in progress and have their $100,000 returned to them for any lame excuse they might offer should they be heavy losers after one or more sessions. Wilson's rules #2, 3, 4 and 5 are not only humorous but self-explanatory.

Soon after, Kane received a letter from Lawrence Revere dated August 14. The letter included Revere's original five challenge rules changes plus those demanded by Braun and Wilson and described above—a total of 9 major challenge rules changes. And we still hadn't heard from Professor Thorp.

By this time it became obvious to me, to Richard Kane, to Roberto Lugo, General Manager of the Caribe Hilton Hotel, and to the officials of the Puerto Rican Gaming Commission that Luckman and the four Black Jack greats were not interested in accepting my challenge but were purposely stalling for time, hoping the Puerto Rican Gaming Commission would call the challenge off. Then they could say that John Scarne backed down on his $100,000 challenge.

To forestall this from happening, Roberto Lugo and I decided to try and smoke the wizards out of their holes by reducing the required front money from $25,000 to $5,000 for each of the four principals to guarantee their challenge participation. John Luckman and the four were notified of this change.

Volume 1, Issue 9 of the *Newsletter* read as follows:
To resolve the rules of play for this Black Jack Challenge contest to the satisfaction of all concerned parties, I request that Richard Kane, John Luckman, or any representative designated by the four Black Jack wizards to meet with Roberto Lugo, General Manager of the Caribe Hilton Hotel, and officials of the Puerto Rican Gaming Commission at the Caribe Hilton Hotel in San Juan, Puerto Rico, not later than October 15, 1976.

However, before the talks take place, Roberto Lugo, General Manager of the Caribe Hilton Hotel and Casino, demands that I deposit a $20,000 check or bond with the Hilton Casino management to guarantee my part in the $100,000 challenge. Roberto Lugo also demands that John Luckman or any other representative Thorp, Wilson, Braun, and Revere may select must do likewise and deposit with the Hilton Casino management a $5,000 check or bond from each of the four Black Jack wizards to guarantee their participation in the $100,000 challenge.

On September 24, 1976, three weeks before the expiration date of my challenge, Lugo received a letter from Allan Wilson. I would not have believed the contents of the letter if I had not read it myself. At this late date, Allan Wilson, Julian Braun and Lawrence Revere did not know the rules for Black Jack as played in Puerto Rican casinos! I quote from Wilson's letter to prove the point.

I am one of the participants in the prospective $100,000 Blackjack Challenge by John Scarne. I would like to know exactly what are the current "Standard Playing Rules" at your casino. Please send to me at the above address a copy of what Scarne refers to as "the government's official Blackjack rules which are posted on the wall of each Puerto Rican casino."

Wilson also requested Lugo to "send a copy of whatever you send to me also to (a) Julian Braun . . . (b) Mr. Lawrence Revere. . . ." Wilson makes no mention of Thorp in his letter. Luckman had previously informed me by telephone that Thorp had refused to participate in the challenge contest. This came as no surprise to me because in early 1964, with the permission of the Nevada Gaming Commission, I challenged Professor Thorp to a $100,000 Black Jack contest to be held at the Sands Hotel Casino in Las Vegas. Thorp's reply was a big "No."

It is really laughable that the three experts, Wilson, Braun, and Revere, conducted correspondence over a five-month period, conditionally accepting my challenge, writing their own stipulations and regulations, when in truth they didn't even know how the game of Black Jack is played in Puerto Rico, the location where the $100,000 challenge match was to take place.

In early October 1976, John Luckman tried telephoning Richard Kane. The call was taken by Robert Bell, production manager of *John Scarne's Newsletter*. Luckman informed Bell that he had a $20,000 check from Lawrence Revere made out to John Luckman to seal the match. Bell in turn told Luckman that the Puerto Rican Gaming Commission demanded that a $5,000 personal check from each of the four Black Jack wizards be deposited with the Caribe Hilton Casino before they sanctioned the match and that Luckman's $20,000 check was unacceptable because Luckman was not a prospective challenge participant.

Later Luckman tried to contact Roberto Lugo by phone in Puerto Rico. Lugo was aware of Luckman's check scheme so he refused to accept Luckman's telephone calls. I arrived at the Caribe Hilton in San Juan, Puerto Rico, on October 13, 1976. Luckman phoned me several times that evening. I refused to accept his calls and instead sent him the following telegram:

Dear Mr. Luckman:
Please be advised that as of October 14, 1976, one day before the expiration date of my proposed $100,000 Black Jack Challenge Match, Richard Kane, my intermediary, has not received any of the four requested $5,000 personal certified checks from Edward Thorp, Allan Wilson, Julian Braun or Lawrence Revere. Furthermore, Richard Kane has not yet received the four requested notarized letters of acceptance from the four principals stating that each accepts my $100,000 challenge and the conditions described in John Scarne's Newsletter some five months ago.

Sincerely
John Scarne

The day after I sent the wire, October 15th, I received a telegram of alibis from John Luckman instead of the four $5,000 checks expected from each of the four Black Jack wizards in order to qualify for the challenge. Since October 15, 1976, was the expiration date of my challenge, I considered my $100,000 Black Jack challenge refused by Thorp, Wilson, Braun and Revere—and the challenge therefore was withdrawn.

Soon after Thorp, Wilson, Braun and Revere refused my $100,000 Black Jack Challenge, many Nevada casinos that previously dealt single and double deck from the hand switched to Scarne's Black Jack Rules with their indicator card and four-deck shoe (pages 75 to 81). Other casinos that switched to my rules unwisely added one, two or four decks to my four-deck shoe, making for a five, six and even an eight-deck game. I'm sure, however, that when this book is studied by Nevada casino operators and they learn that all the advertised winning Black Jack count systems are mathematical hoaxes and can't possibly work even under the most favorable countdown conditions, Scarne's Black Jack rules with their four-deck shoe will become standard in all Nevada casinos—as they now are in casinos in most parts of the world. Some of the Las Vegas major hotel casinos now making use of my rules include Caesars Palace, M-G-M Grand, Dunes, Las Vegas Hilton, Aladdin, Holiday and the Hilton Flamingo.

The reason for these rules changes in Nevada casinos is today's constant presence of thousands of so-called count players working alone or as a count mob (team). Some casino bosses became so alarmed by these count mobs and their unethical casino conduct that in addition to instituting their rules changes they barred many a count mob from their casinos. Other casino bosses switched to my Black Jack rules after being fed up with their single and double-deck reshuffling every time a so-called counter stepped up his bets.

Al (Mokey) Faccinto, casino manager of Caesars Palace, recently asked me the $128,000 Black Jack question: "Scarne, why is it that most of the highly publicized card counters that gambled at Caesars were caught trying to corrupt our dealers to conspire with them to cheat at our Black Jack tables?"

"Mokey, the answer is quite simple. Since each of these phony counters makes his living selling phony Black Jack systems via books, schools, seminars, etc., they'll cheat, steal, and bribe dealers to beat your casino just one time so they can falsely advertise that they beat Caesars Palace with a count system."

6

BANK CRAPS: THE CASINO'S FASTEST GAMBLING GAME

Craps, history's biggest and fastest-action gambling game, is undoubtedly the most widely played game of chance in the United States today; more money is won and lost at Craps illegally and legally each day than at any other form of gambling, with the exception of sports betting and betting on horse races. Today, Bank Craps is played in every major casino in Nevada, Atlantic City, Puerto Rico, the Bahamas, Haiti and elsewhere. Although the casino game of Bank Craps is second to Black Jack in popularity, the sum wagered by the 20 million habitual American crapshooters, of whom 5 million are women, is about 30% more than that wagered at Black Jack.

The Bank Craps tables in casinos the world over look alike, but the Bank Craps layouts (the design printed on the green baize covering of the playing surface) vary in shape, payoffs and bets permitted. The four most popular Bank Craps layouts found in the world's casinos are the Nevada Craps layout, Scarney Craps layout, New York Craps layout and Open or Money Craps layout.

The Nevada Craps layout is found in Nevada, Atlantic City and Puerto Rico. Nevada and Atlantic City pay lesser odds than Puerto Rico on one-roll bets such as the double-aces, double-sixes, eleven, and ace-deuce. Puerto Rico, however, pays lesser odds on the place bets six and eight. The Nevada Craps layout possesses an average house advantage of 4%.

The Scarney Craps layout, which is found in many casinos the world over including Curaçao, Aruba, St. Maarten and Haiti, does not possess a come and don't come betting space. However, the one-roll bets are better than those found in Nevada casinos. The house advantage at Scarney Craps averages about 5%.

The New York Craps layout, which is popular in the Bahamas, England and Monte Carlo, does not possess come and don't come betting spaces, place betting is not permitted, and the bank levies a 5% charge on most bets permitted at its table. The house advantage at New York Craps averages about 5%.

The Money (or Open) Craps layout is found in most illegal gambling joints in operation in the United States. The game is played with cash rather than chips. Players may gamble with each other only on the shooter's point; however, the house advantage averages about 5% when players bet the bank.

The popularity of the American game of Bank Craps has spread in the past two decades to the four corners if the globe. Today, Bank Craps tables can be found in the plush legal gambling casinos of Monte Carlo, England, Puerto Rico, Turkey, Haiti, Bahamas, Curaçao, Aruba, St. Maarten, Panama, Dominican Republic and other Caribbean islands that cater to American tourists. And wherever American servicemen are stationed, at home or overseas, the galloping dominoes are in action.

Bank Craps and Money (or Open) Craps has not only replaced Faro as the favorite casino game of millions of Americans, but has far outdistanced all other casino games in the total sum wagered. Private Craps is the big favorite in the field of friendly or unorganized gambling.

CASINO AND CANDY STORE DICE

Dice have been fascinating people and deciding fates for over 2,000 years. Even the language of dice echoes history. When Caesar made the critical decision to take his victorious army across the Rubicon against the edict of the Roman Senate, he took his retort from the lexicon of the dice player: "Iacta alea est." *The die is cast.*

Primitives all over the globe—the American Indian, the Aztec, and Maya, the South Sea Islander, the Eskimo, the African—have gambled with dice of many curious shapes and markings. Dice have been made from plum and peach stones; seeds; buffalo, caribou and moose bone; deer horn; pebbles; pottery; walnut shells; beaver and woodchuck teeth. In Greek and Roman times, most dice were made of bone or ivory; others were bronze, agate, rock crystal, onyx, jet, alabaster, marble, amber or porcelain.

Almost all modern dice are made of cellulose or some other plastic material. The standard die is marked with a number of small dots (called *spots*) from one to six. The spots are arranged in conventional patterns and placed in conventional relative locations. The spots on the opposite sides always total seven: one opposite six, two opposite five and three opposite four. When the visible vertical sides are two and three and the top side is one, six must be the bottom number while five and four must be on the opposite vertical sides. The combinations of the six spots (sides) plus the number of dice in play determine the mathematical probabilities.

In most games played with dice, the dice are thrown (rolled, flipped, shot, tossed or cast) from the hand or from a receptacle called a *dice cup* in such a way that they will turn at random. The spots that face upward when the dice come to rest are the deciding spots. The sum of the numbers on the top surfaces decides, according to the rules of the game being played, whether the thrower (called the *shooter*) wins, loses, continues to throw or loses possession of the dice.

There are two kinds of dice. *Perfect dice* or *casino dice,* made by hand and true to a tolerance of 1/5,000 inch (dice manufacturers inaccurately advertise perfect dice as true to a tolerance of 1/10,000 inch), are used to play casino Craps. Round-cornered imperfect dice, called *drugstore* or *candy-store* dice, are fabricated by machine and are generally used for social and board games.

Modern casino dice are sawed from extruded rods of cellulose. The spots are drilled approximately 17/1,000 inch into the faces of the die. Then the recesses are filled with a paint the same weight as the celluloid that has been drilled out. The dice are then buffed and polished and, since no recesses remain, are known as *flush-spot dice* or *bird's-eye spot dice.* Most casinos use red flush-spot dice which are transparent and come in sets of five. The standard size used in Nevada, the Caribbean and most casinos the world over is .750 inch. The dice edges are generally either square and known as *razor edge* or slightly turned and known as *feather edge.* Casino dice usually carry a special monogram and coded serial number as a means of thwarting dice cheats. Perfect dice used in various other dice games range from a .250-inch cellulose or bone "peewee" die to an extra large .770-inch die. Perfect concave-spot dice, although still in use, are rarely seen in the best casinos. Besides drugstore, round-cornered dice, pyramidal, pentahedral and octahedral dice, with all sorts of face designs, have been used.

Dice in their various forms are the oldest gambling instruments known to man, and countless games have been played with them. Craps, the most popular gambling house game, is played with two dice. In more social play, Poker Dice and Scarney 3000 are played with five dice; various counter and bar games, such as Twenty-Six, are played with ten dice. In Backgammon and hundreds of "board games," two or more dice are thrown to determine the moves.

NEVADA'S RECORD $400,000 PLAYER WIN AT BANK CRAPS

Although Bank Craps and Money Craps give the player a better shake for his money percentagewise than any other casino game, more money is lost at Craps than at all other casino games combined. I know a man, one of Nevada's top casino owners, who had saved a cool $6 million during his gambling career. He added another $8 million by selling his casino when he retired. Then, with plenty of time on his hands, he became a Bank Craps player, and in three short years of retirement lost all his fortune trying to beat the game on which he had made it. Casino owners and employees call compulsive Craps players who can't control their urge to gamble *dice degenerates.*

This man's story is not unique. Curiously, a great many casino owners and employees lose most of their gambling earnings at Bank or Money Craps. One would think that people who earn fortunes in the gambling business would know better than to try to beat any casino banking game, but when it comes to Craps, with its fast action and big-money wagers, these characters lose all common sense, and many of them become suckers at their own game.

The fair sex has its quota of Craps degenerates, too. The most notable one I met was a 72-year-old widow known to Nevada casino operators as "Ma." I saw her last one day in Vegas in the mid-1950s when she entered the downtown Horseshoe Club and asked Joe Brown, the owner, if he would ante up his $300 Craps limit for her. "Ma," he said, "you can have any limit you want, but your maximum betting limit will be determined by the amount of your first bet." Ma didn't bat an eye. "I understand. My first wager is $10,000 on the front line."

She took her place at the table, began putting ten-grand bets on the layout, and within 30 minutes had won a cool $70,000. About a year later, after having lost more than $2 million, she disappeared from the Nevada casinos. The owner later told me that she was the fastest woman Craps degenerate he had ever seen and that as a big-time bettor she held her own with the outstanding male high rollers.

The biggest Bank Craps player win in Nevada's legalized casino history is the $400,000 won by Nate Jacobson, the fiery and imaginative professional gambler who founded Caesars Palace on the Las Vegas Strip. This huge $400,000 win took place a few years ago at the same downtown Las Vegas Horseshoe Club mentioned above. However, at the time Jacobson won the $400,000, Benny Binion, that amiable professional gambler who hails from Texas was (and still is at the time of writing), the bossman of the Horseshoe Club. Benny Binion became famous in Nevada for his big betting limits at the Horseshoe Club. Binion's betting limit policy is to allow the big-time gambler to bet 10 percent of his cash chip buy-in. Nate Jacobson bought in $50,000 in chips so his maximum betting limit was $5,000 at the time he won the $400,000.

I know of at least 50 players who have lost a million dollars or more at Craps, but I can name only a couple who have, in the long run, won more than $250,000—and they did it at either Money or Private Craps, where they were not bucking house percentages. Big-time winners at Bank Craps over the long run are few and far between.

THE UNFINISHED CRAPS HAND

To my knowledge, the biggest sum of money lost by any illegal casino operator in America at a single Bank Craps table in a one-night session was the $300,000 lost by the operators of the 86 Club in Miami, Florida, in late February 1947. Bigtime gamblers all over America still talk about the "unfinished hand" that night at the 86 Club's $1,000 maximum limit Bank Craps table.

The Craps table was crowded with about 30 bigtime gamblers and racketeers from all over the country who were vacationing in Florida, when, at precisely 2:00 A.M., the stickman chanted "Next shooter" as he pushed the five dice in front of an automobile dealer from Detroit. The shooter selected a pair of dice and, after all bets were placed, threw them across the elastic string stretched across the center of the table. What occurred then made Craps history. At 3:30 A.M., the same automobile dealer still held the dice when Charley Thomas and Jack Friedlander, the casino owners, walked over to the dice table and announced, "Gentlemen, that's all for tonight. The bank is broke." In that 1½ hours of Craps shooting, the Detroit car dealer had shot the owners of the 86 Club out of almost $300,000 in cash.

The shooter pleaded with Jack Friedlander to permit him to finish his hand, but Jack shrugged his shoulders and said, "Gentlemen, it will have to end as an unfinished hand," and it did. I was there, and since I knew that the casino carried a $500,000 nightly bankroll, I later asked Jack Friedlander his reason for stopping the game in the middle of a shot. He grinned. "John, after losing nearly $300,000 on that hot hand I figured that as soon as the shooter threw a miss-out all the players would quit. They had their bundle. All the money I could win back would be on that one miss-out—and who knows how many more point, proposition and place bets these characters were still likely to win if this hot hand continued?"

Despite this $300,000 loss, and after paying all expenses including the ice, which at that time in Florida was high, the operators of the 86 Club divided $1,200,000 in profits for their 11-week season.

Most high rollers or so-called smart gamblers prefer Craps to any other casino game because the percentage favoring the house is much less than at nearly all other casino games. These high rollers, however, lose considerably more at Bank Craps than they lose at any other casino game with a greater house percentage; as a rule they find it is just as impossible to beat the front-line bet at Bank Craps with its 1.41% disadvantage as it is to beat a game with a much greater house P.C. against the player. As a matter of fact, a front-line Craps player bucking the house percentage of only 1.41% is just as big a chump as the racetrack frequenter who bucks the track's favorable percentage of 12% to 20%. This doesn't sound right? I know. But there's a good reason.

The answer is that the major racetracks run only nine races each day, whereas hundreds of front-line decisions are made at the Bank Craps table in the same period of time.

If you add the total house percentages you pay at a Craps table in the time it takes to run off nine races and compare this sum with the total percentages you pay for the privilege of betting a horse in each of the nine races, you will find that the smart Craps player is paying a bigger overall percentage than the horse player.

As my good friend Elmer West, one of Nevada's pioneer gambling operators, once told me, "The only difference between bucking a game with a house percentage of one percent or less compared to bucking a game which has a much higher percentage is that the player bucking the bigger percentage goes broke much sooner."

The main reason why Craps has outdistanced all other games of chance, both in number of devotees and amount of money wagered, is that it offers the players more personal participation. In other casino games the player can only bet that an event will occur; he cannot bet that it will not occur. In Roulette, the croupier spins the ball and wheel, and the player can only bet that the ball will fall in a certain numbered space or in one of a certain group of numbers; he can't bet that the ball will *not* fall into a certain numbered space. In Craps, the players bet with or against the dice, and also have the opportunity of throwing the dice themselves. The thrill they get when they match their luck against the banker or other players is more personal than the one they get when they simply wait and hope that the Roulette ball will drop into their number.

BANK CRAPS, MONEY (OR OPEN) CRAPS, NEW YORK CRAPS, SCARNEY CRAPS AND PRIVATE CRAPS

Very few men have not played a game of Craps at some time or other. Women, however, seldom played Craps until the 1950s. The game was considered undignified before it appeared in Nevada casinos in the form of Bank Craps. My survey shows that today approximately 5 million women have become Craps players.

Let us look at the differences among the five modern variations of Craps: Private Craps, Bank Craps, New York Craps, Scarney Craps and Money (or Open) Craps.

Private Craps is a friendly social game which does not use a casino, Craps table or banker. The only requisites for Private Craps are two or more persons with cash in their pockets and a pair of dice. It can be played on a street corner, in a back alley, private club, army barracks, living room—anywhere the players have room in which to roll the dice.

Bank Craps is the version of the game found in Nevada casinos and other carpet joints throughout the United States, and in foreign countries where American tourists patronize casinos. Bank Craps is played on a specially constructed dice table which has a special betting layout depicting the types of bets permitted. Chips or checks are used instead of cash when wagers are placed on the layout. Players are not permitted to gamble against each other; all bets are made against the bank.

New York Craps is a version of Bank Craps found in most illegal gambling houses in the eastern part of the United States and in the legal casinos of the Bahamas, Yugoslavia and in England. The game is played on a dice table somewhat similar to a Bank Craps table in which place betting is prohibited and the house takes 5% of the amount wagered on the point numbers (4, 5, 6, 8, 9, 10).

Scarney Craps, a creation of the author, is a version of Bank Craps and New York Craps combined. The game is found in casinos in Europe, Curaçao, Aruba, St. Maarten, Haiti and South America. The game is played on a Bank Craps table.

Money (or Open) Craps is so called because, as the inveterate Craps player would say, it is an "open" game and played mostly with cash. It is played on a dice table, and there is a banker called the *book*. The game is found in most illegal sawdust joints and makeshift casinos. The rules permit the players to gamble with each other on the shooter's point number. Players, however, must place all center, flat, off and box-number bets with the book. When he bets the book, the player must pay a charge to him, usually 5% of the amount wagered. Seasoned gamblers, racket guys and other easy-money guys prefer Money Craps to Bank Craps.

ORIGIN AND HISTORY

Craps is of American Black origin. Their colorful slang is still used in the game and dice are often still called "African Dominoes." Around New Orleans, some time after 1800, the Black tried his hand at the English game of Hazard, which the French sometimes called Craps. But the intricacy of the rules and betting odds of this game led him to simplify the playing procedure so greatly that he ended by inventing the present game of Private Craps.

Private Craps moved up the Mississippi and then out across the country, its habitat the steamboats, the river wharfs and docks, the cotton fields and the saloon. About 1890 the game appeared in the form of Bank Craps in a number of American carpet and sawdust joints but made little progress because the layout permitted only one-way action, and the maximum limits (usually a top of $25) were very low. Players could only bet right on such layout spaces as win bets, come bets, field bets, and 6 and 8. Because of this one-way action, many gambling house operators used *six-ace flats,* crooked dice which gave a favorable percentage to the wrong bettor—in this case, the casino. Smart dice players, naturally, avoided these games.

The big banking casino game in those days was the card game of Faro, originally known as Pharaoh or Pharoo, which had been played in France since the middle of the seventeenth century. Faro entered this country by way of New Orleans in the eighteenth century, and shortly after the Louisiana Purchase (1803) became the most widely played gambling-house game in the United States—a position it held until the game of Craps became a successful casino banking game in the early part of the twentieth century.

THE FIRST CRAPS BOOKMAKER

Because of its one-way action Bank Craps remained a small-time banking game until John H. Winn, a dicemaker by trade, decided to book the Craps game by permitting players to bet against him, either right or wrong, for a charge on each $5 bet made. This innovation made him the world's first Craps bookmaker. After several years of intensive searching for him throughout the United States, I finally located him in New York City early in 1944—many years after he had retired as a professional bookmaker—and heard his firsthand story of how he transformed Private Craps into today's successful casino games of Bank Craps and Money (or Open) Craps.

In New York City, in 1907, he began to book the first Craps game—in a back alley near 14th Street and Broadway. He charged both right and wrong bettors a quarter for a $5 bet and 50¢ for a $10 bet. This improvement gave Winn plenty of business and a handsome profit, and other smart dice players, noticing this, began booking Craps games instead of playing. A couple of years later, hundreds of Craps bookies were operating in the principal cities of the United States. The innovation of allowing players to bet both ways demanded that operators use honest and perfect dice and practically eliminated crooked percentage dice in casino games.

THE ORIGIN OF VIGORISH

John Winn invented the Craps book, the quarter charge that developed into the 5% charge, and he is initially responsible for the games of Bank Craps and Money (or Open) Craps. Eventually, because the 5% charge brought in the money so dependably and was so strong, gamblers took the word *vigor,* added a syllable of jargon—as they often do when they would rather the layman couldn't follow their conversation—and called it *the vigorish.* Some gamblers later trimmed the word down to *vig.* Today both are used.

Shortly afterward, Winn also improved the banking layout of Bank Craps in much the same way. He drew a space on the layout "just a little piece off on one side," and lettered in the words *Don't Pass.* This was done in Philadelphia, to which Winn used to commute weekends, and the layout came to be famous as the "Philadelphia layout," the first Bank Craps layout to give the players an opportunity to bet the dice to lose. Winn also charged a quarter for a $5 bet and 50¢ for a $10 bet on the don't pass line.

Later, a gambler who remembered the *bar* on the zero and double zero in the early French-style Roulette, eliminated the direct charge on the don't pass line and substituted the ace-deuce bar (for explanation of the term "bar" see page 199) on the don't pass space. And, finally, when the wrong players' constant complaints that the ace-deuce appeared too often on the come-out became insistent, the bar on the two aces or on the two sixes was substituted and became standard, although there are still a good many gambling houses which, because their clientele is not *dice smart,* still carry the ace-deuce bar. The dice table at Monte Carlo is an example.

A few years later, chips were substituted for cash and, to add dignity, most Bank Craps layouts dropped Winn's 25¢ charge and paid off at less than the correct odds instead. Winn's original quarter charge still exists at Money and New York Craps and in a few Bank Craps games, and is known as the 5% charge. It was Winn's 25¢ charge for each $5 bet, no matter whether the player bet right or wrong, that eventually made Craps the biggest casino gambling game in the world.

By 1910 Bank and Open Craps had replaced Faro as America's number one casino game. There are today probably not more than a few Faro games doing business in the United States, and only one of them is in Nevada. Bank Craps is played today in all major American casinos and in many Caribbean and South American casinos. I was partly responsible for its introduction at Monte Carlo.

Since Bank Craps and Money (or Open) Craps are simply variations of Private Craps, the reader will more readily understand our later analysis if he first takes a look at the official rules for Private Craps.

SCARNE'S OFFICIAL RULES FOR PRIVATE CRAPS

EQUIPMENT

1. Two dice numbered from one to six in such a way that the spots on opposite sides add to seven.
2. A wall or backboard against which the dice are thrown.

PLAYERS

1. Any number may play.
2. The player throwing the dice is the shooter. Any player, by consent of the others, may start the game by becoming the shooter.
3. A new player may enter the game at any time, provided there is an opening in the circle. If no player objects at the time the new player takes his position, he becomes the shooter at his proper turn, even though he may take a position directly at the left of the shooter.
4. The dice pass around the circle of players to the left—clockwise.
5. Players may leave the game at any time (without regard to their wins or losses).

THE PLAY

1. The dice are thrown and the two numbers, added together, that face skyward when the dice come to rest are the deciding numbers.
2. The shooter's first roll and each roll after a decision has been effected is a *come-out.*

3. If, on the come-out, the shooter throws a natural (7 or 11), it is a winning decision called a *pass;* a crap (2, 3 or 12) is a losing decision called a *miss-out.* If he throws a 4, 5, 6, 8, 9 or 10, that number becomes the shooter's *point* and he continues throwing until either:

(a) he throws his point again, which is a winning decision or pass, or

(b) he throws a SEVEN, which is a losing decision or miss-out.

4. When the shooter misses out on the point, the dice pass to the next player on his left, and it becomes his turn to shoot.

5. The shooter may, if he likes, pass the dice to the next player on completion of any decision without waiting to miss-out on the point.

6. Any player may, if he likes, refuse to shoot in his turn, and pass the dice to the next player.

7. When more than one pair of dice are employed, players may call for a box-up or change of dice at any time; the change takes place immediately after the next decision.

THE THROW, OR ROLL

1. The shooter shakes the dice in his closed hand and must try to throw them so that both dice hit and rebound from the backboard.

2. If only one die hits the board, the roll counts, but the players may reprimand the shooter.

3. If this occurs a second time, the other players may designate someone else to complete the shooter's turn at throwing. If they wish, they may also bar him from shooting for the duration of the game.

4. If neither die hits the board, or if, when playing on a table or elevated surface, one or both dice fall off the playing surface, the roll is *no-dice:* it does not count and the dice must be thrown again.

5. If the dice hit any object or person after hitting the board, the roll counts; it is not no-dice.

6. If a die comes to rest cocked at an angle on a coin or any irregularity on the playing surface, and there is a difference of opinion as to which number faces skyward, a neutral player, or any player designated by common consent, or a bystander shall stand at the shooter's position and decide which number counts by stating which top surface of the die appears to be the skyward surface from that position.

7. If, after hitting the backboard, a die rolls out of sight under a bill or any other object on the playing surface, either a neutral player or a player designated by common consent or a bystander shall take extreme care in trying to ascertain the skyward number.

8. The practice of knocking or kicking dice aside on the roll and calling "Gate!" or "No dice!" (known as *gating*) is not permitted.

BETTING

1. All bets must be made before the dice are thrown; they cannot be made while they are rolling.

2. Right bet: A wager that the dice will pass (win, either by making a natural on the come-out or by throwing a point number on the come-out and then repeating it before throwing a SEVEN). Players making right bets are *right bettors*.

3. Wrong bet: A wager that the dice don't pass. Players making wrong bets are *wrong bettors*.

4. Proposition bets: This term is applied in Private Craps to any bet not a point or off-number bet or flat bet.

5. Center bet: Before the come-out the shooter may (but is not required to) bet that he will pass. Players who cover this wager by betting an equal amount against the shooter *fade* the shooter and are known as *faders*. These wagers, placed in the center of the playing surface, are center bets.

If only a part of the shooter's center bet is covered, the shooter may shoot for that amount or he may call the bet off by saying "No bet."

6. Side bet: Any bet not a center bet is placed at one side of the playing surface and is known as a side bet. The shooter may make any side bet including the flat bet.

7. Flat bet: A side bet that the dice pass, made by a right bettor before the come-out, is a *right flat bet*. A side bet that the dice don't pass made by a wrong bettor before the come-out is a *wrong flat bet*. Flat bets are the same as center bets except that the shooter and fader are not involved.

8. Point bet: After the shooter has thrown a point on the come-out, a side bet made by a right bettor that the shooter makes his point is a *right point bet*. A side bet by a wrong bettor that the shooter misses his point is a *wrong point bet*. The right bettor takes the odds on that point. The wrong bettor lays the odds on the point.

9. Any point or off-number bet may be called off by the bettors concerned before a decision is effected.

10. Come bet: A bet that the dice will pass (win), the next roll to be considered as a come-out roll.

Example: Suppose the shooter's point is FOUR and he bets that he comes. If he throws a SEVEN, he loses any bet he has made on the FOUR but wins the come bet because, on this bet, the roll is considered to be a come-out, and the SEVEN is a natural and wins.

If he throws an ELEVEN, the point bet is still undecided, but he wins the come bet.

If he throws a crap (2, 3 or 12), the point bet is still undecided, and he loses the come bet.

If he throws a FOUR, he wins the original point bet, but must continue throwing and make another FOUR before throwing a SEVEN in order to win the come bet. If he then throws any other number (such as 6), it counts as a second point and he continues throwing in an attempt to make either or both points before throwing a SEVEN.

11. Don't come bet: A bet that the dice don't pass (lose), the next roll to be considered as a come-out.

12. The hardway or gag bet: A bet that a specified even number (which may be either the shooter's point or an off number) will or will not be thrown the hard way with two like numbers; that is, a FOUR with double 2, SIX with double 3, EIGHT with double 4, TEN with double 5. If the number is thrown any other way, or a SEVEN is thrown, the bettor loses the hardway bet.

13. One-roll action or come-out bet: A bet that the shooter does or does not throw

(a) *a certain number any way.* Example: A bet that the shooter will or won't throw SEVEN with any of the combinations 1–6, 2–5, 3–4.

(b) *a certain number a certain way.* Example: A bet that the shooter will or won't throw SEVEN with one specific combination such as 3–4.

(c) *any one of a group of numbers on the next roll.* Example: A bet that the shooter will or won't throw any of the numbers in the group 2, 3 and 12 (craps), the group 4 and 10, the group 11 and 3, etc.

14. One-number bet: A bet that a certain number or group of numbers will or will not be thrown before another number.

15. Off-number bet: A bet made at odds that the shooter will or will not throw a specified number other than his point (any of the numbers 4, 5, 6, 8, 9 or 10) before throwing SEVEN.

PRIVATE CRAPS: HUSTLERS AND CHUMPS

For every Bank Craps game found in gambling establishments there are dozens of private games which take place daily, weekly, monthly or annually in homes, convention sites, factories, office buildings, hotel rooms, saloons, clubs and military installations all over the country, no matter what the law may say.

Since the smart wrong bettor in the average Private Craps game enjoys a favorable advantage of about 2% over the sucker right bettor, I estimate that about 900,000 wrong bettors in America took 25,100,000 right or right-and-wrong bettors to the cleaner's.

The great majority of right bettors are plain chumps who accept incorrect odds from the strictly wrong bettors, the *Craps hustlers* (players who knowingly hustle a Craps game by offering right bettors wagers at less than the correct odds). A Craps hustler is half gambler and half cheat. He is the guy who won most of the $1,200,000,000 lost by the millions of chumps in the Private Craps games in 1973.

The casino extracts a house percentage by offering the players less than true odds on all Craps bets, in exchange for supplying a place in which to gamble. In the private game the hustler collects the same or an even greater percentage and supplies, at the most, a pair of dice. More often than not, it is the chumps themselves who supply the dice and the place to gamble. It's as screwy as all that.

A Craps hustler may be anyone: your friend, neighbor, co-worker, fellow club member, in fact anyone who knows more about Craps odds than you do. How does the hustler's extra knowledge of Craps pay off such handsome dividends? In the first place, the whole situation is a setup. In most private games there are three kinds of players. About two-thirds, or 66 out of every 100, are right bettors, or chumps. A little less than one-third, about 31, are right-and-wrong bettors, or half-chumps, who usually bet right when they are shooting and try to bet wrong on the other right player's roll. The remaining 3 out of 100 are strictly wrong bettors, hustlers, who always bet the dice to lose and pass the dice when it is their turn to shoot. Now and then—so you won't recognize them as wrong bettors—hustlers make a right bet, but the amount wagered is always small.

Scratch a consistent winner at your friendly private game and it is 97 to 3 that he's not a right bettor.

The consistent right bettor, or chump, must lose in the long run because the odds are stacked against him. Thousands of Craps hustlers in the country work in industrial plants and hustle the Craps games at noon. I knew one hustler who won $20,000 from his fellow workers during one year of lunch-hour Craps shooting.

There are more than 40 million Craps players in America, 5 million of whom are women, and most of them will accept any sucker bet offered them by Craps hustlers. The correct odds at Private Craps given in the following pages should be of particular interest to these people since a knowledge of the odds will enable them to graduate from the chump category.

There are about 900,000 dice hustlers in this country; about 80,000 of these are women, most of whom learned the business from their hustler or gambler husbands or boyfriends. Some learned the trade by working as dice girls or shills in casinos. Others learned the hard way— by playing Craps in gambling houses, where their constant losses eventually taught them that anyone who has the odds in his favor must grind out a profit in any game.

I once knew a woman dice hustler who had a working knowledge of odds equal to that of any man. After working as a Craps dealer in Reno she turned to hustling Craps and preyed only on women players. Her particular angle was to rent a suite of rooms in a swanky resort hotel and then give a cocktail party to which she invited women guests staying at the hotel. Once the cocktail party was well under way, she and her shill would start a game, rolling the dice on the thickly carpeted floor. If any of the guests did not know how to play, Nina (as she called herself) gave them a fast lesson. The end result was always the same: She won all the folding money in sight simply by offering her guests sucker odds which were almost always accepted because the chumps knew no better. Nina told me that her Craps hustling for a winter season paid all her hotel expenses, the shill's salary, and netted her about five grand.

The novice Craps player must understand that Craps is primarily a mathematical game of numbers, and the only thing the hustler has which the inexperienced dice player doesn't is a knowledge of the correct odds. He simply offers his victim less than the correct odds.

Suppose you agree to take $9\frac{1}{11}\%$ the worst of it on every bet you make in a Private Craps game. This is the same as agreeing to accept $1 every time you win and to pay out $1.20 every time you lose. Anyone who bets in such a foolish manner often enough is a rank sucker, deserves exactly what he gets, and goes broke. These are the sort of sucker odds that the Craps hustlers offer and most players accept. Sometimes the chumps accept odds that are even worse. Here is another example of odds cheating in Private Craps. When a player accepts an even-money bet that the shooter will make his point when it is either a SIX or an EIGHT, he is cheating himself just as surely as if he were playing against *six-ace flats* (crooked dice). The proper odds against making SIX or EIGHT are 6 to 5, and yet most Craps shooters are perfectly content to accept even money on such a bet. They accept $1 for $1 instead of demanding the correct payoff price of $1.20 to their $1. Craps shooters who are unfamiliar with the correct odds accept almost any odds offered because it would embarrass them if they admitted out loud that they didn't know the correct odds. The man who claimed that ignorance is bliss was no gambler. In gambling, ignorance is fatal.

The payoff odds used in 999 out of every 1,000 Private Craps games are actually the gambling house payoff odds casinos use at Bank Craps when paying off right bettors; the payoff odds in Private Craps are permanently fixed against the guy who is either shooting or betting the dice to win. This is why "all right bettors die broke."

Players accept winning payoffs at less than the correct odds in a casino because this is the price charged for the use of the casino and its facilities, but any player who accepts such odds from a Craps hustler in a friendly game, which may even take place in his own home, is making a fool of himself. Any Craps player who studies the following text and then still accepts sucker bets in Private Craps games needs the services of a good psychiatrist. Here you will find everything there is to know about Craps odds.

The first step is to find out how many possible combinations of two numbers can be thrown with a pair of dice, what numbers these combinations form, and in how many ways each number can be formed. Elementary arithmetic supplies the answers. There are six numbers on each die. Multiply 6 × 6 and you get 36 possible combinations, or ways, in which the two numbers on a pair of dice can form the 11 numbers 2, 3, 4, 5, 6, 7, 8, 9, 10, 11 and 12. The table below shows these 11 numbers and the number of possible combinations that form each number.

COMBINATIONS OR WAYS

```
 2 can be made in 1 way:  1–1
 3 can be made in 2 ways: 1–2 2–1
 4 can be made in 3 ways: 1–3 3–1 2–2
 5 can be made in 4 ways: 1–4 4–1 2–3 3–2
 6 can be made in 5 ways: 1–5 5–1 2–4 4–2 3–3
 7 can be made in 6 ways: 1–6 6–1 2–5 5–2 3–4 4–3
 8 can be made in 5 ways: 2–6 6–2 3–5 5–3 4–4
 9 can be made in 4 ways: 3–6 6–3 4–5 5–4
10 can be made in 3 ways: 4–6 6–4 5–5
11 can be made in 2 ways: 5–6 6–5
12 can be made in 1 way:  6–6
```

When we know that there are 36 ways of making these 11 numbers and also how many ways each individual number can be made, we can easily obtain the correct odds on all points and off-numbers. This is done simply by figuring the number of ways the *point* can be made as against the six combinations by which SEVEN can be made. The following chart gives the odds against passing or making the point. The correct odds are also shown in terms of money bets.

ODDS AGAINST PASSING ON THE POINT NUMBERS

The Point Numbers	Correct Odds	Odds in $ and ¢ Bets			
4 can be made in 3 ways, 7 in 6 ways	2 to 1	$.20 to $.10		$2.00 to $1.00	
5 can be made in 4 ways, 7 in 6 ways	3 to 2	.30	.20	1.50	1.00
6 can be made in 5 ways, 7 in 6 ways	6 to 5	.30	.25	1.20	1.00
8 can be made in 5 ways, 7 in 6 ways	6 to 5	.30	.25	1.20	1.00
9 can be made in 4 ways, 7 in 6 ways	3 to 2	.30	.20	1.50	1.00
10 can be made in 3 ways, 7 in 6 ways	2 to 1	.20	.10	2.00	1.00

The trick is to memorize these odds. If you find that they do not tally with those you have been taking, it's a sure sign you have been losing money in your dice playing to dice hustlers or sharpies who have been taking you for a sucker.

Most Craps players think that shooter and fader have the same chance of winning and that the correct odds on a center or flat bet are 1 to 1, 50–50 or even money. In gambling, one thing you should never do is to take something for granted. Let's analyze this bet and find out the correct odds. We first find out how many of the throws made by the shooter will, in the long run, win, and how many will lose. If there are an equal number of each, it's an even-money bet. And if not—well, let's see.

If we calculate how many rolls out of the 36 possible combinations will win and how many will lose, we will complicate matters with fractions. We can avoid fractions by multiplying 36 rolls × 55 to get a lowest common multiple: 1,980 rolls.

Suppose that Joe Doe, a right bettor, throws the ivories 1,980 times; suppose he considers that each roll of the dice is a new come-out and that it results in a decision; and suppose that each of the 11 numbers is thrown exactly as often as probability predicts it will appear in the long run.

Since SEVEN (natural) can be made in six ways out of the total 36, it will be thrown $\frac{6}{36}$ of the 1,980 rolls, and Joe will win 330 times. ELEVEN (natural) can be made in two ways out of 36 and will be thrown $\frac{2}{36}$ of the 1,980 rolls, winning 110 times.

The point FOUR can be made in three ways out of 36 and will be thrown $\frac{3}{36}$ of the 1,980, or 165 times. But, since SEVEN, which now loses, will be thrown 6 times for every 3 times that FOUR is thrown, Joe will miss the point twice for every time that he makes it. Since he only passes one out of three times, he will win only $\frac{1}{3}$ of the 165 rolls, or 55 rolls.

Since TEN can also be made three ways, it will also win 55 rolls.

The point FIVE can be made four ways out of 36 and will be thrown $\frac{4}{36}$ of 1,980 rolls, or 220 times. Since SEVEN will be thrown six times for every four times that FIVE is thrown, Joe will win $\frac{4}{10}$ of the 220 rolls, or 88 rolls.

Since NINE can also be made four ways, it will also win 88 rolls.

SIX can be made 5 ways and will be thrown $\frac{5}{36}$ of 1,980 rolls, or 275 rolls. Since SEVEN will be thrown six times for every five times that SIX is thrown, SIX will win $\frac{5}{11}$ of the 275 rolls, or 125 rolls.

Since EIGHT is also made five ways, it will also win 125 rolls.

If we put these figures in a column and add up the winning rolls, we get 976, as shown in the table on the following page.

When Joe subtracts his 976 winning rolls from his total of 1,980 rolls he finds that he has lost 1,004 rolls. The fader has an advantage of 1,004 minus 976, or 28 rolls. That is his advantage or edge, and it is Joe's disadvantage.

Figure it in percentage by dividing 976 by 1,980, and we find that the shooter, or the right bettor before the come-out, has a $49\frac{2}{99}\%$ chance of winning. The fader or wrong bettor has a $50\frac{7}{99}\%$ chance. The shooter's, or right bettor's, disadvantage is the difference or $1\frac{41}{99}\%$, which expressed decimally is a percentage of 1.414 plus.

SHOOTER'S AND FADER'S CHANCES OF WINNING

	Times Thrown	Winning Rolls
Natural 7	330	330
Natural 11	110	110
Craps 2, 3, 12	220	—
Point 4	165	55
" 10	165	55
" 5	220	88
" 9	220	88
" 6	275	125
" 8	275	125
Totals	1,980	976

There isn't much that can be done to equalize this bet to make the shooter's and fader's chances exactly 50–50. The fader would have to lay odds of $1.0286 to the shooter's $1. Since this would require $\frac{1}{100}$¢ pieces, and since the U.S. Treasury is not likely to go to the trouble of minting such coins just to even up the chances for shooters and faders, it will have to continue being played as an even-money bet. It would just about even things up if everyone would shoot the dice at his turn of play and each player wagered an equal amount when shooting, but this isn't going to happen either.

Whether to shoot money in the center is a decision each player will have to make for himself. If you do shoot money in the center, always insist on the correct odds on all points if you want to stay out of the sucker class. Again, a word of caution. If you don't know the correct odds on all the points by heart and cannot rattle them off as quickly as you can your own telephone number, you should either stay away from Craps and play some game you know something about, or take time out right now and memorize the odds against passing.

Since many one-roll action or come-out bets are often made at Private Craps, and dice hustlers also constantly offer Bank Craps odds on these wagers, you also need to know the correct odds on all the most common one-roll action bets. The odds for each one-roll action bet can easily be calculated by referring to the *Combinations or Ways* table (page 144) and by following the mathematical procedure used in the example below.

Example: Since ELEVEN can be made in two ways, its probability is 2 in 36, or $\frac{2}{36}$. There are 34 chances that some other number will be thrown, and the odds against throwing ELEVEN in one roll are 34 to 2, or 17 to 1.

Here are all the most common one-roll actions odds with each odds figure also translated into terms of dollars and cents.

Even more common than one-roll action bets is the wager that one of the even point or off numbers (4, 6, 8, 10) will or will not be made the *hardway* or with the *gag*.

ODDS ON ONE-ROLL ACTION OR COME-OUT BETS

Numbers	Correct Odds	Odds in $ and ¢ Bets	
A given pair	35 to 1	$1.75 to .05	$35.00 to $1.00
11	17 to 1	.85 to .05	17.00 to 1.00
Any crap	8 to 1 ⎫		
5	8 to 1 ⎬	.40 to .05	8.00 to 1.00
9	8 to 1 ⎭		
4	11 to 1 ⎫	.55 to .05	11.00 to 1.00
10	11 to 1 ⎭		
6	6 1/5 to 1 ⎫	.31 to .05	6.20 to 1.00
8	6 1/5 to 1 ⎭		
Any 7	5 to 1	.25 to .05	5.00 to 1.00
1–2 (3)	17 to 1 ⎫		
3–4 (7)	17 to 1 ⎬	.85 to .05	17.00 to 1.00
5–2 (7)	17 to 1 ⎬		
6–1 (7)	17 to 1 ⎭		

ODDS AGAINST PASSING THE HARDWAY

The Point and Off Numbers	Correct Odds	Odds in $ and ¢ Bets	
4 can be made with 2–2 in 1 way	8 to 1	$.40 to .05	$ 8.00 to $1.00
10 can be made with 5–5 in 1 way	8 to 1	.40 to .05	8.00 to 1.00
6 can be made with 3–3 in 1 way	10 to 1	.50 to .05	10.00 to 1.00
8 can be made with 4–4 in 1 way	10 to 1	.50 to .05	10.00 to 1.00

You are probably all set to give us an argument on this one. Why, since FOUR can be made in only one way with 2–3, and since SIX can be made in only one way with 3–3, are the odds 8 to 1 on number FOUR and 10 to 1 on number SIX?

Most of the Craps players I have met believe that it is just as easy to make a FOUR the hardway with 2–2 as it is to make SIX the hardway with 3–3. They believe the same when shooting for a TEN or EIGHT the hardway.

The fallacy in the average player's reasoning is that when he makes the statement that it is just as easy to throw double-threes and double-fours as it is to throw double-twos and double-fives, he seems to forget that he is talking about the hardway.

The odds against throwing 3–3, 4–4, 2–2 or 5–5 on the come-out roll are the same—35 to 1. But the odds against making a point or off number with those combinations is something else again.

Suppose your point is FOUR and you bet that you can make it the hardway, with 2–2. There are, according to our *Combinations and Ways* table, three ways to make a FOUR, with 2–2, 1–3 and 3–1. If either 1–3 or 3–1 is thrown, you have made your point, but, since you didn't make it the hardway, you lose the bet. You have one way to win and two ways to lose. In addition, you can also lose if you seven out, and since there are six ways to make SEVEN, there are altogether eight ways you can lose, as against one way in which you can win. Consequently the odds are 8 to 1. The same reasoning also applies to making the point TEN with 5–5.

Let's try the same process with the points SIX and EIGHT. SIX, according to the *Combinations or Ways* table, can be made in five ways. Betting on the SIX the hardway means that only one of these ways (3–3) wins and the other four lose. Add the six losing ways that SEVEN can be made, and you have ten ways to lose against one way to win. The odds, therefore, strange as it may seem to players who don't think logically, are 10 to 1. The same reasoning applies to making EIGHT with 4–4.

If the Craps player takes the time to memorize the correct Craps odds listed in the foregoing text, and only accepts bets at correct odds, his chances of winning in any private Craps game will be greatly increased and he will no longer be easy prey for the Craps hustler. That is, provided the dice cheat doesn't use phony dice. For information that will help protect you against crooked dice, see pages 172 to 185.

BANK CRAPS LAS VEGAS STYLE

Bank Craps is the style of Craps played in all Nevada casinos. Money (or Open) Craps is barred by Nevada state law. Bank Craps is the style of Craps favored by the ladies and undoubtedly is responsible for the fact that there are now 5 million women Craps shooters. If you took time out to clock the number of women shooting Craps in the plush casinos on the Las Vegas Strip for a full evening, your clocking would show that about one out of every five Craps shooters is a woman. You'd get the same clocking results in the plush casinos in the Caribbean islands, at Monte Carlo, and wherever legally operated carpet joints are found.

The maximum betting limits at Bank Craps vary throughout the country. The usual top limits in Nevada casinos are $1,000 on the pass and don't pass line, and $1,000 on the place numbers. Some Nevada casinos have a Bank Craps maximum limit as low as $25. The most popular Bank Craps limits in legally and illegally operated casinos in America are $20, $25, $50, $100, $200, $300 or $1,000, and there are a few illegally operated Bank Craps tables catering to seasoned gamblers and racketeers which have $1,000 and $2,000 maximum limits. Many top Nevada casinos will up their $1,000 maximum to as high as $2,000 at the request of an outstanding big-time Craps player.

Betting limits on proposition bets such as the come-out bets and hardways are usually about one-third of the table's maximum betting limit. Example: At a $1,000 limit table the betting limits on the proposition bets (the two aces, two sixes, 11, all craps, all sevens and the hardway bets) usually range from $50 to $100. Occasionally a Bank Craps operator will permit a player to bet the usual maximum betting limit on each of the come-out or hardway bets. A player placing a $1,000 bet on the two sixes coming out and winning would receive a return of $30,000, a figure no casino manager likes to lose on a one-roll bet.

There is little difference between Bank Craps and Private Craps as far as the rules of the game are concerned. The big difference lies in the fact that Bank Craps players cannot bet among themselves; all bets must be placed on the spaces of the Craps layout and made against the bank. Hence the name Bank Craps. Another major difference between Bank Craps and Private Craps is that each bet made at Bank Craps has a percentage in favor of the bank. Bank Craps also has many bets on the layout which are not often made in Private Craps.

Bank Craps is usually played with Craps checks or chips instead of cash, although the Nevada casinos use silver dollars instead of dollar-valued checks. Craps checks in most luxury casinos range in value as follows: $1, $5, $25, $500 and $1,000 checks. Some sawdust joints deal in dime and quarter chips.

Chips have been used instead of cash in European casinos for centuries. The reasons are obvious: (1) Since each casino gaming table is supplied with thousands of dollars' worth of redeemable chips, the casino needs a much smaller bankroll to operate. I know of one casino in the Caribbean which uses $1 million worth of chips nightly, yet its cash bankroll is only about $50,000. (2) Chips in their varied colors make a fine background and make the dealer's job much easier and faster. The possibilities of theft by both dealers and players are minimized because chips are worthless unless they can be cashed.

Bank Craps today is played on a regulation Craps table about the size of a standard pool or billiard table. The first Craps tables actually were billiard tables, and the layout was drawn on the green cloth surface with chalk. A movable wooden rail, about one inch thick and eight inches high, was placed around the outside edges of the table, forming a rectangular enclosure. This served as a backboard and also kept the dice from rolling off the table. The wooden rail was easy to remove, and the Craps table could be quickly converted back to an innocent billiard table in the event of a police raid.

Modern dice tables have grooves on the top edges of the rails in which the players can place their chips during play so that they do not clutter up the playing surface. The inside of the surrounding rail is lined with sponge rubber embossed in various patterns to help ensure that the dice rebound in a random manner. Casino operators, well aware that there are nimble-fingered players who have spent many hours mastering the art of making honest dice roll in a predetermined manner, insist that the shooter throw the cubes so that they strike the rubber-covered backboard before coming to a stop. The rail opposite to the boxmen's seating position is fitted with a nine-inch by six-foot mirror. This is a protection device to help spot crooked misspotted dice that a cheat may have introduced into the game. The mirror permits the boxmen to see the five sides of each die while it's resting on the table layout. On double-end tables, with two Craps layouts, one at each end, and two dealers working, this is not practical, so a string is stretched across the table's center on the cloth. The shooter must throw the pair of dice out and over the string so that they roll before coming to a stop. In most controlled dice shots the dice must hit the table soon after leaving the shooter's hand, and the string serves as a partial protection against such shots. Some spin-and-slide experts can bounce the dice over the string and still bring up the numbers they want, but smart casino operators insist that dice must roll, not merely slide and spin, after they hit the table surface. In most Nevada casinos the string is not used, but the shooter must throw the dice past the spot where the stickman is standing; and at the slightest sign of a controlled shot, the boxman shouts, "Hit the boards!"

The five men required to run a dice table are three dealers and two boxmen. The boxmen sit between the two dealers at the table's center and are in charge. Their duty is to keep their eyes on everything—dice, money, chips, players and dealers. The dealers who stand by the side of the boxmen, after each dice decision, take in the losses and pay off the winners. The third dealer, who stands opposite the boxmen, is in charge of the dice. He calls out the dice numbers as they are thrown and helps with the proposition bets when placed. He is often referred to as the stickman because he retrieves the dice after each roll with a curved stick and holds them until all previous bets have been settled and new bets are made, whereupon he pushes the dice toward the shooter with the stick.

BANK CRAPS LAYOUTS

The Craps layout printed on the green baize covering the playing surface of the table consists of two exactly alike large-sized designs separated at the table's center by another large design allocated for various side bets. The purpose of the two duplicate designs is to accommodate more players and to permit them to make their bets without leaning forward too far or leaving their places at the table. Each of these two designs is divided into spaces of different shapes and sizes representing different bets. The layouts shown here are common ones, and although you may see others differently shaped, the actual difference is small. Some layouts carry wagers that others don't have; some differ more or less in the odds offered. This last variation depends directly upon the players who patronize the particular game, how much they know about odds, and how much of a house P.C. they will stand to buck. The smarter the patronage, the closer the odds offered approach the correct ones; the less they know, the larger the house percentage.

All Craps layouts are clever exercises in mathematical strategy designed to give the player an exciting run for his money and, at the same time, give the bank a mathematical edge on every bet on the layout.

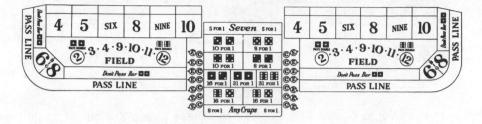

The Scarney Dice Bank Craps layout. The center portion shows the letters C-E which stand for Crap and Eleven. This layout lacks a Come and Don't Come space but pays better odds on most proposition bets.

The present crop of Bank Craps players know little or nothing about the house percentages they are fighting, and, as in Private Craps, this lack of knowledge puts them in the sucker category. The following odds and percentages show you how you can avoid throwing your money away at the Craps table, especially on sucker bets.

Before we continue with our analysis of Bank Craps odds and percentages, you must remember that if you become a Bank Craps degenerate you will eventually lose, no matter how intelligently you bet your dough on the layout. It makes no difference in the long run whether you make bets having only .832% against you, or whether you place bets on the all sevens, which has a big 16⅔% against you. In the long run the bank's percentage will take both the smart Craps player and the dub, the only difference being that the dub loses his shirt much sooner.

But if you play Bank Craps only occasionally, perhaps during your vacation in Nevada or the Caribbean islands, and want to give yourself the best chance to win, give the following text some study.

The house P.C. against the player at most Bank Craps tables can be as low as .832%, provided the player knows which bets to make and which to avoid. The percentages against the bettor on Bank Craps wagers vary from bet to bet.

The difference between the smart gambler and the dub at Bank Craps is simply a knowledge of percentages. I can easily separate the dubs from the expert Craps players by noting on what layout spaces they place their bets. The player must realize that the smaller the percentage he bucks the better are his chances of winning. Give yourself the best break possible by studying the bets, odds and percentages in the following text.

BANK CRAPS BETS

Since layouts vary somewhat as to the bets permitted, odds offered and percentages against the player, the following analysis will cover all the Common Bank Craps bets without regard to any layout.

The Las Vegas Double Side Dealer Bank Craps layout. The center portion shows the letters C-E. They stand for Crap and Eleven.

WIN LINE, DO OR PASS LINE

This is called the *front line* by inveterate gamblers and casino personnel. The players who want to bet the bank that the shooter will win place their chip or chips before the come-out on the long narrow space of the layout marked with any of the following words: WIN LINE, PASS, DO or PASS LINE. The bank pays off at even money (1 to 1) and enjoys the fader's favorable percentage in a private game of 1.414%, or about 7¢ on a $5 wager. This is the most common bet at Bank Craps, and one of the best. But most players are attracted by other bets that pay off at bigger odds, and because they don't know percentages they don't know they are bucking larger house percentages.

Lose, Don't or Don't Pass Line: This is commonly called the *back line*. This bet is favored by smart dice players, but few other players take this action. Because this wager has a standoff they think erroneously that it has a high house perecentage. To illustrate: The player who wants to bet the shooter to lose before the come-out places his bet on the layout space marked either DON'T PASS, LOSE or DON'T. In a private game this bet would give the player a favorable P.C. of 1.414% over the shooter or right bettor. But no bank could stay in business long taking 1.414% the worst of it. It resorts, therefore, to a simple tactical maneuver; it bars either the two sixes or the two aces on the come-out roll. When the barred combination appears on that roll, it is a standoff; there is no action for the wrong bettor. In a private game the fader or wrong bettor would have won the bet, but at the Bank Craps table it is no decision for the wrong bettor only.

In order to see what this means to the bank, suppose we place a $5 bet on the win line and a $5 bet on the lose line. The shooter can be expected to throw two sixes an average of once out of every 36 come-out throws, and whenever this happens, the bank sweeps the $5 off the win line while the $5 on the lose line must remain there until a new decision is effected. If the bank had not barred the two sixes, it would have broken even. Barring the two sixes has earned it $5. The same, of course, holds true for the bar on the two aces.

How much does this cut down that 1.414% advantage? Reference to the *Shooter's and Fader's Chances of Winning* table (page 146) reminds

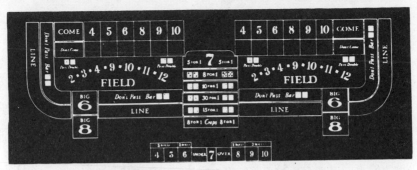

Reno Double Side Dealer.

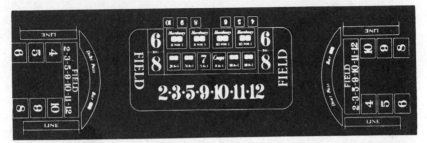

English Double-End Craps Layout.

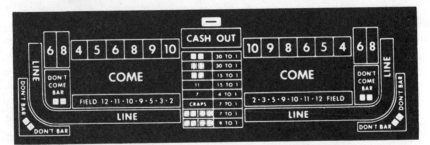

Puerto Rican Double Side Dealer.

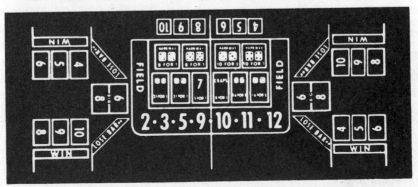

Bahamas style Double-End New York Craps Layout.

us that the right bettor can expect to win 976 rolls and lose 1,004 out of a total of 1,980. One thirty-sixth of those 1,004 losing rolls, or 55 rolls, are double-sixes. (The same is true of double-aces.) When the bank counts those 55 rolls as standoff or neutral rolls, it reduces the 1,004 losing rolls by 55 and stands to win 976 rolls and lose only 949.

The bank thus has a $50^{54}\!/_{77}\%$ chance of winning as against the wrong player's $49^{23}\!/_{77}\%$ chance. Of the 1,925 deciding rolls, there are 27 more rolls that win for the bank than for the wrong player, an advantage of $1^{31}\!/_{77}\%$ or a P.C. of *1.402%, which is about 7¢ on a $5 wager*. If you choose to count the 55 ties as trials, the house edge is $^{27}\!/_{1980} = .01364$ or 1.364%. However, I'll stick with my figure of 1.402%.

The standoff on the two sixes has not only wiped out the 1.414% advantage which the wrong bettor ordinarily has, but has replaced it with a 1.402% disadvantage! This is so nearly the same that for all practical purposes the bank has just as much edge in its favor, no matter whether the players bet the dice to win or lose.

THE ACE-DEUCE STANDOFF

The first Bank Craps games barred ace-deuce instead of double-sixes or double-aces, and some banks still do. Some players think it doesn't make too much difference. And those who do try to figure it out usually decide that since ace-deuce can be made in two ways, and a double-six in one way, ace-deuce must be twice as strong. This may sound good, but the logic is bad and the answer is wrong. The bank won't argue the matter with you, however; it's the customers with the wrong answers who make their business a profitable one.

The correct computation is made as follows: 1,004 losing rolls for the bank which is acting as a right bettor, minus 110 standoff rolls, leaves 894 rolls that lose for the bank as against 976 that win for the bank. The bank's edge is 82 rolls or $4^{72}\!/_{187}\%$. Decimally this is *4.385% or about 22¢ on a $5 wager*.

Consequently, when the bank bars ace-deuce, instead of double-six or double-ace, the P.C. in its favor is not merely doubled, as so many players think; it has more than tripled! And when the ace-deuce is barred, it is a tip-off that the bank is either not patronized by smart-money wrong bettors or doesn't care for that kind of action and is trying to discourage it.

COME AND DON'T COME BETS

The player who wishes to bet the come or don't come places his bet on the spaces of the layout marked "Come" or "Don't Come." The P.C. on these wagers are the same as on the pass and don't pass bets, which is *1.414% or about 7¢ on a $5 wager made on the come, and 1.402% or about 7¢ on a $5 wager made on the don't come.*

BIG SIX AND BIG EIGHT

The player who places his bet on the spaces of the layout marked "Big Six" or "Big Eight" is wagering that the number will be thrown before a SEVEN. He can put his money on that space at any time. The bank pays even money, and most players labor under the impression that it is an even-money bet. The SIX and EIGHT spaces on most layouts are usually made large and are positioned where the players can reach them easily. Why any player should think the bank would emphasize a bet which gives the house no percentage at all is a mystery.

A famous syndicated sports columnist once offered to bet me that SIXES and EIGHTS are thrown just as often as SEVENS. His argument was the common one that each number can be made in three ways (the SIX with 1–5, 2–4, 3–3, the EIGHT with 2–6, 3–5, 4–4, and the SEVEN with 1–6, 2–5, 3–4). He deduced from this that SIX and EIGHT have the same chance of being thrown as does SEVEN and that the correct odds must therefore be 1 to 1, or even money.

What the columnist persisted in overlooking was that the smart-money players who never bet the big six or the big eight would, if his theory were correct, concentrate entirely on those bets. Eventually other players would follow suit and, in the long run, instead of showing a profit, the bank would merely break even on the betting and have nothing in the cashboxes with which to pay operating, maintenance and other costs. Since the bank is a business proposition and the operator is not running it for the thrill of gambling, this just doesn't make sense. The very fact that the SIX and EIGHT spaces are made large and/or convenient to entice bets should be sufficient proof that the SIX and EIGHT can't possibly be even-money bets.

We know from our *Combinations or Ways* and our *Odds* tables (see pages 144 and 147) that since either SIX and EIGHT can be made five ways and SEVEN in six ways, the real odds are 6 to 5 and that the bank should pay off at $1.20 to each $1 wagered. The bank's advantage is $9\frac{1}{11}\%$, which amounts to about 45¢ on a $5 bet.

The SIX and EIGHT spaces on most layouts have grown large and come to be known as the big six and big eight not because they are the best bets on the layout, but because the bank has such a big edge. They are strictly sucker bets.

Take a quick look, for instance, at what happens to the player who puts $1 on one of these spaces and wins five times, letting his money ride. His $1 grows and becomes $2, $4, $8, $16 and finally $32. He takes this down and is more than pleased with $31 profit. But what has actually happened is that his lack of odds knowledge cost the player about $19.54. Want to prove it? Okay. For a bet on the big six at correct odds of 6 to 5, the bank should have paid off $1.20 on the first $1 wager. Then, when the bettor let the whole $2.20 ride, he would, at odds of 6 to 5, have won $2.64 on the second pass and so on. In table form, what happened to him looks like this:

At the Even Money Odds Offered	If the Bank Had Paid Correct Odds
He bets $ 1 and wins $ 1	He bets $ 1.00 and wins $ 1.20
He bets $ 2 and wins $ 2	He bets $ 2.20 and wins $ 2.64
He bets $ 4 and wins $ 4	He bets $ 4.84 and wins $ 5.808
He bets $ 8 and wins $ 8	He bets $10.648 and wins $12.7776
He bets $16 and wins $16	He bets $23.4256 and wins $28.11072
He takes down $32	He takes down $51.53632
His net profit: $31	His net profit: $50.53632

The player won $31 from the bank, but the bank paid him $19.53632 less than it would have had to pay at correct odds.

If you think that $19.54 is merely a paper saving and has not actually earned the bank anything in hard cash, look at it this way. The correct odds are 6 to 5, and the bank that pays even money will, in the long run, collect 6 units for every 5 units that it pays out. The player who continues to place bets of the same amount on the big six or big eight can, consequently, expect to lose the amount of his bet to the bank every 11 decisions.

With these facts staring him in the face, a consistent player of the big six and big eight should not need a crystal ball to dope out whether he will wind up a winner or loser in the long run. If, on some particular evening, he should as much as break even, he should realize that he has been enjoying an exceptional run of luck—luck that, given half a chance, would have won him real money!

FIELD BETS

Most of the women Craps players whom I have observed playing Bank Craps are suckers for field bets. The Craps stickman, at the sight of a woman player, begins to sell the field bets by chanting constantly during the game, "Place your bet on the field." "Nine, that's a field number." "Ten, another field number." When she hesitates he adds obligingly that the field has seven winning numbers and only four losing numbers. After this pitch, she usually begins betting the field.

The field usually bears the numbers 2, 3, 4, 9, 10, 11 and 12. When the player puts her bet on the space of the layout marked "Field," she is betting that one of the group of seven numbers listed there will be thrown on the next roll. The bank pays even money. Since the field shows seven numbers, and there are only four (5, 6, 7 and 8) which can make her lose, the nonthinker figures that her chances are excellent. She may even believe that she has the best of it or, at the very least, an even chance. But appearances are nearly always deceptive, especially in casino games.

If we add together all the ways in which the winning and losing numbers can be thrown, we find that the field numbers can be made in only 16 ways as against 20 ways for the losing numbers. The bank, consequently, has an advantage of four rolls out of 36, which in percentage is $\frac{4}{36}$ of 100 or $11\frac{1}{9}\%$—about 56¢ on a $5 bet.

When the bank pays double on the 2 and 12, as many of them do, the bank's advantage is reduced to $5\frac{5}{19}\%$. And here one of the strangest percentage problems in Bank Craps pops up. Some smart casino operators will tell you that the bank's advantage is $5\frac{5}{19}\%$, and others that the player's disadvantage is $5\frac{5}{9}\%$. Some of them argue for hours over their differences of opinion, but the curious thing is that the argument is unnecessary because both of them are right!

The discrepancy is explained by the fact that they are arguing, not about the same problem, but about two slightly different problems, with two different answers. This fact—which, to my knowledge, no dealer or operator ever realized prior to its first publication in 1945 in *Scarne on Dice*—and the analysis of both problems given below, should clear up the matter and settle the arguments at last.

Suppose that the player and bank each cover the 36 possible field combinations with dollar bets. The player's wagers will total $36 but the bank's wagers, because it puts an extra dollar on the 2 and 12 that are circled for a double payoff, will total $38.

If the dice fall exactly according to probabilities, all 36 different combinations being thrown in 36 successive rolls, the bank wins 20 bets for a total of $40 and makes a profit of $2. The player wins 16 bets, 14 of which have $2 riding and the 2 and 12 pay $3 each. The player therefore takes down $34 and is short $2.

Since the bank wagered $38 and made a profit of $2, its favorable percentage is 2 divided by 38 or $5\frac{5}{19}\%$.

The player, on the other hand, wagered $36 and lost $2. His percentage of loss, or his disadvantage, is 2 divided by 36 or $5\frac{5}{9}\%$.

We have two problems rather than one because the bank and player wager different amounts.

Some banks pay 3 to 1 on double-aces, which supplies the same P.C. as paying double on both 2 and 12. Other layouts are made with a 5 in place of the 4, so that the field bears the numbers 2, 3, 5, 9, 10, 11 and 12. This gives the bank 19 chances against the player's 17, and the bank's edge is $5\frac{5}{9}\%$. Some banks also pay double on two aces, others pay 3 to 2 on double-aces and double-sixes. In each case the bank's advantage is $2\frac{26}{37}\%$ and the player's disadvantage is $2\frac{7}{9}\%$.

The lure of Craps is its fast action, but because wagers on the field are either won or lost *every time* the dice are rolled, the action is so fast and furious that most players can't take it. With a $5\frac{5}{19}\%$ or $5\frac{5}{9}\%$, depending which way you prefer to figure it, grinding away and taking $\frac{1}{18}$ of every bet the players make, the bank can expect to eat up the amount of the player's wagers in 18 rolls.

To show what this means in dollars and cents, let us assume that you place 180 field bets of $10 each, which you can do in an hour's time at many fast-action Craps tables, and assume that the laws of probability work according to expectation. This hour of field betting would cost you exactly $100.

If, after reading the above, you still insist on making field bets, I would suggest that you get yourself a "sponsor" who has plenty of do-re-mi, because, lady, you'll need it!

HARDWAY BETS

When the player places a bet on the layout marked "Hardway," he is betting a specified even point or off number (4, 6, 8, or 10) will be thrown with two double numbers (*hardway*) before it is made the *easy way* (any way other than a hardway), and before a SEVEN is made. Stickmen, when learning their trade, are taught to hustle players into betting the hardway. For that reason, stickmen are constantly chanting, "Folks, place your bets on the hardway. Get yourself 9 to 1 on the hard six or the hard eight," or "Get yourself 7 to 1 on the hard 4 or 10." The reason for this constant hustling of the hardway bets by stickmen is that the bank earns a percentage of $9\frac{1}{11}\%$, $11\frac{1}{9}\%$ or, at times, $27\frac{3}{11}\%$ on such wagers. In spite of this, or because they know no better, most inexperienced Craps shooters go for the hardway bets because the payoff odds of 7 and 9 to 1 are tempting.

Hardway wagers can be found on all layouts, and, once again, most players believe that the odds offered by the bank are fair enough. Some even think they are getting correct odds, a lack of logic that almost classes as not thinking at all!

The layout not only does not offer correct odds on any of these bets, but in many cases offers even less than it appears to. This misdirection, as gamblers call it, is accomplished by wording the proposition so as to mislead players who forget that the two little words *for* and *to* do not mean the same thing. You will see how this deception operates in the following analysis of the hardway wagers.

Four the hardway: There are three ways to make a FOUR and six ways to make a SEVEN. But, since the player wins only one way (by a throw of 2–2) and loses eight ways, the correct odds are 8 to 1.

Most banks offer 7 to 1 on this bet. Its probability is one over the total number of ways that FOUR can win or lose, in this case, $\frac{1}{9}$. This probability times 100 gives the percentage on one way: $\frac{1}{9}$ of 100 is $11\frac{1}{9}\%$. The bank that pays off at 7 to 1 when the correct odds are 8 to 1 thus gains the percentage on one way which is *11 1/9% or 56¢ on a $5 wager*. If it paid off at 6 to 1, it would gain the percentage on two ways or $22\frac{2}{9}\%$.

Some banks do pay only 6 to 1 on FOUR the hardway, although it doesn't look that way. They simply offer to pay 7 *for* 1, and most players take that to mean 7 to 1 and never give it another thought. The difference is this: when paying off at 7 to 1, the bank gives you $7 *and* the $1 you bet. When paying off at 7 *for* 1, the bank pays you $7 but *keeps* the $1 you bet. It pays $7 for your $1. The bank is actually giving you odds of only 6 to 1 on what is really an 8 to 1 proposition! Other layouts try to create the impression that the bank is paying the correct odds of 8 to 1 by offering 8 for 1.

Ten the hardway: Since there are also three ways to make TEN, the bank's P.C. is the same as on the FOUR, for the same reasons.

Six the hardway: A SIX can be made five ways. One way only (3–3) wins, the other four ways lose, as do the six ways SEVEN can be made. Correct odds, therefore, are 10 to 1. Most banks pay off at 9 to 1 and thereby have an advantage of *9 1/11% or 45¢ on a $5 wager*. Other banks, without blinking, pay off 9 *for* 1, with an advantage of *18 2/11% or 91¢ on a $5 wager*.

Eight the hardway: An EIGHT can also be made five ways, and the bank's percentage is, therefore, the same as on the SIX, *9 1/11% or 18 2/11%*.

In tabular form, for easy reference:

HARDWAY BETS

Bet	Bank Pays	Correct Odds	Bank's Percentage	Bank's P.C. on $5 Bets
4 with 2–2 10 with 5–5	7 to 1	8 to 1	11 1/9%	$ .56+
6 with 3–3* 8 with 4–4*	9 to 1	10 to 1	9 1/11%	.45+
4 with 2–2 10 with 5–5	7 for 1	8 to 1	22 2/9%	1.11+
6 with 3–3 8 with 4–4	9 for 1	10 to 1	18 2/11%	.91+

* Some banks pay only 7 to 1 on the hardway *Six* or *Eight* and have an advantage of 27¾/₁₁%, or $1.36 on a $5 wager.

ONE-ROLL ACTION OR COME-OUT BETS

If you make a habit of betting on one-roll proposition bets such as those marked "Two Sixes," "Two Aces," "Eleven," "All Sevens" and "All Craps," you won't be able to stand the percentage pressure very long. Strange as it may seem, most so-called smart dice gamblers laugh at the field player for paying a big 5⅚% for one-roll bets, then turn right around and bet $100 on the two sixes or the 11 on the come out, taking a beating percentagewise of 13⅚% or 11⅑%, as the case may be!

The reason many Craps players are suckers for one-roll come-out bets is, again, the big payoff odds of 15 to 1 on the 11, and 30 to 1 on the two aces or two sixes. To show how foolish these bets are, let's assume that the player places a $1 bet on the two sixes for 360 consecutive come-out rolls, and that the theory of probability works exactly as expected: the two aces appear exactly ten times out of the 360 rolls. Since the player is paid off at the bank odds of 30 to 1, he gets back a total of $310, and he wagered $360—for a loss of $50. Imagine what the bank's earning power on the two sixes adds up to during the evening's play when a dozen or more players are wagering tens, twenties and fifties on this bet at the same time! And many players are not content to make one come-out bet at a time; instead, they make four or five.

Many so-called smart Craps players think they have the best of it when they make two wagers simultaneously in an attempt to insure one or the other. For example, a player places a bet on the win line and tries to protect it against a crap on the first roll by making a come-out bet on all craps. He hopes that if he loses one bet he may win the other, and thus cut down or cancel out his loss. Actually he stands to lose at least one of the bets, and maybe both. Or he may attempt to insure a lose bet after the come-out by taking odds on the point. Since every wager in Bank Craps must be considered as a separate and distinct wager, the only effect of insurance betting is simply to give the bank a P.C. on two bets rather than one. Instead of insuring himself against the loss, the player has merely increased the P.C. against himself!

On any of these one-roll or come-out bets, commonly called proposition bets by casino personnel, the player puts his bet on a specified number or numbers, betting that it will appear on the next roll. He can make the bet before any roll.

Two sixes in one roll: This one can be found on nearly every layout. Since the correct odds are 35 to 1, and since the bank pays 30 to 1, the bank has an edge of 5 in 36 or *13 8/9%, about 69¢ on a $5 wager.*

Two aces in one roll: Payoff odds and P.C. are the same as on the double-six (see above).

Other double numbers in one roll: Although it is not always shown on the layout, many banks will allow you to place come-out bets on other pairs of numbers. The payoff odds and P.C. are the same as on the two sixes.

Eleven in one roll: Correct odds are 17 to 1. Bank pays off 15 to 1 and has an edge of *11 1/9%, or about 56¢ on a $5 wager.*

Three in one roll: Odds are 17 to 1, payoff is 15 to 1, and the bank's P.C. is the same as on the 11.

All sevens in one roll: Odds are 5 to 1. Bank pays 4 to 1 and has an edge of *16 2/3%, or about 83¢ on a $5 wager*.

Any crap (2, 3, 12) in one roll: Correct odds are 8 to 1, bank pays 7 to 1 and has an edge of *11 1/9%, or about 56¢ on a $5 wager*.

3–4, 5–2, 6–1 in one roll: Here number SEVEN must be thrown with the particular combination of numbers on which you place your money. Correct odds in each instance are 17 to 1. Bank pays off 15 to 1 and has an edge of *11 1/9%, or about 56¢ on a $5 wager*.

Horn, Santurce, Miami or Curaçao one-roll bet: Some casino layouts permit the player to make four one-roll bets (2–3–12–11) at the same time. The layout space that permits these one-roll bets is marked differently in various casinos. At Caribe Hilton Casino in Puerto Rico it is marked "Santurce"; in the casinos of Curaçao, it is marked "Miami" or "Curaçao," while in some Nevada casinos it is known as the *horn bet*. For instance, in Puerto Rico, when you wish to place a one-roll Santurce bet, you hand the stickman a $5 chip (or a multiple bet of $5) and call *Santurce*—which means you are betting one unit on 2, one unit on 3, one unit on 12 and two units on 11. The one-roll pay-off odds are the same as one-roll come bets: 15 to 1 or 15 for 1 on the 3 and 11, and 30 to 1 or 30 for 1 on the 2 or 12.

BANK'S PERCENTAGE ON THE STANDARD ONE-ROLL ACTION OR COME-OUT BETS

Bet	Bank Pays	Correct Odds	Bank's P.C.	Bank's P.C. on $5 Wager
Two sixes (6–6) Two aces (1–1)	30 to 1	35 to 1	13 8/9%	$.69
Eleven (6–5) Three (1–2)	15 to 1	17 to 1	11 1/9%	.56
All sevens (7)	4 to 1	5 to 1	16 2/3%	.83
Any crap (2, 3 or 12)	7 to 1	8 to 1	11 1/9%	.56
7 with 3–4 7 with 2–5 7 with 6–1	15 to 1	17 to 1	11 1/9%	.56

Nevada layouts increase their percentage take by listing their odds payoff with the word "for" instead of "to." Their percentages are as follows:

Bet	Bank Pays	Correct Odds	Bank's P.C.	Bank's P.C. on $5 Wager
Two sixes (6–6) Two aces (1–1)	30 for 1	35 to 1	16 2/3%	$.83
Eleven (6–5) Three (1–2)	15 for 1	17 to 1	16 2/3%	.83
All sevens (7)	5 for 1	5 to 1	16 2/3%	.83
Any crap (2, 3, 12)	8 for 1	8 to 1	11 1/9%	.56
7 with 3–4 7 with 2–5 7 with 6–1	15 for 1	17 to 1	16 2/3%	.83

The following one-roll action bets are listed because some smaller banks carry proposition bets on their layouts and include all possible one-roll bets:

Bet	Bank Pays	Correct Odds	Bank's P.C.	Bank's P.C. on $5 Wager
4 in one roll 10 in one roll	9 to 1	11 to 1	16 2/3%	$.83
6 in one roll 8 in one roll	5 to 1	6 1/5 to 1	16 2/3%	.83
5 in one roll 9 in one roll	7 to 1	8 to 1	11 1/9%	.56

The actual figures for the bank's P.C. on a $5 bet are fractional and have been computed here to the nearest cent.

Place or box number bets are counterparts of Private Craps bets such as laying and taking the odds on a point or off number. Most high rollers favor this type of betting and often will take or lay the odds on the six place bets (4, 5, 6, 8, 9, 10) and let the winnings ride whenever a bet is won. Many women Craps shooters favor place betting, but during my casino survey, I saw only a few women taking the odds on the six place bets at one time.

Place betting accounts for a great deal of the action on Bank Craps layouts. Since the bank cannot pay off the place bets at correct odds and stay in business, it resorts to a simple tactical gimmick to make place betting profitable. In insists that the right bettor accept less than the correct odds on each right place bet, and that the wrong bettor lay greater odds than the correct odds when placing a bet to lose. Place bets may be removed, if so desired, at any time during play. Here is a detailed description of place betting odds and the bank's favorable percentages.

PLACE OR BOX NUMBER BETS TO WIN

Four or Ten: The correct odds are 10 to 5 (2 to 1). The right player wagers $5 on FOUR or TEN, the bank pays off winning bets at odds of

9 to 5. This gives the bank an advantage of *6 2/3% or 6.666% or about 33¢ on a $5 wager.*

Five or Nine: The true odds are 7½ to 5, the bank pays off winning right bets at odds of 7 to 5 and takes an advantage of *4%, which is 20¢ on a $5 wager.*

Six or Eight: The correct odds are 6 to 5. The bank pays off winning right bets at odds of 7 to 6. This means that the bank has an advantage of *1 17/33% or 1.515%, or about 8¢ on a $5 wager.*

Some banks pay off this right wager at 11 to 10. This means the bank has an advantage of *4 6/11% or 4.5454%, or about 23¢ on a $5 wager.*

Other banks pay off this right wager at even money or 5 tc 5. This means that the bank has an advantage of *9 1/11% or 9.090%, or about 45¢ on a $5 wager.*

These percentages prove that the so-called smart dice player who places a right bet on the FOUR or TEN is a bigger sucker than the average field players whom most so-called smart dice players ridicule as being novices and suckers.

Obviously the best place bet is placing the SIX or EIGHT when the bank pays at odds of 7 to 6.

PLACE OR BOX NUMBER BETS TO LOSE

These wagers are not as popular as win place bets, since eight out of ten dice players are born right bettors and don't like the idea of laying the odds (putting up more money than they can win). Here are the bank's percentages the player must buck when he lays a place bet.

Four or Ten: The correct odds are 10 to 5. The player must lay odds of 11 to 5. This gives the bank an advantage of *3 1/33% or 3.030%, or about 15¢ on a $5 wager.*

Five or Nine: The correct odds are 7½ to 5, the player must lay odds of 8 to 5, which gives the bank an advantage of *2½% or 2.5%, or about 12¢ on a $5 wager.*

Six or Eight: The correct odds are 6 to 5, the player must lay odds of 5 to 4, which gives the bank an advantage of *1 9/11% or 1.818%, or about 9¢ on a $5 wager.*

Some banks compel players to lay odds of 7 to 5, which gives the bank an advantage of *7 8/13% or 7.615%, or about 38¢ on a $5 wager.*

Most Nevada Bank Craps tables, in addition to permitting players to place their bets on the box numbers, also allow players to buy the box numbers. In Bank Craps games that permit players to place their bets or to buy them at a 5% charge, it would be to the player's advantage to buy the FOUR and TEN and place the FIVE, NINE, SIX and EIGHT. See Bank Craps percentage table on page 168.

NEW YORK CRAPS

As previously stated, New York Craps is a version of Bank Craps found in most illegal gambling houses in the eastern part of the United States and legal casinos in the Bahamas, England, Yugoslavia and wherever gamblers from the eastern United States operate dice games. The big differences between Bank Craps and New York Craps are that the New York dice layout *does not possess come and don't come betting spaces* and that *place betting is not permitted*. Players are compelled to buy the box numbers (4, 5, 6, 8, 9, 10). In buying the boxes, the player is paid off at correct odds, as 6 to 5 on SIX or EIGHT, 3 to 2 on FIVE or NINE, and 2 to 1 on FOUR or TEN. However, for such services, the bank levies a direct charge of 5% on the total sum of right money wagered; this amounts to a charge of 25¢ on each $5 bet. Whether you take or lay $10 to $5 on a FOUR, the bank charges 25¢.

New York Craps is played on a specially constructed dice table that is similar to a Las Vegas or Bank Craps table; but it is shaped somewhat differently and the dealers are posted at each end of the table. A stickman stands at the center of the table and the two boxmen sit opposite the stickman. A lookout, known as a ladderman, sits on a stand high above the table.

Each dealer is supplied with a hundred or more quarters which are spread out on the table in front of him. These quarters are used to help the dealer in taking his 5% charge on a player's box number bet or bets. There is one peculiar fact about the 5% vigorish charge: in most games, the bank's favorable percentage is larger than most players think, but the 5% vigorish charge at New York Craps is less than nearly all Craps players and most casino operators suspect. Here are the correct percentages in favor of the bank when the operators levy a 5% vigorish charge:

RIGHT BETTOR PAYS 4.761 + %, or about 25¢, when taking $5 worth of odds on any point or box number.

WRONG BETTOR PAYS 2.439 + %, or about 12¢, when laying odds of $10 to $5 on point or box number 4 or 10.

3.225 + %, or about 15¢, when laying odds of $7.50 to $5 on point or box number 5 or 9.

4.000 + %, or about 20¢, when laying odds of $6 to $5 on point or box number 6 or 8.

SCARNEY CRAPS

New York Craps has always appeared to me an undignified way to play Craps. The dealer's constant handling of quarters used to make change seems a cheap way of running a modern dice table. Often, while scouting the casinos of the Bahamas and England, I have observed dice players place a $5 bet on a box number (4, 5, 6, 8, 9, 10). The dealer then shouts, "Twenty-five cents, please." The player's usual answer is "What for?" "The 5% house charge," cries the dealer, to the bewilderment of the players.

Some casino operators prefer New York Craps to Bank Craps because New York Craps has a larger house percentage. A casino that opens only in the evening and caters only to gambling junkets—with little or no walk-in business—cannot run a profitable Bank Craps or Las Vegas style of dice game. Many casino operators in the Caribbean where the action is limited to a few hours a day have tried unsuccessfully to operate by dealing Las Vegas odds. The result: They went broke in the attempt, and either went out of business or had to resort to running a bust-out joint.

Early in 1967, the administrator of the Hilton Hotel Casino in Curaçao informed me that casinos in the area, because of the lack of walk-in business (natives are not permitted to gamble), were going broke. Gambling junkets proved to be unprofitable. Then and there I decided to develop a Craps layout that would give casinos such as these a chance to survive and at the same time give the junket player a run for his money. I also took into consideration the fact that for years everything has been increasing in cost—casino rent, salaries, entertainment, drinks, cigarettes, as well as paying for hotel accommodations and plane transportation for junket players. Strangely enough, the only thing that has not gone up is the house percentage at casino tables.

Shortly thereafter, a new Craps layout which I invented appeared for the first time at the Curaçao Hilton Hotel Casino. I have taken the creator's liberty of naming it *Scarney Craps.* I simply dignified New York Craps by eliminating the 5% charge and made use of place betting. Scarney Craps, like New York Craps, lacks a come and don't come space, but the proposition bets at Scarney Craps pay a unit more than most Bank Craps tables in Nevada and throughout the world. Scarney Craps, which is played on a standard Bank Craps table, is being played in many Caribbean casinos as well as in Europe, Asia, Africa and South America.

FREE SINGLE ODDS BETS

Free bet (commonly called *front line odds* and *back line odds*): When the shooter comes out on the point, Nevada and Puerto Rican casinos allow players who have placed bets on the pass and don't pass line or on the come or don't come space to make a second bet, usually equal to the original wager, that the shooter will or will not make the point. However, casinos elsewhere whose limit is $300 or $500 will allow only $150 or $250 respectively as a free maximum-limit odds bet, even though the front- or back-line bet is greater. In brief, the free-bet limit is usually half of the maximum betting limit; any amount over this limit must be bought.

Although a front-line or back-line bet appears to be a free bet, is this actually so? If a right player places a $20 bet on the pass line and the shooter throws a TEN for his point, the bank will allow the player to take $20 to the bank's $40 that the shooter will make it. This bet is paid off at the correct odds and no charge is made for it. How does this affect the bank's percentage? Let's see.

The bank has the usual percentage in its favor of 1.414 on the pass line and 1.402 on the don't pass line. But the second wager on the point is paid off, for a change, at the correct odds. On this bet, the only one of its kind on the layout, the bank has no favorable percentage at all. But, as you might expect, when both wagers are figured together, the bank still has a slight advantage.

On the right bettor's wager to win, the bank has a favorable P.C. of .848. The bank's P.C. on right bets is calculated as follows: The bank has an edge of 28 rolls in every 1,980 rolls before the come-out. Points will appear two-thirds of the 1,980 rolls, or 1,320. Since the two-way bet is made only when a point appears, and since these 1,320 additional rolls have no advantage for either bank or player, the bank's overall advantage is 28 rolls out of 1,320 plus 1,980 rolls or 3,300 rolls. 28 divided by 3,300 gives a percentage of .848 in favor of the bank.

On the wrong bettor's wager to lose, the bank has a favorable P.C. of .832. Barring 6–6 or (1–1) cuts the bank's advantage down to 27 rolls. Since 6-6 (or 1-1) will be thrown 55 times out of 1,980, there are only 1,980 minus 55, or 1,925 decisive rolls. Add the 1,320 that have no advantage either way and the bank has an edge of 27 rolls out of 3,245 rolls, or a favorable P.C. of .832.

Although this is the best bet the Bank Craps player can make, it is strange how few gamblers, even those who know percentages, take advantage of it. Craps shooters are just as unpredictable as the dice. During the thrill, action and excitement of the game, most players bet as their emotions dictate rather than their minds; they follow their intuition rather than their knowledge of P.C. And they seldom do the right thing at the right time.

The free odds bets made on the pass line, don't pass line, come or don't come may be taken down (removed) at any time before the bet is decided. One thing should be remembered, however; the lowest-valued chip in a luxury casino is a $1 chip, and for that reason dealers can't pay off on any part of a dollar. Therefore, when you're taking the free odds make sure that your bet doesn't pay off in cents. For example, if your pass line bet was $1 and the point is 5, taking the free odds for $1 would hurt rather than benefit you simply because the dealer would not pay you the $1.50 your bet should bring. You would be paid one dollar chip—that's all. To receive the correct odds of 3 to 2, you should have made a pass line bet of $2.

The only way to take full advantage of the free odds is to make your bet a minimum (or multiple) of ten ($10). Since the average pass line bettor usually bets only a buck or two he cannot take full advantage of the free odds. Here's why: When you make your pass line bet, you don't know what the come-out number will be. If you bet $1, and the come-out is 4 or 10, you're all right. You can get the full 2 to 1 odds. If the come-out is 5 or 6, or 8, or 9, you can't. You'd get $1 to $1 instead of $1.50 to $1 on the 5 or 9. You'd get even money instead of $1.20 to $1 on the 6 or 8. On every bet up to $10, you'd be blocked from getting full odds on some point. But on a $10 bet, you can get 2–1, 3–2 or 6–5, depending on the come-out number. This is true of any multiple of 10, but not of any other number or multiple. You can figure it yourself. This does not mean that you have to bet $10. With a smaller bet you can still find free odds on some numbers, though not all.

If you happen to be in a situation like that described above, and the Craps dealer tries to talk you into increasing the amount of your pass line bet after the come-out by telling you that it is to your best advantage since it will permit you to take full advantage of the free odds offer, *don't*. Acceptance means taking even money instead of odds that the shooter will make his point and the free odds bet is no longer free. Although "betting the line" and taking or laying the free odds as described above is the smartest way of gambling at casino dice tables it is strange how very few gamblers take full advantage of such a play. I have found that many players are just as unpredictable as the dice. During the thrill, action and excitement of the game, they bet as their emotions, rather than their minds, dictate. They follow their intuition rather than their knowledge of the game, and seldom do the right thing at the right time.

FREE DOUBLE ODDS BETS

A smaller number of banks where the action is highly competitive allow players making free front-line or back-line odds bets to wager double the original amount made to win or lose before the come-out. The bank's percentage in the above instances is .606% on right action and .591% on wrong action. Banks that permit such action would not stay in business long if all the players made only that type of bet, because a casino operation doing fair business requires, on the average, a greater percentage than that on all bets in order to pay its operating expenses before showing a profit. Today, a number of Las Vegas strip casinos, in an attempt to lure the dwindling number of high roller craps players to their dice tables, are advertising "$5,000 Limit, Double Odds" on their marquees.

So that the reader can see the bank's favorable percentages on all the Bank Craps bets at a glance, they have been placed together in the table on page 168. For the hardway bets, see table on page 159; for come-out bets, see page 161.

HOW TO GAMBLE SENSIBLY AT BANK CRAPS

As in any banking game, the house earns a percentage on every bet made at Bank Craps. This is not unreasonable because somebody has to pay for the casino rent, equipment, employees' salaries, etc. But how much you pay for the privilege of shooting Craps in a casino is entirely up to you.

THE CASINO'S P.C. ON BANK CRAPS BETS

Bet	P.C. in Bank's Favor	Bank's P.C. on $5 Bet
Win (pass)	1.414%	$.07*
Come	1.414	.07
Lose (don't pass) bar 6–6 or 1–1	1.402	.07
Don't come, bar 6–6 or 1–1	1.402	.07
Lose (don't pass) bar 1–2	4.385	.22
Don't come, bar 1–2	4.385	.22
Place bets to win		
Bank lays 9 to 5 on 4 or 10	6.666	.33
Bank lays 7 to 5 on 5 or 9	4.000	.20
Bank lays 7 to 6 on 6 or 8	1.515	.08
Box number bets to win (5% charge)		
Bank lays 10 to 5 on 4 or 10	4.761	.25
Bank lays 7½ to 5 on 5 or 9	4.761	.25
Bank lays 6 to 5 on 6 or 8	4.761	.25
Place bets to lose		
Bank takes 11 to 5 on 4 or 10	3.030	.15
Bank takes 8 to 5 on 5 or 9	2.500	.12
Bank takes 5 to 4 on 6 or 8	1.818	.09
Box number bets to lose (5% charge)		
Bank takes 10 to 5 on 4 or 10	2.439	.12
Bank takes 7½ to 5 on 5 or 9	3.225	.16
Bank takes 6 to 5 on 6 or 8	4.000	.20
Field bets		
Field (2, 3, 4, 9, 10, 11, 12)	11.111	.56
Field (2, 3, 4, 9, 10, 11, 12 with double payoff on 2 and 12)	5.263	.26
Field (2, 3, 5, 9, 10, 11, 12)	5.555	.27
Big Six	9.090	.45
Big Eight	9.090	.45
Win bet (pass) line plus free single point odds bet to win	.848	.04
Lose (don't pass) plus free single point odds bet to lose	.832	.04
Win bet (pass) line plus free double point odds bet to win	.606	.03
Lose (don't pass) plus free double point odds bet to lose	.591	.03

* The bank's edge on a $5 wager given in cents has, in each case (except for the place win bet on numbers 5 or 9 and in the box numbers 6 or 8 to lose) a plus fraction which we have omitted.

Nobody can tell you how to win at Bank Craps because if you gamble long enough and often enough the house P.C. will take its toll. But if you still insist on taking a fling at the dice tables, here are several rules to follow which can save you money.

1. Whenever you gamble at Bank Craps, set aside in advance the amount of money you are willing to lose. If you lose that amount, quit the game for the evening; do not borrow money, write a check or obtain credit to continue gambling.

2. Also set for yourself a reasonable amount that you might expect to win, and if you succeed in winning that much, quit the game, no matter how lucky you happen to feel. If you follow this rule you will retain your winnings more often, and you will have more winning plays because you are trying to win smaller amounts.

3. If you lost yesterday, do not gamble today with the object of recouping yesterday's losses. That is the most dangerous course any gambler can follow. Trying to get even has sent more players to the poorhouse than anything else. Write off yesterday's losses and forget them.

4. Naturally, I expect that after reading this text on Bank Craps you will place your bets on the layout spaces which have the smallest percentage against you. If you follow this rule, your chances of winning are greatly increased.

5. Try to win the amount you hoped to win in the fastest time possible. Making bets back and forth all night merely gives the laws of probability a chance to perform as expected in the long run and helps Old Man Percentage slowly but surely to eat up your chances of winning.

If the Bank Craps player follows the above rules, he will be gambling intelligently; his winnings may be greater, and when he does lose, his losses won't hurt him so much.

MONEY (OR OPEN) CRAPS

Open Craps, now often called Money Craps, is the most popular illegal casino form of Craps played in this country today. It is the favorite gambling game of the country's high rollers and big-money gamblers, but it is seldom found in the legalized casinos.

Money Craps, as the name implies, is almost always played with cash rather than chips. Some big-money Craps operators, in order to speed up the game, use small-denomination chips ($5 or $10), but all the big bets are made with currency. The two biggest money games I ever saw were at the 115 Club in Miami (which closed in 1947), and at the Barn, which is described on pages 32–33. The big-time gamblers in both these joints had a cute money gimmick which helped speed up the action; it is now often used. Hundred-dollar bills are made up into packets, each secured by a rubber band. One packet contains one hundred $100 bills ($10,000), another, fifty $100 bills ($5,000), another, twenty-five $100 bills ($2,500) and another, ten $100 bills ($1,000). The original owner pencils his initials on the top bill of each packet so that if the eventual winner should find that it contains less than the stipulated amount, he can be reimbursed by the original owner.

This makes it possible to get big bets down quickly without having to take time to count hundreds of bills. A player laying $20,000 on the point numbers FOUR or TEN simply throws down two $10,000 packets; if laying $7,500 to $5,000 on the points FIVE or NINE, a $5,000 and a $2,500 packet do the trick; and if the player lays $6,000 to $5,000 he simply uses one $5,000 packet and one $1,000 packet. It is not uncommon to see 50 or more such packets being wagered on a single point decision in games presently operated in our big cities. Open (or Money) Craps is now played in most sawdust joints and makeshift casinos, but it is not restricted to gambling houses; big and small games cover the country—in streets, cellars, back lots, factories, hotels, poolrooms and on river wharfs. Nearly every town of any size at all (say, 80,000 population) has at least one game regularly operating, law or no law. It may not always be in the same location, but it's there. Because of its hidden and illegal nature, women are seldom found in the game.

Money Craps in a gambling house uses a dice table similar to a Bank Craps table except that the layout does not have proposition bets such as the field, one-roll come-out bets and the hardway bets. The only betting spaces on the layout are the lose line, the win line, and the box numbers (4, 5, 6, 8, 9 and 10).

The banker at Money (or Open) Craps is known as the *book*. When the book operates in the open (back lot, hotel room or street corner) and does not use a Craps table or layout in order to deal the game, the book visualizes the layout and places the players' bets in the same relative position, as though a layout were being used.

The book's maximum betting limit at Money Craps ranges from a low $25 on up to $1,000 and $2,000, with even that limit lifted in special cases. Fortunes are won and lost nightly at Money Craps; winnings and losses of $200,000 or more in one dice session are common. Such heavy gambling occurs very rarely at Private Craps, and it is impossible at Bank Craps unless the usual betting limits are upped considerably.

It is in games operated in New York City, Chicago, Philadelphia, Detroit, etc., that the big-time gamblers, the horse bookies, the Numbers operators, the thieves and dice and card hustlers of the private game and the underworld big shots gamble with industry's business tycoons, millionaire playboys, stockbrokers, politicians and various other legitimate businessmen.

These people prefer Money Craps because it offers them their biggest opportunity to win large sums of money. Money Craps permits players to take and lay odds on the point number among themselves, something that is not permitted at Bank Craps. Flat or center bets, one-roll come-out bets and hardway bets must be placed with the book, which pays off these wagers at the same odds the bank does at New York Craps (see pages 159, 161–162).

The big action that the book receives is on the off numbers. Players cannot make an off- or box-number wager with each other, and the book gets this action whenever players cannot get other players to take or lay odds on the point.

Open Craps has undergone many betting changes in the past few years. Back in 1945, the book permitted players to make all types of bets among themselves. As the game is played today, it should really be called Semi-open Craps.

Today, most books, when laying or taking the odds on point or box numbers, pay off at the correct odds and charge the player 5% of the right money wagered. The book's favorable P.C. in such instances is the same as the bank's in New York Craps when the right bettor buys the boxes: *4.761%, or 25¢ on $5 worth of right action*. In the wrong bettor's case, the charge is still figured at 5% of the right money wagered (in this case, the book's wager), but the book does not collect the charge. Instead, the charge rides with the player's bet and is picked up by the book only when the player laying the odds loses.

If, for example, the wrong bettor wishes to lay $200 to the book's $100 on a FOUR or TEN, he must put down $205. If the player loses, he is out $205; if he wins, he takes down $305. In this instance he has paid no charge for his bet. The wrong bettor only pays the book a 5% charge when he loses. You may wonder, in these circumstances, not only why two-thirds of all bettors are right bettors, but why there are any right bettors at all. The answer is that the average player knows next to nothing about percentages, and even when he knows a little, he thinks he stands to win more by taking the odds than laying them. He believes in risking a little to win a lot and forgets, or doesn't know, that one of the basic rules is that in the long run the expectation of winning is in direct proportion to the odds.

If they bet the book big and often enough, both the right and the wrong bettor will eventually go broke, regardless of which player pays the greater percentage to the book. For the benefit of the occasional book player, the following table shows the book's favorable percentage on

RIGHT BETTOR PAYS	4.761%, or about 25¢, when taking $5 worth of odds on any point.
WRONG BETTOR PAYS	.813%, or about 4¢, when laying odds of $10 to $5 on point or box number 4 or 10.
	1.290%, or about 6¢, when laying odds of $7.50 to $5 on point or box number 5 or 9.
	1.818%, or about 9¢, when laying odds of $6 to $5 on point or box number 6 or 8.

each of the points, off or box numbers when the book picks up the 5% charge on the right bettor and lets it ride for the wrong bettor.

Some books do not give the wrong bettor such a good proposition as this; they pick up the 5% charge on both the right and wrong action, the same as in New York Craps when buying the boxes. (See page 168 for percentages.)

Some books, in an effort to balance their right and wrong odds action (which is what every book dreams of), charge only 3% and pick it up on both the right and wrong bettor. The exact percentages in both cases are tabulated below:

RIGHT BETTOR PAYS   2.912%, or about 15¢, when taking $5 worth of odds on any point.

WRONG BETTOR PAYS   1.477%, or about 7¢, when laying odds of $10 on point or box number 4 or 10.

1.960%, or about 10¢, when laying odds of $7½ to $5 on point or box number 5 or 9.

2.439%, or about 12¢, when laying odds of $6 to $5 on point or box number 6 or 8.

To sum up, if you insist on playing Money Craps and want to avoid cheating yourself, and if you dislike donating your pay to the Building Fund for the Craps Bookies' Bank Account, paste these simple rules in your hat:

1. Don't bet the book. Know the correct odds on the point numbers, and bet only with other players.

2. Don't bet if you can't afford to lose.

Then, after making sure that the book and his sidekick Old Man Percentage aren't giving you the business, you should also try to make sure that the dice cheat doesn't clip you with his phony dice. Advice on how to do that follows.

HOW TO DETECT CROOKED DICE

As I have mentioned elsewhere, most gambling houses that cater to the masses are *on the square* and earn their profits by employing Old Man Percentage. The same cannot be said for thousands and thousands of Private Craps games or the hundreds of Money or Open Craps floating games. Nearly every Private Craps game has either its Craps hustler or its dice cheat, two characters who are consistent winners in 90% of all friendly games.

Unsuspecting Craps players are fleeced out of several billion dollars yearly by dice cheats who operate in all styles of Craps games. These cheats have increased in numbers in the past decades as a direct result of the indoctrination of 5 million women Craps players.

There are two kinds of dice cheats: the amateur, a player who thinks he has a chance of making money from his friends or co-workers and doesn't care how he does it; and the professional, the skilled dice *mechanic* (sleight-of-hand artist), known in the trade as a *bust-out man,* an experienced cheat who earns his livelihood by hiring out his services to dice mobs who set up their crooked dice games in hotel rooms, poolrooms, private homes, clubs or crooked casinos.

Expert dice mechanics also prey on unsuspecting players in private or floating games, and sometimes make casino operators their victims. Many rug and carpet joints in Nevada and elsewhere have, at one time or another, been cheated out of vast sums of money by bust-out men.

In 1967, a top casino on the Las Vegas Strip was taken for $350,000 in several plays by dice cheats. The management asked me to check it out for them—but when I arrived in Las Vegas, all the casino owners had to show me were the dice—and they were perfect dice. The culprits had long gone. In 1956, three Americans were arrested and jailed in Monaco for switching in crooked dice at Monte Carlo Casino; they had won thousands of dollars before being arrested. Prince Rainier later pardoned one of the three culprits because of his poor health. The others served two-year jail terms.

Bust-out men are not particular who their victims are, and honest casino operators must maintain a constant guard against them. Big-time Money and Bank Craps tables employ laddermen and floormen to protect themselves against such cheats.

An example of the financial possibilities of bust-out men: Working in Miami, Con Baker, the greatest dice mechanic ever to whip in a pair of crooked dice, once fleeced one of America's top oil barons for the tidy sum of $835,000 in a two-hour workday. Con didn't manage to hang on to his money; he died penniless at thirty-seven.

I know of a bigtime horse bookie who was recently taken for $3 million in a six-month gaming period by dice cheats. Bust-out men move around and are not particular where they operate. Wherever a dice game is in progress the chances are a bust-out man will appear on the scene sooner or later.

The art of professional Craps cheating has several branches. Some cheats travel alone, playing single-o against the suckers in private games or wherever they find inexperienced Craps players. But because there is safety and strength in numbers, and because the professional bust-out man, concentrating on the task of switching in his crooked dice, needs someone else to make the wagers, cheats more often work in groups known as *dice mobs.*

Single-o cheats and dice mobs, when detected, often get beaten up by a group of angry players or by casino strong-arm men, but that doesn't deter them. It's all in the day's work—one of the dice cheat's occupational hazards. Dice cheats have little or no fear of arrest and conviction on the charge of cheating, since gambling is usually illegal in the first place, and sleight-of-hand cheating is hard to prove.

My recent survey of Private Craps games reveals that there are crooked dice in about one out of every ten games in daily operation in the United States, usually introduced into the game by some amateur dice cheat who has no special cheating skill. It is easy for anyone to become a dice cheat. Anyone who doesn't care how he wins can achieve this aim. All he needs is a circle of suckers and a pair of gimmicked dice, which can be purchased in many novelty stores and from most suppliers of honest dice. Nowadays, with so many novice Craps shooters in sight, both the suckers and the crooked dice are easy to come by. I don't know how many dice cheats there are in the United States; but I do know that there are a hundred dice manufacturers, many of whom see nothing wrong in making crooked dice, since there is no law against it.

Unfortunately, the average Craps player has little chance of detecting crooked dice, even if he plays with them for weeks. A woman friend of mine phoned me several years ago and asked if I would check a pair of dice which she suspected might be dishonest. I paid her a visit and was told that about ten of her women friends met at her house each Friday night for a Poker game, and that they had gotten into the habit of shooting Craps for an hour or so at the end of the evening. My friend said that she had lost $5,000 during the previous six months and was beginning to suspect that everything was not on the up and up.

It wasn't. The dice turned out to be loaded. "How," I asked, "do you happen to have these loaded babies?"

"About six months ago," she explained, "after one of our Poker sessions, I found them on the floor under the Poker table. I thought someone had dropped them accidentally and, at our next session, I asked if anyone had lost them. No one claimed them, but at the end of the Poker game that night, one of the girls suggested that we shoot Craps for a while."

I did a little investigating and found that one of my friend's Poker-playing pals was formerly a Twenty-Six dice dealer in Chicago. She had planted the loaded cubes where they would be found, knowing that someone, she herself, if necessary, would suggest using them—although I doubt that she expected the loads would stay in use for as long as six months before one of the other players, who were mostly losers, would suspect anything was wrong. If there's a Craps game going on in your home and you aren't sure where the dice came from, it might be a good idea to get a pair that you know are honest.

The former dice-dealing gal, apparently having gotten wind of the fact that somebody had blown the gaff, disappeared, knowing, of course, that my friend couldn't beef to the cops because she would also be subject to arrest for running illegal Poker and Craps games in her home.

There are undoubtedly thousands of pairs of crooked dice in use right now that have been planted on innocent and honest players by dice cheats. There are hundreds upon hundreds of amateur dice cheats, male and female, who win money at Craps by clipping unwary suckers with crooked dice. The most popular forms of *gaffed* (doctored) dice and the methods for detecting them are described below.

Percentage dice: Amateur cheats do not have the skill necessary to switch crooked dice in and out of a game, so they use percentage dice, which can be put into a game and left there. They are gaffed in such a way that some numbers will come up more often than probability predicts. There are two main types: *passers,* which are fixed to favor some of the point numbers and thus favor the right bettors, and *miss-outs,* which are gaffed so that SEVEN will come up oftener than it should, thus favoring the wrong bettors. The dice cheat merely makes his bets according to the bias of the dice and usually shows a profit on every game. To avoid the suspicion that constant winning might create, he occasionally goes broke and then gets back his losses and a share of the winnings from the evening's big winner—a confederate he has planted in the game.

Shapes are the commonest form of percentage dice and can be made either as passers or miss-outs. These are dice whose shape has been altered in one way or another so that they are no longer perfect cubes.

Flats are shapes that have been shaved down on one or more sides so that they are slightly brick-shaped and tend to come to rest more often on their larger surfaces. Shaving off as little as $\frac{1}{5000}$ of an inch will change the probabilities and earn the cheat a profit. The less his suckers know about crooked dice the more he will cut them down. A "strong" pair may have as much as $\frac{4}{1000}$ of an inch, or even more, taken off, and the cheat gets his profit that much faster.

Six-ace flats are the commonest variety of miss-outs. When the 6–1 sides are shaved down, they thus turn up oftener than they would with square dice, and produce more SEVENS. The cheat bets the point numbers to lose.

Flat passers have had the 6–1 sides cut down on one die and the 3–4 sides on the other, so that the points 4, 5, 9 and 10 appear more often. Or the 2–5 sides are shaved on one die and the 3–4 sides on the other so as to favor the points 5, 6, 8 and 9. The cheat bets the points to win.

Two-way flats (fast sevens or four-way sevens) are shapes that have been shaved down on two non-opposite sides. When a few thousandths of an inch is taken off the 6–3 sides, for instance, the 6–1 and 3–4 sides are rectangles having a greater area than the 2–5 sides. The numbers 6, 1, 3 and 4 will appear oftener, and when both dice are cut down in the same way, these numbers will combine to form more SEVENS than normally appear. They are, therefore, miss-outs, and cheaters call them *fast sevens* or *four-way sevens*. The 6–1 and 2–5 sides, or the 3–4 and 2–5 sides, when cut down, act the same.

Bevels are shapes having one or more sides sandpapered so that they are slightly rounded rather than flat. Such cubes tend to roll off the rounded sides and come to rest more often on the flat sides. Bevels can also be made as passers or miss-outs, and as weak or strong as desired. Use the "wobble test" to detect beveled shapes. Hold one die in each hand and rub two sides together, trying different sides. When a beveled surface is rubbed against a flat surface or another beveled surface, the dice will wobble, or rock back and forth.

Cut edges are dice whose edges are not all beveled at the customary 45-degree angle. The four edges on some sides are cut at a 60-degree angle. This gives some sides a larger area than others, and the dice tend to settle on the larger surfaces more often. To detect cut edges hold the two dice together and note the width of the separation line between them. If this varies when you try different sides, the edges have been cut.

Loaded dice: The gaff on shapes is called *outside work;* on loaded dice it is *inside work*. Loads may caliper as perfect cubes, but extra weight just below the surface on some sides will make the opposite sides come up oftener than they should. Loads, contrary to what most people think, are not so heavily weighted that the same sides always appear; this behavior in a game would look very odd indeed. Like shapes, loads are percentage dice which throw certain combinations more often than they should.

Most Craps players know so little about crooked dice that they are cheated out of millions of dollars every year because they think that transparent dice cannot be loaded. Dice makers have never found this very difficult; they simply drill the recessed spots on two or three adjacent sides of the dice a little deeper than usual, and insert thin gold, platinum or tungsten amalgam slugs, which are then covered by opaque paint on the spots. In a well-made pair of transparent loads, the other spots are also drilled deeper and filled with paint, so that when you look through the dice all the spots are seen to be recessed to the same depth.

Many players believe that the practice of throwing the cubes against a backboard is protection against crooked dice. This protects you only against controlled shots, not against shapes or loads.

There are a couple of good tests for loaded dice. The best method is to fill a tall glass with water, hold the suspected cube just above the surface and drop it gently into the water; do this several times, holding the die with a different number up each time. Note whether the die settles evenly or whether it turns over as it goes down. If it turns, and if two or three numbers always show up and others never show, the dice are loaded.

If there is no tall glass of water handy, try this: Hold the cube loosely between thumb and forefinger at diagonally opposite corners so that there is as little pressure as possible. Try all four combinations of diagonally opposite corners. If the cube is loaded, when the weighted sides are on top, the die will pivot as the heavier sides swing around to the bottom. The feeling of movement of the die is unmistakable.

Flush spotted dice: The spots are recessed about $1\frac{7}{1000}$ inch into the die's surface. Most casinos use these today because they are much more difficult to load; however, they are perfect for electric dice (see pages 183–184).

There is little point in testing the dice used in most casinos because most Bank Craps and Money Craps games permit both right and wrong action. Perfectly square dice must be used so that the house will receive its favorable percentage no matter which way the players bet. The use of percentage dice by a crooked casino would serve no useful purpose for the house. This two-way betting action has made it necessary for manufacturers to make dice that are true cubes to a tolerance of $\frac{1}{5000}$ of an inch or thereabouts.

Tops and bottoms (also tops, busters, Ts, misspots): These are the dice used by the professional cheats. They do not use flats, bevels, cut edges or loads because they are usually playing against smart players who would spot these gaffs. Tops are not percentage dice; they do not bring up the same numbers some of the time—they bring up the right numbers all of the time. The cheat's chance of winning is 100%, and the victim's chance of winning is exactly zero.

Since the players can't see more than three sides of a cube at once, they can't see that some numbers are missing and others appear twice. Tops usually bear only three different numbers, each of which is repeated on the cube's opposite side. The players on opposite sides of a Craps circle all see the same three numbers when a top comes to a stop on the playing surface, but since no one individual can be in two places at once, none of them know it. And the misspotting passes unnoticed when they are rolling.

Amateur cheats, however, don't use those sure-fire cubes because, dangerous as they are to the sucker, they are also loaded with danger for the sharp whose sleight-of-hand isn't top-notch. Although the misspotting passes unnoticed during the action of the roll, if the chump ever gets his mitts on a pair of tops and gives them a once-over lightly, he rumbles the gaff immediately. Consequently, tops must be switched in and out at a split-second's notice, with speed and with smooth, undetectable sleight-of-hand. The switch artist who has mastered that never worries about a personal unemployment problem. The mob he signs up with can throw their P.C. dice out the window and depend on tops to corral all the folding money in sight in practically nothing flat and with 100% efficiency.

If the switch man is good, the chance the sucker has of tagging the cubes for what they are is exceedingly slim. Even the fast-company boys can come a cropper when the Ts start rolling! A dice mob can sense a suspicious player with all the celerity of a lie detector. And when someone grabs for and examines the dice, the chances are a thousand to one that he'll pick up fair dice. The tops go in when the player is confident that the game is on the level and is absorbed in the betting and the excitement of the game. When you look for them, they're not there; when you don't, they are.

Tops come in assorted combinations calculated to meet any Craps situation. Gamblers call them busters because that's exactly what happens to the guy who gets in their way—he's busted. If you should ever find yourself in a *steer joint* (crooked gambling joint) and you hear someone ask, "Where's Buster Brown?" you'll know that somebody's baby is going to get new shoes—but it won't be yours. That query is the signal for the *bust-out man* to *bust in** with tops that will bust your chance of winning and leave it looking like a punctured soap bubble.

The method of using busters varies with the game being played. In Private Craps the mechanic uses a pair of tops so misspotted that they make point after point but no SEVEN. Both dice bear three numbers only, each being duplicated on the die's opposite side. Dice misspotted in this way will throw only 9 of the usual 36 combinations. There are numerous combinations, a pair bearing the numbers 1, 3 and 5 on each die, for instance, can only make the combinations 1–1, 1–3, 1–5, 3–1, 3–3, 3–5, 5–1, 5–3 and 5–5 forming the points 2, 4, 6, 8 and 10. The shooter consequently can't possibly throw a 7 and must pass. Tops that pass are known as *hits*.†

---

* Don't say that someone busted in with a pair of flats or loads, however. Those are always *switched* in. The terms *bust in* and *bust out* apply only to switching tops.

† The common passing combinations and the numbers they make are:
1–2–3 and 1–2–3 which make 2, 3, 4, 5, 6.
1–3–5 and 1–3–5 which make 2, 4, 6, 8, 10.
2–3–6 and 2–3–6 which make 4, 5, 6, 8, 9, 12.
2–4–6 and 2–4–6 which make 4, 6, 8, 10, 12.
1–4–5 and 1–4–5 which make 2, 5, 6, 8, 9, 10.
3–4–5 and 1–5–6 which make 4, 5, 6, 8, 9, 10, 11.
3–5–6 and 3–5–6 which make 6, 8, 9, 10, 11, 12.

Many top cheaters claim that a 2–3–6 pair of tops are the best as passers because they throw all the points except 10, make fewer hardway combinations, and consequently arouse less suspicion. Others favor the 2–4–6 combination because the even point numbers 4, 6, 8 and 10 can easily be broken up with a 1–3–5, 2–4–6 set of misses which make only odd numbers.

If the dice mechanic is working single-o, he busts in with the hits when he is the shooter. But if you suspect tops are being used, the shooter is not the only guy you should keep an eye on. When the mechanic has a partner, he busts in both ways—when he is shooting and from the outside when his pal is shooting. The latter throws the dice toward the bust-out man, who picks them up, and busts in with the tops. He repeats the action again later when the shooter wants to have the tops *ripped* (switched) out.

The shooter uses the tops for one or more passes, rakes in the dough, then goes back to fair dice and either continues shooting or passes the dice to the next player. The number of passes he makes before ripping the tops out depends on the action of the players, how well-heeled they are, and the number of passes they'll stand for before scowling suspiciously.

Misses are tops that are made to miss the point. When one die bears only the numbers 1–3–5 and the other only 2–4–6, the only combinations possible are odd numbers. Whenever the shooter is trying for one of the even point numbers (4, 6, 8, 10) with this set of misses, it is impossible for him to throw his point and he must seven out. And when his point is 5 or 9, a set of 1–4–5, 2–3–6 misses makes it impossible for him to throw the point.

Misses are not usually used in private games because the shooter has no legitimate reason to pick the dice up again after he sevens out and thus has no chance to get the tops out of the game. An exception is when the private game has a cutter who may bust them in and out, because, like a house stickman, he has the privilege of picking up the dice and throwing them to the next player.

In house games, the stickman who rakes in the cubes with the dice stick after the roll and tosses them back was originally introduced into the game as a protection against the switching in of phony dice by the players. But in a steer joint the stickman himself is usually the bust-out man who does the dirty work. These boys use several different pairs of tops, both hits and misses, in a manner that gets the money with all the neatness and dispatch of a high-class *cannon* (pickpocket) mob or a *heist* (hold-up) mob.

Bust-out men all have their favorite methods of ripping tops in and out as well as their favorite top combinations. Some dislike to work with the stick, claiming that it slows them up, others can't work without the stick and still others prefer to work from the outside, acting as one of the players. Some use four pairs of tops; others, because it is faster, safer and mistakes are less likely to be made, use only two. In Money (or Open) Craps three are most often used—two pairs of hits and a pair of misses.

In the steer joint, the mechanics of the operation of clipping the chump go something like this: The steerer phones in to say he is bringing a sucker—a big oilman. The boys clear the decks for action and the moment the doorbell rings the game suddenly starts rolling full bloom. The book is behind the bankroll, the stickman behind the stick, the shills betting the money with which they have been supplied, and the bosses with the big dough, acting as players, as doing the same. A little room is left between two bosses so that the mark walks into that position.

The dice in the game at the start are all levels. But as soon as the mark starts to bet and the bosses discover whether he is a right or wrong bettor, the office is given and the tops go in—misses if the chump makes a right bet, hits if he makes a wrong bet. The mark finds that he can get all the action he wants, and then some. The mob always tries to increase the victim's bets as much as possible, figuring that the larger his bets the faster he gets clipped, the fewer moves the bust-out man has to make and the less chance the mark has of detecting the dirty work. Time is also important; another steerer may be on his way with another monkey.

Suppose the mark is a right bettor and has taken $200 to $100 on the FOUR which is the shooter's point. The stickman gets the office and pulls the dice in with his stick. As he draws it back, his right hand comes back close to his body and directly over his coat pocket. This pocket has had a specially designed tailoring job, having been built up on the inside so that it is much shallower than usual and divided by partitions so that the pairs of hits and misses are each contained in separate sections. The stickman's fingers dip in and come out with the 1–3–5, 2–4–6 misses, which do not add up to 4, 6, 8 or 10, any way you look at them.

The chump never glimpses the move because it is covered by the body of the shill who stands close beside the stickman. Sometimes, too, it is the shill's pockets which have been rebuilt and contain the tops, and into which the stickman's fingers dip. The advantage here is that, in case of a blow, the shill walks off and the stickman can stand for a search. An even smarter method, and the one most popular with bust-out men today, not only eliminates the necessity for going into the pocket entirely, but makes the whole move quicker and easier. The stickman's hand goes back between his body and that of the shill and, during the second when the end of the stick is out of sight, the shill simply places the proper pair of tops in the bust-out man's hand.

Once he has the Ts palmed in his right hand, the stickman takes the stick with his left, picks the fair dice up from the table and throws them to the player. Or that is what he seems to do. Actually the tops are thrown out and the fair dice retained, palmed in the right hand, which again takes the stick.

The dice roll out, the shooter sevens and the chump loses his bet. The stickman pulls the dice in, rips the levels in again, and then moves his hand back for an instant and drops the tops into the hand that the shill at his side holds ready and waiting.

The bust-out man's job is a nerve-wracking one that requires the utmost in timing, speed and smooth precision. His life is no bed of roses.

When there are two suckers in the joint, one a right and the other a wrong bettor, he faces a situation he never enjoys. The mark who is a wrong bettor, for instance, has just laid $100 on the FOUR and the stickman has ripped in with a pair of 2–3–6s so that the FOUR must be made. If the other mark wants to take the odds, the bosses pretend they don't hear him. But that stratagem doesn't always work. The right bettor may go to the book and may even take the limit, say $600 to $300.

The moment this happens those hits on the table are a liability. When the shooter passes, the book will lose 500 bucks more to the right bettor than the boss picks up from the wrong bettor. But that can't happen here—not in a steer joint. The bust-out man may have switched the hits in only a moment ago, but suddenly he gets the office to rip in a pair of misses. He has to have them ready and waiting and must bust in on the next roll without fail. Otherwise he's out of a job.

And, if the tops are still in play, when a player calls for a box-up the stickman must do some more fast, smooth work. He has to pick up the tops, switch them for levels as he throws them into the bowl with the other perfect dice and then spill them all out for a selection. And if he gets the office to put the tops back again on the come-out roll, when the player throws him the good dice the stickman must again make the switch as he throws them back. Good bust-out men die young; it's hard on the nervous system.

And so it goes. Whenever the majority of the money bet by the chumps is right money, the misses go in and the dice lose; when most of the suckers are betting wrong, the hits go in and the dice win. But whether the dice win or lose, the chump gets clipped both ways and the steer-joint boys simply can't lose. With a good bust-out man behind the stick, the fattest mark can be broken in almost no time at all. After a few losses he tends to make bigger bets trying to get his losses back, and he's flat before he knows it. Sometimes the boys break him on one roll.

How do you tell a steer joint from a game that is on the up and up? Well, if smart gamblers frequent the place and if the game has been operating for several months or longer, it's no steer joint; those boys don't stick in one spot that long. If the game is a new one, if a stranger brought you there, if there aren't many players around the table and if most of the action is directed your way—then you're in for it. And don't think you aren't. If you think you spot a move and want to object, don't get noisy about it but call the manager and try quietly to get your money back. If you make a fuss that will tip off any other suckers that may be around, you'll get your ears pinned back pronto. The steer-joint boys don't fool.

HOW TO DETECT TOPS AND BOTTOMS

The best way to detect tops and bottoms is to take note of the six sides of the two dice when they stop after each roll. Try mentally to form various combinations of the number 7. If the spots showing on the sides of the dice can form these combinations they can be made. If you do this for a number of rolls and can't see any combinations that will form your point or a 7, don't make a big scene about it; just call off your bet and don't make any more. The same holds true if you see the same three numbers on each cube after each roll.

PERCENTAGE TOPS AND BOTTOMS

Percentage tops and bottoms, also known as *one-way tops and bottoms, double-fives* or *double-deuces,* are the newest innovation in misspots. Only one of the six numbers on a die is duplicated on the opposite side, usually the deuce or five. A die with two deuces is called a *double-deuce* by dice cheaters; a die with two fives is a *double-five.*

A pair of dice may have both cubes misspotted, or it may be composed of one misspot and one square die. Double-deuces are used together, double-fives together, and either a double-deuce or a double-five may be used with a square die. A pair of double-deuces will not throw an ELEVEN; two double-fives will not throw a THREE. When a square die is used with a double-deuce or a double-five all 11 numbers can be made, a fact which makes the misspot difficult to detect in action. A one-way top was recently switched into a Reno casino and remained in action for several hours before the dice-table personnel got wise.

Here is a comparison of the numbers that can be made and the ways in which they can be made with square dice and with the various one-way tops and bottoms:

Numbers	2	3	4	5	6	7	8	9	10	11	12
Ways to make with											
2 square dice	1	2	3	4	5	6	5	4	3	2	1
1 double-deuce and 1 square die	1	3	4	5	5	6	5	3	2	1	1
2 double-deuces	1	4	6	6	5	4	5	2	2	0	1
1 double-five and 1 square die	1	1	2	3	5	6	5	5	4	3	1
2 double-fives	1	0	2	2	5	4	5	6	6	4	1

Percentage tops and bottoms work both as passers and missouts at the same time. Usually, two dice cheats work together; one bets the dice to lose, the other bets the dice to win.

A *double-deuce* paired with a square die gives the right bettor in a private game an advantage of 20% on the point FOUR and $13\frac{7}{11}$% on the point FIVE. The wrong bettor lays the odds on the point NINE and enjoys an edge of $16\frac{2}{3}$%; when he lays the odds on the point TEN he has an edge of 25%.

A *double-five* paired with a square die gives the right bettor a favorable edge on the point NINE of $13\frac{7}{11}$% and on the point TEN an edge of 20%. The wrong bettor lays the odds on the point FOUR and has an edge of 25%; laying the odds on the point FIVE gives him an edge of $16\frac{2}{3}$%.

Two double-deuces used together as a pair are much stronger. They are seldom used against smart Craps shooters unless the cheat is a good dice mechanic capable of switching them in and out of the game. A pair of double-deuces gives the right bettor in a private game an edge of 80% on the point FOUR, 50% on the point FIVE and 22⅖% on the point SIX or EIGHT. The wrong bettor has an advantage of 16⅔% on the point NINE. The point TEN supplies no advantage either way.

Two double-fives used as a pair give the right bettor an 80% edge on the point TEN, 50% on the point NINE and 22⅖% on the point SIX or EIGHT. The point FOUR has no percentage edge either way.

ELECTRIC DICE

These cubes contain steel slugs and are used over an electric magnet built into a Craps table or counter. The slugs used in transparent dice are made by gluing together ⁵⁄₁₀₀₀-inch steel wires to form a grid and punching out circular disks which fit into the countersunk spots. One is inserted in each of the spots on four different sides of the die, leaving the two sides that the operator wants to favor (opposite sides like the 6 and ace) open.

The magnetic field set up by a concealed electromagnet acts and brings one or the other of the unloaded sides up. Since the load is so light and since it is on four sides, neither pivot nor water test will detect electric dice. Furthermore, their roll is not only natural but even honest some of the time. However, the moment the operator puts on the squeeze by pushing the button that controls the electromagnet concealed beneath the playing surface, the electric dice act like trained seals. They are not percentage dice; the action is completely positive. The boys who use these don't intend to give anyone a break.

On the steer-joint Craps table the magnetic plate is close to the rail and just beneath the spot where most shooters will throw the dice. The pull of the magnet is less noticeable and operates more efficiently on the cubes as they drop down from the backboard than if they were simply rolled across the magnetic spot. Throwing the dice against the rail is, ordinarily, a protective measure, but in the steer joint the reverse is true. But don't try *not* hitting the rail; you won't like what happens then either!

Electric dice may be either missouts or passers, the latter being most often used. Six-ace missouts have the disadvantages that, because they always bring up one of the numbers 2, 12 or 7, the juice cannot be applied on the first roll when 2 and 12 lose and 7 wins. Once the shooter has come out on a point he will always lose when the juice is on because 2 and 12 are no decision and 7 loses.

Electric passers on the other hand throw a variety of points. A pair of electric dice, one die having the 2–5 sides and the other the 3–4 sides open, will throw the numbers 5, 6, 8 or 9. A pair of six-ace trey-four passers will throw 4, 5, 9 or 10.

These dice are as deadly as a cobra and completely positive in action.

Either the dealer or a shill on the outside controls the juice by pressing a button concealed beneath the green baize table covering or by pressing a screwhead on the side or under the edge of the table or a foot control. The operation is known either as putting *the squeeze* on or putting *the juice* on.

How to test for electric dice: There isn't any safe method. It can be done very simply by applying a magnet, but there's no point in testing for electric dice in a reputable casino, and if you try it in a crooked one, you'll meet the house bouncer but quick and will find yourself sitting in an alley outside, wishing that an ambulance would come along, and still not knowing for sure if the dice were electric or not. If you ever suspect electric dice are being used, your best protection is to take a quick look around for the nearest exit and use it.

The slick dice cup: The average player believes that use of a dice cup protects him against cheats. Nothing could be further from the truth. More cheating at Craps, Backgammon, Poker Dice, Buck Dice, High Dice and other dice games takes place when a dice cup is in use than when the dice are thrown from the hand. Why? Because it's easier to cheat and less detectable when crooked dice and dice cup are in use. All a cheat requires to take the unsuspecting player is a slick dice cup and a set of two, three, four or five loaded dice called *first flop dice,* depending on the game being played. The cheat places the loaded dice in the crooked dice cup and the dirty work begins.

The slick dice cup has a smooth slicked inner surface and when the cheat shakes the cup with an up and down and slightly rotary motion of his arm, the loaded dice, instead of rattling at random inside the cup, spin around the inside surface like wooden horses on a merry-go-round. The centrifugal force lines the dice up within the cup in a horizontal position. The last sideward shake just before they are thrown causes the loaded dice to top over so that their loaded sides are down. When the cheat throws them, he holds the cup parallel with the playing surface, shoves it forward a bit and jerks it back quickly so that the dice all slide out without turning over and the cheat throws a desired number. When the other players throw using the same cup and dice, they shake and throw properly and the loaded dice do them no good. To avoid being cheated with a slick cup, use a "trip cup," which contains obstructions in its inner surface that make the dice tumble as they are thrown and prevents the shark from sliding them out. Some cups have a trip rim; others are lined with ribbed rubber.

If a trip cup is not available, you can insist that the dice be well shaken —and that the cup be turned completely upside down on the throw so that the dice bounce on the playing surface and do not slide out. Don't hesitate to examine the dice.

CHEATING WITH HONEST DICE

There are still a great many Craps players who don't quite believe the stories about cheats who can make fair dice act like performing seals. "Can fair dice be controlled?" is a question I am often asked. The answer is Yes, but only on certain playing surfaces. The dice mechanic has not yet been born who can bounce a pair of honest dice against a hard back-board and bring up two desired numbers when they drop on a hard play-ing surface. But there are a good many dice cheats who have practiced long and hard and have perfected the ability to make honest dice behave as they want them to under certain conditions.

The spin shot or whip shot, although difficult to perfect, is the com-monest dice-control shot. It works best on soft dirt. The dice are held with the desired numbers on top and rattled in the hand but not actually shaken. A quick whiplike snap of the hand sends them spinning through the air like twin helicopters. When the dice land, the spinning motion keeps them from rolling and they settle down, the wanted numbers still on top. This shot can also be done on hard surfaces; some dice cheats sprinkle a few grains of salt on the playing surface, which helps the dice to spin and slide without turning over. It can also be accomplished on the green baize surface of the Bank or Open Craps table, which is why casinos insist that the player hit the backboard or throw the dice over an elastic string stretched across the center of the table.

The *blanket roll* uses the opposite principle. The dice are thrown in such a way that they roll end over end like wheels. The numbers on the outer sides of the dice do not come up, and certain combinations therefore cannot be made. The shot works best on a blanket, a bed cover or a soft carpet, and it is not difficult to learn. Many players have heard of this one, but not many can recognize it when they see it. Watch the shooter, and if he picks the dice up a bit too carefully and seems to be looking for certain numbers, keep your money in your pocket. If the cheat holds the dice so that the sixes, the aces, or an ace and six face each other, these numbers won't show and a crap or 11 cannot be made.

The *backboard control shot* is a modern percentage controlled shot that makes use of blanket, soft rug or carpet plus a three-foot-high vertical backboard line with foam rubber. As a rule, throwing the dice against a backboard is a protective measure against dice cheats, but not with this gaffed setup. Before releasing the dice from the hand, the cheat gives the dice a phony shake, à la spin shot. Then instead of rolling the dice on the soft surface as in the blanket roll, he lets them fly against the backboard in such a way that both dice hit the backboard at the same time causing them to bounce off the backboard onto the soft surface. The momentum causes them to roll back and over end like a pair of cartwheels without turning sideways. If 3–4 is one hub of the wheel and 2–5 the other, the only way the cheat can seven out is with a three and four.

The *three-cushion controlled dice shot* is a highly secretive private dice-game cheating method. This controlled throw requires the use of a three-foot-high vertical backboard and two sideboards, each lined with foam rubber. The table surface must be smooth—usually a piece of linoleum or plastic—so that the dice will slide to a stop. The three cushion shot is most effective, since few gamblers believe it is possible to hit a sideboard, backboard and sideboard, and still control the dice. To execute this fantastic dice control shot, the cheat shakes the dice, à la spin shot, and throws the dice against the right sideboard where they ricochet off the sideboard onto the backboard and onto the left sideboard. After dropping onto the smooth playing surface, they slide and finally come to rest with the desired numbers uppermost.

The *dice table control shot* is a new casino dice-table control shot. It is the most difficult dice throw to perfect because it requires perfect aim and timing that can be gained only by long and arduous practice on a regulation casino dice table. This dice throw has taken many a casino operator for a bundle. Before I began exposing crooked dice, it is doubtful that more than a handful of gamblers and casino operators had the slightest idea that such a controlled shot existed.

Most modern dice tables have a sponge-rubber embossed zigzag pattern lining the inside of the four 10-inch upright rails that enclose the table's playing surface. However, a bottom inch of this lining, at the juncture of the table surface and the upright rails, does not possess the embossed zigzag patterns—it is plain sponge rubber. And this is exactly the spot the dice cheat must hit to control this shot.

The pickup of the dice in order to execute this controlled shot is difficult to detect because only one die has to be maneuvered into position. Immediately after the dice have been offered to the cheater-shooter, he picks them up in such a manner that one die has the desired number uppermost. This die is held palm down between the thumb and the first two fingers of the cheat's right hand flat on the table surface. The cheat lets the dice fly out of his palm-down hand from the table surface giving the one die he wants to control a whiplike snap aiming at the juncture of the table surface and the sponge rubber sideboard. When the spinning die hits this spot of the sideboard (the bottom inch), it bounces off at an angle and drops into the center of the table without turning over, with the desired number remaining uppermost. If the cheat holds the die so that a five is always uppermost, a hardway ten becomes an even bet. The same holds true for the point numbers 6, 8 and 9.

The use of sleight-of-hand with dice or cards is hard to expose because there is no physical evidence to prove it. Even if you can spot a controlled roll, all you can do is insist on the use of a backboard, and if you are voted down on that, stop playing.

PROTECTION AGAINST DICE CHEATS

At this point you're probably wondering if there is any simple surefire all-around method of making sure that the dice in the games you play are honest. I'm sorry, but the answer is No! Your best protection is to have the information given in this dice chapter in your head. If you are smartened up to all the methods and angles, you will have reduced your chance of being cheated with crooked cubes or a controlled dice throw to a minimum.

The only absolutely certain way of never being cheated at a dice game is not to play. But if this rule proves a little too tough to follow, you should at least take a good look at the cubes and follow these rules:

1. Check that each of the two dice in use total seven on all opposing sides.

2. Check that all sides are level and not concave, rounded or with raised spots.

3. Check that all sides are equally polished.

4. Check that the edges and corners are all straight, square and preferably sharp rather than rounded. If rounded, see that all edges and corners are rounded equally.

5. Check that the spots are all countersunk the same distance and the paint on all spots is the same distance from the cube's surface. Better still, use flush-spot dice.

6. The dice should pass the pivot or water test for loads.

7. Whenever possible, use transparent dice.

8. If the dice cup in use is not a trip dice cup, insist that the dice be well shaken and the cup turned completely upside down on the throw so that the dice drop on the playing platform.

9. Never play dice on a blanket or soft surface and avoid throwing dice against an upright backboard lined with sponge rubber.

If the dice meet the above requirements and you're able to protect yourself against the dice cheat's crooked control throws, your only worry is the dice cheat whose trained fingers can switch a pair of crooked dice for an honest pair as quickly as you can say "Scarne," or if you are playing in a steer joint that is using electric dice.

I have described the most used dice cheating devices and methods, but there are others. For information on such things as the slide shot, the Greek shot, the twist shot, how to switch dice, the dice-cup switch, and (with two dice) the pin gaff, heavy paintwork, busters, etc., see *Scarne on Dice*.

7

CRAPS BETTING SYSTEMS AND THEIR FALLACIES

Today there are more betting systems advertised for sale on how to beat the dice tables in Las Vegas than at any other time in history. A couple of decades ago the only magazine that would publish a gambling system advertisement were the pulp magazines. But today, due to more relaxed standards, periodicals such as *Time, Newsweek, The New York Times,* the New York *Daily News,* the Chicago *Tribune* and other respected publications have dropped their high standards and accept gambling-system ads that guarantee that, when put to use by the buyer, will surely beat the dice tables in Las Vegas, Atlantic City, Puerto Rico, Bahamas, Monte Carlo and casinos the world over. These get-rich-quick betting systems sell from $25 to $100. No wonder these advertisements have graduated from cheap pulp magazines to our leading and respected national periodicals.

The Craps operator and dice hustler earn money by making Old Man Percentage work for them. The dice cheat earns money by beating the dice chumps with crooked dice. And the Johnny-come-lately Craps player, knowing nothing about the mathematics of the game, sees some high roller win a bundle at the Las Vegas Craps table and wishes he were in his shoes. Then when he reads an ad in his local paper or national magazine touting some dice system that the author states is infallible, he promptly invests 35 bucks or more in an instruction sheet that promises to tell him "How to Beat the Las Vegas Dice Tables" simply by following a certain betting method. Here are just a few of the many highly advertised betting systems being sold today.

THE FIVE-WAY CRAPS BETTING SYSTEM

This old five-way craps betting system was recently brought back to life by an extensive advertising campaign in a number of newspapers and national magazines including a full-page ad in *The New York Times, Time* magazine, and *Newsweek.* The advertisement promised that for the sum of $35 the buyer with this system was sure to beat the dice tables in Las Vegas, Reno, Bahamas, Puerto Rico, London and Monte Carlo. The advertisement follows.

"ACTION ON EVERY ROLL!"
BET LIKE THE PROFESSIONAL INSIDERS DO
The most talked about dice instruction in America. Put this new knowledge to immediate use for astounding results. By placing only 5 bets and having all numbers in your favor . . . including the 7. After making his point and your 5 bets are placed any number that comes out in each roll 2, 3, 4, 5, 6, 7, 8, 9, 10, 11, 12. YOU WIN! Only if the shooter's point comes back in two rolls, you don't win. You play two rolls after making his point and make $10 to (approx.) $200 (according to the amount bet).
NOW YOU SAY, PROVE IT! O.K.
Get a pair of dice. Play for as many shoots as you like, and you be the judge. Make your point on the 1st roll, then see if you can repeat the same back in 2 rolls. If you don't, YOU'RE A WINNER EVEN IF YOU HIT A 7. Keep track of the score you make, then see your results after 40 to 50 shoots or more.
BET ON IT! MAKING MONEY IS EASY . . . WHEN YOU KNOW HOW.
BET THE SOURCE THE EXPERTS USE . . .
"ACTION ON EVERY ROLL"
Allow 2 to 3 weeks for Delivery.
Send Money Order plus 80¢ for
Overnight Delivery!

Three weeks after your $35 check has cleared, you receive by special delivery a sheet of instructions as follows:

The following is how the system works. Place a #35 bet on DON'T PASS or lose line before the shooter comes out for a point. The odds are 15 to 1 on the 11, or 4 to 1 on the 7, on the first roll. If you're worried about a 7 or 11 coming out on the first roll, then you could lay the odds on the number he comes out with on the box number of the point made. After he hits his point, you bet the boxes and Field as follows: Place $10 on #6, $10 on #8, $5 on the Field, $5 on Box 4 or 5 whichever number doesn't appear in the Field, depending on where you are playing—in Las Vegas, Bahamas, San Juan or in any legalized casino only. Now, you've GOT TO WIN on every roll—unless he hits his point. We suggest you take your bets down after his 2nd roll.

The first error. The system sheet reveals that the writer knows nothing about Craps odds when he says that the odds on an 11 or 7 on the come-out are 15 to 1 and 4 to 1 respectively. The true odds are 17 to 1 on the 11 and 5 to 1 on the 7. Let's skip this little gem and continue with the analysis of this system.
The system player walks up to a dice table in a Nevada or Puerto Rican casino and places a $35 bet on the Don't Pass or Lose line before the come-out. The shooter on the come-out throws a 7 or an 11 and the system player loses his $35. The odds say that this will occur on the average of eight times out of 36 come-out throws. The system sheet states that if you're worried about a 7 or 11 coming out on the first roll, then you could lay

the odds on the number the shooter comes out with. This statement leaves us breathless. How anyone can lay the odds on the point when a 7 or 11 has been thrown on the come-out is beyond me. But to get on with our analysis of the system—let's skip the 7 and 11 and 2, 3 or 12 (craps) on the come-out and say that the shooter throws a 4 on the come-out and see what happens. As things now stand, the player has $35 riding against the point 4. Now the system instructs the player to switch and bet right, but instead of making one win bet as described in the popular Right and Wrong Way System (pages 195–196) the player is told to make four such win bets. He is told to take $10 worth of odds on the number 6, $10 on the 8, $5 on 4 (no field number) and $5 on the field. The system player has a total of $65 in wagers on the Craps layout. If the shooter throws a seven he collects $35 on the wrong action and loses $30 on the right action. If the player makes his point number 4 and sevens out on the following roll, the system player loses $60 and collects $14 on the place bet 4 for a loss of $46. In short, the system is a very bad adaption of the Right and Wrong Way System because the player is paying a hidden percentage on five bets instead of two.

THE ROTHSTEIN SYSTEM

The Rothstein system uses the general principle on which most dice systems are based. It is our old friend the Martingale, double-up or progressive system in disguise, and it is more commonly employed at the dice table than at any other gambling game. It is advertised this way:

THE ROTHSTEIN SYSTEM

Did you ever try to beat the RACES? It cannot be done. And you cannot beat Craps games any more than you can beat the races. Craps games are MADE TO WIN for the house. Unless you use a SYSTEM.

The Rothstein Craps system is a simple mathematical progressive way of placing bets on the layout. And if the system is adhered to, STICK TO THE SYSTEM, it will win. Figures do not lie and this system is nothing but a simple play of figures.

Anyone that can count 1-2-3-4-5-6 etc., can use the ROTHSTEIN SYSTEM. We sold it to a man in Ohio and he wrote back inside of a week and told us he made $225.00 with the system.

It is guaranteed to win if you FOLLOW THE SYSTEM. The only thing that can keep you from winning is the houseman. He does not like a system player and can, if he wishes, bar anyone. All that is required is that the house fades your bets. Not a crooked move of any kind. . . . $3.00.

It should also be obvious to anyone who "can count 1-2-3-4-5-6" that if a man had a guaranteed winning system, peddling it to all comers at three bucks is the last thing he would do. Actually, this ad does not misrepresent the facts as much as some of them do. After stating that the system is guaranteed to win, it actually tells, in the next-to-last sentence, exactly why the system won't work!

Here's the dope. Your first step is to place 1 chip on the pass line. If you lose, you bet 3 chips, and if you lose that you bet 7 chips. Each time you lose, you double your last bet plus 1. If you win after your first bet, you are ahead 1 chip; after the second bet, 2 chips; after the third bet, 3 chips, etc. And each time you win, you go back and start the progression over again with the 1-chip bet.

"Sometimes," the instructions read, "the dice go clear around the table before they make a pass. This is unusual but it will happen. Nevertheless they *must* pass some time and, while it may take the heart out of players to keep piling chips up, the chips will all come back when a pass is made and there will be surplus chips with them. THIS IS A SYSTEM THAT NO HOUSEMAN LIKES TO SEE USED AGAINST HIS GAME."

That last sentence is strictly off the beam, since stickmen have a habit of crying, "Double up, men! They're bound to change. Double up and beat the bank!" The house likes to see this system used because in trying to win small amounts steadily the player must make many bets; and the more bets he makes, the more the house earns in percentage.

Before I put my finger on the big hitch in the whole scheme, let me first describe another variation of the progressive system known as:

THE WATCHER OR PATIENCE SYSTEM

The instructions on this one lead off my warnings that you must have plenty of patience, and, incidentally, $500 to $1,000 capital. With those two requirements the system is guaranteed to win $10 a day, rain or shine, day in and day out. Don't be greedy, the writer warns, just be satisfied with the ten bucks per day and everything is jake. "This system has been tried and is recommended by some of the smartest dice players in the country."

This time, instead of betting the dice to win, you are to bet the dice to lose. Much stress is laid on the fact that you must watch the dice and not make any bets until after four successive passes have been made. Then bet $10 that they lose on the fifth. This clever little dodge saves you the loss of four $10 bets! Since a penny saved is a penny earned you're already making money!

You have a far better chance betting the dice to lose on the fifth pass than on the first because the odds against five successive passes being made are 31 to 1. It's practically a sure thing. You'll lose such a proposition only once in 32 times. Then you take your $10 and leave. Don't be greedy and be tempted to try the system twice in the same night.

And, if you should lose that 31-to-1 shot? You merely bet $20 that the dice will lose on the next pass. The odds against six passes being made are 63 to 1. If, by any strange streak of fate, you lose that one, too, bet $40 that they don't pass. The odds are 127 to 1 against seven successive passes. You can hardly ask for better odds in your favor than that.

I know one player who bought and played this system for four weeks.

He came away every night wearing a broad smile and with a $10 profit. Of course, sometimes he had to wait hours before four passes were made in a row so that he could begin betting, but he expected that; instructions told him he needed plenty of patience.

But one night he had a little difficulty. When he walked into the casino, he had won $10 a night for four weeks and was $280 ahead of the game. When the fourth pass was made, he bet $10 on the next. The shooter sevened. He bet $20 and the shooter threw an 11. He bet $40 and the shooter sevened again. He bet $80, and a point was bucked right back. He bet $160 and began sweating. But he had faith in the system; it was guaranteed to win. A miss-out *had* to come sometime, and when it did he'd be $10 ahead once more.

Then the shooter crapped out with two sixes and my friend relaxed, all smiles, but only for a moment. The house made no move to pay off.

"Hey," the player asked, "I had $160 down to lose. Don't I get—"

The stickman gave him a sour look. "Something wrong?" he asked, pointing to the space on the layout which read "Two sixes standoff." "In case you don't know, that means there's no payoff, but you don't lose either."

My friend scowled. He was learning fast now. The system sheet hadn't said anything about a standoff, but he began to see that it gave the house two whacks at his dough. There was nothing he could do, however, but let the $160 ride on the next come-out and hope for any crap except two sixes.

The dice came out—a natural with a 6–5. The house raked in the $160, and my friend, now shy a total of $310, reached shakily for his roll, counted off $320 and threw it on the table.

Then he bumped head-on into another very hard fact that the system had failed to stress.

"Sorry, sir," the boxman said, "but you can bet only three hundred. That's the limit at this table."

Now what? If he bet the $300 and won, he would still be a $10 loser. If he lost he'd be shy $610 altogether. The guaranteed system hadn't said anything about a situation in which he'd lose no matter what happened. He'd forgotten that one little line in the ad which read: "All that is required is that the house fades your bets."

While he was trying to make up his mind the dice came out and the shooter sevened. His hesitation saved him $300. But he was still shy $310, thirty bucks more than the $280 it had taken him four weeks of patient waiting to win.

This is also the flaw in the Rothstein system. In fact, every progressive system eventually runs smack up against the house maximum betting limit and explodes in the player's face. Take a close look at the usual house betting limits and you'll see that the spread between the minimum and maximum betting limits prevents the system player from doubling up more than six or seven times. A 25¢ to $25 top, for instance, allows him to bet

25¢ and then double by betting 50¢, $1, $2, $4, $8 and $16. If he loses each bet he's sunk, because the seventh doubling up will take him above the limit. The same thing holds true of the 50¢ to $50 and the $1 to $75 or $100, the $2 to $200 or $300 and the $5 to $1,000 limits.

One book on dice systems even introduces the subject by warning the player to find out the rules governing the limit of the stakes before beginning to play. "The best system," it adds, "is worthless unless the house allows adequate margin for raising the stakes." The writer then wades into a complex explanation of the Patience system as applied to all sorts of games and neglects to mention that *all* houses do have a limit that *does not* allow an adequate margin for raising the stakes. This booklet bears a $5 price on its cover and is sold for $2.50 "while they last." It has been in print for years.

There are also a few things wrong with the advice to watch for four passes before betting and then put your money on the fifth pass because the odds against its being made are 31 to 1. Those are the odds that five successive passes won't be made, all right, but you are *not* betting that five passes won't be made. You are betting that the *next* pass won't be made. There's a slight difference. The odds on that are, as always, slightly less than 50–50. (When the two sixes are barred you have a $49\frac{23}{77}\%$ chance.)

The author of the above-mentioned booklet has a couple of other system secrets that deserve passing mention. "Practice Craps in your home for thousands of shots before you dare enter a gambling house. By doing so you will acquire the necessary intuition for guessing the results of the next shot." Any reader who follows this plan and successfully develops intuition of that kind should set up as a fortuneteller.

And the last word on all the systems in the book is the one in which you are advised to play *against* the player using a progressive system! You always bet the same amount he does and "whenever his guess is wrong you have won as many progressive stakes as he has lost. He has to do the guessing, which is the real trick in every game." This writer not only believes in the maturity of chances (which is what his "watching" tactics imply) but also in the gamblers' superstition that the odds are against the guesser! But even at that, he's a little bit smart; he writes a book on systems instead of playing them.

THE HOT AND COLD SYSTEM

This one is a lulu. The gambler who advertises it for sale promises the player that "with this system you will be betting they win *every time* the dice are *hot* (making passes), and betting they lose *every time* the dice are *cold* (not passing)."

You think this sounds impossible? You'd pass it up because there just couldn't be any way to make certain that you would be betting they win during every hot spell and betting they lose during every cold spell?

Strangely enough, the method given tells you exactly how to do that, and for only $5.

Before you read further, see if you can dope out a way to do it. I warn you, however, that once you've got the answer it won't make a killing.

Here's the method. Whenever a player makes a pass, you begin betting the dice to win. If he continues through a hot spell of passes, you're on it. And the moment he throws a miss-out you begin, with the next roll, betting the dice to lose. Now you're sure to be on any cold spell. And as soon as another pass appears you switch back again. The moment that someone makes a long series of either passes or miss-outs you are in the big money. Sounds good, doesn't it?

Here's the catch. The instruction forgot to say what would happen when a pass is followed by a miss-out, then a pass, then a miss-out and so on, passes and miss-outs coming alternately. What would happen? Playing the hot-and-cold system, you would lose every single bet during the time the dice acted that way.

And, because this system requires that you bet on every decision, the price you'll pay the house in percentage before you discover for yourself what's wrong will be a darned sight more than the five bucks the system cost you. The house and the guy who sells the system make the money— but you lose.

THE PLACE BETTING SYSTEM

This is one of the favorite Craps systems used by some of the so-called smart big-time gamblers. When chance is working in its favor, this system, which first made its appearance in 1940, appears so certain to win money that many a player using it has been told by casino bosses in no uncertain terms to scram and take his business elsewhere.

Here's the method of betting. The high roller usually bets the maximum limit, although lesser amounts can be wagered. For example, he puts $300 to win on each of the six place bets: 4, 5, 6, 8, 9 and 10, wagering a total of $1,800. The moment one of these numbers is made, he collects his winning bet and calls off the $1,500 bet on the remaining five place numbers. Place bets can be called down any time in most casinos throughout the country.

Whenever a FOUR or TEN is made the player wins $540 (at 9 to 5 odds). When a FIVE or NINE is made he wins $420 (at 7 to 5 odds). If a SIX or EIGHT is made he wins $350 (at 7 to 6 odds). The high roller and also the worried dice-game operator figure that he has six numbers, the 4, 5, 6, 8, 9 and 10, going for him, against the bank's lone number, 7. And because he believes he is only paying the bank a percentage on one place bet, he thinks he must eventually beat the bank.

Since those six place numbers can be made in 24 ways and the SEVEN can only be made in six ways, the odds are 4 to 1 in favor of the system player's winning either $540, $420 or $350. But if the losing SEVEN appears before one of the six place numbers is thrown, which is 1 in 5, the system player loses $1,800. Even so, it looks like a good bet to the system player because if he makes a couple of FOURS or TENS he's beating the game.

To find the fallacy here we must discover whether the player pays the bank a percentage on the bets he calls down, and if so, how much? To do this we must analyze a series of 36 bets.

Let's suppose that the system player in a single dice session makes 36 such $1,800 place bets, and let us assume that the dice fall exactly as probability predicts and each of the 36 combinations on the dice are made. Craps and ELEVENS will be made 6 times out of the 36 rolls, but since they do not affect a decision, we can ignore them and consider only 30 bets of $1,800 for a total of $54,000 wagered.

The numbers FOUR and TEN will each be made three times, or six times altogether, and the player retrieves his $1,800 plus $540 in winnings six times out of 30 for a total of $14,040. The numbers FIVE and NINE will each be made four times, or eight times altogether. The player will retrieve his $1,800 eight times plus $420 in winnings each of the eight times, for a total take-in of $17,760. The numbers SIX and EIGHT will be thrown five times each, a total of ten times, and the player retrieves his $1,800 plus $350 in winnings ten times, for a total of $21,500. These winning totals add to a grand win total of $53,300. Subtracting this win total from the $54,000 wagered, we get a loss of $700, or 1.296%.

This brings up one of the most unusual percentage problems in Craps. Why should this system player pay a smaller overall percentage than the percentage on any single place bet? This is because the system player in this instance is actually laying $1,800 to $540, $1,800 to $420, or $1,800 to $350, instead of taking the odds. However, when the percentage is computed on the actual money turnover ($10,800 lost on the 6 sevens and $10,000 won on the 24 place bets), the house percentage increases to 3.35%.

THE RIGHT AND WRONG WAY SYSTEM

This two-way betting system has been a conversation piece for many old-time Private Craps game hustlers for years. It recently popped up again in a booklet published by a Chicago gambling-supply house, and the writer assures the reader that he can beat any Bank Craps game simply by betting the dice to lose and win at the same time.

The writer advises the system player to bet heavily right from the start because in a short time management will realize he has a surefire system and will bar him from further playing. The idea is for the system player to win as much as he can before being barred.

Here's the method the system writer describes.

The system player walks up to a Bank Craps table and places a $60 bet on the don't pass or lose line before the come-out. The shooter on the come-out throws a point number, either 4, 5, 6, 8, 9 or 10, and the system player takes $60 worth of place odds on the point. (See pages 162 to 164 for place bet odds.)

You begin to see what the theory is now? If the shooter fails to make the point, the system player, who has taken $108 to $60 on the point FOUR (or TEN) will lose his place bet, but will win the $60 bet on the don't pass line, thus breaking even. But if the shooter makes the point FOUR, the system player loses the $60 bet on the don't pass line, but wins $108 on the FOUR, for a $48 profit. If the point number is FIVE or NINE, the system player breaks even or wins $24 on either point; on the points SIX or EIGHT, he breaks even or wins $10!

According to the author of this booklet, since the player must either break even or win, he can't lose barring naturals and craps on the come-out.

This statement leaves us breathless. Since this system is based on betting the don't pass line, it is utterly impossible to bar naturals and craps on the come-out.

But let's forget this little gem and go on to our analysis of what actually happens to the player who bets the system over a long Craps session.

Let's take 360 dice decisions and bet $60 wrong and right. We bet $60 on the don't pass line 360 times for a total of $21,600. Out of the 360 decisions, SEVEN or ELEVEN will appear 80 times on the come-out, losing the system player $4,800. Craps will appear 40 times, but since ten of these craps will be standoffs, due to the bar on the two sixes or the two aces, the system player will win only 30 times for a total of $1,800. The points FOUR or TEN will appear 60 times, compelling the system player to wager $60 each of the 60 times for a total of $3,600 more. The system player breaks even 40 times when the point is missed and earns $48 each of the 20 times it is made for a profit of $960. The points FIVE or NINE appear 80 times, compelling the system player to bet $60 each of the 80 times for a total of $4,800. He breaks even 48 times when the point is missed, and he wins $24 each of the 32 times it is made for a profit of $768. The points SIX and EIGHT will appear 100 times, and the player is forced to bet $60 each time for an additional total of $6,000. The system player breaks even the $54\%_{11}$ times when the point is missed, and he wins $10 on each of the $45\frac{5}{11}$ times it is made for a profit of $454.55.

If we add the system player's winnings of $1,800 on the craps, $960 on the FOURS and TENS, $768 on FIVES and NINES and the $454.55 on the SIXES and EIGHTS, we get a winning total of $3,982.55. Subtracting this total from the $4,800 our system player lost on the naturals, we find that his net loss is $817.45, and, since the system player risked a total of $36,000 playing the system, his rate of loss is 2.27%.

SCARNE'S BANK CRAPS SYSTEM

This is the Bank Craps betting system I used at the Craps tables I visited in this country during my casino survey before I was barred.

I used this system not to win money but to cut down my Craps losses during my survey. I selected the Bank Craps bets with the smallest house percentage and systemized them. The bets used were the pass line bet, come bet and free odds bet on the point which carried a house edge of .848%.

Neither the Craps dealers nor the casino bosses like to see this system used at their tables. Not because they are afraid it will break the bank—the dealers don't like it because it makes considerably more work for them than usual; the casino bosses don't like it because each bet made involved in the system gives the house the smallest favorable percentage at Bank Craps.

This system is not guaranteed to beat the bank because, like all other systems, the player is bucking adverse odds. But it will cut the bank's earning power to a rock-bottom minimum and increase your chances of winning as against those of the average Craps player.

Here's the method:

Bet $10 on the pass line before the come-out. If the shooter throws a natural or crap, again bet $10 on the pass line. If the shooter throws a point number, 4, 5, 6, 8, 9 or 10, you take the odds on the point. You received the correct odds on this bet since the bank levies no charge. (See page 164.)

On the next throw of the dice, you bet $10 on the come, and if a 4, 5, 6, 8, 9 or 10 is thrown, you take one chip's worth of odds on this number. You again receive the correct odds because of your come bet.

With a rate of loss of .848%, you can expect to pay $84.80 on $10,000 worth of action, and $848 on $100,000 worth of action. So, you see, all systems are worthless, even the best of them.

If you want to shave the bank's percentage down a bit more—to .832% —simply bet the don't pass and don't come space and lay the free odds.

8

ROULETTE: THE GLAMOUR CASINO GAME

Roulette, the glamour European casino game, is the favorite gambling game of millions of Americans. Visit any casino in Nevada, Atlantic City, Puerto Rico, the Bahamas, Aruba, Curaçao, Haiti, Europe and South America, and you will find that on the average three out of five players seated at a roulette table are women.

Roulette is said by some historians to have been invented in 1655 by the French scientist Blaise Pascal, during his monastic retreat, and first played in a makeshift casino in Paris. Other historians say it was invented by a French monk to help break the monotony of monastery life. Still others say it originated in an old Chinese game whose object was to arrange 37 statuettes of animals in a "magic square" of 666, but they fail to describe the method of play. They add that the game was later played in Tibet and eventually by French Dominican monks, one of whom transposed the statuettes into numbers from 0 to 36 and arranged them haphazardly along the rim of a revolving wheel. Since the early French wheels of the 1800s had both the 0 and 00, this theory does not sound plausible.

ROULETTE WHEELS—YESTERDAY AND TODAY

Despite considerable research, I have not found any reliable evidence on the true origin of the game, but I did discover that the modern game historians who say that the first Roulette wheels to appear in French casinos were identical with those used today in French and other European casinos are wrong. The *American Hoyle,* printed in the mid-1800s, describes in detail the playing rules and the design of the wheels and layouts used in France and America at that time. Both the French- and American-style Roulette of that day differed considerably in structure and rules of play from the present European and American wheels.

My research shows that from the day Roulette was first introduced into American casinos and up until about 1890 the American wheels were of a special design unlike the European wheels. They had 31 numbers and symbols: the numbers 1 through 28, a single 0, a double 00, and a picture of an American eagle which was the equivalent of a triple 000. When the ball dropped into either the 0, 00 or Eagle, the bank won all bets on the layout except those bet on the winning symbol. These winning single-number bets were paid off at odds of 27 for 1.* All other winning single-number bets also paid off at 27 for 1, and the only other bets permitted were bets on red and black, which paid even money, and on the four columns, each comprised of seven numbers, which paid off at 3 to 1. The bank's favorable percentages on this Roulette wheel were: single-number bet, $12\frac{28}{31}\%$; red or black color bet, $9\frac{21}{31}\%$, and seven-number-column bet, $9\frac{21}{31}\%$. This high percentage take for the bank is obviously the main reason why Roulette did not become popular in American casinos at that time.

The French Roulette wheel of the middle 1800s was built like the modern American wheel with its single 0 and double 00. Although there were 36 numbers, the bank paid off at odds of only 34 to 1 on a single-number bet. Also, the single 0 was black, the double 0 was red, and when the ball dropped into either the 0 or 00 all bets on the corresponding colors were considered *bars*. This meant that when the ball dropped in the single 0 all bets on black neither won nor lost, and when the ball dropped in the double 0 all bets on red neither won nor lost. We have the same situation today in Bank Craps with its bar on the don't pass line of either two aces, two sixes or the ace-deuce (see pages 152 and 154–155). There is no doubt in my mind that the bar used at Bank Craps was taken from French Roulette.

Roulette wheels found today in Monte Carlo, Deauville, San Remo and other European casinos have 36 numbers (1 to 36) and a single zero (0). When zero appears, all bets paid off at even money such as red, black, odd or even are "imprisoned" and their ultimate fate is determined by the next spin of the wheel. They are either lost or are returned to the winning player, who gets back only his original bet. The player loses half of his wager on red, black, odd, even, 1–18 and 19–36 when the zero appears. The bank's favorable percentage, in this case on red, black, odd, even, 1–18, or 19–36, is $1\frac{13}{37}\%$, and on all other types of bets it is $2\frac{26}{37}\%$.

The modern American-style Roulette wheel with its single 0 and double 0 is similar to the wheel discarded by French and European casino operators decades ago. This indicates that the first American Roulette op-

---

* In odds terms this is 26 to 1. If a player bet $1, the Roulette dealer would first collect his $1 winning bet, then pay him $27. The player was really collecting $26 in winnings, and getting back the $1 bet. This misdirective device, which led some players to think they were winning more than they really did, is no longer used at Roulette. The odds are quoted at 26 to 1, the dealer pays $26, and the winning bet is left on the table. This procedure tends to give the casino additional action because the player may make the bet again by leaving his bet on the layout. This former gimmick of using the word *for* in odds quotes is, however, still found on many American Craps layouts.

erators of the early colonial days used the early French-style wheel with its 28 numbers and three symbols for a total of 31, rather than the 36 numbers and single zero used in European casinos today.

These changes in Roulette wheels and layouts are caused by the fact that players shy away from the game after suffering constant losses and after discovering the percentage they must buck. When this happens, the operators, in an attempt to retrieve their lost business, make changes which give the player a better percentage break. Example: the first Roulette wheels in American casinos had the 0, 00 and Eagle. Present-day wheels have the single 0 and the double 0. I predict that soon after this book hits the bookstores American Roulette wheels will have only the single 0, as do the present European wheels.

Fortunes have been won and lost by women and men at Roulette. The biggest Roulette winnings I recently witnessed were those of a Japanese businessman at Mike McLaney's swank Royal Haitian Hotel Casino in Port-au-Prince, Haiti. The Japanese Roulette player asked for, and McLaney agreed to, a $500 limit on straight, splits, corners, streets, columns and sections bets. After an hour's play, McLaney had the Japanese down $200,000. However, this wasn't for long. The Japanese in the next three hours of play not only recouped his $200,000 loss but quit the game a $300,000 winner. Quite a profitable business trip for the Japanese Roulette player.

A California woman, the wife of a retired oil magnate, once confided to me that during the past five years her total losses at Roulette in European and American casinos exceeded the $3 million mark.

The largest sum of money known to have been lost at a single roulette session in the United States was $1,250,000 lost by an American industrialist at a Saratoga casino one evening during the month of August 1946. The special limit put into effect for the industrialist was $25,000 on an even-money bet and $1,000 on a single number, with an additional $1,000 any way he could reach the number, such as a split, corner, or street bet. For example, a $2,000 limit bet on a single winning number paid $72,000 ($70,000 in winnings plus the original $2,000 wager).

P.S. The high limit didn't worry the casino operators because the wheel was gaffed! The industrialist settled his losses for $500,000.

Europeans and Latin Americans play Roulette much more than Americans do, but Roulette tables can now be found in most legal and illegal gambling casinos in this country, especially in the luxury rug joints. More than any other casino game, Roulette has an aura of glamour that makes it especially attractive to women. When a woman enters a casino for the first time, it is almost a sure bet that, after playing the slot machines, the first game she tries will be Roulette.

This is the game which the handsome hero and well-dressed heroine have played for years in countless motion pictures, books and short stories. It has been publicized as the game of millionaire playboys, of kings and princes. It is celebrated in many stories of fortunes won and lost, of mathematical wizards who have spent years developing Roulette systems, and even in a song: "The Man Who Broke the Bank at Monte Carlo." Roulette is the world's oldest banking game still in operation, and through the years it has given rise to many true stories, as well as much that is legend and myth.

A great part of Roulette's fascination also lies in the beauty and color of the game. The surface of the handsome mahogany table is covered with a blazing green cloth which bears the bright gold, red and black of the layout. The chromium separators between the numbered pockets on the wheel's rim glitter and dance in the bright light as the wheel spins. The varied colors of the wheel checks stacked on the table's apron and before the croupier and scattered on the layout's betting spaces, the evening clothes of the women, the formal dress of the men, the courteous croupiers —all add to the enticing picture.

The neophyte soon discovers that although the betting layout looks complicated the game is easy to learn. The women are also attracted by the odds the bank offers, which are higher than most other casino games. One chip on a straight winning number is paid off at 35 to 1 and the player receives a stack of 20 and a stack of 15 chips.

Before entering on a detailed discussion of the game, we need to examine the equipment used. In the description that follows you will find a detailed explanation of the construction and inner workings of the Roulette wheel itself.

STANDARD ROULETTE EQUIPMENT

Roulette tables: There are two styles of Roulette tables found in American casinos. One is the standard table, which has one betting layout with the Roulette wheel at one end; the other, called the double-end table, has two layouts with the wheel in the center between them.

Roulette layout: The layout is a multicolored design printed on green baize that covers the players' side of the table and forms the betting section. The main portion of the design is comprised of 36 numbered rectangular spaces arranged in three long columns of 12 spaces each. The spaces at the head of the columns are numbered 1, 2, 3, and are nearest the wheel. The numbering continues in sequence across the columns, ending with 34, 35 and 36 at the foot of the columns farthest from the wheel. Directly below these numbers are three blank spaces. A chip placed on one of these indicates that the player is betting on the 12 numbers on the long column directly above the space on which the chip rests. (On some layouts these squares are marked "2 to 1" and are located on the player's side of the table.)

Along one side of the long columns are three rectangular spaces marked "1st 12," "2nd 12" and "3rd 12." A chip placed on one of these spaces indicates that the player is betting on the first 12 numbers, 1 through 12; on the second 12 numbers, 13 through 24, or on the third 12 numbers, 25 through 36.

Next to these are six more spaces which read from left to right: "1–18," "Even," "Red," "Black," "Odd," "19–36." Above the three long columns are two spaces with pointed tops containing the figures 0 and 00.

Roulette balls: The balls used are made of ivory or plastic. They vary in size from ½ inch to ¾ inch in diameter.

Wheel checks, or chips: The standard Roulette table employs five, six or seven sets of wheel checks (usually called chips). Each set is differently colored, each consists of 300 chips, and there is one set for each player. The chips are usually valued at 25¢ each, and the minimum number a player can buy is 20, $5 worth. Some sawdust joints also sell 5¢ and 10¢ chips. The color of the chips indicates the player, not the value of the chips. If a player wishes to buy 50¢ or $1 chips, the croupier places a 50¢ or $1 marker on top of the stack of chips in the table's chip rack whose color corresponds to the chips purchased. Five-dollar and $25 chips, which may be used at any gambling table in the casino, may also be purchased. These, unlike the other chips, do have a color indicating value. Sometimes $100, $500, or $1,000 chips are used when dealing a big money Roulette game in Las Vegas.

Roulette wheels: There are two styles. The American wheel has 36 numbers and the signs 0 and 00. The French or European wheel, which has 36 numbers and only the single 0, is found mostly in European and South American casinos and is seldom seen in this country.

The American wheels used in the United States and the Caribbean islands are, except for the double 0, similar in construction to the French wheels. They are made up of two separate parts; the table, which is stationary, and the wheel itself, which is movable and manually rotated.

Most of the table's area consists of the betting section and a large wooden, bowl-shaped recess called the *bowl*. This contains the wheel, which is called the *wheel head*. The interior diameter of the bowl is approximately 32 inches. It has a back track made of sturdy wood which contains an inch-wide groove running around the bowl's circumference. It is in this groove that the croupier spins the Roulette ball. When the speed of the ball diminishes it falls on to the bottom track of the bowl. The revolving wheel head and the bottom track are marked off by black lines into eight equal sections. In the center of each section on the bottom track there is a small metal obstacle 2 inches long, ½ inch wide and ½ inch thick. These obstacles are placed alternately vertically and horizontally and the rolling ball, as it strikes them, is given a random and unpredictable motion.

The bowl's bottom underneath the wheel is open, and below it there is a flat wooden base from the center of which rises a steel spindle, ¼ inch in diameter and 4 inches high.

The wheel head, the only moving part, consists of a solid wooden disk or plate, slightly convex in shape. Around its rim are metal partitions known as *separators* or *frets,* and the compartments or pockets between these are called *canoes* by Roulette croupiers. These pockets are metal, painted alternately red and black, except for two pockets which are green. Each of the red and black compartments bears a number from 1 to 36 in gold. The green pockets carry the signs 0 and 00, also in gold.

Most players and croupiers believe that the numbers 1 through 36 are arranged on the rim of the wheel head in a haphazard manner, except that red and black numbers alternate. There is nothing haphazard about the arrangement. An attempt has been made to alternate low, high, odd and even numbers as well as the red and black colors in such a way that each group of numbers and each color is spaced out in a mathematically balanced fashion. A perfect mathematical balance is not possible, since the sum of the numbers 1 through 36 is 666, and the 18 odd numbers add to only 324, while the 18 even numbers add to 342. In order to attain the best possible mathematical balance, Roulette manufacturers use the following arrangement:

The signs 0 and 00 are directly opposite each other on the wheel-head

Roulette wheel showing number arrangement.

rim, separated on each side by 18 numbers. The 0 pocket is between two black-numbered pockets and the colors alternate in both directions around the wheel, ending in two red pockets, one on each side of the 00. Odd numbers alternate with even numbers. In order to get the best possible distribution of high and low numbers, the sum of each two successive numbers of the same color must equal 37. There are two exceptions: the numbers 9 and 28 and the numbers 10 and 27 are not the same color; each pair is made up of a red and a black number.

A shining steel ornament rises about eight inches above the exact center of the disk. Inside it, a four-inch hole runs upward from its bottom. This fits over the steel spindle, crowned with a ball bearing, which rises from the center of the bowl. The wheel, perfectly balanced at its center on this single ball bearing, spins in an almost frictionless, smooth and precise manner.

ROULETTE PERSONNEL AND THEIR DUTIES

A Roulette table with a single layout is usually worked by two croupiers. A double-end table with two layouts is operated by either three or four croupiers. The croupier who spins the wheel and deals the game is called the *wheel roller* by casino employees. To keep our explanation simple we'll call him the *dealer,* and call his assistant a *croupier.* We will describe the operation of a table with a single layout.

The dealer is in charge of the conduct of the game. His main duties are selling chips to players, spinning the wheel, throwing the Roulette ball, announcing winners, collecting losing bets and paying off winning bets. The croupier separates and stacks the losing chips that have been collected or swept from the layout by the dealer. He stacks the chips in piles of 20 of the same color and places them in the chip rack on the table's apron. He helps the dealer pay off winning bets by stacking the correct number of chips in a convenient place to the left of the table's apron.

All large casinos use an additional employee, the *pit boss* or *inspector.* He stands in the pit ring, watches the game and is in charge of its conduct. He makes out cash-out, credit and fill slips, corrects any errors made by the croupiers or players and watches for cheating.

SCARNE'S RULES FOR PLAYING ROULETTE

The players begin making their bets placing chips on the spaces of the layout in any manner permitted by the rules. The dealer starts the wheel spinning in a counterclockwise direction, then flips the ball on to the bowl's back track so that it travels clockwise. Players may continue placing bets while wheel and ball are in motion until the dealer calls: "No more bets!" He does this as the ball slows down and is about to drop off the back track. Bets placed on the layout after this announcement are not valid and must be returned to the player or players.

When the ball falls and comes to rest between any two metal partitions of the wheel, it marks the winning number, a zero or double zero, the winning color, and any other permitted bet that pertains to a winning number or symbol. The dealer immediately announces the winning number and its color, and he points with his index finger to the corresponding number on the layout. Some dealers place a plastic peg (a half inch in diameter and two inches tall) on the winning number for all to see. He collects all losing bets, not disturbing the chips resting on winning spaces, and pays off the winner or winners with the correct amount of chips due each winning bet. The signs 0 and 00 win for the bank all bets except those placed on 0 and 00.

On the first spin the dealer has no fixed point from which to spin the wheel or ball. Thereafter he must spin both from the winning pocket into which the ball dropped. The croupier dealing the wheel is obliged to spin the ball with the hand nearest the wheel.

Some casinos give the player the privilege of asking the inspector or casino operator to substitute another dealer, and this may be done provided one or more of the other players at the table do not object. No such substitution may take place until after the dealer has thrown the ball five times.

POSSIBLE ROULETTE BETS, ODDS AND PERCENTAGES

Since Roulette layouts do not vary in bets permitted, odds offered and percentages against the player, the following text covers all of the common bets permitted on any layout.

Straight bet or single-number bet: The player places his chips squarely on one number on the layout, making certain that the chips do not touch any of the lines enclosing the number. This indicates that the player is betting that number to win. Since there are 36 numbers on the wheel, plus the signs 0 and 00, making a total of 38, the correct odds are 37 to 1. The bank pays off at 35 to 1 and consequently has the advantage of the 0 and 00. In terms of percentage this is $\frac{2}{38}$ of 100, or $5\frac{5}{19}\%$ (about 26¢ on a $5 bet).

The signs 0 and 00: These can be played the same as any straight or single-number bet. The bank's favorable percentage is the same as on a straight bet: $5\frac{5}{19}\%$ (about 26¢ on a $5 bet).

Split bet or two-number bet: The player places his chips directly on any line separating any two numbers. If the winning number is one of the two wagered on, the player wins.
Payoff odds: 17 to 1
Correct odds: 18 to 1
Percentage favoring bank: $5\frac{5}{19}\%$ (about 26¢ on a $5 bet)

Street bet or three-number bet: The player places his chip or chips on the outside line of the layout. This indicates that he is betting the three numbers opposite the chips, going across the layout. If the winning number is one of these three the player wins.

Payoff odds: 11 to 1

Correct odds: 11⅔ to 1

Percentage favoring bank: 5⁵⁄₁₉% (about 26¢ on a $5 bet)

Square bet, quarter bet, corner bet or four-number bet: The player places his chips on the intersection of the lines between any four numbers. If any one of these four numbers wins the player collects.

Payoff odds: 8 to 1

Correct odds: 8½ to 1

Percentage favoring bank: 5⁵⁄₁₉% (about 26¢ on a $5 bet)

Line bet or five-number bet: The player places his chips on the line separating the 1, 2, 3 from the 0 and 00 spaces at a corner intersection. This indicates that he is betting that one of the numbers 1, 2, 3, or 0 or 00 will win.

Payoff odds: 6 to 1

Correct odds: 6⅗ to 1

Percentage favoring bank: 7¹⁷⁄₁₉% (about 39¢ on a $5 bet)

Note that the house percentage differs from the 5⁵⁄₁₉% which is the bank's edge on all other Roulette bets. From the player's viewpoint it is therefore a bet to avoid because it has 2¹²⁄₁₉% more against the player.

Line bet or six-number bet: The player places his chips on the intersection of the side line and a line between two "streets." If any of these six numbers wins, the player collects.

Payoff odds: 5 to 1

Correct odds: 5⅓ to 1

Percentage favoring bank: 5⁵⁄₁₉% (about 26¢ on a $5 bet)

Column bet or 12-number bet: The player places his chips on one of the three blank spaces at the bottom of the layout (some layouts have three squares marked "1st," "2nd," "3rd"). This indicates that the player is betting the 12 vertical numbers above the space wagered on.

Payoff odds: 2 to 1

Correct odds: 2⅙ to 1

Percentage favoring bank: 5⁵⁄₁₉% (about 26¢ on a $5 bet)

Dozens or 12-number bet: The player places his chips on one of the spaces of the layout marked "1st 12," "2nd 12" or "3rd 12." The 1st 12 indicates that the player is betting on the numbers 1 to 12 inclusive; the

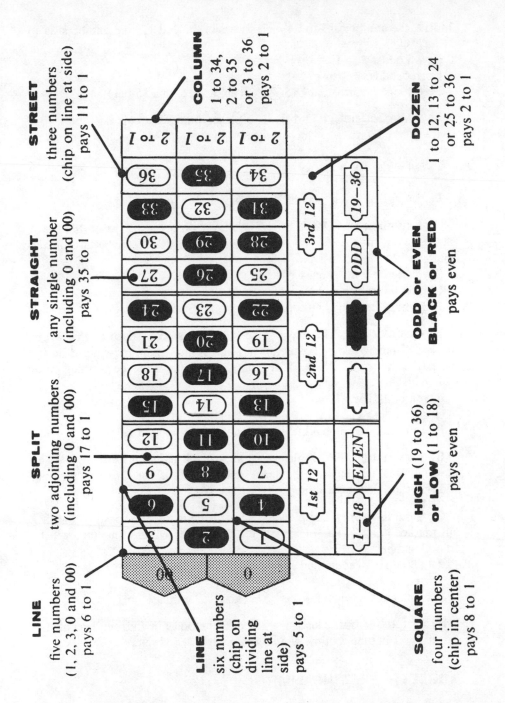

COLUMN
1 to 34,
2 to 35
or 3 to 36
pays 2 to 1

DOZEN
1 to 12, 13 to 24
or 25 to 36
pays 2 to 1

STREET
three numbers
(chip on line at side)
pays 11 to 1

STRAIGHT
any single number
(including 0 and 00)
pays 35 to 1

SPLIT
two adjoining numbers
(including 0 and 00)
pays 17 to 1

LINE
five numbers
(1, 2, 3, 0 and 00)
pays 6 to 1

LINE
six numbers
(chip on
dividing
line at
side)
pays 5 to 1

ODD or EVEN
BLACK or RED
pays even

HIGH (19 to 36)
or LOW (1 to 18)
pays even

SQUARE
four numbers
(chip in center)
pays 8 to 1

Players indicate the bet or bets they make by the placement of chips on the layout as shown here.

2nd 12, the numbers 13 to 24 inclusive, and the 3rd 12, the numbers 25 to 36 inclusive.
Payoff odds: 2 to 1
Correct odds: $2\frac{1}{6}$ to 1
Percentage favoring bank: $5\frac{5}{19}\%$ (about 26¢ on a $5 bet)

Low-number bet (1 to 18): The player places his chips on the layout space marked 1 to 18, which indicates that he is betting on the numbers 1 to 18 inclusive.
Payoff odds: Even money
Correct odds: $1\frac{1}{9}$ to 1
Percentage favoring bank: $5\frac{5}{19}\%$ (about 26¢ on a $5 bet)

High-number bet (19 to 36): The player places his chips on the space of the layout marked 19 to 36, which indicates that he is betting on the numbers 19 to 36 inclusive.
Payoff odds: Even money
Correct odds: $1\frac{1}{9}$ to 1
Percentage favoring bank: $5\frac{5}{19}\%$ (about 26¢ on a $5 bet)

Black color bet: The player places his chips on a space of the layout marked "Black." (Some layouts have a large black diamond-shaped design instead of the word "Black.") The player is betting that the winning color will be black.
Payoff odds. Even money
Correct odds: $1\frac{1}{9}$ to 1
Percentage favoring bank: $5\frac{5}{19}\%$ (about 26¢ on a $5 bet)

Red color bet: This is the same as a black color bet except that the player places his chips on the space marked "Red," or the red diamond, and is betting that the winning color will be red.

Odd-number bet: The player places his chips on the space of the layout marked "Odd." The player is betting that the winning number will be an odd number.
Payoff odds: Even money
Correct odds: $1\frac{1}{9}$ to 1
Percentage favoring bank: $5\frac{5}{19}\%$ (about 26¢ on a $5 bet)

Even-number bet: This is the same as the odd-number bet, except that the player is betting that the winning number will be even.

ROULETTE BETTING LIMITS

The maximum amounts permitted to be wagered on different spaces of the layout vary with each casino. The minimum bet allowed is usually four chips, be they 5¢, 10¢ or 25¢ chips. A player betting 25¢ chips must bet a minimum of four chips on one spin of the wheel, although the four chips can be spread over the spaces on the layout as desired, excluding even-money and 2 to 1 spaces. A minimum of four chips or a bet valued as $1 is required on all even-money or 2 to 1 bets.

The standard maximum betting limits in Nevada are as follows: $100 on a straight, split, street, corner or line bet and $1,000 on any 2 to 1 or even-money bet. However, major casinos in Nevada will up their maximum betting limits at the sight of a high roller. Casinos in the Bahamas adhere to the same betting rules as Nevada. Puerto Rican casinos, where betting limits are government regulated, and various other casinos in the Caribbean permit the following maximum limits: $10 on a single-number bet and any other way you can reach it (split, street, corner, line); $180 on black, red, odd, even, high and low, and $120 on dozens and columns. Although maximum limits may vary from casino to casino, the following maximum limits on all possible roulette bets are fairly standard in most major casinos throughout the world:

MAXIMUM BETTING LIMITS AND PAYOFF ODDS

Type of Bet	Maximum Limit	Bank's Payoff Odds
Straight	$100	35 to 1
Split	100	17 to 1
Street	100	11 to 1
Quarter or corner	100	8 to 1
Line (1–2–3–0–00)	100	6 to 1
Line (six numbers)	100	5 to 1
Columns	500	2 to 1
1st, 2nd, 3rd dozen	500	2 to 1
Color (red or black)	1,000	Even
Even	1,000	Even
Odd	1,000	Even
1 to 18 (low)	1,000	Even
19 to 36 (high)	1,000	Even

A single number may also be played with $100 straight and another $100 placed on split, corner, street, line or other bets. In other words, a $100 maximum can also be bet any way you can reach the number. Many casino operators will increase these limits for big-time bettors. Some casinos have lower maximum betting limits than those listed above. Usually, when the limit on one bet is smaller, the limits on all others are proportionally smaller. Example: If the maximum straight bet of $100 is reduced to $25, all other bets would also be reduced by about 60%.

THE $400,000 ROULETTE WIN AT HARRAH'S CASINO

Roulette happens to be a very tricky game, and raising the standard maximum betting limits may not be too wise if the player is mathematically smart and knows more about betting systems than the casino manager suspects. This is especially true when the deviations from the standard maximum limits are increased from $500 to $7,000. Here's a good instance of this.

While on a recent casino inspection tour at the Curaçao Hilton Casino in the Netherlands Antilles, I received several long-distance telephone calls from the casino manager of Harrah's Casino in Lake Tahoe, Nevada, asking me to make a hurried trip there to analyze a Roulette betting system being used by a high roller. The first phone call I received informed me that the high roller had won $250,000 in five days of play, an average of $50,000 per day. Since my mission in Curaçao was not completed, I asked the casino manager to call me back in three days. When I received the phone call three days later, he informed me that the high roller was now a $400,000 winner.

As I could not leave the islands at the time, I asked the excited casino manager to brief me about the details of the player's system. This is what he told me: The high-rolling Roulette player asked for special limits before he began his play. After some back-and-forth bickering, the casino manager agreed to a $7,000 maximum betting limit and a $25 minimum on all 2 to1 and even-money bets (red, black, odd, even, high, low, dozens and columns). In addition, a $400 maximum limit and a $25 minimum bet were permitted on a straight, split, corner, street and line bet.

After analyzing the data the casino manager had given me, I had the answer to the system. The high roller was making use of a sophisticated progressive system betting on the color black. That is, he used an irregular progressive betting system, sometimes doubling his previous bet, sometimes betting the same amount as his previous bet, and sometimes nearly tripling the size of a previously lost bet. And whenever he was a winner of $100 or more, he began his progressive system all over again.

To best describe this progressive system, let us assume that Mr. High Roller lost ten consecutive bets. His bets would be made as follows: He would start with a $25 bet on black and continue his black progressive system as follows: $50, $50, $75, $100, $100, $500, $1,500, $3,500, $7,000 for a total loss of $12,900. The chance of Mr. High Roller losing ten black bets in a row is about 1 in 970. If Mr. High Roller lost nine consecutive bets and won the tenth bet, his profit would be $1,100 and he would start his progressive system again with $25 for his first bet. If he lost eight consecutive bets and won the ninth bet, his profit still would be $1,100 and he would start his system anew. If he lost seven consecutive bets and won the eighth, he would win $600 and start his progressive system over again. If he lost six consecutive bets and won the seventh, his profit would be $100 and he would start his system anew. The most he could stand to lose on five consecutive losing bets would be $300. The $400 maximum betting limit on the straight, split, corner, street and line bets were also placed on the layout in an irregular fashion, as were bets on the color black.

After explaining to the casino manager the reason for the success of the high roller's betting system, I instructed the manager to increase the minimum betting limit on the black and all other 2 to 1 and even-money bets from $25 to $100. His mistake, I explained was not in giving Mr. High Roller the $7,000 limit but in giving him a $25 minimum limit. This small limit permitted the high roller to double each previous losing bet nine consecutive times and still show a profit: for example, $25, $50, $100, $200, $400, $800, $1,600, $3,200, $6,400. The spread between the low and the high limit given by the casino manager violated the basic concept of professional gambling limits which, of course, is not to allow more than six or seven consecutive doublings up. For instance, Puerto Rican casinos have a $200 maximum limit and a $5 minimum. Note the double-up sequence: $5, $10, 20, $40, 80, $160, cannot bet $320. This also holds true for a maximum of $300 and a $5 minimum. A $500 maximum limit and a $5 minimum permits only seven consecutive double-up bets. P.S. The introduction of the $100 minimum bet by the casino manager was first refused by Mr. High Roller, but he eventually went along with it. In the end, he lost the $400,000 back to the house.

THE $1 MILLION ROULETTE LOSS AT THE M-G-M GRAND HOTEL CASINO

Several years ago an Arabian prince came to Las Vegas with a million dollars in cash to try to beat the Roulette tables. His first stop was at Caesars Palace. The management provided him with a limit of $600 a number. This was $600 any way he could get to it—with splits, corners, streets, columns and sections. The Prince's first bet was $600 on number 11, $600 on each of the four splits, and $600 on each of the four corners for a total of $5,400 a spin. After the Prince had placed his bets, the croupier started the wheel spinning in a counterclockwise direction, then flipped the ball clockwise on the Roulette wheel's back track. Bob Wilkinson, Caesars capable pit boss, alert as always, watched as the little Roulette ball dropped into the Prince's lucky number 11 for an $81,000 winning payoff. The Prince varied his play, sometimes circling a single number, other times circling two, three, or four numbers. At the end of five hours' of play and an $850,000 loss, the Prince called for an hour's recess in play, saying that he was hungry and tired. The management prepared a deluxe spread to be served at the Roulette table, the food from the hotel's Bacchanal Room which is as fine as any that can be obtained in Las Vegas. When the waiter placed the gourmet spread on the apron of the Roulette table, the Prince took one look and asked if there was a McDonald's in town.

Then the Prince hopped a cab, rode to McDonald's, picked up two Big Macs, and returned with them to the casino. While eating his sandwiches he again began to play, his luck began to turn, and in a couple of hours he had recouped his $850,000 loss and called it a day.

The next day the Prince visited the M-G-M Grand Hotel Casino just across the street from Caesars Palace and received the same Roulette limits he had received at Caesars Palace. At the Grand Hotel Roulette table the Prince ran into a streak of bad luck and lost his million in cash. The public relations director of the Grand Hotel released the million-dollar-loss story to the wire services. Result—he got fired. Casinos only like player-winning publicity to be reported, not player losses. Reporting player losses is bad for business.

ROULETTE BETTING SYSTEMS

Undoubtedly more betting systems have been created in an effort to beat the bank at Roulette than at any other casino game. Every now and then one of our national magazines carries an article describing a surefire system for winning at Roulette. The authors of these articles usually swear that the system was successfully used by a friend at Monte Carlo and promise the reader that if he is not greedy he can earn $50 to $100 a week playing the system. I am sure that some of these magazine editors must know better. They apparently print the articles because they know they will sell magazines, and they are not much concerned about the fact that some readers may actually try the system and lose their shirts. I do know that whenever an article touting a system appears in print the casino operators silently thank the author, editor and publisher.

I recently saw a young lady lose $5,000 at a Roulette table in a Las Vegas Strip casino playing a system which had been described in a leading men's magazine. I am sure she would never have lost so much if she had not believed implicitly that the system was workable. When I told her afterward that the only thing the system did was to help her lose her money faster, she replied that she had won several hundred dollars using the same system several months before and wanted to know how I explained that. I said, "That's easy. You won simply because you had a streak of good luck. The system had nothing to do with it."

Whenever a player wins a little money using a system, he is convinced that he has found one that works and immediately envisions himself winning great sums. And if a system player has a winning streak that lasts for a month or so he will spend so much time thinking about the millions that will soon be his that he will never get any sleep. Systems are even bad for a player's health.

THE MARTINGALE AND GREAT MARTINGALE SYSTEMS

The two oldest and most popular Roulette betting systems in casinos the world over are the Martingale and the Great Martingale. The basic idea of the Martingale system is that whenever a player loses a bet, he doubles or increases his next bet or bets until he makes a win that recoups all his previous losses and leaves him with a one-unit profit. Though it was invented for Roulette, the Martingale is used in many games in which the payoff odds are even or about even, like the red, black, odd, even, high or low bets made at Roulette, the banker or player's bets at Baccarat and the pass and don't pass line bets at Bank Craps.

The Great Martingale is based on the player's doubling his previous losing bet and added one unit. For example, $1 + 2 = 3$, $6 + 1 = 7$, $14 + 1 = 15$, $30 + 1 = 31$, etc. The system player must win, so he believes, the logic being that if he keeps betting the same even-money bet (red, black, odd, even, high, or low) he must win sooner or later.

Let's analyze this system: The system player bets $5. If he loses, he doubles his bet and adds $5 to it making his second bet $15. If he loses again, he doubles his bet and adds $5 for a total of $35. On paper, five consecutive losses and one win look like this:

Number of Bets	Lose	Win	Total Losses
1	$ 5		$ 5
2	15		20
3	35		55
4	75		130
5	155		285
6		$315	—
	Won	$315	
	Lost	−285	
	Profit	$ 30	

If the player wins the sixth bet, he recoups all his losses and makes a $30 profit. If he starts with enough money to cover seven consecutive losing bets ($1,235), it looks like a sure thing he'll catch one winner out of seven spins of the wheel. If he plays the system several times a day, he can spend the rest of his vacation having fun. After all, how often does the same color come up seven times in a row? It sounds wonderful. But, first of all, if he loses six times in a row, that's the end of his Great Martingale system. He will have lost a total of $600. His next bet must be $635 in order to make $35. And he can't make that bet because the maximum bet permitted in most casinos is $500. If he bets $500 instead of $635, his predicament becomes worse: he's placing a bet which may cause him to lose a total of $1,100, and the best thing that can happen to him is that he will lose a total of $100. If he believes it's not possible for an even-choice bet (red, black, odd, even, high or low) to lose seven times in a row, I would like to point out that the odds state that it is expected to happen about once in every 121 spins of the wheel.

D'ALEMBERT SYSTEM

The most popular roulette system used by players at Monte Carlo and Latin American casinos is the d'Alembert system. It is based on what its proponents call the "law of equilibrium." This is nothing more than the doctrine of the maturity of chances, which mathematicians call the gambler's fallacy (see page 325). The theory is that any two opposite chances, such as red and black, odd and even, must sooner or later win an equal number of times. If red, for instance, dominates for a series of spins, it is only a question of time until black will make up its retard. The d'Alembert system player, therefore, after every losing bet, adds an additional chip or chips to his bet on the next spin, and after every winning bet, reduces his bet by one or more chips. These players misinterpret the theory of probability. They think that opposite chances will even up in a short run, whereas probability theory only gives an approximate statement of what can be expected to happen in a very long run.

The bank's favorable advantage of the 0 and 00 will, in the long run, break all the players.

CANCELLATION SYSTEM

Players who have never been in a casino or seen Roulette played are always impressed by the stories they have read or heard about some mathematics professor who, without even having seen the game played, has spent years doping out a Roulette system. I have met several hundred men and women who have never set foot inside a casino who believe they have a winning Roulette system, and most of them, ironically, are intelligent, well-educated people.

One of them once phoned me at my home from Dallas, Texas, with the exciting news that after ten years she had developed the perfect system. Mrs. Blank, as I shall call her, offered to let me in on this marvelous get-rich-quick system if I would deposit $15,000 to her credit in her Dallas bank, and added that if I was able to find a flaw in the system the money would be returned to me. If I failed to find a flaw in it, then she would keep the $15,000 and I could go to Vegas, use the system and win it back in an evening of play.

When I pointed out that this proposition already had one flaw because the Las Vegas operators won't permit me to play at their dice or Roulette tables she suggested that I could easily get some friend to play the system for me. I told her to read the chapter on systems in *Scarne on Dice* which would tell her what I thought of systems in general. "I have," she replied, "but those were dice systems; mine is for Roulette." She thought she had an answer for everything and she ran up quite a phone bill before I could shake her, which I did by saying that I might be playing a convention date in Dallas shortly and that I would look her up when I got there.

I heard no more from her until one day in February 1959 a woman walked up to me in the casino of the Caribe Hilton Hotel in San Juan, Puerto Rico, where I was then, and still am, gambling consultant. It was Mrs. Blank.

"My husband and I are spending our vacation here," she said.

"How is that perfect system of yours working?" I asked.

She replied, "My husband has been playing it here all week. He's won an average of $100 for each night's play. So, you see, Mr. Scarne, it does work."

"Shouldn't you warn your husband," I asked, "that I'm here? I might learn your system by watching him play."

She shook her head. "We discovered that your casino manager knows it already."

"I saved myself the fifteen grand you wanted for it, didn't I?"

She laughed. "Yes. I guess it isn't worth quite as much as I thought then. But it still works."

Just then a man walked up to her and said, "I just won another $110 at the Roulette table. We're $868 ahead of the game on eight nights' play."

Mrs. Blank introduced me to her husband, who turned out to be a professor of psychology at a Texas college. I had seen him playing at the table, and I knew the system he was using. System gamblers at Monte Carlo have used it for years and it has appeared in several magazines under different names. Gamblers call it the Cancellation system.

It consists in writing down a column of figures in serial order beginning with 1. Suppose we use the sequence 1, 2, 3, 4, 5, 6, 7, 8, 9, 10. The player begins by betting the total of the top and bottom figures—in this instance, 11 chips. If he wins, he crosses out the top and bottom figures and then bets the total of the new top and bottom figures—in this case, 9 + 2, or 11. If the player loses, he adds the amount lost at the bottom of the column and then bets the total of the new top and bottom figures. In this instance he would bet 11 + 2, or 13 chips. This procedure of betting and crossing out and adding numbers continues until all the numbers in the column have been crossed out.

As in the Progressive or Double-Up system, the player must increase the amount of his bet after each loss. In the Cancellation system the player sticks to bets which pay even money, and the theory is that since he crosses out two numbers of his series when he wins and adds only one number when he loses, he must eventually cross out all the numbers. When this happens, he will have won 55 betting units.

On paper it looks good, and I don't blame Mrs. Blank for thinking she and her husband were on to a good thing. But, as she had already found out, there's no fortune in it. Her husband wasn't winning $15,000 in a night's play as she originally thought could be done; he was winning small amounts. What she still didn't know was that if he continued using the system he would lose in the end.

There are several catches. First, of course, is the fact that the player is forgetting that 0 and 00 win for the house. In the long run the player will lose 38 bets for each 36 that he wins. Even with the system he is still bucking that house advantage of $5\frac{5}{19}\%$.

The Cancellation system, like the Progressive or Double-Up system and others, sooner or later is interrupted by the fact that the player goes broke. Since in this system the player increases his bets by small amounts, it takes him longer until his bets increase to the point where he is stopped by the house limit. But when a long losing streak hits the player he may find himself so far in the hole that he has reached the limit of his own bankroll. Or he discovers that the constantly increasing size of his bets has put him in the position of having to risk a large amount of money to win a small amount. At this point, afraid that the losing streak will continue, he quits a loser, saying, "Well, it didn't work that time. I'll try again tomorrow."

Another catch is that if the table is busy the croupier views this process of placing a long series of small bets with distaste. The player is giving him a lot of work and he is very likely to drop a broad hint that he doesn't want your business. "Look, buddy," he'll say, "play your system somewhere else. We're busy now."

It doesn't matter how you place your bets; in the long run you can't beat the $5\frac{5}{19}\%$ that the Roulette bank has stacked against you.

SYSTEM PLAYERS

Thousands of inveterate Roulette players refuse to believe this. Many of them haunt the casinos day after day, endlessly recording statistics, noting how often certain numbers, colors or combinations have or have not appeared in the last few hours, nights and even weeks. No casino operator is ever worried that these players will come up with a workable system. In fact, on request, they will supply the addict with a chart on which the Roulette numbers are printed so that he can save time, paper and pencil by merely checking off the winning numbers instead of having to write them down.

Some addicts compile all this data for a different reason. They compare their statistics with all sorts of probability calculations, hoping to find some indication that the wheel is biased. A wheel very seldom goes haywire of its own accord, and I can't think of any fault a wheel could develop by itself that would not be spotted by the croupiers in very short order.

Other addicts believe that their figures will indicate when a wheel has been gaffed and allow them to take advantage of it. The only advantage these addicts have is that they spend so much time making notes that they do less betting and hence lose less money.

THE MENTAL BET

Another type of Roulette watcher is the character who stands for hours by the wheel making mental bets. When he has lost a number of bets in succession he begins to play, believing that the wheel must even things out and that the tide must turn in his favor. He forgets that the little ivory ball can't read his mind, can't see where it is going, and has no memory of what it has been doing. These players are never convinced of this until after they are dead broke.

One of my favorite gambling stories is about mental bets. A few years back in a Houston, Texas, casino an elderly, distinguished-looking gentleman slightly in his cups wavered back and forth behind a group of women players at the Roulette table. Nobody paid any attention to him until he began complaining how unlucky he was.

"What do you mean, unlucky?" the croupier asked.

"Number thirty-two just won, didn't it?" the grumbler said.

"Yes, but you didn't have a bet down. What's unlucky about that?"

"Oh, yes, I did," the drunk groaned. "I made a ten-dollar mind bet on twenty-six and lost!" Then he handed the croupier a $10 bill. "I always pay my losses—even on mind bets."

The croupier tried to return the money, but the old gentleman stubbornly refused to take it. Since this argument was creating a commotion and interrupting the game's action, the croupier finally shrugged, smiled wryly and shoved the bill into the money box.

The drunk, apparently satisfied, disappeared in the direction of the bar, but he was back again before long. He walked up to the table just as the croupier spun the ball. He wobbled unsteadily and watched until the ball dropped; then he came to life, shouting exciedly, "That's me! That's me! I bet ten bucks on number twenty and I won!"

The croupier tried to continue the play, but the drunk, who suddenly seemed much more sober, interrupted loudly, demanding to be paid the $350 he had won on his mind bet. He kept this up until the casino manager was called. After hearing what had happened, he ruled that since the croupier had accepted a $10 losing mental bet, he must pay off on the winning mind bet. You can be quite sure that this was the last mental bet which that croupier or any other in that casino ever accepted.

And don't try this stunt yourself; everybody in the casino business knows about it.

THE SCIENTIFIC SYSTEM

Another type of Roulette watcher is the Scientific system player who clocks the wheel for hours and hours at a time without making a bet, or if he does bet, it's the minimum the casino will allow. This type of player watches the wheel for days and even weeks until he's detected a pattern, or until he believes he's detected a pattern. Certain numbers or sections of the wheel are turning up more than they should, he feels. The wheel must be off. There must be something wrong with the mechanism. "At last," he says to himself, "I have found a defective roulette wheel. Now, I'll clean up."

The classic story of this type has as its hero an English engineer, Charles Jaggers, who latched on to a biased wheel at Monte Carlo and won a big

$100,000 before the casino caught on to the bias and switched wheels on him.

In most major casinos throughout the world, a Charles Jaggers, or anyone who wants to emulate him, is wasting his time and any amount of money he might bet on such a wheel. The reason is that every wheel is periodically thoroughly inspected. It is checked with a balance, and each fret or partition in the wheel head is examined for the smallest sign of wear and unevenness. And whenever a wheel shows a loss of some magnitude, the wheel head is replaced with another and thoroughly examined in the casino's workshop. No, the myth that the Scientific system player or those unknowledgeable gambling writers would have you believe, that there are defective wheels in major casinos, is just that, a myth and to put it bluntly, "just bunk."

While on the subject of biased wheels, I once discovered one in a Caribbean hotel casino in my early days of work as a gambling consultant. I arrived in the casino several minutes before closing, but early enough to hear an unfamiliar sound at one of the Roulette tables. The Roulette ball in play failed to echo the familiar sound of tock-tock-tock-tock. I immediately knew that a magnetized Roulette ball was in play and that several of the wheel head's pocket separators or partitions were made of steel since the ball slowed up more abruptly than it normally would when it hit a particular section of the partitions. After the casino closed, I ran a magnet over the partition or pocket separators and found that six partitions separating the adjacent pockets numbered 7, 20, 32, 17, 5 and 22 were made of steel instead of the nonmagnetic chromium-plated metal used in honest wheels. The gaffed roulette ball had a magnetized steel core in its center which accounted for the strange bouncing sound when it dropped into the bottom of the wheel head. A former casino manager was the perpetrator of this swindle.

THE PERFECT ROULETTE SYSTEM

This Roulette system first appeared in 1959 in *Bohemia,* a Cuban monthly magazine sold throughout Latin America. The writer introduced it with this glowing testimonial:

This, dear reader, is a sure-fire system to win at any roulette table in the world. Don't say it can't be done. It can. The mathematical calculations prove it. The system to be divulged to you proves it. The many times I have tried it at Monte Carlo proves it. The results you will get will prove it to you.

Everybody knows, of course, that in normal betting at Roulette the odds are against the player, which is caused by the fact that the zero and double zero work for the operator. However, by playing this system I can assure you that not only will you overcome this mathematical disadvantage, but will supplant it with a favorable percentage.

To say simply that this article increased the Roulette action in the

Caribbean and other Latin American casinos is the understatement of the year. I saw at least 20 players betting the system within a few weeks. I did *not* hear any of the operators complain about it.

The system works, the *Bohemia* writer explains, because the third column of the layout possesses eight red numbers and only four black numbers, an arrangement that is a mathematical flaw in the layout. Here is the simple betting method and mathematical proof that he says is guaranteed to make any Roulette player rich.

You make two bets on each spin of the wheel. Bet one $1 chip on the color black, which pays even money. And bet one $1 chip on the third column which contains eight red numbers, 3, 9, 12, 18, 21, 27, 30 and 36, and the black numbers 6, 15, 24 and 33. This bet pays odds of 2 to 1.

There are 36 numbers plus the 0 and 00 on the layout. Suppose you make 38 two-chip bets for a total of $76. In the long run this should happen:

1. The zero or double zero will appear 2 times in 38, and you lose 2 chips each time—a loss of 4 chips.

2. Red will appear 18 times out of 38. Each time one of the ten red numbers listed in the first and second column appears you lose two chips— a loss of 20 chips on those ten numbers. But when the eight red numbers in the third column appear you win two chips on each for a total win of 16 chips. This gives you a net loss on red of four chips.

3. Black will also appear 18 out of 38 times. Each time one of the 14 numbers in the first and second column appears, you lose one chip— a total loss of 14 chips. But since you also bet on the color black, you win 14 times for a gain of 14 chips. This loss and gain cancel out and you break even 14 times. But when the four black numbers in the third column (6, 15, 24 and 33) appear, you win three chips each time (two chips on the number and one chip on the color) for a profit of 12 chips on black.

Having lost four chips on the zero and double zero, and four chips on red, and having won 12 chips on black, you come out ahead with a final profit of four chips. Divide your total bet of $76 into your profit of $4 and you find that you have not only overcome the house advantage on the zero and double zero of $5\frac{5}{19}\%$ but have actually supplanted it with an advantage in *your* favor of $5\frac{5}{19}\%$.

The system has turned everything upside down and it is the house that is bucking a $5\frac{5}{19}\%$ disadvantage! But don't withdraw all the money in your savings account and make tracks for the nearest Roulette table. Not yet. Stop long enough to ask yourself: If the *Bohemia* writer won with the system at Monte Carlo, as he says, why is he still in the position of having to earn a living selling articles to magazines? And why does he want to let everyone else in on this marvelous, money-making secret?

The editor who bought the article apparently couldn't spot any flaw in what the writer claims is "mathematical proof that this system in the long run will beat any Roulette game." As in all systems, there is a fallacy here—one little monkey wrench that louses up the system's mathematical machinery. Can you find it before you read the answer below?

The joker is in the statement that "when the eight red numbers in the third column appear, you win two chips on each for a total win of 16 chips." This is incomplete. When those eight numbers win and pay off 16 chips, *you also lose eight chips on black,* making the net payoff only eight chips. Since you lose 20 chips on the red numbers in the first and second columns, your net loss on red is not four chips, as stated, but 12 chips. Having lost 12 chips on red, won 12 chips on black, and lost four chips on the zero and double zero, you end up losing four chips. And that washes that system out completely. The house still has its favorable edge of $5\frac{5}{19}\%$, as usual, and the casino operator is the guy who is going to get rich—not you.

THE CONCENTRATION SYSTEM

Another recent betting system to make its appearance on the American gambling scene is the Concentration betting system, and it is, for my money, the most ridiculous of them all. It results from the many magazine and newspaper articles describing the experiments of Dr. Joseph Banks Rhine in his parapsychology laboratory at Duke University in Durham, North Carolina.

Dr. Rhine is a psychic researcher who claims that his PK (psychokinesis) experiments have proved that the mind can influence and control the action of inanimate objects. He says that some people have a mysterious supernormal, possibly psychic, power, which enables them occasionally to make desired numbers come up on dice, just by wishing, much oftener than probability predicts. He even believes that this mental force, for which he admits he has no explanation, can control the position of playing cards during a shuffle.

The fact that he is a college professor and that Duke University appears to approve his conclusions has convinced a lot of newspaper and magazine readers that he must have something. Many of them decide that if Dr. Rhine's subjects can emit thought waves that make dice and cards behave as desired, perhaps they can, too. So they hunt up the nearest casino, hoping that these mystic powers will bring them a fortune.

I stopped in at the Casino de Capri in Havana one evening before Castro took it over to say hello to my friend, movie star George Raft, who was casino host there. George said, "I've got something to show you, Scarne. Look over there." He nodded toward a lone player at a nearby Roulette table whom I recognized as a personable young master of ceremonies then appearing on a national TV musical quiz show back in the States. I couldn't figure out what had attracted George's interest, but I got it as soon as our hero made a bet. He pushed a stack of $5 chips on the red number 3 and then, as the croupier spun the wheel and the ball, turned his head up and gazed steadily at the ceiling. He held this position until the last clicking sound of the ball indicated that it had come to rest in one of the pockets.

I turned to Raft. "No," I said.

He nodded. "Yes. He concentrates that way every time the wheel spins and he won't let anyone talk to him while he's projecting thought waves. I expect to see Dr. Rhine walk in here any day now to try it himself."

We watched him concentrate for a while and then, over a cup of coffee, Raft said, "He came in here several nights ago, and Nick, Larry, Joe and some of my other partners watched him concentrate. They were quite amused—at first. But later in the evening he was a five-thousand-dollar winner, and the boys began to look thoughtful. As a matter of fact, three nights later he was still ahead, and Harry, one of the pit bosses, decided he wasn't going to take any chances that Doc Rhine might be right, so he went over to the table and did some anti-concentrating to cancel out our friend's thought-wave advantage."

"How did that work?" I asked.

George grinned. "I guess Harry concentrates better. Our friend started to lose."

The TV personality joined us at our table a bit later. He looked glum. "I've had it," he said. "No more Roulette. I'm $17,000 in the hole."

"You've been reading about Dr. Rhine?" I asked.

"Yeah. According to what I read, the laws of probability have been taking quite a licking at Duke University."

"He's been working with dice and cards, not Roulette," I said.

"I know, but I figured a Roulette ball should be even easier to control. Just one little mental nudge from a thought wave ought to have even more effect on a falling Roulette ball than on rolling dice. But when PK experiments cost $17,000, I'll let somebody else experiment. I'm through."

Hundreds of people have also been trying this concentration at dice and cards, and their faith in Dr. Rhine loses these Concentration system players a good many hundreds of thousands of dollars every year. If you want my further comments on his dice-rolling experiments, see *Scarne on Dice,* where I have discussed them at some length.

One final word about Roulette system players: Most of them seem normal enough, except that they all have a greater capacity for self-deception than non-system players.

CHEATING AT ROULETTE

Here is a paragraph taken from a recent book on gambling whose author claims to be an authority:

An experienced croupier (even with an honest wheel) is able to plunk that little ivory ball into a section almost as accurately as you could make a ringer in horseshoes if you played every day of the year. On more than one occasion I have seen a croupier at an absolutely honest table give some attractive lady a break who had lost too much. He would tell her which numbers to play and when the excessive loss was retrieved somewhat, send her away with a "That's all now." I have seen that happen more than once and am certain that his charity was due merely to the experienced rolling of the ball.

When this statement appeared in print I was bombarded with letters from Roulette players asking whether this was possible. My answer in capital letters was and is a great big NO. The modern wheel, with its obstacles on the bottom track of the bowl, together with the fact that the croupier must spin the wheel and ball in opposite directions and must spin the ball from the last number into which it dropped, makes it an impossible feat even for the greatest of all Roulette croupiers. I once heard a lady friend of mine ask a croupier in a Las Vegas casino if he could drop the ball into any slot he wished. "Lady," he said, "if I could do that I wouldn't be working here. I'd have been worth millions years ago."

In some makeshift casinos throughout the country you may, however, find croupiers who can drop the little white ball into any predetermined group of 12 adjacent numbers on the wheel. Doc Winters, an old-time crooked Roulette dealer, could even drop the ball into any six-numbered section he desired. But this can only be done by spinning wheel and ball in the same direction and using a wheel that has no obstacles. You can guard against this sort of cheating by not placing your bets until after wheel and ball are spinning, just before the croupier announces that no further bets are allowed.

GAFFED ROULETTE WHEELS

Few, if any, of the top casinos resort to cheating at Roulette or any other game; it isn't necessary. But there are crooked wheels operating in many *sneak* (illegal) games throughout the country.

The misinformation in print on crooked Roulette wheels and how they are gaffed is amusing. Each one of the self-styled gambling experts and computer experts who write on the subject believes that one of the others may know more about the subject. They, therefore, copy from each other and are, consequently, wrong. The same situation existed as to dice and cards until the two standard reference works, *Scarne on Dice* and *Scarne on Cards,* were published. Since then, the writers who have done their copying from those books are getting their facts straight. From now on perhaps the writers on Roulette will also be able to get some facts straight.

"The most common method of rigging a Roulette wheel," one of these writers said, was "by the installation of several small electromagnets under several desired numbers. In this case the ball is not solid ivory, as it appears, but contains a steel slug in its center. When the croupier wishes to protect the casino against some heavily-backed number or combinations, he touches a concealed switch activating one or more of the electromagnets, drawing the ball into a numbered slot not covered by the players."

This description gave some law-enforcement agents in New Jersey a headache a few years ago. They had raided a gambling joint in a shore resort town and confiscated a Roulette table. Dry batteries hidden in the money drawer indicated that the wheel was crooked. The prosecutor wanted to introduce the wheel as evidence and needed to find the hidden electromagnets. He read several books on gambling which contained information like that quoted above, and he and the county detectives went to work with hammer and chisel in an effort to get under the numbers. They chiseled and chopped until the wheel was in a hundred pieces without finding a single electromagnet. The crooked gambling charge was finally dropped for lack of evidence.

Neither the writers, the prosecutor nor the detectives stopped to ask themselves how the electric current coming from the batteries could possibly feed into electromagnets concealed inside a spinning wheel. Inaccurate and misleading information supplied by self-styled experts who are merely guessing is worse than useless. It actually aids the cheats when it leads investigators to look for something that isn't there and causes them to conclude that the game must be honest when it is not.

The electromagnets, as the batteries indicated, were there, but they were in the table, not the wheel. This is one of the commonest methods of cheating at Roulette. There are four magnets equally spaced around the track and they are inside the woodwork of the bowl directly behind the back track in which the ball spins. Wires lead from the magnets through the batteries, which are usually hidden in the bowl or in the table's money drawer, and to the concealed switch, usually under the green baize of the table top. The switch is controlled either by a croupier or a cheat acting as a player.

The ball is gaffed with a magnetized steel core in its center. When the ball has slowed and is almost ready to drop, the cheat studies the now slowly rotating wheel. When he judges that the ball and the desired number are properly positioned, he presses the hidden control, putting the juice on for just an instant. The ball hesitates, then drops like a homing pigeon into the desired section of the wheel.

Unsuspecting players are fleeced of tens of thousands of dollars each year with wired Roulette wheels. I can't tell the occasional gambler any sure way of detecting a wired wheel while it is in operation, but I can give him a few tips as to what to watch for. The croupier in a *juice joint* (gambling house which has an electromagnetic wheel) can successfully operate the gaff only when the wheel is spinning very slowly. If he gives the wheel a slow spin and you see him or some other casino employee, hands on the table, watching the revolving wheel and ball with concentrated intensity just as the ball is about to drop, it's quite possible that the wheel is rigged.

The little ball doesn't always land just where the cheat wants it; considerable skill is required to judge the precise moment to apply the juice. The cheat, therefore, usually aims the ball at the 0 or 00. If the big bets are on red, he sends the ball toward the 0, which has a black pocket on either side. If the big money is on black, he aims for the 00, which has a red pocket on its left and right. This gives the croupier three chances to drop the ball into a losing pócket. So, if you see the ball head for the signs 0 and 00 more often than it should, you'd be wise to take your Roulette business elsewhere.

Some operators don't like the magnetic wheel because they fear that the hidden control button may stick. If this happens when there are big losers in the joint and they see the ball defy gravity by adhering to the wheel's back track instead of dropping into a number, there is bound to be trouble.

Embarrassing situations of this sort can be avoided by the use of the pointed needle gaff, a mechanical non-magnetic gimmick. A cable runs from the back of the money drawer to a tiny hole in the bowl's back track on the side nearest the 0 and 00 on the layout. A long, flexible rod inside the cable has a pin-pointed end which fits into the hole and can be made to project and retract. When the operator presses his body against the money drawer, the long rod moves forward in the cable and its tiny pointed end projects slightly from the small hole in the back track. This knocks the spinning ball off the back track and down toward the desired section of the slowly spinning wheel. As with the magnetic wheel, the operator aims for the 0 and 00. The hole, because of its location, cannot be seen by the seated players, and it is so small that it is difficult to see even when one is looking at it.

Rigged wheels, which, at the time of writing, cost about $7,500 more than an honest wheel, may be purchased from at least a couple of manufacturers throughout the country. There are no laws against the sale of rigged wheels or other crooked gambling devices, and such laws would probably be ineffective in any case, since the boys who deal in such equipment pay no attention to anti-gambling laws. Widespread exposure of these devices is the public's best protection because the more the players know about such gimmicks the riskier their use becomes for the crooked operator.

There is another way to protect yourself against a magnetic wheel, but I don't advise you to try it unless you are adept at sleight of hand. In 1935 James J. Braddock, who was heavyweight champ at the time, and I were on vacation and staying at the Dempsey Vanderbilt in Miami Beach. One evening Jim said, "I'd like to play a little Roulette tonight, John. How about you?"

"This isn't the place to do it," I told him. "You won't find an honest wheel in any rug joint in Dade County."

"You're kidding," Jim said.

I shook my head. "No, I'm not."

"I'd still like to play," Jim said, "even if it is a crooked game."

I pulled open a bureau drawer. "Maybe we can, at that," I said. "I've got an idea." I took out and opened a box containing some of the exhibits I used in my gambling lecture demonstrations.

Jim said, "You've got enough dice there to open your own casino, John."

I nooded. "A crooked casino. These are all gaffed—loads, shapes, cut edges, tops—I've got them all, but this is what I wanted to show you."

I took out two Roulette balls, placed them on the dresser top close together. When I released them they rolled toward each other and stuck together.

"Magnetized," Jim said. "Where did you get them?"

"I picked this pair up in a casino in Memphis about a year ago. I have quite a few of them and I think we can add another to my collection tonight." I took another ball from the box and handed it to Jim. "This is an honest ball." I held it a few inches above the dresser top and let it fall. It bounced several times, giving out a solid ring before coming to a stop. "Now, you bounce one of the magnetic balls."

Jim did. It only bounced twice and stopped with a thud. "Quite a difference," Jim said. "It has a dead sound, too. What does a crooked ball like this cost?"

"Anywhere from a hundred bucks up. It has a magnetized steel core." I told him about the electromagnets behind the wheel's track and explained how the gaff works.

"I see," Jim said. "If we could get an honest, unmagnetized ball into the game the croupier could switch on the juice all he wanted and nothing would happen."

"That's just what we're going to do," I said. "For one night at least, we'll make an honest man out of the croupier."

I gave him a few instructions and then we drove out to the Drum, a nightclub on the outskirts of Miami. The owner and several of the guests spotted Jim as we entered and came over to get the champ's autograph or shake hands. Inside the casino I whispered to Jim, "Look at the legs on the Roulette table. Notice how much thicker they are than the usual. That's where the batteries are."

We took seats at the table and the croupier said, "Good evening, champ. What will it be, quarter or dollar chips?"

Jim bought fifty $1 chips and I did the same.

Then, as we had planned, Jim asked the croupier, "Okay if I spin the ball on my first play? I feel luckier if I always do that."

"It's okay with me, champ," the croupier said, handing him the ball. Jim placed it on the table to his right, took his handkerchief from his pocket and wiped off his hands. It was a hot, sticky night. Then, just before Jim picked up the house ball I reached over and pushed it closer to him. At least, that is what seemed to happen. Actually, I switched the house ball for an honest one I had palmed.

Jim gave the ball a perfect spin. "You spun that like a pro," the croupier remarked.

"Thanks," Jim grinned and put four chips on number 24. I made a few split bets and put a few chips on straight numbers. I also kept one eye on the croupier. As the ball slowed I saw him press downward slightly on a stack of chips. I knew now where the switch was concealed.

I also saw a brief surprised look on the croupier's face as the ball spun smoothly on past the spot where he had expected it to drop. Later he pressed the control a few more times without any effect on the spinning ball, and he finally gave up, apparently figuring that the batteries were dead or there was a bad wiring connection. Jim and I played for a couple of hours and were lucky enough to win about $300, bucking the house P.C. of $5\frac{5}{19}\%$.

And then Jim asked me for the magnetized ball. I slipped it to him, and he approached the casino owner who had just come in. The first croupier, having been relieved, had probably reported that the gaff wasn't working, and the owner had come to take a look for himself.

Then Jim did something I don't advise you to try unless you are the world's heavyweight champ. He held up the crooked ball, and in a loud voice that carried across the casino, he asked the owner, "Hey, boss, how would you like to buy a magnetized Roulette ball?"

The owner, who was walking toward the table, stopped as suddenly as if he had walked into a brick wall and his face went white. He knew now why the gaff wasn't working. His mouth opened and closed a couple of times, but nothing came out. He was still trying to think of something to say as we made a quick exit.

CHEATING WITH AN HONEST WHEEL

There are also a few methods of cheating with an honest wheel. Several years ago I was retained by an American high roller who asked me to find out if the Caribbean casino in which he had lost $200,000 had got it honestly. I won't mention his name, or that of the casino, which is still operating but under new management and honestly. Under the name of Pietro Orlando, which I sometimes use on such investigations, I registered at the hotel of which the casino is part. I also sported a new mustache, long sideburns and an Italian accent. I played Roulette for several hours the first night and lost about $20 but could see nothing wrong with the operation of the wheel. For the next few nights the action at the wheel was small, and there was no indication that the croupiers were cheating. I did, however, spot a dice mechanic working at one of the Craps tables, and I know that if one game in a casino is crooked they all are.

I hung around for another week and still found no cheating at the Roulette table. But on Saturday night an American tourist began betting $100 on each spin, placing his bets on straight, split and corner bets. After he had made a few such bets I noticed that several casino employees had unobtrusively gathered around the table. A woman shill had taken the seat nearest the table's apron, and another casino employee stood directly at her left close to the wheel and directly opposite the croupier who was dealing. Cheaters always tense up just before they do their dirty work, and I could sense the tenseness around this table.

After a few more spins, the tourist asked for $5,000 worth of black $100 chips. He spread them all over the layout, but put none on the 0 and 00 spaces. I was tense myself now, and I watched the play closely. The croupier spun the wheel and ball in the usual manner, and, just as the ball was about to drop, the woman shill stood up, leaned forward and began putting chips all over the layout. She was still leaning over when the ball dropped into a slot.

Since the woman was between all the other players and the wheel, none of them could see the ball at the moment it dropped into the slot, but when she moved back and sat down again, there it was, resting innocently in the green 0. We had been *screened out*. Just to make absolutely sure this wasn't accidental I stuck around until I had seen the same thing happen several more times. Since I knew the dodge, I also knew, without actually having to see it, what had happened behind her. When she leaned across the table to place her bets (honest players often do the same), she always did it just as the ball had slowed and was almost ready to drop. Under this cover, the casino employee at her side and right next to the wheel simply lifted the ball from the track and dropped it into the green 0.

There is always more than one way to skin a cat—or fleece a chump.

HOW TO PROTECT YOURSELF AGAINST SHORT PAYOFFS

It's easy to learn how to play Roulette, and yet surprisingly few players know exactly how many chips they should receive when they win on a combination of several bets, particularly if the wager involves single, double or four-number wagers. When a croupier pushes over several stacks of chips, only about five out of 100 players have any idea of whether or not the payoff is correct. I have seen a good many players shorted on chips in many of our top casinos. It is often an honest mistake on the croupier's part, but whether it is or not, if you are going to play Roulette you'd be smart to learn how to calculate your winnings. Why should you pay an extra charge by being short-changed?

Here is a mathematical shortcut the reader can use to calculate men-

ROULETTE PAY CARD

Straight 35 to 1		Split 17 to 1		Street 11 to 1		Quarter 8 to 1		Line 5 to 1	
1	35	1	17	1	11	1	8	1	5
2	70	2	34	2	22	2	16	2	10
3	105	3	51	3	33	3	24	3	15
4	140	4	68	4	44	4	32	4	20
5	175	5	85	5	55	5	40	5	25
6	210	6	102	6	66	6	48	6	30
7	245	7	119	7	77	7	56	7	35
8	280	8	136	8	88	8	64	8	40
9	315	9	153	9	99	9	72	9	45
10	350	10	170	10	110	10	80	10	50
11	385	11	187	11	121	11	88	11	55
12	420	12	204	12	132	12	96	12	60
13	455	13	221	13	143	13	104	13	65
14	490	14	238	14	154	14	112	14	70
15	525	15	255	15	165	15	120	15	75
16	560	16	272	16	176	16	128	16	80
17	595	17	289	17	187	17	136	17	85
18	630	18	306	18	198	18	144	18	90
19	665	19	323	19	209	19	152	19	95
20	700	20	340	20	220	20	160	20	100

tally the number of chips to be paid off on single-number bets on which the odds are 35 to 1. For any even number of chips, simply divide by 2, multiply by 7, and tack a zero onto your answer. Example: You bet 16 chips on a single number and win. Divide 16 by 2, which gives you 8, multiply by 7 which gives you 56, add the zero, which gives you 560— the correct number of chips due you.

If you wager an odd number of chips, you make the same calculation except you subtract 1 before you start and add 35 at the end. Example: You wagered 15 chips. Subtract 1, getting 14, divide by 2, getting 7, multiply by 7, getting 49, add a zero, getting 490, and add 35 for a final answer of 525.

If you want to avoid mental calculation, give the following chart a little study and memorize the payoffs on the more complicated bets. Here are all the correct payoffs on straight, split, street, quarter and line bets when wagering one to 20 chips. Simple multiplication will enable you to extend the chart to payoffs on more than 20 chips.

Curiously enough, there are many more methods used by cheats to beat a Roulette game than there are cheating methods to beat the player. Roulette mobs have on several occasions secretly got into Monte Carlo during the night, gaffed the wheels and then won considerable amounts from the house before the casino discovered what had happened. This also happened in a good many other casinos. The methods they use to gaff the wheel are much easier to install than the two I have described, but I won't discuss them here because I'm not trying to smarten up any casino owners. Also, this cheating doesn't affect the honest players at the table; only the cheats who know about the gaff gain by it, and it's only the house that loses.

HOW TO GAMBLE SENSIBLY AT ROULETTE

The best way to avoid losing at Roulette is to stop playing the game, but since it is such a favorite with so many millions of people I doubt that very many of them will take this advice. And I can't give a best bet at the game because, unlike all other casino games, all but one of the bets have the same $5\frac{5}{19}\%$ against the player. The best I can do to save you money is to suggest you avoid the five-number combination bets with their $7\frac{17}{19}\%$ advantage for the bank.

You may be lucky and win at Roulette over a short period, but your chances of beating the wheel if you play continuously through several long sessions are very dubious.

If you intend to play for several sessions, budget yourself. Divide the amount of money you can afford to lose by the number of times you expect to play, and don't exceed that loss limit in any session. If you should at any time find yourself ahead of the game by a good sum, pack the game in. Tomorrow is another day. This advice will at least prevent you from becoming a Roulette degenerate.

SCARNE'S ADVICE TO CASINO OPERATORS: SWITCH TO EUROPEAN ROULETTE

Roulette, the biggest and most glamorous betting game found in European casinos, was never given a chance to prove its big-time betting potential in Nevada casinos. Prior to 1950, legal casinos in Nevada were owned and operated by former bootleggers and racketeers whose gambling knowledge consisted only of 5% New York Craps, Slot Machines and Black Jack. The word Roulette was seldom used in their gambling vocabulary. Thus, when Nevada state gaming officials insisted that Roulette was a must for all major casinos in Nevada, these former underworld casino operators introduced Roulette as a casino side game rather than as the fashionable big-time betting European casino game.

For years Roulette, as played in Nevada and the Caribbean, has been considered a sucker's game by most casino gamblers because of its outrageous house advantage of $5\frac{5}{19}\%$ or 5.26%, and for this reason most present-day casino high rollers avoid playing Roulette like the plague.

Now I ask this question: "Isn't it time that the casino operators in Nevada, Atlantic City and the Caribbean return Roulette to its rightful place as a big-time money casino game?" And when they do so, I'm sure that Roulette will bring to the American casinos a new breed of wealthy and fashionable American and foreign high rollers who are noticeably missing from the American casino scene today.

For Roulette to become competition for Craps, Black Jack and Baccarat, the 5.26% favorable house percentage must be drastically reduced and its *even money* paid-off bets listed on the Roulette layout which are marked red, black, odd, even, 1–18 and 19–36 must offer the player as good a bet percentagewise as the 1.41% house edge on the Pass Line at Bank Craps, the 1.34% house edge when a player bets the banker's side at the game of Baccarat, the house's edge of 2% at Black Jack when the Scarne strategy is used intelligently, or the house's edge of 1.30% at Scarney Baccarat when the player makes use of expert strategy.

In my opinion, the only good thing about European Roulette is that its house percentages are considerably better for the player than those found in American Roulette. However, European Roulette equipment and the croupiers' method of dealing the game are outdated, the game-dealing style being too slow for American casino gamblers. To overcome these obstacles, I have devised a plan to take the lower house percentages from European Roulette but retain the American Roulette equipment, such as the style of table, layout, wheel checks (chips) and the game workings of the Roulette personnel. With my plan we need do just two things: replace the American wheel with a European wheel that is minus the double zero (00), and replace the present-day layout with one exactly like it except it will possess only the single zero (0), the double zero having been discarded. The absence of the double zero automatically eliminates the five number bet that possesses a player disadvantage of 7.89%, the most outrageous Roulette sucker bet of all.

When my plan is adopted, the American wheel, like the European Roulette wheel, will possess 36 numbers (1 to 36) and a single zero (0). Each and every bet found on the Roulette layout such as straight, split, street, corner, line, column, dozens, low, high, black, red, odd, even, etc., are paid off at present-day existing odds. However, when the zero appears, all bets paid off at even money such as red, black, odd, even, 1–18 and 19–36 are "imprisoned" (the chip bet or chips bet are taken by the croupier and centered on the outside line of the section wagered on nearest the player's side, half the chip or chips resting on the section wagered on and the other half resting off the layout design). Their ultimate fate is determined by the next spin of the wheel. They are either lost or returned to the player who gets back only his original bet. In short, the player loses half of his bet on red, black, odd, even, 1–18 and 19–36 when the zero appears. The house's favorable percentage, in this case on red, black, odd, even, 1–18 and 19–36 is 1.35%. All other types of Roulette bets which originally had a favorable house percentage of 5.26% are now reduced to 2.70%, due to the absence of the double zero.

My advice to casino operators in Nevada, Atlantic City and the Caribbean is to get wise, stop treating the American Roulette players like suckers and adopt my plan of European Roulette.

9

SLOT MACHINES:
THE ONE-ARMED BANDITS

Automation came to the gambling industry in 1887, when Charles Fey placed the first nickel-in-the-slot machines in the gambling palaces of San Francisco. Today the slot machine, long known as the "one-armed bandit," is without any doubt gambling's most consistent money-maker. There has never been any other gambling device which has produced such enormous profits with so little effort on the part of the operator.

My survey shows that in 1978 17 million Americans, of whom 12 million are women, played the 70,000-odd slot machines found in casinos in Nevada, Atlantic City, Puerto Rico, the Bahamas, Aruba, Curaçao, Haiti and other Caribbean islands.

The 65,000-odd slot machines found in the 100-odd casinos in Nevada gross about 70% as much money as all other casino games such as Bank Craps, Black Jack, Roulette, Baccarat-Chemin de Fer, Keno, etc. In other words, about 40% of the entire casino industry's gross earnings comes from these 65,000-odd slot machines, of which about 2,000, the largest number under one roof, are to be found in the M-G-M Grand Hotel Casino in Reno.

New South Wales, one of Australia's six states, with a population of 4.77 million, runs second to Nevada in the number of slot machines in operation. There is a total of 44,000 slot machines in the 1,525 clubs registered to operate them in New South Wales. This past year, the 44,000 slot machines grossed $157 million, more than the country's entire national defense budget for 1978–79.

England's private gaming clubs (casinos) harbor about 256 slot machines known as "fruit machines." The reason for so few slot machines in England is due to the government's regulation permitting only two fruit machines to each of the country's 128 legalized private gambling clubs.

LEGAL CASINO SLOT MACHINES

At the present time the only legal casino slot machines under the American flag are found in Nevada, Atlantic City and the Commonwealth of Puerto Rico. Slot machines in Puerto Rico's casinos are owned and operated by the government. The government pays the casinos 40% of the gross revenue for the use of the casino.

The biggest loss suffered by a slot machine degenerate (what else would you call them?) was $250,000 which a California woman lost over a two-year period in the Reno area.

I know at least 20 casinos in Nevada and the Caribbean whose individual yearly slot take is from $5 million to $20 million and more. This leaves a very handsome net profit when you consider that a modern machine costs $4,200 or more, and that such a casino operation may require about 40 employees—change girls, collectors, mechanics, cashiers and inspectors. Slots are found not only in casinos; they are in hotel lobbies, taverns, clubs, lodges, bowling alleys, bus-stop restaurants, grocery stores and even airline terminals such as McCarran Airport in Las Vegas. Where slots are legal, you'll find them almost any place where people congregate—except churches.

It may interest the reader to know that slot machines situated in Las Vegas' downtown casinos account for more than 60% of gross casino revenue. Slots in Reno casinos account for more than 65% of their gross casino revenue. However, in the Las Vegas Strip casinos the table games get the most action.

The slot machine is the only gambling device with a mechanical banker that collects losing bets, pays off winning bets and makes fewer mistakes than any human dealer in any casino banking game.

My survey estimates that for every legal slot machine in the country, there are four operating illegally. Although some illegal slot machines have been known to earn $2,000 or more per week, my survey shows that the average national weekly take for such a machine is only $100.

The slot machine is essentially a cabinet housing three or more narrow cylindrical drums, commonly called *reels,* which are marked with symbols. Vertically disposed on a common axis, the reels are caused to revolve freely when a player activates the machine and pulls a leverlike handle affixed in the side of the cabinet. Awards or payoffs, which are generally paid automatically, are usually based on the horizontal alignment of symbols, when the spinning reels come to a position of inertial rest.

The nickel and quarter machines are the most popular, and their action accounts for about 85% of the yearly slot handle. They are followed by the dime, half-dollar and silver-dollar machines, in that order.

There is also a two- to seven-coin, flat-top type of electrically controlled machine known to the industry as a *console.* This is actually two or more one-armed bandits in one. Because they look different and are not called slots, thousands of these consoles can be found in localities where the slot machine is illegal.

The modern super deluxe one-armed single-coin bandit with its shining chromium finish, its array of glowing neon lights and its progressive

San Francisco Chronicle
April 15th, 1887
San Francisco, Calif.

San Francisco Machinist Unveils New Nickel Operated Machine

A group of owners of Saloons and Restaurants, of Market, Mission Enbarkadera and Barbary Coast gathered this morning in the small machine shop of Charley Fey at 631 Howard St. to view Mr. Fey's entirely new Liberty Bell, a machine featuring 3 reels mostly hidden with Horseshoes, Spades, Diamonds, Hearts, Bells symbols on reels. The device is operated by depositing a nickel in a slot to release the handle, when the right combination of symbols stop in the window the player is awarded coins ranging from 2, on 2 Horseshoes to 20 for 3 Bells. Most of those present agreed the machine should be a great success.

Clipping from San Francisco Chronicle, *1887.*

jackpot sells for as high as $5,000—the retail price of a modern Bally slot machine one-to-eight-coin three- or four-wheeler, progressive jackpot ranges from $4,000 up. The price of a standard single-coin three-wheeler machine ranges from $3,000 to $4,000, and consoles sell for from $5,000 up.

The latest change in size is the six-feet-tall machine dubbed Big Bertha. This machine accepts half dollars or dollar bills and pays back about 80% of its gross take. At present, no casino has more than one Big Bertha; it is used primarily for propaganda purposes and to make a few bucks at the same time.

The success of Big Bertha is responsible for its enlarged counterpart, Super Big Bertha, a six-by-ten-foot slot machine which is said to have cost $150,000 to design and engineer. It makes use of a five-horsepower electric motor to power the 20-inch-wide chain-driven wheels. The Super Big Bertha possesses eight reels, each containing 20 symbols for an overall 25.6 billion different combinations, only one of which will pay out the $1 million promised by its developer, that is, providing you play eight Eisenhower dollars at the same time. Smaller amounts will be paid off when fewer coins are played. Though the probabilities are one in 25.6 billion of hitting the $1 million jackpot, and since you have to play eight coins at one time to do so—our mathematics shows that on the average, the player would have to pump close to 205 million silver dollars into the machine to win the $1 million jackpot. The biggest jackpot payoff at time of writing was $165,000 won on a one-dollar progressive jackpot slot at the Flamingo Hilton Hotel Casino in Las Vegas on April 9, 1978.

Except for horse bookmaking and Policy Numbers, the slot machine in the past 50 years has been the cause of more legal indictments, court decisions and police raids than all other forms of gambling combined. In spite of all attempts at restriction, the slot business keeps growing. Perhaps the biggest reason for this is the manner of play. It is doubtful that any other form of gambling has the hypnotic fascination of the slot machine. It is difficult even for a person who believes gambling is morally wrong not to drop at least one coin in the slot and pull the handle, if only to watch the wheels spin.

Slot players seem to get more excited when they hit a jackpot than do players winning much greater sums at Black Jack, Craps, Roulette, Big Six, Numbers and horse racing. When I was the gambling consultant at the Habana Hilton Casino in Cuba, before Castro's time, I was watching a bigtime Roulette game in which winning numbers were paying off as much as $25,000. The game, naturally, was tense. Suddenly everyone's attention was diverted by cheers and howls of delight from a group of women across the room. One woman had just hit a nickel jackpot and collected $7.

CHARLES FEY AND THE FIRST SLOT MACHINES

The slot machine, an American invention, is now found in all parts of the world—Europe, Africa, South America, Asia, the Caribbean and of course the United States.

A 29-year-old mechanic, Charles Fey, made the first slot machine in 1887 in a small machine shop in San Francisco; he began manufacturing them by hand and placed them in the local gambling palaces on a 50% rental basis. He is, therefore, not only the inventor but also the first slot machine operator.

His first machine was not, as some gambling historians say, cruder and bulkier than modern machines, nor did its reels carry the fruit symbols commonly used today. His original one-armed bandit, called the Liberty Bell, was somewhat smaller than present-day slots, although mechanically very similar. It had three wheels carrying bright lithographed pictures of playing-card symbols—hearts, diamonds and spades—and bells, horseshoes and a star. This original machine can be seen today in the collection of old machines at the Liberty Belle Saloon and Restaurant in Reno, which is owned and operated by Charles Fey's grandsons, Marshall and Franklin Fey. Charles Fey also developed many other slots which old-timers may remember: Draw Poker, On the Square, Little Chief, Duo, Little Vender, Silver Cup and Silver Dollar, the first one-armed bandit designed to take that large a coin.

The wheels on the first machine were smaller than those used today; each had only ten symbols instead of the 20 now used; only the three symbols on the pay line could be seen through the small window. Also, there was no jackpot. Fey's wheels, like the present-day three-wheelers, were vertical. The player inserted a nickel and pulled the lever to spin the wheels. If the three symbols showing when the wheels stopped were a winning combination, the machine paid out the correct number of coins. A colored reward chart on the machine's front listed the payouts for each winning combination as follows:

Three bells	10 drinks
Flush of hearts	8 drinks
Flush of diamonds	6 drinks
Flush of spades	4 drinks
Two horseshoes and star	2 drinks
Two horseshoes	1 drink

Although the reward chart listed drinks, the machine's payout mechanism paid out nickels. At that time there was a 2¢ Federal revenue tax on a deck of playing cards, and Charles Fey thought it wise to buy the tax stamp and paste one on each of his slot machines because he used playing-card symbols. A shrewdie, I must say.

His machines were an immediate success, and he couldn't manufacture enough of them in his small workshop to supply the demand in and around San Francisco. Gambling equipment manufacturers soon discovered this and tried to buy the manufacturing and distribution rights, but Fey refused all offers. His invention remained an exclusive California phenomenon until 1907, when Herbert Stephen Mills, a Chicago manufacturer of arcade-type machines, began production of a machine whose automatic payout principle was similar to Fey's.

The Mills machine was named the Operators Bell, and because its mechanism was encased in iron as the modern slots are, players nicknamed it the "Iron Case." It had three wheels, each bearing 20 symbols, and was the first machine to carry the symbols of bars, bells, plums, oranges, cherries and lemons. Nine symbols could be seen through the window. By 1910, slot machines could be found in every city and nearly every hamlet in the country.

The company started by Herbert S. Mills in 1889 still bears his name —Mills and Company. The Jennings Company was founded in 1906. The Pace Company was founded shortly thereafter. Today the Bally Manufacturing Company is the largest company producing slot machines. Mills has factories in Chicago and Reno, Jennings and Bally are in Chicago and Pace is in Maryland. There are several foreign companies manufacturing slot machines, two in Australia and one in Japan.

FEDERAL TAXES AND LAW ENFORCEMENT

The public and many Federal and state legislators believe that the slot machine industry, from the top level on down, is largely controlled by racketeers and hoodlums. This is not quite the case. The majority of slot machine manufacturers are educated men, highly respected in their communities and active in civic and church affairs. But there is a minority which is not exactly beyond reproach; its members sell slots to some real shady characters.

At the distributors' level, in states where slots are banned, the business of selling coin-operated music machines and legitimate vending machines is used as a front for the illegitimate slot machine business.

At the operators' level, the picture changes. This is where we find the racketeers, hoodlums, and their *animals* (professional strong-arm men) working hand in hand with corrupt public officials and law-enforcement agents on all levels.

On the other hand, in states where the machines are legal, most of the operators are ordinary businessmen, although racketeers can sometimes be found hiding in the background.

As evidence of the size of the slot machine industry I'll cite a yearly report of the Bureau of Census of the Department of Commerce which disclosed that in one year 49,271 slot machines (including consoles) were shipped to distributors and casinos.

In the late thirties and throughout the 1940s, there was a concerted drive against the slots. The result was to outlaw them in most states. In 1951, Congress made it a Federal offense to transport slot machines or consoles or even their components across state lines unless the ultimate destination is a state or foreign country where slot operation is legal. The Department of Commerce reports since then don't tell the whole story, since they have no figures on illegal shipments.

The Bureau of Internal Revenue, however, tries to collect an annual license fee of $200 for each machine in operation, legal or illegal. If we add the state and local taxes to the Federal license fee, the total levy on a legally operated machine averages about $500 a year. It costs the illegal operator considerably more. My findings indicate that he pays in *ice* (bribes to officials) from $1,000 to $5,000 per year on each machine, depending on locality and circumstances.

In spite of the Federal law prohibiting interstate commerce in slot machines, the operators in states where they are illegal manage to make out. They open a receiving office in a legal state, then reship the machines secretly by motor vehicles. Federal agents in Pennsylvania recently confiscated a truck loaded with 67 slot machines. There is, apparently, little or nothing that Federal agents can do to eliminate or regulate the 200,-000 illegal slot or console machines. They are much too popular with both operators and players, and too many public officials like the ice they get.

HOW TO SPOT A CROOKED SLOT MACHINE

Most of the slots in operation prior to 1940 were real one-armed bandits for sure. Although each of the three wheels bore 20 symbols, every other one was a dummy that could not appear on the pay line. Since only ten symbols could appear on the pay line, these machines were known in the trade as "ten-stop machines." The brakes which slowed the spinning wheels were so set that the wheels, as they stopped, fitted into a cog that allowed a stop only on alternate symbols. The dummy symbols were very effective bait because they often formed winning combinations which could be seen by the player just above or below the pay line. If you played the slots in those days, this explains why you found yourself saying so often, "Boy! I just missed the three bars and the jackpot! See, they're just above the pay line."

This happened with great regularity because the manufacturers placed the symbols on the wheels in such a way that many more fake winning combinations appeared above or below the line than appeared on the pay line itself. A machine, for instance, might have three bars on each wheel. Normally this would mean that the three-bar jackpot combination could be hit in $3 \times 3 \times 3$, or 27, ways. But when two of three bars on each wheel are in positions at which the wheel cannot stop, there is only one way the player can line three bars up on the pay line, and there are eight ways the fake bars can show near-hit winning combinations above or below the pay line. Payoff combinations of the other symbols were gimmicked the same way so that the player saw a great many more paying combinations that were near misses. This induced him to continue feeding in nickels as he tried to hit combinations that would never show.

Many slot operators didn't like to give the player even that one chance to hit the jackpot three-bar combination, so they came up with another gimmick—the *bug*. This is a small, flat half-circle of iron about an inch long, which looks something like a bug. It was screwed onto and closed a cog which controlled one of the three bars, usually the one on the third wheel. When the wheels stopped and the bugged bar was about to appear on the pay line, the brake hit the bug and couldn't slip into the opening of the cog. The bar symbol came to rest just above or below the pay line instead. The best you could get on a machine bugged this way was a two-bar combination.

Sister, if a bar symbol on the machine you are playing has a habit of slipping down or jumping up past the pay line after the wheels have come to a stop, it's an even bet that the machine is bugged. It also means that you're playing an old-timer, because modern machines are all 20-stop machines and no longer gaffed in this way.

Slot machines built during the thirties usually had a payback of about 50% when they weren't bugged. When half the money you feed in is retained, it doesn't take long before the machine has it all. And when the bug was used, you lost even faster. It was this type of machine that was first called the one-armed bandit. The story is that a couple of professional bandits in the Midwest were playing a gaffed machine. After losing consistently, one of them remarked, "You sure don't need a gun to hold up anyone, not if you own a couple of machines like this."

"Yeah," the other crook agreed, as he pulled the handle once more, "and this bandit has only one arm."

The use of this phrase hasn't hurt the slot machine business. On the contrary, it seems to help. Several Nevada casinos have slot machines built into a multicolor cast iron figure of a scowling, bearded Western outlaw. The figure is minus a right arm, and his upraised left, the machine's lever, holds a six gun.

In the early twenties one slot company tried to circumvent the anti-gambling laws of certain states by making a slot that pretended to be a candy-vending machine. Candy mint rolls were contained in a tube at the side. Purchase of the candy entitled the buyer to give the three wheels a spin. When he hit a winning combination, he received slugs which could either be played back into the machine or redeemed for cash.

The innovation didn't last long. There were several court decisions which ruled that, mints or no mints, the machine was a gambling device. The operators argued that it was a candy-vending machine because the players always received a roll of mints for each coin deposited. The courts didn't agree; they knew that most players kept putting in money without bothering to take more than a few of the candies and continued to do so even when the candy tube was empty. By the early thirties, after thousands of machines had been confiscated and the seizures upheld by the courts, the mint-vending machines became extinct.

FRANK COSTELLO: HISTORY'S BIGGEST SLOT MACHINE OPERATOR

The biggest slot machine operator in history was Frank Costello, the one-time racket boss of New York City. The Tru-Mint Company of New York City, which Costello and his partner, Dandy Phil Kastel, organized, had at its height of business in 1933 some 7,000 slot machines in speakeasies, stationery stores, candy stores, and other locations in New York. The Tru-Mint Company had seventy branch offices and warehouses throughout the city. Frank Costello's take from these slot machines was approximately $2,800,000 a year—and this was during the height of the Depression.

At the time, Costello's slot machine empire did not need political protection since slot machines had not yet been classified illegal either by state or Federal government. Costello, however, used the law to protect his empire by the use of state and Federal injunctions against the confiscation of his slot machines by the police.

Then along came Mayor Fiorello LaGuardia and my friend Police Commissioner Lewis J. Valentine, considered by many to be the best police commissioner in New York's history, and, in spite of Costello's court injunction, his 7,000 slot machines were confiscated by the New York police and smashed to smithereens. Mayor LaGuardia's Fusion Administration fought Costello's slot machine injunction up to the United States Supreme Court and obtained a dismissal of the ruling against the seizure of the candy-mint slot machines. By May 7, 1934, it obtained an amendment to the state penal code, which gave the police the authority to seize and destroy all gambling machines.

MODERN SLOT MACHINES AND PAYBACKS

An innovation that was unquestionably a great stimulant to the industry, occurred in the middle twenties. A simple box-shaped enclosure with a glass front was built into the front of the machine and called the *jackpot,* the term coming from Draw Poker. The machine automatically fed coins into the jackpot, building it up, and the operator also filled it when necessary. When the three bars hit the pay line the jackpot opened and added its contents to the customary three-bar payout of 20 coins.

Millions of slot players and even some people in the gambling business who should know better believe that the operator can adjust a slot machine to pay out any percentage desired merely by turning some sort of screw inside the machine. The belief has arisen because a good many authors of game books write about slots without really knowing what the machines are like on the inside. It is simply not true; the mechanism of a slot machine is quite complicated, and the payback odds cannot be changed unless the reel's symbols are repositioned and the payoff slots adjusted to coincide with the changed combinations on the reel. The one exception is when the machine is bugged.

To change the payoff odds the machine must be partly dismantled. The reels must be changed and the internal disks which correspond to the reels must also be changed. In the new multiple-coin machines there are electronic controls containing a maze of wires and complicated circuitry. This makes a payout change equivalent to a major overhaul. It takes a good mechanic half a day to accomplish the change.

Most major casinos maintain a slot machine workshop where slots are repaired and payout changes can be made. Competition generally determines the percentage payout on most slot machines. In areas where major casinos are next door to each other, the slots in each casino will pay back from 70% to 95%. The few slots with a payback of 95% are usually situated in a conspicuous part of the casino. The machines' payout percentages aren't posted on them. Only the casino operator and his slot mechanic know the percentages and the location of each machine.

Recently, however, many Las Vegas and Reno casinos have been advertising a 97% payback on their one-dollar slot machines. And according to the action on these machines, the advertising of the 97% payback is getting results.

Nevada and the Caribbean governments set no payout percentage regulations, feeling competition will take care of that. What they do care about is the honesty of the posted payoff winners. Are they correct? When a sign says 21 ways to a jackpot, there must be 21 ways to the jackpot, and all other posted payouts must be possible also. State or government inspectors are always on hand to make periodic checkups on all slot machines. Violations are treated severely.

Wherever slot machines are illegal, the payback is usually 50% or less. This also holds true for legal slot machines situated in private clubs, airports, drugstores, supermarkets and shoeshine parlors.

In the middle thirties the first substantial change in the appearance and design of slot machines came about with the introduction of the flat-top, electrically driven console. Since more than one person can play at a time, the makers hoped it would replace the one-armed bandit. It failed to do this because the slot player seems to be happier bucking the machine on his own and pulling the lever himself. There are few such machines now in operation in the United States.

Although the symbols on many modern machines are still Charles Fey's and Herbert Stephen Mills's original bars, bells, plums, oranges, cherries and lemons, some machines now use other symbols. Slot machine manufacturers try to distinguish their own make of machine from others by using their own symbols: the words Tic, Tac, Toe; the numeral 7, pictures of watermelons, star symbols, a cowboy on horseback known as a "buckaroo" and others. Also, many slots pay out double or twin jackpots and giant awards.

Another important slot innovation appeared in the late 1950s. Actually it was just four single-coin slot machines bolted together, but the only handle was placed between the two center machines. The player had to insert four coins—one in the slot of each machine. He would "hit" the jackpot when he got "Three Bars in Any Position." That meant that the bars which appeared below and above the pay line were also counted. In other words, one bar on the pay line, one above and one below it would add up to a jackpot; or any such combination on a single machine meant a winner. Since four machines were working in tandem, it was possible for a player to hit up to four jackpots simultaneously.

These machines, which were often called monsters and Frankensteins, never became too popular and eventually disappeared from the slot machine scene. However, the idea of multiple-coin play was introduced and finally led to the development of single-machine multiple-coin play.

Many top casinos make use of the jackpot *light-up board*. This is a large electric sign which hangs from the ceiling and can be seen by all the players in the room. Each slot machine has its own number and is electrically connected to the light behind a corresponding number on a glass square on the board. If you hit a jackpot on machine 42, the number 42 on the board lights up, a chime rings and one of the lovely jackpot payoff girls appears at your side pronto. She verifies the jackpot and gives you the cash. The slot machine business has certainly taken on a new look in the past 15 years, yes sirree.

Then in the 1950s came the four-reeler, with four reels instead of the usual three. The first of these to appear, the Jennings Buckaroo, can still be found in some of the top casinos in Nevada. When you line up four buckaroo symbols, this machine's special jackpot pays $250 for 5¢, $500 for 10¢, $1,250 for 25¢, $2,500 for 50¢ and $5,000 for $1. This jackpot is in addition to the regular three-wheel jackpots which run from a guaranteed $7 on a nickel machine to $140 on the dollar machine. This type of four-reeler with the special buckaroo award is usually geared to pay back from 80% to 90%.

In the 1960s, the "hold and draw" class of slot machines became quite popular in the downtown casinos in Las Vegas. This style of machine offers a player a "second chance" to win. That is, after a nonwin spin, a hold signal is lit. A player may then press hold buttons to hold any desired reel or reels in a locked position, deposit a second coin and spin the reel or reels not held to try again for a win. For example, if a bell appears on the first and third reels and another symbol on the middle reel, a player may hold the bells and spin the middle reel in hope of "drawing" another bell to fill out a triple bell win.

Also in the sixties we had the introduction of three-line-pay machines. One of these machines may be played with a single coin, which qualifies only the basic central row of symbols as the win line. Or, at his option, a player may deposit up to three coins before pulling the handle. When the second coin is deposited, both the central row and the visible row are qualified as win lines. When three coins are deposited, all three visible rows—the central row and the rows above and below the central row—qualify as win lines. Today, in most casinos, we'll find five-line-pay machines which may be played with a single coin—or a player may deposit up to five coins before pulling the handle. The first coin qualifies the basic center line as the win line; and each additional coin qualifies an additional line as a win line. If five coins are played, five lines—three horizontal and two diagonal—are win lines. Wins in this type of machine are not generally multiplied by the number of coins played, but the player can win on any lines qualified as win lines. An inducement to most multiple-coin play is provided by the fact that the fifth line—qualified by the fifth coin—is a special jackpot line.

Actually, the introduction of the multiple-coin machine, of which the

A progressive five-coin multiple slot machine whose two super-jackpots show possible payouts of $382.02 and $779.36, should either appear on the fifth line. However, for the fifth line to be active, five coins must be played at one time. (Bally, Inc.)

"hold and draw" and "three-line-pay" types were the forerunners, is probably the most important design change since the invention of the slot machine. Most casinos are replacing their conventional single-coin machines with multiple-coin machines on which a player can wager from one to eight coins at a time with corresponding multiple payoffs. The reason, of course, is to give the player an opportunity to pump more coins into the machine in the hope of hitting the five-, six- or eight-coin super-multiple jackpot which amounts to $500 on a five-coin four-reeler 25¢ machine, $1,500 on a 50¢ six-coin four-reeler, etc. Here's the way some five-coin multiple machines work: the superjackpot on a three-wheeler, which can be three bars, three sevens (or any other three identical symbols) pay off at the basic rate of 200 to 1 multiple if one, two, three or four coins are played. Example: $50 for one quarter, $100 for two quarters, $150 for three quarters, $200 for four quarters. But if the player wagers five quarters, the jackpot is worth not $250, but $500, which is a potential bonus of $250.

Another new type of machine which steps up the slot action is the "progressive type." Actually, this is a machine in which the top jackpot—called the *superjackpot*—continuously increases in a predetermined ratio to the number of coins played into the machine. The jackpot can in some $1 or 50¢ machines reach a high of $100,000 or more. The superjackpots are usually displayed on two separate superjackpot counters, which advance alternately, while red arrows light alternately to indicate the superjackpot which may be won at each moment of play. Thus, when one counter is reduced to the minimum figure by a superjackpot win, the other counter remains an inducement to continued play.

Progressive slot machines are available in single win-line models and multiple line models, as illustrated above. The numbers 38202 on the top line and 77936 on the bottom mean that if the superjackpot is won the payoff, since this is a nickel machine, is either $382.02 or $779.36. Of course, if this was a $1 or 50¢ machine, the payoff would be $3,820.20 or $7,793.60. But note the gimmick in front of the player: to be eligible for the progressive jackpot the player must wager six coins at a time. Otherwise he is only paid off at the conventional 200 to 1 odds.

These machines, fairly rare a few years ago, are now so common that in many casinos in Nevada or the Caribbean islands a player is hard put to find a single-coin slot machine. The reasons for the sudden influx of multiple-coin slots in casinos throughout the world are: (1) Hourly income per square foot of floor space is notably increased. (2) Players are free to increase or decrease their bets at will. (3) Players like the action of the big jackpot. The payout percentage of these babies is the same as the single-coin slots—but, except for an exceptional jackpot win—you'll go broke much faster.

SLOT MACHINE ODDS

Most present-day three-wheel slot machines have 20 symbols on each wheel. The number of combinations that can appear on the center pay line is 20 × 20 × 20 = 8,000. To get the number of possible combinations on a four-wheel machine, you multiply once more by 20, for a total of 160,000.

If the number of possible payouts on a three-reeler totals 7,200 coins, you can divide this by the 8,000 possible combinations, getting 90%. That is the percentage of the total handle the machine will pay back in the long run, leaving a profit to the owners of 10%.

If I were a slot player and in a position to play any machine on the market today, I would select the Twenty-One Bell three-wheel nickel machine. This pays a jackpot in 19 ways and permits the bell symbol on the first reel to pay off either as a bell or as a bar. The payback to players is $94\frac{9}{20}\%$. The chances of hitting a jackpot are 1 in 421.

I'd be playing it just for fun; I wouldn't expect to beat it in the long run. Bucking even the low favorable percentage to the machine of $5\frac{11}{20}\%$ is an impossible winning task.

I'll use the Twenty-One Bell three-wheel machine to illustrate how slot machine percentages are calculated. First, here are the payoff combinations:

PAYOFF COMBINATIONS

	Cherry	Anything	Anything	Pays 2 Coins
	Cherry	Cherry	Anything	5
	Orange	Orange	Bar	10
	Orange	Orange	Orange	10
	Plum	Plum	Bar	14
	Plum	Plum	Plum	14
	Bell	Bell	Bar	18
	Bell	Bell	Bell	18
Jackpot:	Melon	Melon	Bar	100
Jackpot:	Melon	Melon	Melon	100
Jackpot:	Bar	Bar	Bar	100
Double Jackpot:	7	7	7	200

And here is a list of the 20 symbols on each reel:

Space	1st Reel	2nd Reel	3rd Reel
1	Orange	Cherry	Bell
2	Melon	Plum	Orange
3	Plum	Cherry	Plum
4	Cherry	7 & orange	Bell
5	Plum	Cherry	Orange
6	Orange	Bell	Lemon
7	7	Plum & bar	Bell
8	Bell & bar	Bell	Melon & orange
9	Orange	Cherry	Bell
10	Cherry	Orange	Plum
11	Bar	Bell	Lemon
12	Plum	Melon & orange	Bell
13	Orange	Plum	Plum
14	Plum	Bell	Bell
15	Melon	Cherry	7 and bar
16	Plum	Bar	Lemon
17	Orange	Orange	Bell
18	Plum	Cherry	Melon & orange
19	Bar	Bell	Bell
20	Plum	Melon & orange	Lemon

Note that in some instances two symbols show in a single space, as in space 8 on reel 1 where a bell and a bar are together. When this shows in the window, it counts either way—as a bell or a bar.

We now count the number of times each symbol appears on each reel:

	Reel 1	Reel 2	Reel 3
Cherries	2	6	0
Oranges	5	5	5 (including 2 melons, 1 bar)
Plums	7	3	4 (including 1 bar)
Bells	1	5	9 (including 1 bar)
Bars	3	2	1
Melons	2	2	3 (including 1 bar)
7s	1	1	1

This gives you the information you need to figure the number of payoff combinations for each symbol that can be expected to occur in the long run in each 8,000 plays.

Single-cherry combinations: The 2 cherries on reel 1 each pay off with all the symbols on reel 2 that are not cherries (14), and all the symbols on reel 3, which has no cherries (20). Then $2 \times 14 \times 20 = 560$ single-cherry combinations. Since each combination pays 2 coins, there are $560 \times 2 = 1,120$ coins paid out.

Two-cherry combinations: The 2 cherries on reel 1 each pay off with the 6 cherries on reel 2 and any of the 20 symbols on reel 3. Multiply $2 \times 6 \times 20 = 240$ combinations, each paying 5 coins for a total of 1,200 coins.

Three-symbol combinations: These are all figured alike. Take plums as an example. There are 7 plums on reel 1, 3 plums on reel 2, and 3 plums plus a bar that counts as a plum on reel 3. Multiply $7 \times 3 \times 4 = 84$ combinations. Each pays 14 coins for a total of $84 \times 14 = 1,176$ coins.

The following table shows the calculations for all symbols. Two oranges and bar are lumped in with 3 oranges, etc.

	Symbols					
	1st Reel	2nd Reel	3rd Reel	Ways	Payoff in Coins	Total Payoff
1 cherry	2 ×	14 ×	20 =	560	× 2	= 1,120
2 cherries	2 ×	6 ×	20 =	240	× 5	= 1,200
3 oranges	5 ×	5 ×	5 =	125	× 10	= 1,250
3 plums	7 ×	3 ×	4 =	84	× 14	= 1,176
3 bells	1 ×	5 ×	9 =	45	× 18	= 810
3 melons (jackpot)	2 ×	2 ×	3 =	12	× 100	= 1,200
3 bars (jackpot)	3 ×	2 ×	1 =	6	× 100	= 600
3 sevens (double jackpot)	1 ×	1 ×	1 =	1	× 200	= 200
				1,073		= 7,556

There are, as you see when you add the last three entries in the ways column, 19 ways to hit a jackpot.

There are 1,073 ways to hit a payoff combination. Divide 1,073 by total number of 8,000 plays and you find the player can expect to get a payback of some sort on an average of 13.4% of his plays. Of 8,000 coins put into the machine the player gets, in the long run, a return of 7,556 coins. Dividing 8,000 into 7,556 gives a coin-return percentage of $94\frac{9}{20}\%$. The machine retains, in the long run, 444 of each 8,000 coins played, a favorable percentage for the operator of $5\frac{11}{20}\%$.

Most machines in use are still three-reelers, but the popularity of four- and even five-reelers is on the increase. Most reels in these larger machines have 20 symbols; some casinos, however, use a limited number of slots with 22 symbols on each reel (22 stops or positions at which each spinning reel can stop), and a few 25-symbol, 25-stop machines. The latter type gives the three-reeler thousands of additional combinations so that the jackpot or bonus awards can be made much larger. You can, for example, have a $50 jackpot on a three-reel nickel machine and still retain all the lesser payouts. The number of possible combinations on this machine is $25 \times 25 \times 25$, or 15,625, which is nearly double the 8,000 on the usual three-reeler. The same applies to five-, six- or eight-coin machines, if you remember that an additional single-coin payout comes with the insertion of each additional coin.

CALCULATING THE PAYOUT PERCENTAGE ON OTHER MACHINES

How does a slot player figure the payout percentage of a particular machine or find out which of a group of machines has the best payout percentage? If you ask the machine's operator, the chances are he doesn't know. Even if he gives you an answer, how do you know it's right? You probably wouldn't believe him anyway.

The only sure way to get this information is to open the back of the machine, count all the symbols and calculate the percentage as I did on the Twenty-One Bell machine. The catch here is that there is almost no chance that an operator will permit you to do this. So you try to count the number of like symbols through the machine's little glass window, after the spinning reels come to a stop. They spin too fast for you to do this when they are in motion. This isn't any help. You can see only nine of the 60 symbols, and you don't know whether or not the bell that shows on the first reel is the same bell that appeared on a previous spin or a different one.

Although I can't give you any sure way of obtaining the information that will allow you to figure the correct percentage, I can give you a system by which you will be able to determine which of a number of machines is the "loosest" and gives the best percentage of return. That will have to do.

It's a system that was first used by an old-time slot player who had been a slot mechanic working in Reno years before the machines were legalized in Nevada. He started with $50 worth of nickels—1,000 coins. He would select a machine and play the 1,000 coins into it—a little more than an hour's work. He pocketed all the coins the machine paid out and did not play any of them back into the machine. Jackpot winnings, if any, were kept separate. When the original 1,000 coins were gone he counted his payback returns, not counting the jackpot money. Then he repeated the same procedure with other machines and compared the payback returns from each. The machine that returned the most coins, he figured to have the best payback percentage for the player. This system of spotting the loosest and tightest machines is not 100% accurate, but it does work about 95% of the time.

SLOT PLAYERS

If you think that playing the slots is nothing more than a pleasant pastime, watch a few slot addicts at work. I can name a dozen women players who have lost as much as $20,000 a year to the machines. For many addicts, putting coins into one machine isn't fast enough, so they tackle two, three or four machines at the same time. The left hand puts a coin in, the right pulls the handle down with a practiced rhythmic motion, the player takes a sideward step and repeats with the next machine, and the next and the next, then back to the first machine—hour after hour. Many women addicts wear a glove on the right hand to avoid getting calluses.

Here's an incident that illustrates the fascination the slot machine holds for men and women in all walks of life. Five friends of mine—the socially prominent Chicagoan Mrs. Blanche Sundheim, her husband, Harry, and three friends, Ralph Leonardson, Milton Henry and Victor Goldberg, were walking through the casino at the Habana Hilton on the afternoon of August 6, 1958. Mr. Goldberg found a lost nickel on the floor, handed it to Mrs. Sundheim, and suggested she play it in one of the machines that line the walls. She dropped the coin in the slot, pulled the lever and found herself a five-coin winner.

Four hours later I came by and found the group glued to the same machine. Blanche, with a handful of nickels, was playing, and the four men were rooting for her to hit the jackpot. Mr. Goldberg, seeing me, said, "Scarne, this is all happening with a found nickel."

I turned to Mrs. Sundheim. "Why don't you play the nickel four-reel Buckaroo machine? You might hit the four buckaroos and collect the hundred-and-twenty-five-dollar bonus award."

"Let's go," she said, and a moment later was pulling madly at the Buckaroo machine lever, occasionally switching from right to left hand.

After about 15 minutes of average slot-machine payouts, Whammo! Four buckaroos on the pay line. The four friends let out a whoop that could be heard all over the casino, and play stopped momentarily at the dice, Black Jack, Roulette and Baccarat tables. A few minutes later, with the $125 award, Blanche and her rooting section moved to a quarter Buckaroo machine. She played in about $10 and Lady Luck smiled again—a broad grin. She had hit the four buckaroos for the $625 prize award. More cheers rocked the casino.

After five hours of play Blanche and party adjourned for dinner. After dinner they were back at the slots again. And they did little else for the next six days. They put in about 60 hours of slot play, during which Blanche hit about 40 jackpots. After the first 40 hours, that found nickel had grown to $1,700. This would have been a good place to stop.

For the last two days of play they moved over to the silver-dollar machine, whose Buckaroo award is $2,500. An hour before leaving the hotel to catch a plane for home, Blanche lost her last silver dollar. The found nickel had gone; both her hands were callused, and black from handling the coins. I told her she had pulled the slot handle approximately 54,000 times.

She smiled and said, "I enjoyed every one of those fifty-four thousand pulls."

BEATING THE ONE-ARMED BANDIT

Today the slot machine manufacturers seem to be winning their long battle with the slickers who are out to cheat the machines. Years ago slot cheats sometimes managed to empty the coin tube and jackpot by drilling a tiny hole with a special tool through the wood of the cabinet directly opposite the payout slides. They would insert a hooked wire, catch the bottom payout slide, pull it and receive a payout after each play, no matter what combination appeared on the pay line. The manufacturers countered that by lining the wooden interior with a drill-proof steel sheet.

Other slickers used *spooning* devices. The spooner pushed the handle of a teaspoon into the coin-return opening, wedged open the little trap door, put a coin into the slot and pulled the lever. The slide now paid off on any combination. Another method was to insert long flexible rods up through the payout hole into the payout chute. A back-and-forth manipulation of the slide brought the coins out on any combination. Slot manufacturers stopped this by putting two sharp angles on the pay chute, thus making it impossible to insert anything up the chute and still keep leverage.

THE RHYTHM SYSTEM

The manufacturers thought they had outwitted the slot cheats. Then, one day some years ago, a mysterious stranger walked into the Golden Nugget on Fremont Street in Las Vegas. He began playing a nickel slot and about ten minutes later had emptied the machine's coin tube and the jackpot. Within an hour he had hit jackpots on a dozen more machines. The slot inspectors and the Golden Nugget owners watched him hit jackpot after jackpot and eventually walk out with $500 in winnings. Some figured he was just a lucky guy. Others suspected that he might be smart and have something on the machine; but they couldn't prove a thing. He hadn't been drilling or using spooning devices.

That same evening the stranger emptied a dozen tubes and jackpots at the Flamingo and then went on to the El Rancho Vegas, where he had equal success. During the next week he had hit jackpots on about 300 machines all over Las Vegas. He caused quite a lot of talk among the gambling fraternity. "Who is he?" "Can anybody be that lucky?" "Nobody could hit three hundred jackpots in a week; he *must* have something on the machines." "Maybe he's a scientist using some top-secret radar gimmick."

His phenomenal run of luck continued and he checked out after another week's play with about $30,000 in winnings. Not bad for two week's work.

He dropped out of sight for a month. Then the operators in Reno began to notice a player who was emptying slot tubes and jackpots almost as fast as the attendants could fill them. After a week he disappeared again, and the slot owners, who had begun to wonder if something had gone wrong with their machines, were relieved to find that they were again paying out winners in the usual fashion.

As the months passed, slot manufacturers noticed that they were getting more and more complaints from their customers in various parts of the country. Always the same complaint: a stranger was giving the law of averages a terrific beating.

Early in 1948, operators of casinos in Reno and Las Vegas again noticed that their daily receipts were dropping off; but they didn't remember the stranger who had been so lucky a couple of years before.

Several operators returned machines to the manufacturers and asked for replacements because the machines were no longer earning the expected revenue. The makers replaced the machines with new ones which proved to be afflicted with the same trouble. The entire slot handle in Nevada took a nose dive.

I heard about the situation and went to Las Vegas to get a look for myself. I interviewed a dozen casino managers and they all reported a revenue drop. I also discovered that the same mysterious stranger was in town again, only now he had four companions, all of whom were being much too lucky.

One casino manager had this to say:

"A couple of days ago in walks a guy who the day before had emptied tubes and jackpots of fifteen machines. I figured he must have some gaff so I watched him. He hadn't been playing five minutes when I heard *Klump!*—the sound of a falling jackpot. The machine inspectors refilled the jackpot with thirty dollars in quarters. I moved closer, kept watching, and began counting the coins he dropped in. At forty, the old familiar jackpot sound—another *Klump!*

"Not again, I told myself. I walked over and took a good look. Sure enough, the three bars were lined up on the pay line."

"What did you do then?" I asked.

"What could I do? I paid off. Scarne, after this character hit five more jackpots within the next half hour I knew for sure he had something on the machine. I studied the way he dropped his coin into the slot and the way he pulled the handle. I looked for every cheating gimmick ever used to beat a machine. The only thing unusual I could spot was that he didn't have the usual slot-player's swing. Once he pulled the handle immediately after inserting the coin; other times, after dropping the coin, he waited a bit before he pulled the handle. There were many pauses between plays, some much longer than others. But I wasn't sure this meant anything. And there was nothing I could do about it anyway; a slot player can do as he pleases when playing his own dough."

My next stop was the Golden Nugget. When the then owner, Jake Kozloff, spotted me, the first words he said were, "I'll bet you're in town checking on the rhythm players." This was the first time I had heard the expression "rhythm players."

Jake added, "You're lucky, Scarne; a representative of the Mills Company is arriving in town in about an hour."

"What's so unusual about a slot manufacturer's representative showing up in Las Vegas?" I asked.

Jake grinned. "I've got a ten-thousand-dollar wager with him that I'll empty the coin tube he's bringing with him from Chicago."

"I'll say I'm lucky, Jake, if what you say is true."

He wasn't joking about the $10,000 bet or his ability to do what he said. The next morning, in the basement of the Golden Nugget, I saw Jake Kozloff feed about a dozen quarters into the new slot machine and pull its lever in the usual fashion with the usual results. Then he turned to the Mills Company man and said, "I'm going to put two cherries on the machine's pay line."

Before anyone could reply, he put in another quarter, pulled the handle and sent the three wheels spinning. Sure enough, when the reels stopped there was a cherry on each of the first two reels. Nobody spoke. The only sound was the jingle of several quarters rattling down the payout tubes.

Jake pulled the handle again and got two cherries again. He repeated this four times in a row—always the same two cherries. It was obvious that all he had to do to empty the tube was to keep going. He did. It took him about 20 minutes.

The Mills man said in an unhappy voice, "Jake, I'm sick. Not about losing the ten-thousand-dollar bet, but about the thousands and thousands of dollars that the slot operators are losing. If we don't find an answer to this rhythm gimmick fast, slot machines are doomed."

Before I left the Golden Nugget that morning Jake gave me an hour's lesson in "rhythming" a machine, and I knew that the slot representative had called the turn. Unless a cure for rhythming could be found, the slot industry would fold.

Shortly after I returned home I heard from my friend Clifford Jones, then Lieutenant Governor of Nevada, that a group of players who called themselves the Rhythm Boys had opened a school in Las Vegas and were charging $500 for a complete course in how to beat the slots by the rhythm system. This was apparently a pretty successful school and it graduated a good many students summa cum laude. During 1949 a couple of thousand rhythm players, most of whom were women, were beating the slots all over Nevada and various other sections of the country. Hundreds were barred from the slot rooms, and slander suits (which were later dropped) were filed by some of the barred players.

My findings show that national slot machine revenue took a real nose dive, dropping from the 1948 figure of $700 million to a rock-bottom low of $200 million in 1949. The rhythm players beat the slots during 1949 for half a billion dollars.

How did the original mysterious stranger happen to come up with his bright idea? And who was he? I did some further detective work and discovered that he was an Idaho farmer who, during his spare time, had been helping a slot-mechanic friend repair out-of-order machines. He discovered that the three wheels in certain makes of machine made exactly the same number of revolutions when the handle was pulled. He studied the clock fan which controls the length of time the reels spin and found that on some machines the clock went dead from seven to eight seconds after the reels stopped spinning. He also memorized the position of each symbol on each reel. In actual play, since he knew the relative positions on the reel of all the symbols, he could deduce from the nine visible symbols he could see through the window just where all the others were. Then, by timing himself to pull the machine's lever at precisely the right instant and before the clock gear went dead, he found that he could manipulate the desired symbols onto the pay line. Most of the rhythm players who learned the system later could, as a rule, control only the cherry on the first reel, but even that was good enough to empty the payoff coin tube; it just took a little longer.

In 1950, a ten-page pamphlet explaining how to rhythm a slot machine appeared, selling for $5. Here is a quote from it that gives you more details on the system:

First of all remember the system of the "Rhythm Boys" is based on timing. Each machine has a clock gear which determines the number of revolutions that each reel will make. As each reel has 20 symbols, the timing must be precise; i.e., if you aim at a cherry, you don't want to hit the orange above or below the cherry. The average clocks become dead in from 7 to 8 seconds. After that time has elapsed there will be nothing that can be done to control the reels.

The average slot machine has a payback of between 80 to 92 percent of the money that is placed into it. Using our timing system the rate of payback is raised to between 110 and 125 percent.

Although the system is based on timing, standing at a machine with a stop watch would, of course, appear too obvious. So we do the next best thing: we have a "watch" in our minds.

As the first lesson, get a watch and time yourself by the second hand; count under your breath from 1 to 20 in exactly five seconds, then learn to count from 11 to 30 in exactly five seconds. Practice this until you become absolutely perfect. When you are positive you can do this without the help of a watch, we will proceed to the next step, which is learning to play the machine and learning how to apply the count.

Place your money in your left hand, taking each coin out with the right hand, insert the coin in the slot and carry the right hand on over to the handle. Pull the handle, starting the mechanism.

The reason for holding the money in the left and operating the mechanism with the right is to stall when you have a long count or to be ready immediately when you have a short count. You will have a count varying from five to twenty-five.

Now start your count with the stopping of the last reel. Practice this until you count one at exactly the same time the third wheel stops. When we say exactly, we mean exactly; it has to be, as the whole system is based on precision. After you have learned this you are now ready for the most important part of the operation, which is learning how to memorize the reel strips.

We cannot stress too much the importance of this part of the system because you will have complete control over any one reel. So when the object you are trying to control goes out of sight you will have a count to bring it right back.

Every machine has a "hold" count. To understand this hold count, say we're playing a machine and the hold count is 16. For example, if the last bar is in the window and if we give it an exact count of 16 from the time the third reel stops until we trip the mechanism with the handle, the last bar should come right back in the pay slot or if it fluctuates, should be no further than three emblems away on each side of the pay slot, which is giving you control of the reel. This eliminates from the pay slot all the dead emblems, lemons, etc., which are no good.

Use a short count to bring symbols up, use a long count to bring symbols down, going on a basis of one count to each symbol.

For example, if the hold count is 16, 1 up from center, count 17; 2 up from center, count 18; 3 up from center, count 19, etc. If 1 down from center count 15; 2 down from center, count 14; 3 down from center, count 13. Center means payoff position.

Each machine has a different hold count. To find this hold count get the object in the window which you are trying to hold, count 14, pull off the mechanism and let it stop. If the object goes down from center, for example, subtract 5 from 14 and the approximate hold count would be 9.

Another example: if the object went up 6 from center, add 6 to 14—an approximate hold count of 20 which, as you start to play the machine again, you will be able to jockey the machine to the exact hold count. If the machine jumps too far away from center the machine is erratic. Try another machine.

This was too good a thing to last. By 1951 all the slot manufacturers knew exactly what was happening and had solved the problem. They simply added another gimmick to the machines—a variator. This mechanical device controls the clock mechanism so that the spin starts at different times.

The variator put an end to what was, for a lot of players, the most exciting period in the history of the slot machine.

THE $7 MILLION CASINO SLOT MACHINE RIPOFF

The biggest and most successful slot-machine ripoff in casino history came to light on May 18, 1976, when Nevada state agents raided the slot-machine section of the Las Vegas Stardust Casino. Information leaked to me by a high Nevada official revealed that top slot-machine personnel at the Stardust Casino were able to steal $7 million in quarters over a two-year period.

In Nevada casinos, slot-machine coins are weighed, not counted, and for the reader's information I add that $7 million in quarters weighs 175 tons. To steal 175 tons of quarters without detection is a feat in itself.

This is how the slot thieves were able to steal 175 tons of quarters over a two-year period. The chief feature was a coin scale, among several, that had been ingeniously rewired to register only $66\frac{2}{3}\%$ of its actual weight. In other words, the scale registered only two of every three coins placed on it. The coins were then wrapped in rolls and stored in a large vault that was part of a change cage right out on the casino floor. By selling the quarters to the casino's change girls for paper money, the casino culprits were able to avoid the logistical problem of removing 175 tons of quarters from the Stardust Casino. This scam is still under investigation at the time of writing.

PINBALL MACHINES

Pinball machines today are primarily amusement devices and are not used for gambling to the extent they once were. Slot machines and pinball games are, however, related in one way: When slots are banned in a territory, the slot operators, instead of closing up, switch over to pinball machines. They want to stay in business so they'll be ready if the one-armed bandits come back.

Pinball machines evolved from a very old game known as Bagatelle which, under various names, can still be purchased in toy stores. Several versions of this have been used for gambling by carnival operators since the early 1900s. One of the earliest, the Drop Case, consists of a vertical board studded with brads, under glass. Marbles dropped in through openings at the top roll down through the maze of brads into numbered pockets at the bottom. Reference to a chart tells the player whether he has won or lost. Drop Cases are usually gaffed so that they can be controlled by the operator. They are still to be found in carnivals.

In larger sizes the pinball machine was designed as a glass-covered wood box with an inner inclined playing surface studded with nails or brads. When the player pulled back a plunger at one side and then released it, a ball was propelled to the upper end of the board and rolled back down through the obstructing pattern of nails into winning and losing sections.

Pinball manufacturers later added many electrical gadgets, flashing lights and sound effects.

About 1928 a Chicago manufacturer took the game out of the carnival class and began making it for sale in quantity. By 1931 the first electrically operated pinball machines appeared with their more complicated high scoring systems.

These first machines were intended for use in locations where slots were prohibited. They were advertised as "skill" games, but the purchaser was told that they were perfect gambling devices for closed territories. The gimmick was that high scores paid off a specified number of winning games which were redeemable in cash over the counter. This subterfuge didn't fool the courts for long, and the machines were banned when used for gambling.

The manufacturers discovered that the public liked to play the pinball game even when it didn't pay off in cash, so they discarded the gambling feature and installed a "free play" feature. A winning score gave the player the right to continue playing without more coins.

Even now, there are many storekeepers who will redeem the winning scores for cash; but the great majority of pinball games are amusement devices only.

ADVICE TO SLOT PLAYERS

As a gambling consultant I see a great many gamblers every day. The biggest gambling fool I've ever encountered is the slot machine degenerate who feeds the machines for hours at a time, day in and day out, in the belief that he can make a killing.

The slot machine player has less chance of winning in a long or short run than does the player at any other casino game: Bank Craps, Roulette, Black Jack or even the Big Six. His chance of beating the slots for even a few bucks over a period of time is exactly zero.

This isn't due, as most people believe, to the slot machine's percentage take, but rather to a betting restriction. "Slot machines," you may object, "don't have realistic minimum and maximum betting limits like other casino games."

Sure. You can bet one to eight coins on a modern multiple-coin machine. But what kind of a limit is that? A three-time double-up (2–4–8) and you reach the machine's maximum betting limit. In other casino games, when you feel lucky, you can step up your action.

If you were playing Bank Craps, Black Jack or Roulette and the rules restricted you to betting one to eight dollars per round or hand, you wouldn't stay in the game for long. You'd soon learn that your chance of winning any decent amount of money was very small. Millions of slot machine players never seem to realize this as they keep feeding in one to eight coins at a time.

Of the thousands upon thousands of slot players I have seen here and in other countries I can't recall one who ever quit a small winner over a long period of playing time, slot cheats excluded. But I can recall easily the names of a dozen slot degenerates who lost fortunes vainly trying to beat the slots.

At a Caribbean casino I once overheard a woman slot player making the old, familiar slot player's complaint to the casino host, Allen Kanter.

"Mr. Kanter, I just dropped twenty dollars in that quarter machine and only got four quarters back. Don't these slot machines ever pay off?"

Allen's reply was classic: "Lady, they sure do. They pay the casino's rent, the light bills, all the casino employees' salaries and a cool half million dollars a year in profits. Sure, they pay off."

My last piece of advice to the degenerate slot player who thinks he can beat the one-armed bandit consists of four little words: It can't be done.

10

CHEMIN DE FER
AND BACCARAT

Baccarat and its variations, Punto Banco and Chemin de Fer, are the most popular games in European and Latin-American casinos, and are undoubtedly the most important and get the biggest play of any banking card games. Baccarat, or Baccarat–Chemin de Fer as it is known in Nevada, is played in most major casinos in Las Vegas, Reno and Atlantic City. Before 1960, Chemin de Fer, usually called Shimmy by American gamblers, was the type of Baccarat most often played in fashionable casinos in the United States. Another variation, found in European casinos, is Baccarat-en-Banque. The present-day Baccarat and Chemin de Fer are French variations of the Italian game of Baccara, which was first introduced into France about 1490 during the reign of Charles VIII. It was for years the favorite private gambling game of the French nobility and did not make its public appearance in the European casinos until many years later.

HISTORY

Baccarat, under its earlier name Baccara, first made its appearance in America in 1911, and by 1912 several New York City sawdust joints, including Big Thompson's on Houston Street, featured Baccara tables. It disappeared from the American scene a few years later when the structurally similar Black Jack was introduced into American casinos.

Chemin de Fer was first played in this country in 1920, shortly after World War I, in the homes of wealthy Americans vacationing in Palm Beach, Florida. It had its biggest boom here during the 1940s, when every big rug and sawdust joint had a Chemin de Fer table. The Star Dust Hotel in Las Vegas introduced a Shimmy table into its casino early in 1958, the first legalized game of Chemin de Fer in the country. Soon after, other Strip casinos also introduced it, but for reasons which I'll explain later it didn't click in the big way the operators hoped it would.

Almost two years later, on November 21, 1959, Carl Cohen, then manager of the Sands Hotel Casino in Las Vegas, began operating a Baccarat–Chemin der Fer table. Early that year, Aaron Weisberg, a Sands casino executive, came to see me at the Habana Hilton Hotel Casino in Cuba, where I was consultant. He wanted to know all the necessary information— house's favorable percentage, method of play, etc.—on Punto Banco. After our discussion, he decided that the game was for Las Vegas and borrowed several Cuban dealers from the Habana Hilton Casino to accompany him to Nevada to deal and teach the Sands casino employees the game. An interesting fact was that the first hours of play cost the operators $251,000, which was paid to a dozen winners, the biggest a Texas rancher who pocketed $172,000. But Baccarat–Chemin de Fer proved to be a big success at the Sands.

Las Vegas style Baccarat is similar to the Baccarat found at Monte Carlo, Deauville and the municipal casinos in San Remo, Italy, plus a few Cuban trimmings.

The biggest single loss that I have ever witnessed at a Baccarat session was $1,500,000 lost by a titled English high roller at the Knightsbridge Sporting Club in London. The biggest loss in Nevada to my knowledge at Baccarat–Chemin de Fer took place recently at the Sands Hotel Casino when several Japanese high-rolling businessmen lost the gigantic sum of $2 million in a week's play at the game. At about the same time I saw a well-groomed young Chinese woman run a $200 bet into a $250,000 profit in a week's play in a number of Las Vegas Strip casinos.

There is only a slight difference in the playing rules of Shimmy and Baccarat, or Baccara. In Baccarat, as it is played in Monte Carlo and other European casinos, the game is banked by the casino operators or by concessionaires (usually a Greek syndicate) who pay the casino operators 50% of their monthly winnings for the banking privilege. Players who bet the bank to win are charged 5% of their winnings on each bet. Players who bet the bank to lose do not pay a direct charge, but they do play a hidden percentage.

Chemin de Fer is played exactly the same as Baccarat, with the exception that the casino operators take no risk, since the players bet against each other. The house acts as a *cutter,* the same as the operator of a Poker game. For a standard *cut* (charge) of 5% taken out of the player banker's winning *coup* (bet), the house rents out the Shimmy equipment and supplies three croupiers to operate the game. In return for the 5% charge, the croupiers run the game, manage the banker's money, collect winning bets and pay out losing bets.

During the early forties, when Shimmy was the gambling rage in America, the casino's 5% cut on the banker's winnings was not quite as sure a thing as the income of the Internal Revenue Bureau, but " 'twill do, 'twill do." One night, during that period, I clocked the casino take at the Shimmy table at Ben Marden's Riviera casino in Bergen County, New Jersey. It was approximately $30,000. Further detective work revealed that the yearly house cut at this one Shimmy table during World War II was about $3 million. On a capital investment of the price of a gambling okay, this seems a tolerable dividend.

The vocabulary of Chemin de Fer used in the United States is partly French (*banco, la grande, la petite*), partly Black Jack lingo (Hit me!) and partly from Craps (next shooter, the bank's faded). Unlike the Baccarat games in French casinos, *checks* (chips) are seldom used in Shimmy games in the United States; the green stuff makes for a more interesting game.

The bets at Shimmy vary from a low of $5 to $50,000 or more, depending on the amount of the player-banker's winnings and the amount anted into the bank. The usual Chemin de Fer banker's ante limits run from a low of $100 to $10,000 or more. The largest sum ever anted into a Shimmy bank in an American casino was the $500,000 bank of an American oil tycoon in a Florida casino one night in the winter season of 1946. The oil tycoon lost $847,000 that evening. Note: He was cheated.

The Chemin de Fer equipment is bulky. The game requires a heavy kidney-shaped table, its surfaces padded and covered with a fancy green baize layout divided into numbered sections for nine or 12 players. Other requirements are six or eight decks of cards, a mahogany *sabot* or *shoe* (card-dealing box), a *money box* which holds the casino's gambling revenue, and a discard cylinder. The croupier, who handles the dealt cards, sits in the concavity of the kidney-shaped table and uses a wooden *palette* to slide the cards, cash or chips around to the players.

The two croupiers who sit opposite him also have a palette to facilitate handling the bets. A lookout sits on a stand overlooking the Shimmy table. Although Shimmy and Baccarat are as fair percentagewise as any other banking game, until the first publication of *Scarne's Complete Guide to Gambling* in 1961 many American gamblers didn't realize this and rarely sat down to play either game.

SCARNE'S RULES FOR CHEMIN DE FER

REQUIREMENTS

1. From two to as many players as there are player spaces available on the layout. Some tables have nine, others 12. The banker plays against only one player at a time, but any or all the other players may bet on that one player's hand against the bank, provided the bank possesses enough money to cover the wagers.

2. A regulation Chemin de Fer table with a *discard box* into which the played cards are dropped and *money box* to receive the casino's 5% charge.

3. A card-dealing box called a *sabot* or *shoe.*

4. Eight standard decks of 52 cards, four red-backed decks and four blue-backed decks, plus two advertising cards which are used as indicators. (In some casinos only six decks are used.)

5. Three Chemin de Fer *palettes,* long thin paddles which enable the seated croupiers to transact business at the far reaches of the table.

OBJECT OF THE GAME

To win a *coup* by holding a combination of two or three cards totaling 9 or as close as possible to 9, or to a two-digit number ending in 9. When the total of the cards is a two-digit number, only the latter digit has any value. Examples: A count of 19 has a value of 9; a count of 23 has a value of 3, and so forth.

VALUE OF THE CARDS

The ace is the lowest ranking card and has a point value of 1 (one). Kings, queens and jacks have a value of 10 each. All other cards have their numerical face value. The suits have no comparative value.

THE SHUFFLE AND CUT

At the start of the game, the dealer-croupier spreads the eight decks of cards on the table and all the players and croupiers are permitted to take a group of cards and shuffle them. On later deals when the discard receiver is emptied on to the layout and some cards are face up, some face down, the croupiers and players turn the face-up cards down and shuffle them.

After the players have shuffled groups of cards, the croupier gathers all the cards and shuffles them together, usually shuffling about two decks at a time. Finally, the croupier assembles all eight decks into one packet and hands a player an indicator card and says, "Cut, please." The player inserts the indicator card into the packet to show where he wants the cards cut. The croupier cuts the cards at this position, putting the indicator and all the cards above it on the bottom. He then inserts the second indicator card seven, eight or ten cards from the bottom of the packet, and places all the cards into the shoe face down. The croupier next deals three cards from the shoe and drops them through a slot in the table into the discard receiver. This is called *burning* the top cards. (Some operators burn five or six cards instead of three.) The shoe is now ready to be dealt by the first banker-player.

SELECTING THE FIRST BANKER

The first player on the croupier's right has the privilege of being first banker. If the first player declines the bank, the privilege passes to the player to his right, and so on, counterclockwise (or the bank may be auctioned to the highest bidder).

The banker-dealer at Chemin de Fer continues to deal until he *misses a pass* (loses a bet). When the active player wins a bet the croupier passes the shoe to the player on the dealer's right. It always moves on counterclockwise. In mid-game, as at the start, the bank may be declined.

When the first advertising card shows, the croupier announces, "One more hand, please." Upon completion of this last hand, a reshuffle takes place which is governed by the rules for the original shuffle and cut.

PREPARATION FOR THE PLAY

The croupier slides the shoe to the first designated banker, who places on the table an amount of money within the house betting limits. This amount may be from a low of $100 to a high of $5,000, $10,000 or more, all depending on the banker's gambling spirit. A lucky bank may at times hold several hundred thousand dollars, and a player can bet all or any part of it as he wishes.

THE BETTING

Before any cards are dealt, the players must make their bets (called *fading*). If a player wants to fade the bank for its total worth, he calls "Banco." A banco bet has precedence over any other. The player to the right of the dealer has the first privilege of bancoing. If he does not banco, the privilege passes to the next man on the right, and so on around the table. Then, any watcher or former nonplayer may call banco.

If no one bancos, then partial bets are accepted, with the first man on the right placing his bet, for whatever amount he chooses, on the table before him. Then the player on his right bets, and so on around the table until the bank is partly or completely faded. If the bank is not completely faded, the amount which has not been faded is set aside for the banker.

Anyone who bancos, whatever his position around the table, has the right of *banco suivi* (following banco) if he loses. His right to call banco on the next deal has precedence over all others; if he fails to call banco and more than one other person calls banco, the player nearest the dealer starting from the right has precedence, even though he may call banco after another player has done so. This right is known as *banco prime*.

The player who bancos becomes the active player. If no one has bancoed and there are partial bets, the player who has bet the most money is designated by the croupier as the active player.

Because the rules of Chemin de Fer are so many and so complicated, each player is supplied with a card, as shown, describing the player's and the banker's rules.

THE COUP, OR PLAY

The banker slides one card out of the shoe and deals it to the active player; then he deals one card for himself, a second card to the player, and finally a second card to himself. All four cards are dealt face down.

THE FIRST TURN OF PLAY

The active player now examines his cards. If they total a count of 8 or 9, he turns them face up on the table. If the count is 8, he calls, *"La petite!"* If it is 9, he calls, *"La grande!"* The croupier verifies the count. The banker must now turn his two cards face up.

CHEMIN DE FER

Game Must Be Played According to Rules

PLAYER

H	0 – 1 – 2 – 3 – 4	Always Draws a Card
A		
V	5	Optional—*Stand or Draw*
I		
N	6 – 7	Never Draws—*Stands*
G	8 – 9	*Turn* Cards Face Up

BANKER

		Draws If Giving	Does Not Draw in Giving		O
H					P
A	3	1, 2, 3, 4, 5, 6, 7, 10	8	9	T
V					I
I	4	2, 3, 4, 5, 6, 7	1, 8, 9, 10		O
N					N
G	5	5, 6, 7	1, 2, 3, 8, 9, 10	4	A
	6	6, 7	1, 2, 3, 4, 5, 8, 9, 10		L

Banker Always Draws When Having 0, 1, 2
Banker Never Draws When Having 7
Banker Faces 8, 9
If Player Takes No Card, Banker Stands Only On 6, 7

— NO MISTAKES ARE ALLOWED —
IF ANY ARE MADE IT IS COMPULSORY
For The DEALER to Reconstruct The COUP

1. If the active player's count is higher than the banker's, the croupier pays off all the winning players. If the active player's count is lower than the banker's, the banker wins, and the croupier collects all the bets for him.

2. If the active player holds a count of less than 8, he says, "Pass," and the banker now examines his own cards. If they total 8 or 9, he turns them face up, and the croupier collects all the bets for him.

3. If the banker does not hold a count of 8 or 9, play reverts to the active player.

4. If the banker's count is the same as the player's count, it is a *legal tie,* or *standoff,* and neither banker nor player wins or loses.

These four rules apply with equal force to the player's and banker's second turn of play.

ACTIVE PLAYER'S SECOND TURN OF PLAY

1. If the active player holds a count of 1, 2, 3, 4 or 0, he must draw a card.

2. If the active player has a count of 5, the draw is optional; he may elect either to *get hit* (draw) or to *stay* (not draw). This is the only discretionary play the active player has at Chemin de Fer.

3. If the active player has a count of 6 or 7, he *must* stay.

BANKER'S SECOND TURN OF PLAY

1. If the banker holds a count of 0–1–2 he must draw a card.

2. If the active player stays and the banker holds a count of 4 or 5 he must draw.

3. If the active player stays and the banker holds a count of 6 or 7 he must stay.

BANKER HOLDS A COUNT OF THREE

1. If the active player in his turn of play has drawn a card valued at 1, 2, 3, 4, 5, 6, 7 or 10, the banker must draw.

2. If the active player has drawn an 8, the banker must stay.

3. If the active player has drawn a 9, the banker's play is optional; he may draw or stay.

BANKER HOLDS A COUNT OF FOUR

1. If the active player fails to draw a card, the banker must draw.

2. If the active player draws a card valued 2, 3, 4, 5, 6 or 7, the banker must draw.

3. If the active player draws a card valued 1, 8, 9 or 10, the banker must stay.

BANKER HOLDS A COUNT OF FIVE

1. If the active player did not draw a card on his turn of play, the banker must draw.

2. If the active player draws a card valued 5, 6 or 7, the banker must draw.

3. If the active player draws a card valued 1, 2, 3, 8, 9 or 10, the banker must stay.

4. If the active player draws a 4, the banker's play is optional; he may either stay or draw.

BANKER HOLDS A COUNT OF SIX

1. If the active player fails to draw, the banker must stay.

2. If the active player draws a 6 or 7, the banker must draw.

3. If the active player draws a card valued 1, 2, 3, 4, 5, 8, 9, or 10, the banker must stay.

BANKER HOLDS A COUNT OF SEVEN

Regardless of the active player's draw, the banker must stay.

RULES GOVERNING THE BANK

If the bank loses a coup the deal passes. If the bank wins, the same player holds the bank and all the money in the bank is now at stake—the banker's original bet and his winnings, less the 5% charge (in some casinos the 5% is not collected from the first win by the bank). The banker does not have the privilege of *dragging down* or reducing his bank. It is all or nothing. He may, of course, pass the bank at any time; but if he wants to retain the bank he risks the entire bank, except when the bank exceeds the house limit or the bettors have not faded the full amount of the bank. In either case, the excess is put aside for the banker by the croupier.

When the banker passes, the croupier holds an informal auction of the bank, and gives it to the player who will put up a bank equal to the one that has just been passed. If the high bidder happened to be the player to the right of the banker, that player now gets the bank, in his regular turn.

The bank can pass at any time up to the actual dealing of the cards.

I once saw a friend of mine at a casino in Palm Springs, California, roll up a bank from $500 to about $30,000, never hesitating to continue playing. When it was $30,000 or nothing, he watched the players' bets go down. It happened that only $10,000 was covered, so $20,000 was put aside. My friend dealt the cards out—and lost. But he still received the $20,000. Later he said to me, "John, I must have been crazy to let that thirty thousand ride in the center. I should have passed the bank. I was in a fog and I didn't realize what I was doing." That is how most Shimmy players react when the betting gets big.

BACCARAT LAS VEGAS STYLE

Since many European and South American casinos have 40 or more Baccara tables in action at one time, it is surprising that Nevada gambling operators have waited almost 30 years before giving Baccara, or Baccarat as they call it, a try. They will do this when they discover that Baccarat gets more action than Chemin de Fer, and thus earns more money for its operators, for the following reasons:

1. Because the house banks the game of Baccarat, one lone player can play, whereas at Chemin de Fer, players may sit around for hours (as in Poker), waiting for enough players to arrive to get the game started.

2. Baccarat has the advantage that a player can bet two ways: on the bank or on the player's hand. Hence, players often switch their betting from the bank to the player's hand—or vice versa.

3. Baccarat has a bigger draw for the bigtime player than Chemin de Fer: the player knows that if he gets lucky he can win big, because the casino's entire bankroll is at stake. At Chemin de Fer, the amount a player can win is limited by how much the other players are willing to lose.

The betting limits for Baccarat in Nevada casinos run from a low of $5 to a maximum of $2,000, with, of course, special betting limits for well-known high rollers, usually the amount of their first bet: $2,500, $5,000, $10,000 or even more.

The Baccarat table and equipment are similar to those for Chemin de Fer, except that the Baccarat layout has two betting spaces at each end of the table, one marked "Bank" and the other marked "Players." There are spaces for 12 players at the table, numbered from 1 to 12. In European and Latin American casinos checks or chips are used to deal the game and run from a low of 50¢ to a high of $100. The 50¢ chips are used to facilitate the croupiers' taking the 5% house charge from winning players who have bet on the bank. Until a few years ago, Nevada casinos used money rather than chips in dealing the game. After several scandals of stealing from the casino bankroll, the Nevada Gaming Control Board ruled that Baccarat-Chemin-de-Fer Las Vegas style, like all other casino table games, must use chips to deal the game.

In most Las Vegas Strip casinos players do not have to keep track of the 5% charge on their winning bets when placed on the bank. The croupier keeps track by placing chips or markers indicating how much each player owes the casino in a small rectangle marked with each player's seat number. The numbered rectangles are marked clearly and are located in a row on the layout directly in front of the croupier. When the 5% charge money owed the house reaches a certain amount, or at the end of a dealt shoe, the player is asked to pay up.

A bet placed on the space of the layout marked "Bank" indicates the player is wagering that the shooter will win or pass; a bet placed on the layout marked "Players" is a lose bet and against the shooter. A count of 0 in Baccarat is known as *baccarat;* a count of 9 is known as a *natural*.

Several shills are used at a Baccarat table to stimulate action.

SCARNE'S RULES FOR PLAYING BACCARAT LAS VEGAS STYLE

The playing rules for Baccarat Las Vegas or Cuban style are the same as for Chemin de Fer, except that the optional plays, such as the banker's optional when holding a count of 3 and dealing the player a 9 and when holding a 5 and dealing the player a 4, are compulsory draws. The same holds true for the player when holding a count of 5. The abolishment of these optionals at Baccarat make the game mechanical; all a croupier can do is follow the rules. It does, however, eliminate those arguments which arise in Chemin de Fer caused by a player's hitting or staying against the wishes of another player.

The rules of Baccarat, like those of Chemin de Fer, are many and complicated, and each player is given a card like that on the opposite page, describing rules for players and banker.

PERCENTAGES AGAINST THE PLAYER AT BACCARAT AND CHEMIN DE FER

The rules governing Chemin de Fer and Baccarat seem unnecessarily complicated, but before we blend our voices in with the Shimmy and Baccarat addict's immemorial complaint, "Why don't they simplify the laws?" let's re-examine one of the inner secrets of all banking games.

That secret may be stated as follows: Nothing in gambling is unreasonably complicated. If it's complicated, there's a reason. The reason for the strange and apparently unnatural statutes governing the play at Chemin de Fer or Baccarat is that in their complication lies the hidden percentage against the player.

Before giving a mathematical analysis of the game, I would like to point out to the reader that the source of the banker's advantage is the fact that, as in Black Jack, the player must always play first. Although the Baccarat or Chemin de Fer player cannot bust his hand as in Black Jack, he does expose his possible card count to the banker by his decision of play. From there on, the rules of the game do the rest. They are devised to give the bank or dealer a percentage edge over the player.

Example: It is the player's second turn of play. He draws a card. This indicates that he holds one of these counts: 1, 2, 3, 4, 5 or 10. His drawn card is face up. We see that it is an 8, and we know his total count now must be 9, 10, 11, 12, 13 or 18.

Now the dealer faces his cards. He has a count of 3. Under the rules, he cannot draw a card. He stays, poor devil, and what happens? It is a 3 to 2

BACCARAT
—RULES—

PLAYER	HAVING	
	1–2–3–4–5–10	Draws a Card
	6–7	Stands
	8–9	Turns Cards Over

BANKER	HAVING	DRAWS WHEN GIVING	DOES NOT DRAW WHEN GIVING
	3	1–2–3–4–5–6–7–9–10	8
	4	2–3–4–5–6–7	1–8–9–10
	5	4–5–6–7	1–2–3–8–9–10
	6	6–7	1–2–3–4–5–8–9–10
	7	STANDS	
	8–9	TURNS CARDS OVER	

PICTURES AND TENS DO NOT COUNT

bet in his favor that his low count of 3 will beat whatever count is in the player's hand.

Another example? The player stays. The banker-player holding a count of 5 *must draw*. We know, of course, from the player's staying action that he has a count of 5, 6 or 7. If, on his own turn of play, the banker player elected to stay, he couldn't possibly win; so the rules compel him to draw a card and give him a possible chance to beat the player.

These are just two of the countless number of situations I had to analyze to figure the banker's and player's chances of winning. I did not realize when I started this mathematical analysis on Baccarat and Chemin de Fer that it would take so many weeks of laborious computing. I had to fill sheaves and sheaves of paper with numerous and varied computations in order to obtain the following answers: the chance of winning for the player is $49\frac{33}{100}\%$ and the chance of winning for the banker-player is $50\frac{67}{100}\%$. These percentages apply to the Baccarat rules in use in Nevada casinos or a similar strategy of play used at Chemin de Fer. The player's disadvantage is the difference of $1\frac{34}{100}\%$, which expressed decimally is 1.34%.

If the casino did not extract its 5% charge on each of the banker-player's winning bets, the banker-player would naturally have a 1.34% advantage over the other players. Since the banker-player must pay a standard charge of 5% on his winning bets, which occur $50\frac{67}{100}$ times out of every 100 dealt hands in the long run, the 5% casino charge on the banker-player's winnings is actually 2.53%. Subtracting from this the 1.34% advantage the banker-player enjoys over the other players, we find that the banker-player pays the casino 1.19%. The casino enjoys a 1.34% advantage over the player and 1.19% advantage over the banker at either Shimmy or Baccarat, and no matter how you look at it, "If you play, you must pay."

When the casino extracts a 3% charge on the banker-player's winnings, the bank's advantage dwindles to less than $\frac{1}{5}$ of 1%: to be exact, .18%. This is the best bet to be found in any casino in the world. I doubt, however, that you'll be able to find this bet in any American casino.

When the casino extracts a 3% charge from the banker-player before the hand is even dealt (win or lose), the banker-player's disadvantage is 1.66%. When the casino charges the banker-player $2\frac{1}{2}\%$ (win or lose), his disadvantage is 1.16%. The player's disadvantage always remains the same at 1.34% and is not altered by the percentage charge which the casino extracts from the banker-player.

In addition to the above wagers, Baccarat layouts have bank spaces marked 9 and 8, and below each number the legend: "10 for 1." A bet placed on the 9 means that the player is betting that the dealer on the next turn of play will hold a count of 9 with his first two dealt cards. The casino pays off such winning bets at 10 for 1, actually 9 to 1. And since the correct odds are $9\frac{23}{64}$ to 1, the operators enjoy an advantage of 3.46%.

When a player places a bet on the 8 (same rules apply as on the 9) he is paid off at 9 to 1. But since the correct odds against being dealt a count of 8 in the first two cards are $9^{43}\!/_{62}$ to 1, the casino enjoys a favorable edge of 6.48%.

Some Baccarat operators permit players to make bets that the dealer will hold either an 8 or 9 count in his first two dealt cards. This bet is paid off at 4 to 1. The correct odds are $4^{11}\!/_{42}$ to 1, for a favorable casino advantage of 4.98%.

In 1964 Nevada casino owners eliminated the bank spaces marked 8 and 9 from their layouts and replaced them with a bet marked "Ties Pay 10 for 1," which means that if a bet is placed on ties, the player is betting that the banker's and the player's hand will have the same count. This change occurred because casino owners became alarmed by a Baccarat winning system hoax that appeared in *Life* magazine the week of March 27, 1964, plus the appearance of a trio of card counters who lost $15,000 at the Dunes Hotel Casino when they tried unsuccessfully to beat the Baccarat side bets by clocking the eights and nines on the old layout. However, if I had been consulted at the time, I would have recommended, rather than changing the layout, that the casino add another 52-card deck to the original eight-deck packet—and before placing the cards into the shoe for dealing, insert a second indicator card about 60 cards from the bottom of the packet to determine the end of the deal. For further information on this kind of anti-card-casing device, see pages 74–75.

When the bank pays ties at 10 for 1, the house advantage is 4.80%. To make the situation worse, most Nevada casinos pay ties at 9 for 1. This means that any bet placed on such a space is paid off at 8 to 1 odds should the bank and player tie. Since this bet has a house advantage of 14.36%, it is a sucker bet and should be eliminated from the layout.

ADVICE TO BACCARAT AND CHEMIN DE FER PLAYERS

If you still insist on casino gambling after having read this book, and you find yourself in a casino that harbors all the standard casino games including Chemin de Fer and Baccarat, and you would like to give yourself the best possible chance to win, sit yourself down at the Shimmy or Baccarat table. The low house percentage which the player and banker-player must buck in these games makes the 1.34% and 1.19% bets the best available at any casino banking game, with the exception of two bets permitted at Bank Craps: a "front-line or come bet plus the front-line odds" and a "back-line or don't come bet plus the back-line odds."

However, I must again remind the reader that any gambler must lose in the end if he *repeatedly* takes the worst of any game percentagewise, whether his disadvantage is a low 1% or less, or a high 10% or more. The higher the house P.C. the faster the player is sent to the cleaner's.

CHEATING AT BACCARAT AND CHEMIN DE FER

Reputable and long-established casinos do not resort to cheating at their Baccarat or Chemin de Fer tables. When dealing Chemin de Fer, the management is not itself a participant in the game; it is a beneficiary, and there is no economic motive for cheating. Since the casino's edge at Baccarat will eventually get all the money in sight anyway, it would be foolish to spoil the casino's reputation by cheating the game. All it wants is a well-heeled, high-rolling betting crowd with nothing at all (certainly not suspicion) on its mind, and plenty of action. The 1.34% edge which it enjoys over the player and the 1.19% edge it has over the banker-player will eventually earn all the money it needs.

However, because some operators will always cheat and their Baccarat or Chemin de Fer tables are crooked, and because others aren't capable of protecting their players against card-cheat players who have infiltrated the games, much cheating does take place. Chemin de Fer and Baccarat are the international card cheat's paradise because of the high stakes. It requires an exceptionally skilled card cheat to beat these games when they are protected by three croupiers and a lookout, but it does happen regularly. I once proved this to a doubting casino operator.

It happened in 1958 when Mike McLaney, then owner of the Habana Nacional Casino, and 19 other operators of American- and Cuban-owned casinos decided to set up a standard code of regulations and a Cuban Gaming Control Board. I was asked to meet with them and they offered me the chairmanship of the board, which, for personal reasons, I had to decline. During the meeting I was asked a great many questions about gambling, and at one point I made this remark: "Every casino which has a Chemin de Fer or Baccarat table—in Cuba, the United States, Monte Carlo or anywhere else—will at one time or another be cheated by international card sharps."

Analito Batisti, then owner of the Sevilla Biltmore Casino in downtown Havana, immediately jumped to his feet. "Scarne," he objected, "I think no card thief can steal at my Baccarat game. I got the best croupiers in all Cuba workin' at my casino."

I didn't argue with him about it then. I merely smiled and replied, "The best croupiers in all Cuba should certainly be able to detect any crooked moves at your table." But three weeks later I walked into the Sevilla Biltmore one evening and had a private talk with Batisti. "I'd like to make sure that the best croupiers in all Cuba can spot a Baccarat cheat when he's working. Suppose we test them and find out."

He wasn't sure he liked the idea at first, so I put the proposition to him as a wager.

"I'll bet you $500 I can cheat the game using methods your boys won't detect. I'll play until I either win or lose $10,000, and that money won't be involved in the wager; you'll give me credit for that amount. If I lose it or am caught in the act of cheating, I'll pay you $500. If I win ten grand by cheating and am not caught, you pay me $500."

Batisti is a gambler, and he figured this was an easy way to pick up five bills. It was early in the evening and the Baccarat table hadn't yet obtained any action. The five players seated at the table were all shills. There were three croupiers and the ladderman.

Bastiti told the croupier that I could have $10,000 worth of credit and took his seat on the ladder stand overlooking the Baccarat table. My first bet was $100 on the player's side, which I lost. I continued making $100 bets on the player's side for about 20 minutes. I took a quick glance at Batisti and saw that he wore a puzzled scowl. I could guess what he was thinking: How does this character expect to win $10,000 by wagering only a hundred dollars on each hand?

I was even when I decided to make my move. I turned to the croupier and said, "Ten thousand dollars on the player's side." The croupier looked up at Batisti who nodded in assent, and placed a $10,000 marker on the Baccarat layout marked "Player." The croupier turned to a shill who had the card-dealing box and said, "Deal the cards, please."

After the player's two cards and the banker's two cards had been dealt, the croupier scooped up the player's two face-down cards with his palette and slid them directly in front of me. My left hand reached for the two cards and I held them face down for a split second, then rapidly turned them face up and called, "Nine," dropping them face up on the layout. As pretty a jack and nine of spades as you'll ever see.

The croupier turned to the shill who still had the banker's two cards in his hand and asked him to turn them over. The croupier saw a 6 count, called, "No cards, player wins." He scooped up the four dealt cards with his hand and dropped them through the slot in the table into the discard cylinder.

As I got up from the table after the croupier had paid the bet, I noticed that Batisti's face was covered with a "What happened?" expression. The croupier and shills acted as if nothing unusual had happened; a $10,000 bet at the Sevilla Biltmore Casino Baccarat table was nothing to get excited about. Batisti quickly jumped down from the ladder stand, walked rapidly over to where I was standing and said, "You don't cheat; you lucky!"

"That's what you think," I said. I told Batisti to remove the discard cylinder from under the table and examine the last four cards that were dropped in by the croupier. Batisti found two Tally-Ho cards possessing a different back design from the Bicycle cards that were in use. He turned red in the face. "You change cards?"

"Yeah, I change cards." I reached into my inside coat pocket and brought out the two Bicycle cards I had switched for the two Tally-Ho cards. I collected my $500, and as I was leaving I could hear Batisti and the croupiers buzzing excitedly in Spanish.

Later that same year, casino owner Batisti learned another, more expensive, lesson in the art of gambling. This time it was at Black Jack and at a cost of $59,700 (see The $1 Million Freeze-out, pages 68 to 70).

Since the average Baccarat or Chemin de Fer player has little if any chance of spotting a slick card cheat in action, the best advice I can offer him is to keep his bets down to a minimum when not playing in a long-established casino.

The most common method Baccarat or Chemin de Fer operators use to cheat players is to insert a previously stacked packet into the card slot. Some operators have been known to switch the entire shoe containing the eight decks for a previously prepared one during play. To avoid being fleeced by such swindles, keep your eyes on the cards as they are being shuffled and placed in the shoe.

CROOKED DEALING SHOES USED TO CHEAT AT BACCARAT AND CHEMIN DE FER

Some crooked casinos here and abroad cheat at Chemin de Fer, Baccarat and Punto Banco by using a crooked dealing shoe. This shoe contains a hidden pocket near the mouth of the dealing box. The secret pocket holds about eight cards which are released singly by the dealer simply by squeezing the box with his left hand near its mouth when dealing with his right. The squeezing pressure opens a slit in the pocket about ¼ inch from the mouth of the dealing shoe, permitting the dealer's right thumb to touch and deal the top card of those hidden in the pocket instead of the card that should be dealt. The eight cards secreted in the pocket of the dealing shoe usually are arranged 9–10–9–10–9–10–9–10. When the big-money hand makes an appearance, the crooked dealer deals his player confederate two cards from the hidden pocket, a crooked 9 and 10 for a natural 9 count. To eliminate crooked dealing shoes, I recommend that the manufacturers of casino dealing boxes make a transparent plastic dealing box, which will prevent any cards from being secreted in the shoe's interior.

PRIVATE CHEMIN DE FER, OR SLOGGER

Private Chemin de Fer, or Slogger, is a simplified and demechanized version of Chemin de Fer and was described in print for the first time in *Scarne on Cards*. With Baccarat now being played in Nevada casinos, Slogger could become a serious rival to private Black Jack when played among friends. The special virtue of the game is that the banker and player each have a 50-50 chance to win, which is not true of Black Jack. If you want to play a dead-even banking game at your next private Black Jack session, give Slogger a try; you'll like it.

The game is played exactly like Chemin de Fer, with the following exceptions:

1. One standard 52-card deck is used.

2. Selecting the first banker: Players may sit anywhere they like. By mutual consent, any player may shuffle the cards, any player may cut the cards, and the acting dealer deals each player one card at a time, starting with the player at his left and dealing clockwise until some player is dealt an ace. That player becomes the first banker.

3. The shuffle and cut: The banker shuffles. Any player may ask for the right to shuffle at any time, but the banker has the right to shuffle last. After the shuffle, the banker-dealer puts the cards on the table to be cut. Any player may cut. More than one player may cut. If no other player cuts, the banker must.

4. *Dead cards* (cards which have been played) are *burned* (placed upside down) on the bottom of the pack as in single-deck casino Black Jack.

5. When the deck is exhausted or it is a new dealer's turn to bank, a new shuffle must be made.

6. There is no restriction in this game—as there is in casino Chemin de Fer—on any player's drawing a card or staying on any count below 8. This includes the banker. Regardless of his count on the first two cards, the banker or the player may draw or stay, at his own discretion.

7. The count of 9 with two cards is called *Big Slogger,* and is immediately turned up by the holder. The same holds true for the count of 8, called *Little Slogger.*

All the cheating methods discussed under Black Jack (pages 107 to 110) are applicable to private Chemin de Fer, or Slogger.

BACCARAT-EN-BANQUE

Baccarat-en-Banque, also called Baccarat à Deux Tableaux (double table), is an old-time cousin of Chemin de Fer played mostly in France. The game is usually banked by the casino operators or by concessionaires (usually from a Greek syndicate), who pay the casino operators 50% of their monthly winnings for the banking privilege. Unlike Baccarat or Chemin de Fer, there is a permanent bank and three hands are dealt instead of two. There is one hand for the bank and two player hands, one at each side of the table. The table layout is divided at the center by a heavy line.

Players may wager on either player hand, right or left; or they may wager on both by placing their money *à cheval,* that is, across the line. If one side wins and the other loses, a bet placed in this manner is a stand-off and no one wins or loses. If both sides lose, the bet is lost; if both sides win, the bet is won.

When all wagers have been placed, the croupier deals one face-down card to the player on his right, one to the player on his left and one to himself. He repeats this procedure and, when each has two cards, the hands are checked. If any of the three has a count of 8 or 9, it must be turned face up and the other two hands are exposed, ending the play. Bets are paid off as in Chemin de Fer. When either player holds an 8 or 9, the player on the dealer's right acts first. He draws or stands, according to the Chemin de Fer rules, and has the option to draw or stand with a 5. Then the player on the left acts and is guided by the same rules.

When the players have completed their hands, it becomes the bank's turn to play. Here is where considerable judgment and skill on the banker's part come into play. In this version of Baccarat-en-Banque, the banker doesn't have any restrictions: he may stand or draw a card as he pleases; he is really the only one who has any opportunity to exercise judgment in the play of his hand. It must be remembered that the banker will mentally total the amount wagered on each side of the table, and will draw or stand to try and beat the side betting the most money. Example: The banker has 5, the player on his left has drawn a 10 and the player on his right did not draw. The banker will stand or draw depending on which side has bet the most money. If the left-hand player is the big bettor, the bank will stand on 5. The reasoning is that the player on the left, having drawn a 10, has a count of 0, 1, 2, 3, 4 or 5. The banker is about a 5 to 1 favorite to win the big bet. If the right side has the big wager, the banker will calculate the difference between bets and then decide whether to draw or stay.

One reason Baccarat-en-Banque has not made any headway in the United States is that it is open to all sorts of cheating—especially player cheats who signal their card count to a banker cheat so that, in a short time, the bank must win all the money in sight. The cheats split the take later, and the honest player hasn't a chance.

11

SCARNEY BACCARAT

HISTORY OF THE GAME

Scarney Baccarat, my own casino card game invention, takes the legendary European game of Baccarat a giant step further. Scarney Baccarat combines the principles of Las Vegas Baccarat and Black Jack, plus several entirely new game principles. Scarney Baccarat is destined to become a rival to Black Jack as the number one card game in casinos the world over. Scarney Baccarat possesses all the strategies of Black Jack plus the following player advantages: (a) as in Black Jack, a player may draw, stand, split pairs, double down and take insurance; (b) unlike Black Jack, a player cannot bust (lose his bet by going over 21). A player's cards are always in play until the dealer completes his play and the payoff takes place; (c) the house advantage at Black Jack is more than double that of Scarney Baccarat. Black Jack's house advantage is 5.90%, whereas the house advantage at Scarney Baccarat is a low 2.44%. (Scarney Baccarat is a "proprietary" game—its designs and names are trademarked and its rules of play are copyrighted. No part of this game can be reproduced in any form without written permission from the owner and distributor, John Scarne Games, Inc., 4319 Meadowview Ave., North Bergen, N.J. 07047.)

SCARNE'S RULES OF PLAY FOR SCARNEY BACCARAT

Requirements: The following are required to play Scarney Baccarat:

1. A regulation Scarney Baccarat table with six or seven betting spaces on its layout.

2. A dealer (houseman) who deals the game and functions as the banker, collecting player's losing bets and paying off player's winning bets.

3. One to six or seven players, each of whom may bet on one to three hands, depending on the betting spaces available.

4. A card-dealing box called a shoe.

5. Four standard packs of 52 cards each, shuffled together and used as one, a total of 208 cards dealt as a single deck.

6. Two indicator cards. One is used by players to cut the deck and the other indicator card is used to determine the end of the deal.

Value of cards: The ace is the lowest-ranking card and has a point value of 1. Kings, queens and jacks have a value of 10 each. All other cards have their numerical face value. The deuce is counted as 2, the three is counted as 3, the four is counted as 4, etc. The suits have no value.

Object of the game: Each player tries to obtain a higher total card count than the dealer by holding a combination of two or three cards totaling nine or as close as possible to nine, or to a two-digit number ending in nine. Examples: $1 + 8$ gives point 9; $2 + 5$ gives point 7, $3 + 1$ gives point 4; and so forth. When the total of the cards is a two-digit number, only the last digit has any value. Examples: $10 + 9$ gives point 9; $9 + 3 + 1$ gives point 3; $1 + 3 + 10$ gives point 4; $6 + 7 + 9$ gives point 2; and so forth.

A player, at his proper turn of play and at his own discretion, regardless of the value of his two-card count, may stand or may draw a third card in an attempt to better his card count.

The shuffle and cut: The cards are shuffled by the dealer, who then hands a player an indicator card and says, "Cut please." The player inserts the indicator card into the deck to show where he wants the cards cut.

The dealer cuts the cards at this position, putting the indicator and all the cards above it on the bottom. The indicator goes to the bottom of the pocket. The dealer then inserts the second indicator card 60 cards or thereabouts from the bottom of the deck and places all the cards into the dealing box face down. The dealer next deals three cards from the shoe and puts them to one side out of play. The shoe is now ready to be dealt by the dealer. When the indicator card inserted by the dealer makes its appearance, and enough cards from below the indicator card have been dealt to complete the round in progress, the deal ends. The dealer must begin a new shuffle, repeating the above procedure.

Betting: Before the deal begins, each player must place his bet, in chips, in one of the rectangular betting spaces that are painted on the playing surface; all bets are in full view of the dealer. I repeat, players may place bets on one to three betting spaces providing there are available holes (betting spaces). When a player places bets on more than one betting space at a time, he must play the hand farthest to his right to completion before being permitted to play his next hand or hands.

The deal: After all players' bets are down, the dealer, starting with the player on his extreme left, begins dealing clockwise. He gives one card face up to each player and one face up to himself. He next deals each player, starting with the player on his extreme left, a second face-up card and one face-down card to himself.

Player's turn at play: The player to the dealer's extreme left makes the first play of the hand. He may elect to stay or draw.

1. To stay: Either he is satisfied with his two-card count or he fears that a third and final card may reduce his count. He says, "No card," "I have enough," "I stand" or "Good."

2. To draw the third and final card: When a player is not satisfied with his count, he says, "Hit me," "Give me a card," makes a beckoning motion by closing his hand or makes a come-on motion with a finger. The dealer then deals a third and final card from the shoe face up before the player and next to his original two face-up cards. A player isn't permitted to draw more than one card. Each dealt hand remains in front of the player or players.

The play moves to the player's left, clockwise, around the table until all players have played out their hands. At this time it becomes the dealer's turn.

The dealer's turn at play: After all the players have played out their hand or hands, the dealer must play his hand and abide by the following rules:

1. He turns up his hole card so that his two cards are exposed.

2. If his count is 5, 6, 7, 8 or 9, the dealer must stay. He is not permitted to draw a third card.

3. If his count is 0, 1, 2, 3 or 4, he must draw a third and final card, after which he must stay. However, if a dealer's three-card count totals zero (0), and is made up of three 10-count cards, he must continue to draw cards until his total count is anything except zero (0). This is called the *Scarney baccarat* or *baccarat*. With the above exception, every Scarney Baccarat hand is made up of either two or three cards.

Final settlement: At the end of his play, the dealer starts with the first active player on his extreme right and moves around the table to the left; he pays off players who have a higher count than his with an amount equal to the bet they placed, and collects the placed bets from players showing a lesser count. If a player and the dealer have the same count, it is standoff or tie, and no one collects or loses. A total three-card count has the same value as a similar total two-card count. Example: A 9 count made with three cards ties a 9 count made with two cards. (The same holds true for a Scarney Baccarat hand of three, four, five or more cards.)

Splitting pairs: Any two aces, cards that are identical, regardless of their suits, may be treated as a pair. Also, any two cards each having a count of 10 (totaling zero) may be treated as a pair, such as two tens, two jacks, two queens, two kings, or a combination of any of the two above 10-count cards; such a combination is called baccarat. Each of the above pairs, at the discretion of the player, may be treated as the first card dealt of two separate hands.

A player being dealt two cards forming a pair on the initial round may, if he chooses, separate one from another and treat each card as the first card dealt in two separate hands.

When the pairs are split, the player's original bet is placed on one of these cards and an equal amount must be bet on the other card. The player is then dealt a second and final card face down on the face-up card on his right and then a second and final card face down on the other face-up card. When splitting pairs, at no time is a player permitted to draw a third card on any hand.

Players are not permitted to look at a face-down card until the dealer turns it face up after the deal has been completed.

The double-down bet: A player after being dealt his first two cards (which may be any two cards) may elect to double his original bet before drawing his third card. This is known as a double down or *down for double*. A player at his turn of play, and before calling "Down for double" or "Double down," must place an amount equal to the original bet on the betting space. The player is then dealt a third and final face-down card on the two face-up cards. The player isn't permitted to look at his face-down card until the dealer turns it face up after the deal has been completed.

The Scarney insurance bet: If the dealer's face-up card is a 9 count, players (at the dealer's turn of play) may elect to make an insurance bet against a loss or standoff to the dealer's possible two-card 9 count (9 + 10), called *Scarney*. The dealer, before turning his hole card face up, inquires if any player wants *Scarney insurance*. A player who desires insurance places an amount equal to half his present wager toward the center of the table.

After the dealer faces his hole card, if it is a 10 count, he calls "Scarney" and each insurance bettor is paid off at the rate of 2 to 1 for each unit wagered. If the card is not a 10 count, the dealer collects the player's insurance bet and continues to play out his hand.

The Scarney Baccarat insurance bet: After the dealer faces his hole card (at dealer's turn of play) and his initial two dealt cards are both 10 counts, players may elect to make the Scarney Baccarat insurance bet. The dealer, before drawing his third card, inquires if any player wants Scarney Baccarat insurance. A player who desires the Scarney

Baccarat insurance places an amount equal to half his present wager toward the center of the table.

After the dealer draws his third card, if it is a 10 count he calls "Scarney Baccarat" and each insurance bettor is paid off at a rate of 2 to 1 for each unit wagered; the dealer continues to play out his hand. If the card is not a 10 count, the dealer collects the players' insurance bets and that ends the play. If the dealer's third dealt card is a 10 count, a second Scarney Baccarat insurance bet is permitted. Should the dealer's fourth dealt card be a 10 count, a third Scarney Baccarat insurance bet is allowed; and so its goes, insurance bet after insurance bet, until the dealer fails to draw a 10-count card and the hand ends.

The side bets: Scarney Baccarat layouts have betting spaces marked 5–6–7–8–9, and above these numbers appears the phrase "Each **Pays** 10 for 1." Before a new deal begins, the player places his side bet by betting on a specified number of numbers, betting that on the next round of play the dealer's first two cards will total the count he bet on. The dealer pays off such winning bets at odds of 10 for 1. These wagers are also called *propositions*.

Field bet: The field bears the numbers 5, 6, 7, 8, 9. When a player puts his bet on the space of the layout marked "Field," he is betting that on the next round of play the combined count of the dealer's first two dealt cards will be 5, 6, 7, 8 or 9. The dealer pays off winning bets at even money. If the dealer's first two cards total 0, 1, 2, 3 or 4, the players lose their field bets.

A dealer's two-card 9 count comprised of a 9 and 10 is known as "Scarney." A count of zero with two or three cards is known as "baccarat." A dealer's count of zero with three or more 10-count cards is known as "Scarney baccarat."

A player is not permitted to double down on a split pair.

Optional protective deal rule for Scarney Baccarat: To help protect both casino management and players from being cheated by worn, bent, defaced or marked cards by either house employees or player cheats, and to help avoid a conspiracy between both house cheats and player cheats, the following optional deal rule is recommended.

After all players bets are down (field and side bets included) the dealer, starting with the player on his extreme left, begins dealing clockwise dealing one card face up to each player and one face up to himself. He next deals each player starting with the player on his extreme left a second face-up card—but omits dealing himself (the dealer) a second card. After all players have finished playing their hands, the dealer removes (discards) the top card of the card packet and places it in the discard receiver without showing its face value. Next, the dealer deals himself his second face-up card and the standard rules follow. However, if the dealer's first upcard is a nine spot, he must inquire if any player desires a Scarney insurance bet immediately after players have played their hands and prior to discarding the top card of the card packet.

SCARNEY BACCARAT STRATEGY

Before giving a mathematical analysis of the game, I would like to point out that in Scarney Baccarat a player can't bust his hand as in Black Jack. A player's cards are always in play until the dealer completes his play and the payoff takes place. In Scarney Baccarat the house advantage is the result of the dealer's special play of the game. If the dealer's three-card total is zero and is made up of three 10 count cards, the dealer continues to draw cards until his final count is different from zero. This is the only time a Scarney Baccarat hand contains more than three cards. It isn't feasible, of course, to figure the exact percentage against individual players because their playing differs so much. Some players will stay on a count of 5 or more; some will draw on 5 and 6; others stay on 4 or more; and there's always the hero who will hit a 7 or an 8. However, the rules allow the dealer no choice of staying or drawing: he must draw to a count of 4 or less and stay on a count of 5 or more. A house P.C. can be calculated for a player who matches dealer's play (and thus does not split pairs or double down).

If the player adheres to the dealer's fixed strategy, and doesn't split pairs or double down, the house percentage in which a hand consists of a play of the game which terminates in a win, loss or tie is a low 2.44 percent. If a tie isn't counted as a trial, then the house advantage is 2.71 percent. In other words, Scarney Baccarat will appear on the average of about once in 37 deals. I must reemphasize one fact you should not forget: the only positive advantage in favor of the bank is the 2.44 percent that it gains through a Scarney Baccarat.

There are several situations which, played properly, give the player an opportunity to cut down this house percentage. Most players handle these situations so inexpertly that, instead of reducing the percentage they are bucking, they add to it. Here are the playing factors which can be utilized to the player's advantage:

1. The player actually knows a little more than the dealer because one of the dealer's two initial cards is dealt face up—this gives the player important information about his possible card count. The rules governing the dealer's play prevent him from making use of similar information about the player's hand, even if the latter's first two cards were dealt face up.

2. Unlike the dealer, the player can stay or draw on any count he

wants. At one turn of play he may draw to a count of 3, 4, 5, or more; and at other times he may stand on the same count. In some situations this is advantageous to the player.

3. The player can decide whether or not he wants to double down or split pairs, a strategy denied to the dealer.

4. The player may play one to three hands when there are available betting spaces; the dealer can only play one hand.

5. The player is the one who decides the amount of the bet and can raise or lower it at will within the prescribed betting limits.

6. The player may case the deck. If he can remember the cards previously dealt or exposed, this knowledge will greatly improve his chances of winning.

If you adhere to the strategy that I shall outline for you in the following pages, I promise that you can cut down the house 2.44 percent considerably. The strategy utilizes these factors: the dealer must hit a 4 or less and stand on 5 or more; the knowledge of the dealer's face-up (exposed) card; the player's total count; when it is to your advantage to stand, to draw, to split pairs, and to double down.

Playing according to upcoming information will assure you that you are fighting an average house advantage of considerably less than 2 percent. However, my strategy doesn't guarantee that you will win—it simply cuts down the house percentage to its lowest possible level and gives you a much better opportunity to win than any other method of Scarney Baccarat play.

SCARNEY BACCARAT BASIC STRATEGY TABLE

Hit-and-stand strategy:

1. When the dealer's upcard is anything, stand on a count of 6. 7, 8, or 9.

2. When the dealer's upcard is anything, draw to a count of 0, 1, 2, 3, or 4.

3. When the dealer's upcard is 0, 1, 5, 6, 8, or 9, draw to a count of 5.

Splitting pairs:
1. Split threes when the dealer's upcard is 7, 8, or 9.
2. Split fives when the dealer's upcard is 1, 2, 3, 4, or 5.
3. Split sixes when the dealer's upcard is 0, 1, 2, 3, 4, 5, or 6.
4. Split sevens when the dealer's upcard is 0, 1, 2, 3, 4, 5, 6, or 7.
5. Split eights when the dealer's upcard is 7.

Doubling down: Double down on a count of 4 when the dealer's upcard is 0, 1, 2, 3, or 4.

Double down on a count of 3 when the dealer's upcard is 0, 1, 2, 3, 4, or 5.

Double down on a count of 2 when the dealer's upcard is 0, 1, or 2.

Scarney insurance bet: Whenever the dealer shows a nine as his upcard, he will invite you to place an additional wager (called Scarney insurance) equal to half the amount already bet, which will pay you 2 to 1 if the dealer's down card is a 10-count card, and which you will lose if it is not. In this optional bet, you are thus "insuring" your hand against the possibility of a loss to a dealer Scarney. In order for this bet to be a profitable bet, more than one-third of the undealt cards must be 10-count cards. This is not very often the case, so let's take a look at the usual odds. If the dealer's upcard is a nine, and you have no knowledge of any other cards, the quadruple deck would contain 64 10-count cards.

Suppose you do not look at your own cards, nor do you see any of the other players' cards prior to taking the insurance. Then the dealer's down card may be considered drawn at random from the 207 cards that remain unseen. Clearly, 64 of these cards are 10-counts and the other 143 are not 10-counts. The odds are 143 to 64 against the dealer having a 10-count in the hole. The payoff is 128 to 64, approximately 7% against the player. As a general rule, I don't recommend insurance betting. However, the casual card caser (counter) can use the insurance bet advantageously if he has been keeping track of 10-count cards in previous hands. *Example:* Suppose half the deck (104 cards) has been dealt and the casual card caser recalls that only 12 10-count cards have been dealt. If an

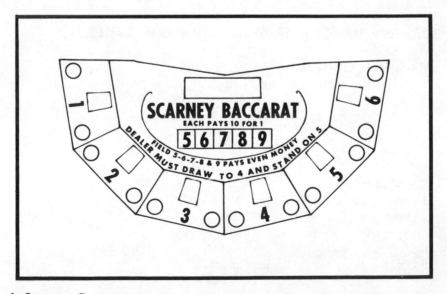

A Scarney Baccarat layout, the first new casino banking game in the past century.

insurance bet could be made on the next deal, it would be wise to take insurance because the player has an edge of more than 33% over the house on this bet.

Scarney Baccarat insurance. The house advantage in Scarney insurance also holds true when placing a Scarney Baccarat insurance bet.

Proposition or side bets. In addition to the preceding wagers, Scarney Baccarat layouts have spaces marked 5, 6, 7, 8, or 9, and above these numbers appears the statement "Each Pays 10 for 1." A bet placed on a 5 means that the player is betting that the dealer, on the next turn of play, will hold a count of 5 with his first two dealt cards. The dealer pays off such winning bets at 10 for 1, and since the correct odds are $9\frac{23}{64}$ to 1, the house enjoys an advantage of 3.46%. The same house percentage holds true for the numbers 7 and 9.

When a player places a bet on the 6 (same rules apply as on the 9), he is again paid off at 10 for 1. But since the correct odds on being dealt a count of 6 in the first two cards are $9\frac{48}{62}$ to 1, the house enjoys an advantage of 6.80%. The same holds true for number 8.

Field bet: When a player places a bet on the space of the layout marked "Field" he is betting that the dealer's first two dealt cards on the next round will total a count of 5, 6, 7, 8, or 9. The dealer pays such winning bets at even money. The dealer may be dealt 1,326 different two-card counts, of which 632 comprise the field (5, 6, 7, 8, and 9) and 694 comprise the losing numbers (0, 1, 2, 3, and 4). When we subtract 632 winning two-card counts from the 694 losing two-card counts, we find the field bettor has a disadvantage of 62 two-card counts for a dealer's edge of 4.67%.

12

KENO:
NEVADA'S SOLITAIRE
BINGO-TYPE GAME

Racehorse Keno, a variation of old-fashioned Keno, is played in most gambling establishments in Nevada and many illegal gambling joints situated in the western United States. Before the acquisition by big business of the major casinos on the Las Vegas Strip, Keno, by Strip standards, was looked down at as a cheap gambling pastime for tourists. Today, however, Strip casinos such as Caesar's Palace, Dunes, Las Vegas Hilton, Frontier, and Sands have replaced their cocktail lounges (which previously boasted of round-the-clock star-studded entertainment) with Keno parlors. Their electric Keno tally boards are situated throughout the casino and adjacent restaurants, and if you happen to be in the restaurant, a traveling Keno girl will place your bets for you while you're dining.

PLAYING RULES

Racehorse Keno—today generally called just Keno—differs from regular Keno in several ways. The old Keno, like Bingo, required large numbers of players for successful operation; the purchase price of a Keno or Bingo ticket was the same for all players, and games were usually run one night a week, each session lasting only a few hours. Racehorse Keno, on the other hand, can be dealt to one or more players; each player can wager any amount he likes on a single ticket provided it is within the house betting limits, and the Racehorse Keno parlors in Nevada operate 24 hours a day, with a new game dealt every few minutes.

Racehorse Keno parlors seating from 50 to over 300 players are usually located in a prominent part of the casino. They contain several tables loaded with Keno *outside tickets,* and the players are supplied with ink and brushes or black crayon. Each ticket bears the numbers 1 through 80 and the player marks on his ticket the numbers he wishes to play and the sum he is wagering. He presents his cash and the marked outside ticket at the Keno counter where the dealer makes two duplicates by punching out the

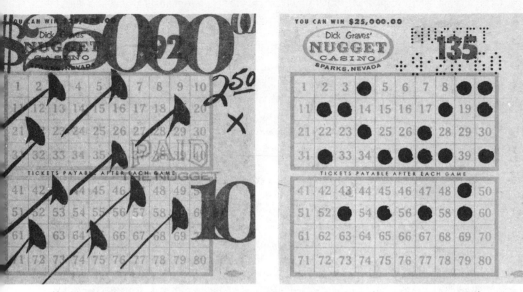

(Left) Outside ticket marked by the player and, after the game, stamped and displayed to show that player won $25,000. *(Right)* An inside ticket is a duplicate of player's ticket with punched holes replacing ink marks. (Dick Graves' Nugget)

numbers on an *inside ticket* which bears the 80 numbers and also the number of the game to be played and the name of the casino. The dealer gives the player one copy and retains the original and the other copy. These are checked after the game has been played and are paid off if the ticket wins. If seated in a casino restaurant, the player simply marks his ticket with a black crayon and hands the marked ticket and cash to a traveling Keno girl who handles all the details.

A Bingo blower behind the Keno counter contains 80 numbered Ping-Pong balls, and 20 of these are drawn. As each ball is drawn, its number is called and flashed on the electrically lighted tally board. When the 20th ball has been drawn, the game ends. A great number of different bets can be made at Racehorse Keno because the players can select various combinations of numbers. A 1-spot ticket is one on which a player has marked, and is betting on, a single number. If that number appears in the 20 drawn numbers, the player wins. If he marks two numbers it is a 2-spot ticket, and he wins if both numbers appear among the 20 which are drawn. He may mark and bet on groups of as many as 15 numbers, but the most popular ticket is the 10 spot.

The player selects ten numbers, marks his ticket, gives it with the amount of his bet to the dealer and receives a punched duplicate. The player wins if five or more of his numbers appear in the 20 drawn numbers.

Many different combinations can be bet. On a high-low ticket the player marks three groups of four connecting numbers. If one, two, three, four or none of his 12 selected numbers is drawn, he wins nothing. If he catches five spots, the payoff varies according to the location of the numbers. If two numbers are in one group, two in a second and one in the third, he is paid 20¢. A 3–1–1 arrangement of the numbers is paid 25¢; a 3–2 arrangement, 30¢, and a 4–1 arrangement, 35¢. The payoffs for catching 6, 7, 8, 9, 10 and 11 spots are shown on the high-low ticket list below. The high payoff for catching all 12 spots (4–4–4) is $1,296.

The player can also bet groups of 4, 5, 2 and 3 spots as shown under high-low ways, 10 spot, deuce ways and 9 spot. A typical casino's payout chart listing the bets permitted and the payoff odds on each is reproduced on page 285.

Other bets not listed on the chart are used by some casinos, such as the three-way eight ticket in which the player marks three groups of four adjacent numbers. He must catch four numbers in each of two groups to collect the minimum payoff. A four-way 10 spot is four groups of three adjacent numbers plus a single number called a "king." For a minimum win the player must catch five numbers within three groups, plus the king. There are also three-way nine tickets and others.

CALCULATING THE HOUSE PERCENTAGE AT RACEHORSE KENO

First, let us analyze the simple 1-spot ticket on which the player has marked only one of the 80 numbers and which, when his number appears among the 20 drawn numbers, pays him $3.20 for a $1 bet.

To figure the house percentage let's assume that you mark 80 tickets, betting on a different number on each. At $1 per ticket this costs you a total of $80. Since you are betting on every possible number, each of the 20 drawn balls gives you a winner. You collect $3.20 on each for a total of $64. Subtract this from the $80 bet and your loss is $16. Divide $16 by $80 and you find that the house has a favorable edge on a 1-spot ticket of 20%.

On the 2-spot ticket the player has marked 2 of the 80 numbers, and if they appear among the 20 drawn numbers he is paid off at 13 for 1. Here we must find the number of two-digit combinations which are possible with 80 numbers. The calculation is $\frac{80 \times 79}{1 \times 2} = 3160$. Suppose you bet $1 on each of these 3,160 two-number combinations for a total wager of $3,160. After 20 numbers have been called, you will hold $\frac{20 \times 19}{1 \times 2}$, or 190 winning tickets and, at 13 for 1, will collect $13 on each, a total of $2,470. Since you bet $3,160, your loss is $690. Divide your loss by the total amount

$25,000.00
LIMIT --- EACH GAME
TO AGGREGATE PLAYERS

HIGH-LOW TICKET, 12 SPOTS
3 groups of 4—35c rate pays

5 Spots	2-2-1 pays	$	.20
	3-1-1 pays		.25
	3-2 pays		.30
	4-1 pays		.35
6 Spots	2-2-2 pays		1.50
	3-2-1 pays		1.80
	3-3 pays		2.40
	4-1-1 pays		2.40
	4-2 pays		2.65
7 Spots	3-2-2 pays		11.35
	3-3-1 pays		14.25
	4-2-1 pays		17.15
	4-3 pays		23.00
8 Spots	3-3-2 pays		76.50
	4-2-2 pays		87.70
	4-3-1 pays		98.85
	4-4 pays		132.30
9 Spots	3-3-3 pays		194.40
	4-3-2 pays		198.00
	4-4-1 pays		205.20
10 Spots	4-3-3 pays		432.00
	4-4-2 pays		450.00
11 Spots	4-4-3 pays		756.00
12 Spots	4-4-4 pays		1296.00

HIGH-LOW WAYS
(Groups of 4)

12 Spots,	1 way	Cost	$	.35
16 Spots,	4 ways	Cost		1.40
20 Spots,	10 ways	Cost		3.50
24 Spots,	20 ways	Cost		7.00
28 Spots,	35 ways	Cost		12.25
32 Spots,	56 ways	Cost		19.60
36 Spots,	84 ways	Cost		29.40
40 Spots,	120 ways	Cost		42.00

10 SPOT
5c Per Way Ticket
(Groups of 5)

15 Spots,	3 ways	Cost	$	.30
20 Spots,	6 ways	Cost		.30
25 Spots,	10 ways	Cost		.50
30 Spots,	15 ways	Cost		.75
35 Spots,	21 ways	Cost		1.05
40 Spots,	28 ways	Cost		1.40
45 Spots,	36 ways	Cost		1.80
50 Spots,	45 ways	Cost		2.25
55 Spots,	55 ways	Cost		2.75
60 Spots,	66 ways	Cost		3.30
65 Spots,	78 ways	Cost		3.90
70 Spots,	91 ways	Cost		4.55
75 Spots,	105 ways	Cost		5.25
80 Spots,	120 ways	Cost		6.00

DEUCE WAYS
(Groups of 2)

12 Spots,	6 ways	Cost	$	.30
14 Spots,	21 ways	Cost		1.05
16 Spots,	56 ways	Cost		2.80
18 Spots,	126 ways	Cost		6.30
20 Spots,	252 ways	Cost		12.40

9 SPOT
(Groups of 3)

9 Spots,	1 way	Cost	$	.35
12 Spots,	4 ways	Cost		1.40
15 Spots,	10 ways	Cost		3.50
18 Spots,	20 ways	Cost		7.00
21 Spots,	35 ways	Cost		12.25
24 Spots,	56 ways	Cost		19.60
27 Spots,	84 ways	Cost		29.40
30 Spots,	120 ways	Cost		42.00

9-SPOT RATE

Spots	35c Ticket	70c Ticket	$1.05 Ticket	$4.20 Ticket
4	$ .15	$ .30	$ .45	$ 1.80
5	1.80	3.60	5.40	21.60
6	17.80	35.60	53.40	213.60
7	110.70	221.40	332.10	1,328.40
8	1,000.00	2,000.00	3,000.00	12,000.00
9	2,250.00	4,500.00	6,750.00	25,000.00

Spots	50c Ticket	$1.00 Ticket	$2.00 Ticket	$4.00 Ticket
4	$ .20	$ .40	$ .80	$ 1.60
5	2.55	5.10	10.20	20.40
6	25.40	50.80	101.60	203.20
7	158.10	316.20	632.40	1,264.80
8	1,428.55	2,857.10	5,714.20	11,428.40
9	3,214.20	6,428.40	12,856.80	25,000.00

10-SPOT RATE

Spots	25c Ticket	50c Ticket	$1.00 Ticket	$2.50 Ticket
5	$ .50	$ 1.00	$ 2.00	$ 5.00
6	4.50	9.00	18.00	45.00
7	45.00	90.00	180.00	450.00
8	325.00	650.00	1,300.00	3,250.00
9	650.00	1,300.00	2,600.00	6,500.00
10	2,500.00	5,000.00	10,000.00	25,000.00

11-SPOT RATE

Spots	$ .55 Ticket	$1.10 Ticket	$2.75 Ticket
5	$ .60	$ 1.20	$ 3.00
6	5.10	10.20	25.50
7	42.30	84.60	211.50
8	267.00	534.00	1,335.00
9	845.00	1,690.00	4,225.00
10	1,800.00	3,600.00	9,000.00
11	5,500.00	11,000.00	25,000.00

12-SPOT RATE

Spots	$ .40 Ticket	$ .80 Ticket	$2.40 Ticket
5	$ .25	$ .50	$ 1.50
6	2.25	4.50	13.50
7	14.95	29.90	89.70
8	85.20	170.40	511.20
9	299.25	598.50	1,795.50
10	720.25	1,440.50	4,321.50
11	1,533.25	3,066.50	9,199.50
12	4,000.00	8,000.00	24,000.00

1-SPOT ($1.00 Minimum)

Spots	$1.00 Ticket	$2.00 Ticket	$3.00 Ticket
1	$ 3.20	$ 6.40	$ 9.60

2-SPOT (25c Minimum)

Spots	$ .25 Ticket	$ .50 Ticket	$1.00 Ticket
2	$ 3.25	$ 6.50	$ 13.00

3-SPOT (25c Minimum)

Spots	$ .25 Ticket	$ .50 Ticket	$1.00 Ticket
2	$ .25	$ .50	$ 1.00
3	11.75	23.50	47.00

4-SPOT (25c Minimum)

Spots	$ .25 Ticket	$ .50 Ticket	$1.00 Ticket
2	$ .25	$ .50	$ 1.00
3	1.25	2.50	5.00
4	29.50	59.00	118.00

5-SPOT RATE

Spots	50c Ticket	$1.00 Ticket	$5.00 Ticket
3	$ 1.50	$ 3.00	$ 15.00
4	13.00	26.00	130.00
5	166.00	332.00	1,660.00

6-SPOT RATE

Spots	50c Ticket	$1.00 Ticket	$5.00 Ticket
3	$ .50	$ 1.00	$ 5.00
4	2.80	5.60	28.00
5	55.00	110.00	550.00
6	620.00	1,240.00	6,200.00

8-SPOT RATE

Spots	50c Ticket	$1.00 Ticket	$7.00 Ticket
4	$ .80	$ 1.60	$ 11.20
5	7.20	14.40	100.80
6	53.90	107.80	754.60
7	402.50	805.00	5,635.00
8	1,920.00	3,840.00	25,000.00

13-SPOT RATE

Spots	$ .95 Ticket	$2.85 Ticket	$5.70 Ticket
5	$ .35	$ 1.10	$ 2.20
6	2.85	8.55	17.10
7	17.70	53.10	106.20
8	100.10	300.30	600.60
9	360.10	1,080.30	2,160.60
10	950.30	2,851.00	5,702.00
11	2,035.00	6,105.00	12,210.00
12	4,110.00	12,330.00	24,660.00
13	9,540.00	25,000.00	25,000.00

14-SPOT RATE

Spots	$1.25 Ticket	$5.00 Ticket	$10.00 Ticket
5	$ .30	$ 1.25	$ 2.50
6	2.30	9.25	18.50
7	13.40	53.50	107.00
8	70.65	282.65	565.30
9	253.25	1,013.05	2,026.10
10	694.00	2,775.90	5,551.80
11	1,552.40	6,209.50	12,419.00
12	3,060.00	12,240.00	24,480.00
13	5,900.00	23,600.00	25,000.00
14	13,000.00	25,000.00	25,000.00

15-SPOT RATE

Spots	$1.50 Ticket	$7.50 Ticket	$15.00 Ticket
5	$ .25	$ 1.25	$ 2.50
6	1.80	9.00	18.00
7	9.80	48.85	97.70
8	48.85	244.20	488.40
9	172.35	861.70	1,723.40
10	480.00	2,400.00	4,800.00
11	1,107.45	5,537.30	11,074.60
12	2,225.00	11,125.00	22,250.00
13	4,130.00	20,650.00	25,000.00
14	7,700.00	25,000.00	25,000.00
15	16,000.00	25,000.00	25,000.00

DEALER WILL BE GLAD TO EXPLAIN ANY TICKET TO YOU

bet and you find that the house has a favorable edge of 21.8%. The same method can be used to find the house percentage on all the other tickets.

THE BREAKDOWN ON THE 10-SPOT TICKET

Of the tens of millions of dollars wagered annually at Racehorse Keno, about 80% is bet on the 10-spot ticket. This one isn't easy to figure. Thousands of Keno players have wondered just what their chances were of hitting the ten numbers on a 10-spot ticket. During 1960, many Nevada Keno operators, hearing that I had worked out the mathematical breakdown of the ten-spot ticket, asked me for it, but I withheld it for the publication of *Scarne's Complete Guide to Gambling,* where it appeared in print for the first time.

To calculate the probability that a specified ten numbers will appear among 20 numbers which are drawn from a group of 80, we must first find out how many different combinations of ten numbers can be formed with 80 numbers. In mathematical language, we are looking for the number of combinations of n things taken r at a first time. The formula is: $\dfrac{n(n-1)(n-2)\cdots(n-r+1)}{r!}$. We substitute 80 for n and 10 for r and get the equation that follows.

Keno charts which players receive listing the various wages that may be made. (Dick Graves' Nugget)

$$\frac{80 \times 79 \times 78 \times 77 \times 76 \times 75 \times 74 \times 73 \times 72 \times 71}{10 \times 9 \times 8 \times 7 \times 6 \times 5 \times 4 \times 3 \times 2 \times 1} = 1{,}646{,}492{,}110{,}120$$

Step number two consists in discovering how many different combinations of ten numbers can be formed with the 20 drawn numbers:

$$\frac{20 \times 19 \times 18 \times 17 \times 16 \times 15 \times 14 \times 13 \times 12 \times 11}{10 \times 9 \times 8 \times 7 \times 6 \times 5 \times 4 \times 3 \times 2 \times 1} = 184{,}756$$

Step number three: We find the number of combinations of groups of nine numbers which can be formed with 20 drawn balls:

$$\frac{20 \times 19 \times 18 \times 17 \times 16 \times 15 \times 14 \times 13 \times 12}{9 \times 8 \times 7 \times 6 \times 5 \times 4 \times 3 \times 2 \times 1} = 167{,}960$$

We must then calculate the number of ways these winning nine-group combinations can be formed with the 60 remaining numbers in the total of 80 balls: $167{,}960 \times 60 = 10{,}077{,}600$. This is the total possible number of ways 9 numbers plus one other number can be made.

We apply this same method to find the total possible combinations of eight numbers, seven numbers, six numbers, five numbers, four numbers, three numbers, two numbers, one number and 0 (zero) numbers.

Groups of 8 numbers:
$$\frac{20 \times 19 \times 18 \times 17 \times 16 \times 15 \times 14 \times 13}{8 \times 7 \times 6 \times 5 \times 4 \times 3 \times 2 \times 1} = 125,970$$

$$\frac{125,970 \times (60 \times 59)}{2 \times 1} = 222,966,900$$

Groups of 7 numbers:
$$\frac{20 \times 19 \times 18 \times 17 \times 16 \times 15 \times 14}{7 \times 6 \times 5 \times 4 \times 3 \times 2 \times 1} = 77,520$$

$$\frac{77,520 \times (60 \times 59 \times 58)}{1 \times 2 \times 3} = 2,652,734,400$$

Groups of 6 numbers:
$$\frac{20 \times 19 \times 18 \times 17 \times 16 \times 15}{6 \times 5 \times 4 \times 3 \times 2 \times 1} = 38,760$$

$$\frac{38,760 \times (60 \times 59 \times 58 \times 57)}{4 \times 3 \times 2 \times 1} = 18,900,732,600$$

Groups of 5 numbers:
$$\frac{20 \times 19 \times 18 \times 17 \times 16}{5 \times 4 \times 3 \times 2 \times 1} = 15,504$$

$$\frac{15,504 \times (60 \times 59 \times 58 \times 57 \times 56)}{5 \times 4 \times 3 \times 2 \times 1} = 84,675,282,048$$

Groups of 4 numbers: (Since no payoffs are made on 4 numbers or fewer of a 10-spot ticket, the double calculation above can be combined into one.)
$$\frac{(20 \times 19 \times 18 \times 17) \times (60 \times 59 \times 58 \times 57 \times 56 \times 55)}{(4 \times 3 \times 2 \times 1) \times (6 \times 5 \times 4 \times 3 \times 2 \times 1)} = 242,559,401,700$$

Groups of 3 numbers:
$$\frac{(20 \times 19 \times 18) \times (60 \times 59 \times 58 \times 57 \times 56 \times 55 \times 54)}{(3 \times 2 \times 1) \times (7 \times 6 \times 5 \times 4 \times 3 \times 2 \times 1)} = 440,275,888,800$$

Groups of 2 numbers:
$$\frac{(20 \times 19) \times (60 \times 59 \times 58 \times 57 \times 56 \times 55 \times 54 \times 53)}{(2 \times 1) \times (8 \times 7 \times 6 \times 5 \times 4 \times 3 \times 2 \times 1)} = 486,137,960,550$$

Groups of 1 number:
$$\frac{(20) \times (60 \times 59 \times 58 \times 57 \times 56 \times 55 \times 54 \times 53 \times 52)}{(1) \times (9 \times 8 \times 7 \times 6 \times 5 \times 4 \times 3 \times 2 \times 1)} = 295,662,853,200$$

Groups of no-hit numbers:
$$\frac{60 \times 59 \times 58 \times 57 \times 56 \times 55 \times 54 \times 53 \times 52 \times 51}{10 \times 9 \times 8 \times 7 \times 6 \times 5 \times 4 \times 3 \times 2 \times 1} = 75,394,027,566$$

Placed in tabular form, the total number of possible combinations in a 10-spot ticket are as follows:

	Number of Ways	Odds Against
10 numbers	184,756	8,911,710 + to 1
9 numbers	10,077,600	163,380 + to 1
8 numbers	222,966,900	7,383 + to 1
7 numbers	2,652,734,400	619 + to 1
6 numbers	18,900,732,600	86 + to 1
5 numbers	84,675,282,048	18 + to 1
4 numbers	242,559,401,700	5 + to 1
3 numbers	440,275,888,800	2 + to 1
2 numbers	486,137,960,550	2 + to 1
1 number	295,662,853,200	4 + to 1
No numbers	75,394,027,566	20 + to 1
Total number of combinations	1,646,492,110,120	

We then add all the ways that the winning groups of five or more numbers can be formed:

10 numbers	184,756
9 numbers	10,077,600
8 numbers	222,966,900
7 numbers	2,652,734,400
6 numbers	18,900,732,600
5 numbers	84,675,282,048
	106,461,978,304

Now we divide the total number of winning ways into the total number of possible ways: $\dfrac{1,646,492,110,120}{106,461,978,304}$.

We get an answer of 15+, which means that the odds are 14 to 1. For every fifteen 10-spot tickets you purchase you can expect in the long run to collect on one winning ticket.

THE HOUSE PERCENTAGE ON THE 10-SPOT TICKET

To figure the house percentage on the ten-spot ticket we must refer to the payoff chart below which lists the payoffs on catching five, six, seven, eight, nine and ten numbers.

5 numbers pay 2 for 1
6 numbers pay 18 for 1
7 numbers pay 180 for 1
8 numbers pay 1,300 for 1
9 numbers pay 2,600 for 1
10 numbers pay 10,000 for 1

Again we suppose that you mark all the possible ten-spot tickets (1,646,492,110,120), which, at $1 each, will cost you $1,646,492,110,120. After the 20 numbers are drawn, you will find you have 106,461,978,304 winning tickets ranging from five to ten numbers. And here is what you collect:

Winning Numbers	Number of Winning Tickets		Amount Won on Each Ticket		Total Amount Collected on Each Winning Number
10	184,756	×	$10,000	=	$ 1,847,560,000
9	10,077,600	×	2,600	=	26,201,760,000
8	222,966,900	×	1,300	=	289,856,970,000
7	2,652,734,400	×	180	=	477,492,192,000
6	18,900,732,600	×	18	=	340,213,186,800
5	84,675,282,048	×	2	=	169,350,564,096
Total	106,461,978,304		Total money won		$1,304,962,232,896

Our final step is to subtract the total money won from the total amount bet: $1,646,492,110,120 minus $1,304,962,232,896. This gives a loss of $341,529,877,224, a favorable edge to the house of 20.74%.

When the house pays 25,000 for 1 on ten numbers, 2,800 for 1 on nine numbers, and 1,400 for 1 on eight numbers, as some Nevada casinos do, the house edge is 19.10%.

HOUSE PERCENTAGES ON ALL TICKETS

The table that follows shows the percentages in favor of the house on all tickets from the 1 spot through the 15 spot, calculated on the payoff prices shown on page 285.

The 12-spot high-low ticket, 10-spot groups of five, deuce ways groups of two, 9-spot groups of three and similar tickets average about 25% against the player.

Ticket	House P.C.	Ticket	House P.C.
1 spot	20.0%	9 spot	21.2%
2 spot	21.8%	10 spot	20.7%
3 spot	26.4%	11 spot	25.6%
4 spot	24.7%	12 spot	18.9%
5 spot	21.5%	13 spot	20.1%
6 spot	21.3%	14 spot	23.1%
8 spot	20.2%	15 spot	23.8%

A final bit of advice to Racehorse Keno players. Don't gamble your money away expecting to win $25,000 on the 10-spot ticket, because this is about nine times more difficult than winning the $50,000 top prize in the New Jersey or New York State lottery, in which, by the way, the odds happen to be one in a million to win.

KENO AND THE FEDERAL TAX PROBLEM

The most bewildering topic among gamblers who make a big hit is the tax procedure employed by the Internal Revenue Service in the collection of income taxes on a player's gambling winnings. From a technical and legal standpoint, the IRS regulation states "that a gambler's total yearly winnings must be included in his income. However, he is permitted to deduct his gambling losses incurred during the same year, but only to the amount of his winnings." That is the law, but since all consistent gamblers who buck adverse odds are losers over the long run, where does that leave the poor sucker who happens to be lucky enough one day to win $1,000 or more in a Las Vegas Keno game?

To begin with, few gamblers (and none that I know of) keep a record of every bet they make during the year. So even assuming that in early December in any given year, a Craps shooter in Las Vegas gets lucky and manages to get a hot hand at the dice table and wins $6,000 or more, who is to say whether this puts him in the winner's circle for the year? To further complicate matters, no legal casino keeps records of an individual's gambling transactions—especially those on a cash basis. Therefore, the matter of what to report is up to a gambler's conscience. Sure, there are many cases where gamblers report winnings of $25,000 or more made at a gambling casino, but many of these individuals are racket guys who list their alleged winnings as earnings rather than reveal illegitimate sources of revenue.

From a practical standpoint there are only three games played in Nevada today where the Internal Revenue Service requires that a report be made of sizable wins. These are Keno, Bingo and Slot Machines. Some of the Keno lounges, in fact, post a detailed schedule citing the size of the winning tickets that the casino must report to the IRS. The schedule is as follows:

Cost of Ticket	Minimum Winnings Which Must Be Reported
$ .00–$ .59	$ 600
.60– .89	1,200
.90– 1.19	1,800
1.20– 1.79	2,400
1.80– 2.39	3,000
2.40– 2.99	3,600
3.00– 3.59	4,200
3.60– 9.99	6,000
10.00 and over	10,000

The IRS policy creates, for winning at Keno, as many questions as it does answers. For example, a Keno player buys a $3.60 Keno ticket and gets lucky and wins $6,000. In accordance with the casino policy a report of the $6,000 winnings is made to the Internal Revenue Service, which, we will assume, expects the $6,000 winnings to be added to the taxpayer's gross income for that year. The trouble is that during the same year the player lost $18,000 at the casino Black Jack and Craps tables. However, since no records were kept of these betting transactions, the player has no way of proving this except by his own statement, which the IRS will not accept unless it is documented. At the racetrack, for instance, such documentation of loss is possible. The player can produce losing tickets on horse races, Keno and lotteries, canceled checks to casinos, etc.

On the basis of the above information, we would have to conclude that anyone who plays the horses, buys lottery tickets, plays Keno, Bingo, Slot Machines, or gambles in Las Vegas, and intends to apply gambling losses against potential gambling winnings, better start keeping records of his gambling transactions—the more comprehensive the records are the better. Because, based on past performances, it's a sure bet that your word and undocumented statements won't carry much weight with the Internal Revenue Service. On the brighter side, there are probably 50 million gamblers in America who just for once would like to make a big winning of $6,000 or more and be faced with the problem of whether or not the IRS will permit them to deduct their gambling losses on their income tax returns.

13

CASINO
SIDE GAMES

Since casino operators, legal and illegal, seldom overlook an opportunity to grab an extra buck, any available space not suitable for a major standard casino game like Bank Craps, Black Jack or Roulette is usually occupied by one or more minor banking games known as *side games*. Most of these are games of chance of the carnival variety such as one finds at amusement centers, county and state fairs, American Legion and firemen's carnivals, and church bazaars.

The most popular side games, listed in order of their popularity, are: the Big Six, the Money Wheel, the Racehorse Wheel, Chuck-a-Luck, Hazard, Beat the Shaker, Under and Over Seven, Barbouth, Four Five Six or the Three-Dice Game, Monte, Trente et Quarante, and Bingo Casino Style.

These side games are all clever exercises in mathematical strategy designed to give the operators a big favorable percentage and at the same time make it as difficult as possible for the player to calculate the percentage. Casino operators and carnival hustlers have learned by experience that these games will get the players' dough much faster and more surely than any of the major casino games. The reason is that the house percentage averages three or four times more, running from a minimum 8% to a high of more than 20%. Betting limits vary, ranging from 10¢ to $10 for some games and for others from $1 up to $100 and sometimes $200 or $300.

In casinos today it is the novice gamblers, male and female, who give the side games their big action. Any gambler who knows even a little about house percentages and how they work avoids these games like the plague.

THE BIG SIX

The Big Six, or Jumbo Dice Wheel, is a giant wheel of chance five feet in diameter which, with its pedestal, stands eight feet high. It is the most popular of the casino side games and often earns the house $1,000 or more per day.

There are 54 spaces around the rim of the wheel's surface, each of which shows one side of three dice bearing different combinations of the numbers 1 through 6. There is a layout which also bears the numbers 1 through 6. The players *cover* (put their money on) one or more numbers on the layout and the dealer spins the wheel in a clockwise direction. Projecting *posts* (nails) on the outer edge of the wheel's rim separate the spaces and pass by a leather indicator at the top. When the wheel comes to a stop, the section in which the indicator rests is the winning combination.

This is how one of the "Gaming Guide Souvenir Booklets," which most luxury casinos distribute free to hotel and casino guests, describes the pay-off odds.

IT'S THE BIG SIX FOR BIG THRILLS. You'll enjoy a thrill a minute at this spell-binding Wheel of Fortune. If you put $1 on 1 and the wheel stops at 1–2–3, you get back $1 plus the $1 you invested since the 1 showed only once. If the wheel stops at 1–1–2 you get back $2 plus the $1 you invested since the $1 shows twice. This holds true for all the numbers, i.e., if you play $1 on 5 and the wheel stops on 4–5–6, you get back $1 and your dollar. If it stops at 5–5–5, you receive $3 and your $1.

If you are still not convinced that this is the game for you, the Big Six dealer will explain further advantages of the game. He tells you that "there are three winners and three losers on each and every spin of the wheel." He illustrates this by putting a silver dollar on each of the six numbers on the layout, then he points to a space on the wheel marked 1–2–3 or a space marked 4–5–6 and tells you that if the wheel stops on either of these spaces the player who wagered $1 on each of the six numbers on the layout can't lose any money. The player would win three $1 bets and lose three $1 bets, thus breaking even. He demonstrates this by collecting the three silver dollars on the losing numbers and uses them to pay off the three winning numbers. "Nothing," he adds, "could be fairer than that."

But what the casino booklet and the dealer fail to point out is that there are only six sections on the wheel that are dead even and contain three different numbers. The other 48 sections contain 24 doubles (pairs), and 24 triplets (three of a kind). This arrangement gives the Big Six operator a favorable advantage of $22\frac{2}{9}\%$, which is much too large for any player to overcome.

Here, without the help of algebra, trigonometry or differential calculus, using only simple grade-school arithmetic, is the proof that this is the correct percentage.

The wheel bears 54 sections of which 6 have no pairs, 24 have pairs, and 24 have three of a kind. Let's put a $1 bet on each of the six numbers on the layout, spin the wheel 54 times, and assume that the "laws of probability" are strictly enforced and that each of the 54 spaces appears once as a winner. We wager $6 on each of the 54 spins for a total of $324.

In 6 spins of the wheel we get "no pairs," winning $3 and losing $3 each time. We come out even, having bet $36 and taken down $36.

A casino Big Six wheel found in many Nevada casinos and elsewhere.

On the 24 spins in which pairs appear, we have wagered a total of $144. We take down $72 on the double numbers at 2 to 1, and $48 on the single numbers at even money, a total of $120. Our loss is $24.

On the 24 spins in which three of a kind appear, we have wagered a total of $144 and at 3 to 1 take down only $96 for a loss of $48.

Our total loss of $72 divided by the total $324 wagered gives us the percentage in the operator's favor of 22⅑%, or, in decimals, 22.22+%.

Since your average rate of loss is 22⅑¢ on each dollar wagered, do you still think the Bix Six is as attractive a proposition as the booklet and the dealer tried to make out?

Some Big Six wheels have fewer than 54 sections—48 or 30 or some other number—and the dice arrangements on their winning sections vary as well. The more often triplets appear on the wheel, the greater the operator's percentage.

THE MONEY WHEEL

At present this is the most popular casino side game found in the major Las Vegas hotel casinos. The mechanical structure and rules of play of the Money Wheel are very much like the Big Six except that it uses a different betting layout and has a different number of sections on the wheel's rim. This changes the payoff odds and the operator's favorable P.C.

The rim of the wheel is divided into 50 sections covered with glass, and in 48 of these are new American greenbacks in denominations of $1, $2, $5, $10 and $20, or just dollar figures to indicate the same. The remaining two sections bear a picture of the American flag and a joker. There are seven corresponding betting spaces on the layout showing $1, $2, $5, $10, $20, flag and joker.

The values of the bills indicate the payoff odds to winners. A winning bet on the $1 bill is paid off at even money or 1 to 1 odds. A winning bet on the $2 bill is paid off at 2 to 1 odds, on the $5 at 5 to 1 odds, on the $10 at 10 to 1 odds, on the $20 at 20 to 1 odds. A winning bet on the flag pays off at 40 to 1 odds, and you also receive 40 to 1 for a winning bet on the joker.

Some Money Wheel players think that the big odds offered cut down the operator's edge, and some even believe that the game is almost dead even. This logic, or rather lack of it, is what makes Money Wheel operators rich. The operator's favorite percentage is calculated in the same way as on the Big Six.

Of the 50 sections on the wheel, 22 contain a $1 bill, 14 contain a $2 bill, 7 contain a $5 bill, 3 contain a $10 bill, 2 contain a $20 bill, and there is one flag and one joker. There are 7 betting spaces on the layout corresponding to the betting groups.

If we cover each of the 7 betting spaces with a $1 bet, spin the wheel 50 times and assume that each of the 50 sections wins once, we will wager $7 on each spin for a total of $350.

The wheel stops at the $1 bill 22 times and we take down $44.

It stops at the $2 bill 14 times and we take down $42.

It stops at the $5 bill 7 times and we take down $42.

It stops at the $10 bill 3 times and we take down $33.

It stops at the $20 bill 2 times and we take down $42.

It stops at the flag once and we take down $41.

It stops at the joker once and we take down $41.

Our winnings add up to $285. We subtract this from the total $350 wagered and get a loss of $65. Divide this $65 by the $350 total wagered and we find that the operator has a percentage in his favor of $18\frac{4}{7}\%$, or, in decimals, $18.57+\%$.

There are other types of money wheels. All are basically the same in structure and method of operation, but some give the operator a greater favorable percentage. This runs from a low 18% to a high of 30% or more.

THORP'S WINNING SYSTEM FOR THE MONEY WHEEL

During my lifetime I have read a lot of fairy tales by many a self-styled winning gambler describing some fantastic but impractical method that he used to beat a casino game, but Professor Edward O. Thorp, of *Beat the Dealer* fame, takes the cake with this baby. Following is a quote from a story about Thorp that appeared in *Life* magazine on March 27, 1964.

BEATING THE WHEEL WITH THE BIG TOE

At one point, to beat the "wheel of fortune" which stands at the entrance of most casinos, he [Thorp] built a device which measured off a second with an all but inaudible click and installed it in one shoe where he could start it with his big toe. Thus armed, with his hands innocently free, he was able to time the velocity of the turning rim well enough to predict its 40 to 1 payoff and quickly enough to put down a bet almost as soon as its carny-voiced operator gave it a spin.

The wheel of Fortune used in Nevada casinos with its 40 to 1 payoff as described above is the Money Wheel. If this mysterious gadget controlled by Thorp's big toe informs him when this giant size (five feet in diameter) wheel will stop on the 40 to 1 payoff, I assume it would be less work for Thorp's big toe if he geared this magical gimmick to predict the lesser payoff sections, since they appear on the rim of the wheel many times more than the two sections which pay off at 40 to 1 odds.

While I'm on the subject of gambling fantasies, here's another lulu that rivals the big toe gimmick, which appeared some time ago in the book *Gamblers Don't Gamble* by Michael MacDougall. Incidentally Mr. MacDougall was Thorp's adviser on the card-cheating chapter in *Beat the Dealer,* and what a chapter of misinformation it turned out to be!

Mr. MacDougall is the man who achieved considerable fame among old-time gamblers when he wrote, "I could tell by the mere sound that the dice were phony. I can't describe that sound but it's unmistakable once you catch it." A few pages later, we learn the dice referred to were loaded.

I can well understand why he has difficulty describing the sound. In all my years as a gambling consultant and investigator, I have never heard any such sound and I am willing to bet MacDougall any amount he cares to put up that his ears aren't that good either.

Believe it or not, good old Professor Thorp has done it again. Not being satisfied with his phony winning systems at Black Jack, Baccarat, and the Money Wheel, he informs us that he has developed a computer-tested method for beating the casino game of Roulette. However, he adds there are certain electronic problems with the method that have kept him from using the system on a large scale against casinos.

In conclusion, I must state that Professor Thorp treats his readers as if they were gambling idiots.

THE RACEHORSE WHEEL

The Racehorse Wheel is very much like the Big Six and the Money Wheel. The number of sections on the wheels varies, with layouts to correspond, and the sections bear pictures of racehorses and numbers specifying payoff odds. Man o' War may pay 40 to 1, Morvich 20 to 1, Teeko 5 to 1, etc.

The operator's favorable edge on most Racehorse Wheels runs from a low of 15% to a high of 25%.

CHEATING AT WHEELS OF CHANCE

The Big Six, Money Wheel and Racehorse Wheel in a permanently established casino are almost never rigged for two very good reasons: (1) The house advantage is so great that the wheels will win all the loose money around, and cheating is not only unnecessary but downright foolish. (2) The day-in-and-day-out casino operation of a gaffed wheel would be certain suicide for the owner, because even the rank suckers would sooner or later *rumble* (catch on) to the mechanical gaff.

CHUCK-A-LUCK

Chuck-a-Luck, commonly called the Bird Cage, is the game from which Big Six was derived. Since the introduction of Big Six into the casinos the popularity of the Bird Cage has hit a new low. Smart casino operators prefer Big Six because their take is triple that of the Bird Cage. You'll still see the Cage occasionally in some rug or sawdust joint, and it is still widely used by carnival hustlers working around outings, picnics, carnivals, fair grounds and bazaars.

The Bird Cage equipment and rules of play are simple. Three two-inch dice are tumbled in a wire cage shaped like an hour glass. The slim waist of the cage is encircled by a metal band connected to an axle on which the cage turns. The three captive dice tumble from end to end of the cage when it is spun, and they come to rest on one of the drumlike coverings at the ends of the cage.

As in Big Six, the layout bears the numbers 1, 2, 3, 4, 5, 6. Players put their bets on one or more of the layout numbers. After the cage is spun and the dice come to rest, if a player's number appears on one die he gets even money (1 to 1); if his number appears on two dice, he gets paid off at 2 to 1; and if all three bear his number he gets paid off at 3 to 1.

Many casino operators whom I have questioned believe, since the payoff odds at Chuck-a-Luck and the Big Six are the same, that the house advantage must also be the same. Nothing could be further from the truth. The operator's edge of $22\frac{2}{9}$% at the Big Six is considerably more than his edge of $7\frac{47}{54}$% at Chuck-a-Luck.

This big percentage difference arises from the fact that there are only 54 three-dice combinations painted on the Big Six wheel, most of which are pairs and three of a kinds, whereas the three dice used in Chuck-a-Luck possess a total of 216 combinations comprised of 120 no pairs, 90 pairs, and only six three of a kinds. I won't repeat the calculations here, but if you follow the same procedure as was used to figure the Big Six house percentage, and don't make a mistake, you'll find that the operator's favorable P.C. is $74\frac{7}{54}\%$.

CHEATING AT CHUCK-A-LUCK

Some Bird Cage operators who want a stronger P.C., because they believe implicitly in the cheater's adage "Never give a sucker an even break," employ a gaffed Bird Cage outfit when dealing the game. Steel-loaded dice (known as *electric dice*) are used in the cage and an electromagnet is concealed in the table on which the cage rests.

Electric dice are so loaded as to bring up either of two opposite sides. Opaque celluloid dice are loaded with steel slugs. The slugs used to load transparent dice are circular disks punched out of a grid of $\frac{5}{1000}$-inch steel wires. These are placed in the countersunk spots. One is inserted in each of the spots on four different sides of the cube, leaving the two opposite sides which the operator wants to control unloaded. All three dice are loaded the same way, and when the juice is on, either a pair or three of a kind must appear. If the unloaded sides are the six and ace, the dice will show three sixes, three aces, a pair of sixes and an ace, or a pair of aces and a six.

The tip-off on the electric cage is the distance between the bottom of the cage and the table top in which the electromagnet is concealed. If this is so small that the cage just barely clears the table when it turns, it may mean that the cage is gaffed.

HAZARD

Today's most popular dice games, Private, Bank and Money Craps, are descended from the 700-year-old private game of Hazard. The casino banking game of Hazard, originally known as Grand Hazard, using three dice, had an era of great popularity during the early 1900s, both in our western sawdust joints and in our fashionable casinos. I first saw it played in Colonel Bradley's famous Beach Club in Palm Beach, Florida, in 1932. Players placed their bets on the Hazard layout, and the dealer, standing behind it, dropped three dice through a device called a *Hazard chute*. A series of inclined planes called steps, inside the chute, tumbled the dice as they went through the chute and out onto the layout surface.

Years later, after Black Jack was introduced into the casinos, Hazard's popularity waned and it became a side game. About the same time, a Chicago manufacturer marketed the first Chuck-a-Luck cage, and since then most operators have discarded the chute and dealt Hazard with a Chuck-a-Luck cage.

In the top casinos today Hazard runs a poor fifth in popularity behind the Big Six, Money Wheel, Racehorse Wheel and Chuck-a-Luck. It is still popular, however, in many western sawdust joints and with carnival hustlers.

Hazard is now played much like Chuck-a-Luck except that the layout permits 25 additional wagers not found in Chuck-a-Luck. Here is the percentage breakdown on the more important bets:

Raffles: The player bets that any specific three of a kind (three aces, three deuces, etc.) will appear. This bet is paid off at odds of 180 for 1; the correct odds are 215 to 1, which gives the bank a favorable edge of $16\frac{2}{3}\%$.

Any raffle: The player bets that *any* three of a kind will appear. This bet is paid off at odds of 30 for 1 and the correct odds are 35 to 1; the bank's advantage is $16\frac{2}{3}\%$.

Low bet: a bet that the total count on the dice will be 10 or below.

High bet: a bet that the total count on the dice will be 11 or more.

Odd and even bet: a bet that the total count on the dice will add up to the number selected by the player.

Since the player loses when his selection appears if it is made up of three of a kind, the bank has an edge on each of these wagers (low, high, odd-and-even) of $2\frac{7}{9}\%$. This low percentage makes it much the best bet for the player.

Numbers bet: The player bets that he can pick the exact winning number of the total count such as 4, 5, 6, 7 and so on, up to and including 17. The bank's favorable edge runs from a low $9\frac{13}{18}\%$ on a count of 7 to a high $30\frac{5}{9}\%$ on a count of 8.

Chuck numbers: These are the same bets as in Chuck-a-Luck, and they get the most action at Hazard. The player bets on the numbers 1 through 6, and a winning number pays even money if it appears on one die, 2 to 1 if it shows on two dice, and 3 to 1 if it shows on three dice. The bank's edge is the same as in Chuck-a-Luck: $7\frac{47}{54}\%$.

CHEATING AT HAZARD

The electric cage is gaffed as in Chuck-a-Luck (see page 298).

BEAT THE SHAKER

In various sections of the country this is also known as *High Dice, Beat the Banker, Beat the Dealer, Beat the Shake* and *Two-Dice Klondike.* This side game is popular in honky-tonk gambling houses, where it is operated as a counter game and usually dealt by dice girls. It is such a simple and deceptive game that the average gambler believes it should be easy to beat. He's wrong.

When operated as a counter game, the dice are thrown from a cup. When dealt in a sawdust joint or by a carnival hustler, the dice are on a high perch, and when the operator pulls a string they drop through a transparent chute out on to the playing surface. Two dice are used, and the banker and the player each get one throw. The banker goes first. To win, the player must get a higher total count on his throw than the banker; the banker wins on all ties.

The game is a dead-even proposition except for the ties; they constitute the bank's advantage. To calculate this we simply find out how many ties can be expected in the long run. The banker stands to throw the number 2 (two aces) once out of 36 throws. The player's chances are the same. The chance that they will tie by throwing two aces each is $\frac{1}{36} \times \frac{1}{36}$, or $\frac{1}{1,296}$.

If we multiply the probabilities on each of the numbers 2, 3, 4, 5, 6, 7, 8, 9, 10, 11 and 12 and then add, we find that in the long run ties can be expected 146 times. Dividing the favorable chances of 146 by the total chances of 1,296 gives us a percentage in favor of the bank at Beat the Shaker of $11\frac{43}{162}\%$, or, in decimals: 11.26+%.

Some carnival operators who want to speed up the action and take the chump even faster use only one die. The operators advantage in this case is $16\frac{2}{3}\%$.

CHEATING AT BEAT THE SHAKER

The most common method, when the dice are thrown from a cup, is the use of a *slick dice cup* which is gaffed by having its inner surface slicked or polished, and a pair of first-flop dice which are so heavily loaded that, when properly thrown from the slick cup, they will always show fives and sixes (making the combination 10, 11 or 12). On the dealer-cheat's turn, he shakes the cup with an up-and-down and slightly rotary motion of his arm. Instead of tumbling at random inside the cup, the dice spin around the slicked inner surface like horses on a *chump twister* (merry-go-round).

The centrifugal force created by the rotary up-and-down motion of the cup causes the loaded sides of the dice to face the cup's inner surface. When the cheat slides the two dice out and across the playing surface, the desired unloaded sides are up and he gets a high count of 10, 11 or 12. He can win whenever he likes—which is most of the time.

For information on how to spot loaded dice see pages 172 to 185.

UNDER AND OVER SEVEN

This game, also called *Over and Under,* is an old-time carnival game which is still going strong at outings, picnics, carnivals, fairs or wherever the carnival hustler is found. It is also very popular in many honky-tonk gambling joints. Like Beat the Shaker, it is usually dealt from a chute when played outdoors, and indoors by dice girls from a cup.

A pair of dice, the cup (or chute) and a betting layout with three betting spaces are used. The center is marked with a large 7, the space on the left reads "Under 7," that on the right, "Over 7." The player puts his money on any one of the three spaces, and throws. A bet on under 7 wins if he throws a 2, 3, 4, 5 or 6, and the player is paid off at even money; he loses if he throws 7 or more. A bet on over 7 wins if he throws an 8, 9, 10, 11 or 12, and he is paid off at even money; he loses if he throws 7 or less. If he puts his bet on the 7 space and throws 7 (a natural) he wins and is paid off at odds of 4 to 1; any other number loses.

It looks as though the operator is leaning over backward to give his customers a fair chance to win. He's leaning all right, like the leaning tower of Pisa, but in the other direction. Since there are six ways to make 7, the player who bets on that space can expect to win $\frac{1}{6}$ of the time. If the operator paid off at 5 to 1 it would be an even-up proposition. He pays 4 to 1 and has an advantage on that bet of a big $16\frac{2}{3}\%$.

Of the 36 combinations with a pair of dice, 15 will total less than 7; the player has 15 chances out of 36 to win a bet on under 7, making the correct odds 7 to 5 against him. The operator pays off at even money and again has a favorable edge of $16\frac{2}{3}\%$. The same holds true for the over 7 space.

It doesn't matter on which space you put your money, that stiff $16\frac{2}{3}\%$ P.C. will grind down your bankroll almost as fast as if your pocket was being picked.

CHEATING AT UNDER AND OVER SEVEN

Since the operator seldom handles the dice and since that take of $16\frac{2}{3}\%$ is plenty big enough, the operator rarely cheats. Player cheats however, have been known to beat operators by switching crooked dice into the game.

BARBOUTH

A favorite among Greek and Jewish players, Barbouth (also known as Barbudey, Barbooth, Barabout) is now popular in this country and often played for large stakes. It is a dead even game, shooter and fader each having an exactly even chance.

Any number can play, usually as many as can sit around a regulation Poker table. Two peewee dice (small .375-inch dice) and two dice cups are used. Each player rolls one die and the high man becomes the first shooter. The shooter does not specify the amount of his wager the way he does in Craps, but the player on his right, called the *fader*, bets any amount up to the limit that the shooter will not win and places it in the center of the playing surface. The shooter may cover the bet, allow other players to take all or part of the bet, or he may refuse the wager and pass the dice to the player on his right. The fader also has the privilege of refusing to fade and passing his opportunity to fade. The other players make side bets on whether or not the shooter or fader will win.

After his bet has been covered the shooter throws out the dice for one roll. If the number thrown does not effect a decision the dice pass to the fader, who takes one roll. If his roll is also no decision, the shooter throws again; and shooter and fader continue to throw alternately until a decision is effected. If the shooter or a fader throws 3–3, 5–5, 6–6 or 6–5 he wins. If he throws 1–1, 2–2, 4–4 or 1–2 he loses. All other throws are meaningless. If the shooter loses with a throw of 1–1, 2–2, or 4–4, or if the fader wins with a throw of 3–3, 5–5, or 6–6, then the dice pass to the player on the shooter's right who becomes the next shooter and the player on the right of the new shooter becomes the new fader. But if the shooter loses with a throw of 1–2 or the fader wins with a throw of 6–5, the shooter retains the dice and continues to shoot.

A house employee known as a *cutter* takes the charge of 2½% of each winning bet. A bookmaker or banker is usually available to accept side bets for a charge of 5%, which is divided equally between the bookmaker and house cutter.

Since the small opaque dice used in Barbouth are easy to switch and load, and considering the present method of play in which the shooter and fader each use their own dice and dice cup, a player must be on guard against a slick cup used with first-flop dice, controlled shots with the cup, and switching of tops and bottoms.

FOUR FIVE SIX, OR THE THREE-DICE GAME

This game is popular throughout the northwestern United States, including Alaska, and western Canada. Most players believe it is an even-up game with no advantage for the banker.

As many players may play as can crowd around the playing surface. Three dice are used, and are thrown from a cup. Each player puts the amount he desires to wager in front of him and the banker, who covers all bets, plays against each player in turn. After the first round, the player on the banker's left becomes the banker and so on.* The banker shoots first.

When either banker or player throws (1) the combination 4–5–6, (2) any pair and a six or (3) three of a kind, it is a winning decision. If (1) 1–2–3 or (2) any pair and an ace is thrown, it is a losing decision. When any pair is thrown and the third die is a 2, 3, 4 or 5, the number on the

---

* Except when the game is operated by the house, in which case the bank does not rotate. The bank usually has a $25 limit.

third die becomes the shooter's point. If his opponent fails to score a winning or losing decision, and also throws a point, the player whose point is highest wins.

A tie is a standoff. When a player does not get a pair and does not throw either 4–5–6 or 1–2–3, the roll is neutral and he must continue shooting until he wins, loses, throws a point or ties.

Since the banker wins and loses according to the same deciding throws as the player, there would seem to be no advantage in his favor—until we break it down. There are 216 different combinations possible with three dice, of which 120 are no pairs, 90 are pairs and six are three of a kind.

Of the 90 pairs $\frac{1}{6}$ can be expected to have a 6 as a number on the third die, a total of 15. There are six ways to throw three of a kind and six ways to throw 4–5–6, a total of 27 winning ways.

The losing throws: Any pair with an ace and 1–2–3 can be made in 15 ways and six ways respectively for a total of 21 losing ways.

Point numbers (any pair with a 2–3–4–5) can be made in 60 ways (the 90 ways pairs can be made minus the 30 ways pairs with aces and sixes can be made).

All these winning and losing and point number ways added together show that just half of the possible 216 ways are of importance, or 108 ways. The other 108 rolls are neutral and do not affect any decision.

The banker's advantage lies in the fact that he always throws first. Out of 108 decisive rolls he can expect to win 27 times, lose 21 times and throw a point 60 times. Considering only the first throw, he has an advantage of six winning ways in his favor, a P.C. of $\frac{6}{108}$ times 100 or $5\frac{5}{9}\%$.

If he throws a point, his opponent takes the cup and throws, and the $5\frac{5}{9}\%$ is now in the opponent's favor. But while the bank always has this P.C. on his throw, the player has it only when the banker throws a point, or $\frac{60}{108}$ of the time. (On the other 48 throws, the player never gets a chance to shoot.) $\frac{60}{108}$ of $5\frac{5}{9}\%$ leaves a favorable percentage of $3\frac{7}{81}\%$ for the player.

Subtracting the player's percentage from the banker's percentage leaves a $2\frac{38}{81}\%$ advantage in the banker's favor. This is about 12¢ on a $5 bet.

Because they think Four Five Six is an even-up game, many players pass up their opportunity to be the banker when it is their turn. The $2\frac{38}{81}$ P.C. is always working against those players and grinding them down. The game is an even-up proposition only if each player takes his turn at banking so that the P.C. works for as well as against him.

MONTE

This game is also called *Spanish Monte* and *Monte Bank*. Due to its big moneymaking feature and its lack of bulky equipment, which minimizes police raids and arrests, Monte has replaced Bank Craps as the number one banking game in most illegal gambling clubs operating in the big cities of the United States.

REQUIREMENTS

1. A standard deck of 52 cards from which the eights, nines and tens have been removed, making a 40-card deck.

2. A banker chosen from two or more players. As a rule, the admissible maximum is the number that can crowd around the card table.

3. A houseman, called a *cutter,* whose official duty is to aid the player-banker in his dealing chores, including the payoff, collection of losing and winning bets, and collection of a 25% charge from each player's door or gate winnings. This 25% charge is known as a "cut" and is divided equally between the banker and the house at the end of a player's banking role.

Object of the game: To win a bet that one or more face-up cards on the table layouts will be matched before one or more of the remaining face-up cards on the Monte layout.

Value of the cards: The cards have no special value relative to each other, and neither do the suits.

Selecting the banker: By mutual consent any player shuffles the pack, then puts it in the center of the table. Each player cuts a group of cards off the pack. The player cutting the low card is the first dealer and banker. In case of a tie for low card, the tied players cut until one is low. On completion of the banker's deal, the deck and the deal pass to the player on the dealer's left; thereafter, it rotates to the left, clockwise. At any time, the dealer may pass the bank (i.e., decline to bank the game), if there are no unsettled bets on the table. To announce that he means to pass the bank, the dealer utters the word "Aces!"

Betting limit: The dealer is privileged to place as much money in the bank as he chooses. If a player wagers more money than is in the bank, and the bank loses the bet, the largest wager is paid off first; the second largest is paid off next, etc. Other bets are called off. The banker is only responsible for the money in the bank. The wagers are always in cash.

Shuffle and cut: The dealer shuffles the pack. Any player may call for a shuffle before the cut, but the dealer is entitled to shuffle last. After the shuffle, the dealer puts the cards before the player at his right to be cut. That player must cut, although the other players may also call for the right to cut before the player to the dealer's right completes his own cut.

Start of the deal: After the cut the banker, holding the pack face down, deals two cards off the bottom of the deck, facing these two cards and putting them in the center of the table two or three inches apart. This is known as the *top layout*. Then the dealer takes two cards off the top of the deck, and puts them face up two or three inches below the first two cards, about the same distance apart, forming the *bottom layout*. Should the two cards of the bottom layout be of the same rank, there is no play and a new deal is in order. If the two cards of the top layout are of the same rank, the dealer places one card on top of the other and then deals a third card alongside it. Bets placed on a pair indicate that a player is betting against two same-rank cards of the opposite color of the other card in the top layout. Example: If the other card is red, the player is betting against a black card (spades or clubs) of the same rank; or vice versa. Should three cards of the same rank appear in the top layout, they are grouped in threes and a bet on a triple means that the player is betting against the same color and same rank of the other card. The above bets are all paid off at even money.

TYPES OF MONTE BETS

Crisscross bet: To bet that a selected one of four face-up cards will be matched before a designated card of the other three cards. (A card is matched whenever one of three remaining cards of the same denomination is dealt from the pack.) Example: Face up on the table are the ace, two, three and four of clubs. The player puts his bet on the ace, placing his cash in such a way that it points to or just touches the deuce. He's now betting that one of the three remaining aces will be dealt from the pack before one of the three remaining deuces.

Doubler or doubler bet: To bet that a card in the top layout will be matched before a card is matched in the bottom layout, or vice versa; or that one of the two cards resting on the dealer's left will be matched before one of the two cards on his right, or vice versa. This bet is paid off at even money.

Circle bet or circling a card: To bet that one card will be matched before any of the three others. This bet is paid off at 3 to 1 odds.

Monte Carlo bet: To make a combination of the three bets at one time. The payoff of such bets is determined by the sum wagered on each. All Monte Carlo wagers are indicated by the placement of the money (bills) as described under the crisscross bet. Bets can be placed any time during a deal.

THE PLAY OF MONTE

After the bets have been placed, the cutter tells the dealer, "That's all," which formally terminates that phase of the game, and the dealer turns the deck face up in his hand. From then on the cards are dealt face up one at a time. Some gambling joints insist that after each decision the deck be turned face down and future bets placed before the deck is turned face up.

If the top card of the deck matches one of the four layout cards, either the dealer or a player (or players) wins; and the dealer keeps taking cards off the pack until (1) all the cards bet on are matched or (2) the cards the players are betting against are matched. As a card is matched, it is removed from the board. When all bets are won or lost the deal is completed and a new deal starts.

THE HOUSE TAKE

When a player places a bet (any time during the game) and the next (first) dealt card matches his winning card, the cutter takes 25% of the player's winnings. This is called the *door* or *gate*. This cut is put aside and divided equally by the banker and house at the end of the player's banking session. Percentagewise, this 25% cut amounts to an overall advantage of about 3%.

TRENTE ET QUARANTE

Also known as *Rouge et Noir* (red and black), Trente et Quarante is a standard European casino banking card game and is most popular in French and Italian casinos, and the world-famous Monte Carlo Casino, where its popularity is only surpassed by Baccarat and Roulette. The name Trente et Quarante ("30 and 40") is derived from the fact that the winning point always lies between these two numbers.

REQUIREMENTS

1. A regulation Trente et Quarante table with a double layout. See the illustration showing half of the Trente et Quarante layout.

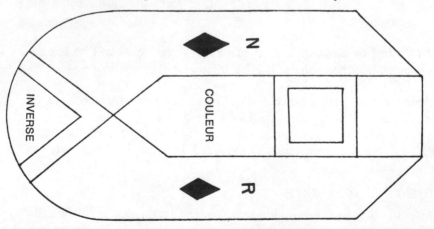

Trente-et-Quarante layout as seen in European casinos including Monte Carlo.

2. Any number of persons can play against the bank, as many as can be accommodated at the gaming table.

3. Five croupiers. Four serve as banker and one as dealer (tailleur) and count caller. A supervisor sits on a stand overlooking the Trente et Quarante table to see that no errors are committed.

4. Six standard packs of 52 cards each, shuffled together and used as one deck of 312 cards.

Value of cards: The ace is the lowest-ranking card and has a point value of 1. Kings, queens and jacks have a value of 10 each. All other cards have their numerical face value. Deuce is counted 2, three is counted 3, etc. Suits have no value. Only colors count: hearts and diamonds are called red; spades and clubs are called black.

Shuffle and cut: At the start of each round of play, the dealer spreads the six packs of cards on the table and all players and croupiers are permitted to take a group of cards and shuffle them. On later deals, when the discard receivers are emptied onto the layout and some cards are face up and some are face down, the croupier and players turn the face-up cards down and shuffle them.

After the players have shuffled groups of cards, the croupier gathers all the cards and shuffles them together, usually shuffling about two packs at a time. Finally, the croupier assembles all six packs together and then hands a player an indicator card, saying, "Cut, please." The player inserts the indicator card into the packet to show where he wants the cards cut. The dealer cuts the cards at this position, putting the indicator and all the cards above it on the bottom.

Object of the game: To bet that a specific color (black or red) will produce a count of 31 or a total nearer to 31 than the opposite color. The player may also place his bet on *rouge* (red), *noir* (black), couleur or inverse.

THE PLAY

All betting is done against the casino or bank. Before the deal begins, the players place their bets. The dealer takes about 50 cards off the top of the pack and deals out the first card face upward onto the noir (black). He then deals a second, a third, etc., which he places in the same row, right and left, announcing the cumulative total of the spots with each card dealt. The dealing stops with the card which causes the total to reach or exceed 31. The second row, rouge (red) is dealt below the noir row in the same manner.

The row with the total nearer to 31 is the winning row. For example, a bet on noir wins if the count of the first or noir row is 34 while the rouge row totals 36. A bet on couleur wins if the very first card dealt is the same color as the designating the winning row. If this card is of the opposite color, a bet on inverse wins. The dealer traditionally announces the result for red and color only, calling "Rouge gagne" (wins) or "Rouge perd" (loses) or "couleur gagne" or "couleur perd." All bets are paid off at even money (1 to 1).

If both rows total the same count (tie), it is called a *refait* and all bets are called off. If there is a refait at 31—refait de trente-et-un—the bank takes half of all bets; however, the player has the option of leaving his bet in *prison,* where it remains for the next game or coup. If he wins on this coup, he withdraws his bet; but if he loses, he loses the whole.

As bets are settled, the cards dealt for that coup are brushed into the discard receiver. When there are insufficient cards for the next coup all the cards are reshuffled.

Refait insurance bet: Before the cards are dealt, players may insure their bets against a possible loss of half their bets when a refait at 31 takes place. The insurance charge is 5% of the amount wagered.

Probabilities: Of the ten numbers from 31 to 40, the number 31 appears more often than any other:

Number	Times
31	13
32	12
33	11
34	10
35	9
36	8
37	7
38	6
39	5
40	4

Our mathematics informs us that a refait (tie) of 31 will happen about once in 41 dealt hands of play, which is about 1½% when the bank takes 50% of each player's bet when a standoff of 31 occurs.

BINGO CASINO STYLE

Bingo, that great American women's pastime, is a popular attraction in many gambling casinos in Nevada and the Caribbean islands. Many gambling casinos in Nevada now run free Bingo parties in order to attract customers to their gaming tables. Some charge a fee, usually $1 for each Bingo card. These games, with attractive $1,000 to $10,000 jackpots, do draw the crowds, both men and women. One Nevada casino operator told me: "Bingo is a much better draw for us than any name act from movies or television."

Some writers on Bingo say it is of English, Swedish or Dutch origin. My research shows that it is actually a more complicated version of the still popular Italian parlor game of Lotto, which is in turn derived from the more than 440-year-old Italian national lottery. Other writers say that Lotto is a direct descendant of Keno, a form of lottery popular in the gambling dives in and around New Orleans in the early 1840s. The truth of the matter is the reverse: Keno is a descendant of Lotto, because the latter was played in Italy centuries before Keno made its appearance in New Orleans saloons.

Almost every casino patron knows how to play Bingo. You buy a printed paper or cardboard card that bears a printed design of five rows of five squares each, 25 squares in all. The letters B–I–N–G–O appear above this design, each letter above one of the vertical columns. All the squares contain numbers except the center square, which is considered a free play.

The first vertical row on the left under the letter B contains any five numbers from the group 1 through 15. Under I there are any five numbers from the group 16 through 30. Under N, the center vertical row, there are only four numbers from the group 31 through 45. The middle square of this row is the center square of the card, and it is either blank or bears a printed O or X of the words "Free Play." This is always considered a covered square of free play. Under G in the fourth vertical row there are any five numbers from the group 46 through 60, and under O in the fifth row any five numbers from the group 61 through 75.

The most popular device for selecting numbers is the Bingo bowl, often called the Bingo cage, a spherical wire-mesh cage about 9½ inches in diameter, in which the Bingo balls are placed. It is mounted on a wooden or metal base and has an electric crank-turning ball-selecting device. There are 75 Bingo balls, each of which bears one of the letters of the word "Bingo" and a number. The B balls bear numbers from 1 through 15 group: the I balls, from the 16 through 30 group, and so on—the same grouping arrangement as the cards.

When the operator presses a button the wire cage revolves and the players can see the balls being mixed. When the cage stops revolving, an opening at the bottom of the cage releases one ball.

Another popular device for mixing and selecting the balls is the Bingo blower, which consists of a glass enclosure into which 75 lettered and numbered Ping-Pong balls are placed. An electric air compressor sends a stream of air into the glass case which agitates and mixes the balls until one ball falls into a small pocket and then drops out of the enclosure.

The game commences when all the players have purchased as many cards as they want, plus a pile of markers to keep track of possible winners.

As the selected numbers are called one by one, each player places a marker on any selected number that appears on his card. The object of most casino-style Bingo games is to be the first person to cover (1) five numbers in a straight line (2) four numbers at the four corners of the card (3) eight numbers which surround the center "free play" square, and (4) the one which is rewarded by the big cash prizes—the covering of all numbers on the board.

BIG-TIME CASINO BINGO GAMES

Because of the interest of Bingo, many Las Vegas casinos have initiated interesting Bingo gimmicks. For instance, the Aladdin Hotel Casino has come up with a form which can best be described as "Super Bingo" for high rollers. The cost to each participant is $25 and the game session is limited to 400 players. The Bingo session consists of ten games with a guaranteed payout of $7,500. The tenth and final game is a giant cover-all prize with $6,000 guaranteed payout to the winner regardless of how many numbers must be drawn to cover all or black out the entire card. Since the Aladdin takes in $10,000 and pays out $7,500, its percentage take is $2,500 or 25% for each such Bingo session.

Recently the Aladdin Hotel Casino began running 56 Bingo sessions a week, offering a grand prize of $10,000 at each session to anyone getting a coverall in 48 numbers or less. Other Nevada casinos offer Cadillacs, Mark V Continentals, mink and sable coats for a coverall in 50 numbers or less. The Las Vegas Showboat Hotel Casino offers a daily 11 A.M. Bingo Breakfast to help stimulate early business at the slot machines and gaming tables. Sunday's Bingo Breakfast features a progressive coverall which starts at $300 awarded to anyone covering his card in 50 numbers or less and builds up to $3,000 awarded for calling Bingo in 56 numbers or less.

Sportsman Mike McLaney, in his plush Royal Haitian Casino in Port-au-Prince, Haiti, has the most interesting variation of Bingo I have ever seen. The last day of each month, he runs a Bingo special which gets plenty of action both from tourists and local gamblers alike and brings many players to the gambling tables of his fashionable casino. The charge for each Bingo card, which is good for the whole session, is $40. In addition to the regular big prizes of from $500 to $1,000 for a dozen games, the night's jackpot special for a coverall in 50 draws or less is $25,000. The jackpot special for a coverall in 51 draws is $15,000, $10,000 in 52 draws, $5,000 in 53 draws, $4,000 in 54 draws and $3,000 in 55 draws; and if no coverall is made in 55 draws or less, $2,000 is paid to any player who made a coverall, no matter how many draws were required. When I told McLaney that with an average of 400

Bingo participants in the game of coverall in 50 or less drawn numbers, the chance of one of the players winning the $25,000 top prize was rather remote and that the odds were approximately 529 to 1 against such a happening, he replied, "Scarne, I know all about that, but listen to my side of the story. With 400 paid customers I take in $16,000 and pay out some $12,000 in prizes, plus my expenses which come to another $1,000. I believe I'm entitled to pocket $3,000 a session to protect myself against a possible loss of $10,000, $15,000, or $25,000."

CASINO BINGO PROBABILITIES

Since the number of players in any paid casino Bingo game varies and the number of cards purchased by each player in any specific game session varies, and since the top jackpot cash prize varies from one casino to another as they compete for gaming clientele, it becomes obvious that an exact analysis of the casino's percentage take is well-nigh impossible to make. But my survey of some 20 different casino Bingo sessions in action in Las Vegas and Reno infer an average casino Bingo take of approximately 25%.

Since in many casino Bingo games in the Caribbean islands and elsewhere the top jackpot prize of $10,000 to $25,000 is won by the first person covering all 24 numbers on his card in 50 or less drawn numbers, I deem it necessary to list the chances of a coverall in 50, 51, 52, 53, 54, or 55 draws and give my computational method of achieving these results.

If you like to dabble in arithmetic, have plenty of time and don't mind headaches, you can check the following figures, but it's a 100 to 1 shot you'll quit, deciding that the answer isn't worth all that work.

Here's what you have to do. First find the number of possible ways that 75 Bingo balls can be arranged in groups of 24. The mathematical formula for discovering the number of combinations of n things taken r at a time is written like this:

$$\frac{n\,(n-1)\,(n-2)\ldots(n-r+1)}{r!}$$

Substitute 75 for n and 24 for r and you begin to see how much work is involved:

The numerator becomes this: $75 \times 74 \times 73 \times 72 \times 71 \times 70 \times 69 \times 68 \times 67 \times 66 \times 65 \times 64 \times 63 \times 62 \times 61 \times 60 \times 59 \times 58 \times 57 \times 56 \times 55 \times 54 \times 53 \times 52$. This multiplication results in a product of 15,-994,352,952,548,504,498,502,271,753,960,292,352,000,000.

The denominator $r!$ (factorial r)becomes: $24 \times 23 \times 22 \times 21 \times 20 \times 19 \times 18 \times 17 \times 16 \times 15 \times 14 \times 13 \times 12 \times 11 \times 10 \times 9 \times 8 \times 7 \times 6 \times 5 \times 4 \times 3 \times 2 \times 1$, which equals 620,448,401,733,239,439,-360,000.

Divide the larger of these answers by the smaller, and you find that

75 Bingo balls can be arranged in groups of 24 in the following number of ways: 25,778,699,578,994,555,700.

A simplified method which saves considerable multiplication is to set up the formula as a fraction (below) and cancel out before multiplying.

$$\frac{75 \times 74 \times 73 \times 72 \times 71 \times 70 \times 69 \times 68 \times 67 \times 66 \times 65}{24 \times 23 \times 22 \times 21 \times 20 \times 19 \times 18 \times 17 \times 16 \times 15 \times 14}$$

$$\frac{\times 64 \times 63 \times 62 \times 61 \times 60 \times 59 \times 58 \times 57 \times 56 \times 55}{\times 13 \times 12 \times 11 \times 10 \times 9 \times 8 \times 7 \times 6 \times 5 \times 4}$$

$$\frac{\times 54 \times 53 \times 52}{\times 3 \times 2 \times 1} = 25,778,699,578,994,555,700$$

Since we want to find out the number of coveralls that can be formed with the first 50 drawn numbers, we must next find out how many ways 50 numbered Bingo balls can be arranged in groups of 24. We substitute 50 for n and 24 for r in the formula and get this:

$$\frac{50 \times 49 \times 48 \times 47 \times 46 \times 45 \times 44 \times 43 \times 42 \times 41 \times 40}{24 \times 23 \times 22 \times 21 \times 20 \times 19 \times 18 \times 17 \times 16 \times 15 \times 14}$$

$$\frac{\times 39 \times 38 \times 37 \times 36 \times 35 \times 34 \times 33 \times 32 \times 31 \times 30}{\times 13 \times 12 \times 11 \times 10 \times 9 \times 8 \times 7 \times 6 \times 5 \times 4}$$

$$\frac{\times 29 \times 28 \times 27}{\times 3 \times 2 \times 1} = 121,548,660,036,300$$

Finally, we divide the total number of ways 75 balls can be arranged in groups of 24 by the number of ways 50 balls can be arranged in groups of 24.

$$\frac{25,778,699,578,994,555,700}{121,548,660,036,300} = 212,085$$

That's the answer: if you purchase only one card for the jackpot or coverall game, your chance of winning by covering all the 24 numbers on your card in 50 or less drawn numbers is 1 in 212,085. It does not matter how many other players there are; you and each of the other players have the same chance of 1 in 212,085. If you use two cards your chance will be 2 in 212,085; if you use three cards, 3 in 212,085, and so on. (Actually, multiplying by 2, 3 and so on is an approximation of the mathematically exact method; but for any practical number of Bingo cards the approximation is more than accurate enough.)

The Bingo operator will be interested to learn that if he sells a complete set of 3,000 Bingo cards for a session his chances of *not paying* the jackpot in 50 or less drawn numbers are 212,085 divided by 3,000, or about 70 to 1 in his favor.

Here in tabular form are the chances a one-card holder has of making a coverall in 50, 51, 52, 53, 54 or 55 drawn numbers:

Total Numbers Drawn	Chances of Making a Cover-all with One Card
50 or less	1 in 212,085
51 or less	1 in 112,284
52 or less	1 in 60,458
53 or less	1 in 33,081
54 or less	1 in 18,379
55 or less	1 in 10,359

Just for curiosity, while we are on this subject, let us calculate how many Bingo cards could be printed without having two cards on which the number arrangement is duplicated. Each card bears 5 of a group of 15 numbers under each of four columns headed by the letters B, I, G and O, and 4 out of 15 numbers under the letter N. The formula that supplies the answer is this:

$$\underset{\text{UNDER B}}{\frac{15 \times 14 \times 13 \times 12 \times 11}{5 \times 4 \times 3 \times 2 \times 1}} \times \underset{\text{UNDER I}}{\frac{15 \times 14 \times 13 \times 12 \times 11}{5 \times 4 \times 3 \times 2 \times 1}} \times \underset{\text{UNDER N}}{\frac{15 \times 14 \times 13 \times 12}{4 \times 3 \times 2 \times 1}} \times$$

$$\underset{\text{UNDER G}}{\frac{15 \times 14 \times 13 \times 12 \times 11}{5 \times 4 \times 3 \times 2 \times 1}} \times \underset{\text{UNDER O}}{\frac{15 \times 14 \times 13 \times 12 \times 11}{5 \times 4 \times 3 \times 2 \times 1}} = 111,007,923,832,370,565$$

This is the number of cards it is possible to print without duplicating a single card. And remember that Bingo card manufacturers usually print only 3,000 different cards to a set.

Now let me ask a hypothetical question: What would you think of a promoter's running a Bingo game, charging 1¢ for each card and agreeing to pay a jackpot prize of $1 million to any person who succeeded in covering his or her entire card in the first 24 drawn numbers? Crazy? No. He's real smart, because your chance of winning that million bucks is only 1 in 25,778,699,578,994,555,700. If the same Bingo promoter succeeded in selling every possible different Bingo card, he would collect, at 1¢ each, the astronomical sum of $1,110,079,238,323,705.65! $1 million compared to this sum is truly a drop in the bucket. He would have a tough time doing this, however, because with a world population of 3,860,000,000, every single person on the face of the earth would have to buy 28,758,528 cards and each pay $287,585.28.

14

THE MATHEMATICS AND SCIENCE OF CASINO GAMBLING

WHAT IS CASINO GAMBLING?

Casino gambling consists of wagering money upon the outcome of a casino game of chance or a casino game that combines both chance and skill. Casino games of chance include all forms of Craps, Roulette, Baccarat, Slot Machines, Keno and all types of casino side games. The two casino games that combine both chance and skill are Black Jack and Scarney Baccarat.

The verb "gamble" and the noun "gambler" first appeared in print in the English language around the 1750's. From that period until 1931, with the legalization of casino games in the state of Nevada, both terms had an unsavory meaning. At best, a gambler was regarded as an undesirable, a cheat, and/or a criminal. These names surely did fit most professional gamblers and operators of that era.

Today, with government regulation of legalized casinos in Nevada, Atlantic City, Puerto Rico, Bahamas, Aruba, Curaçao and Haiti, casino games are usually honest. However, there are still some legalized casinos in operation in these areas which will take a pot shot at an extremely high roller and cheat him whenever they possibly can.

Modern dictionaries define a gambler as one who makes a practice of wagering money on a game or event, and the term does not carry any connotation of evil. However, millions of Americans and various law enforcement agencies, most of whom are gamblers themselves, consider any casino operator or big-time casino gambler a potential lawbreaker.

GAMBLERS AND SCIENTISTS

Dice are the oldest of all gambling devices. Man's earliest written records not only mention dice and dice games but crooked dice as well. Dice of one sort or another have been found in the tombs of ancient Egypt and the Orient, and in the prehistoric graves of both North and South America.

The earliest gamblers thought that the fall of the dice was controlled by the gods, and although a few of them tried to outwit divinity by loading the cubes, most of them probably considered that any prying into the matter was sacrilegious.

In the sixteenth century at least one gambler began to wonder if the scientists who were beginning to make valid predictions about other matters might not also be able to fortell how the dice would fall. An Italian nobleman asked Galileo why the combination 10 showed up more often that 9 when three dice were thrown. The great astronomer became interested in dice problems and wrote a short treatise which set forth some of the first probability theorems. His reply to the gambler was that $6 \times 6 \times 6$ for a total of 216 combinations can be made with three dice, of which twenty-seven form the number 10 and twenty-five the number 9.

In France, in 1654, the philosopher, mathematician and physicist Blaise Pascal was asked a similar dice question by one of the first gambler-hustlers on record. The Chevalier de Méré had been winning consistently by betting even money that a six would come up at least once in four rolls with a single die. He reasoned from this that he would also have an advantage when he bet even money that a double-six would come up at least once in 24 rolls with two dice. But he had been losing money on this proposition, and he wanted to know why.

Pascal worked on the problem and found that the Chevalier had the best of it by 3.549% with his one-die proposition. Throwing a double-six with two dice, however, would theoretically require 24.6+ rolls to make it an even-money proposition. In practice it can't ever be an even-money bet, because you can't roll a pair of dice a fractional number of times: it has to be either 24 or 25 rolls. The exact chances of rolling two sixes in 24 rolls are: 11,033,126,465,283,976,852,912,127,963,392,-284,191 successes in 22,452,257,707,354,557,240,087,211,123,792,674,-816 rolls.

This means that dice hustler De Méré had been taking a beating of 1.27+% on the bet. If he had bet that two sixes would come up at least once in 25 rolls he would have enjoyed a favorable edge of .85%.

Pascal corresponded with mathematician Pierre Fermat about this and similar gambling problems, and these two men formulated much of the basic mathematics on the theory of probability.

History doesn't state how many francs Chevalier de Méré lost on his double-six betting proposition before Pascal explained why he was getting the worst of it, but I do know that nearly 300 years later, in 1952, a New York City gambler known as "Fat the Butch" lost $49,000 by betting that he could throw a double-six in 21 rolls.

Fat the Butch, although a smart gambling-house operator who has made millions booking dice games, went wrong on the bet because he figured it this way: There are 36 possible combinations with two dice, and a double-six can be made only one way—so there should be an even chance to throw a double-six in 18 rolls. Consequently, when "The Brain," a well-known bigtime gambler, offered to bet $1,000 that a double-six would not turn up in 21 rolls, Fat the Butch thought he had the best of it and jumped at the opportunity.

After twelve hours of dice rolling, Fat the Butch found himself a $49,000 loser, and he quit because he finally realized something must be wrong with his logic. He was, later, part owner of the Casino de Capri in Havana, and when I told him it would need 24.6 rolls to make the double-six bet an even-up proposition, and that he had taken 20.45% the worst of it on every one of those bets, he shrugged his massive shoulders and said, "Scarne, in gambling you got to pay to learn, but $49,000 was a lot of dough to pay just to learn that." "That is for sure," I agreed.

Although most of the odds and percentage problems you will encounter in this book can be calculated simply, a few, like the double-six problem above, are more complex. Here is the formula for figuring problems of this type. To find out when the chances are *approximately* equal in any single event, multiply the "odds to one" by .693, the co-log of the hyperbolic log of 2. This will give the approximate number of chances, trials, rolls, guesses, etc., needed to make any event an even, or fifty-fifty proposition.

For example: the odds are 35 to 1 against throwing double sixes with two dice in one roll. Multiply 35 × .693 and you find that a double-six can be expected to appear in the long run once in approximately 24.255 rolls. (The figure of 24.6+ given earlier is more exact.) To calculate the approximate number required for a double event such as throwing double-sixes twice, multiply the "odds to one" by 1.678. For a triple event multiply by 2.675; a quad event, by 3.672; and a quint event, by 4.670.

The theory of probability is essentially a method of getting an approximate answer when part of the factors are unknown. It is used to calculate what can be expected to happen when some of the factors are not at hand or when the information is too complex to be easily broken down.

The modern physicist uses the theory of probability in studying the behavior of the atom, and the secrets of energy and matter; the biologist and bacteriologist use it in their studies of heredity; the whole insurance business depends on the mortality tables that are based on the theory of probability; and any businessman who uses statistics or combinational analysis owes a debt to the gamblers who first asked Galileo to consider their problems.

Paradoxically, however, the gamblers who are the godfathers of a whole branch of mathematical science today know little about it. They got lost by the wayside when the professors began answering their questions in an argot even stranger than the gamblers' own—the language of mathematical symbols. As a consequence, although modern man has tossed the superstition that dice can divine the future into the discard, many gamblers still believe that the fall of the dice or the turn of the wheel is still controlled by some supernatural force.

The proof of this lies in the fact that many casino gamblers carry good luck charms; some of them ask to have the dice changed or call for a new stickman when they begin to lose; some won't bet at all unless they stand at a certain spot at the table; some of them back away from the Black Jack table when a new dealer begins his stint; some of them won't play at a Roulette table if a women player is wearing a hat; others won't sit down to play Baccarat or Chemin de Fer unless they get a certain numbered spot at the table. Some quit the game when they are losing and walk around the casino to change their luck; other avoid playing the one-armed bandits in the morning. One casino manager I know changes his suit during a casino losing streak or wears the same suit day after day while the casino is winning. I know a Keno player who won't allow her beautician to cut one particular hair on her head because if it is clipped, she never wins, or that's what she thinks.

Many gamblers don't seem to realize that the correct answers can all be obtained with figures—and that the mystic symbols having to do with black cats and four-leaf clovers can be thrown out the window. As a class, gamblers are superstitious for the usual reason—ignorance. They don't understand how chance operates or know what luck really is.

LUCK AND HOW IT WORKS

The dictionary defines luck as a person's apparent tendency to be fortunate or unfortunate. Most people who use the word, however, forget that this tendency is not real but only apparent. Anyone who believes that one player has a better chance of winning a bet because he is luckier than another is no smarter than the customers of the sorcerers and witches of the Middle Ages, the African voodoo doctor or the gypsy fortuneteller who reads tea leaves.

If you gambled and won yesterday, you may correctly say that you were lucky, because you are merely stating that you placed your bets in such a way that they agreed with the fall of the dice or the turn of the wheel. But the fact that you were lucky yesterday or that you have been consistently lucky in your affairs does not guarantee you a better break than the next guy tomorrow. The odds on dice, cards, Numbers, Roulette or any other gambling game are not different for different people at different times. If your past luck has any effect on your future luck, then some supernatural force is working for you because you carry a rabbit's foot.

The supernatural will continue to get a foot in at the door just as long as we try to investigate chance as it applies to a single person. But if we consider chance as it applies to a large group of players and a long series of wagers, then we begin to make sense, and superstition gets a quick brush-off.

One of the first things we discover is that the marvelous run of luck you had yesterday or last week isn't always as astonishing as it seems. At Bank Craps, the gambler who puts his money on two aces and takes 30 to 1 that they will appear on the next roll feels that he is a very lucky guy indeed when the two aces are thrown four times in a row, and he bets on each roll—especially if he happens to know that the odds against such a thing happening are 1,679,615 to 1. He is amazed that some mysterious fate has singled him out for such a favor. But the guy who was betting the limit on the front or pass line and lost four big bets when those two aces appeared four times in succession would consider himself as being the champion hard-luck guy in the world.

Both players forget that the statement that the odds are 1,679,615 to 1 against such an event also means that the event can be expected to occur on the average once in every 1,679,616 times. They forget that on the night when that succession of double-aces appeared there were thousands of other Craps games in progress and several millions of dice throws were made. It would have been more amazing if someone somewhere had *not* thrown a double-aces four times in a row. If you had stayed at home with a good book or a blonde, the run of double-aces would probably have happened just the same in some game somewhere, and someone else would have exclaimed over his remarkable luck or, if he was betting the front line, his bad luck.

Prolonged winning or losing series in various forms of gambling are not unusual for individual players. And every few years a gambling record of one sort or another is established in some casino at some gambling activity by someone, somewhere. Here are several examples to prove the point.

The longest successive single number of wins at Roulette I have witnessed occurred on July 9, 1959, at the El San Juan Hotel in Puerto Rico. I watched the little ivory Roulette ball drop into the number 10 pocket six times in succession. The chance of this happening is 1 in 133,448,704.

The longest color win recorded at the game of Roulette in an American casino occurred at the Arrowhead Casino in Saratoga, New York, in August 1943, when the color red won 32 consecutive times. The odds against this happening are 22,254,817,519 to 1. You may call it a miracle, but remember that the odds are exactly the same—22,254,817,519 to 1— against a series of 32 alternate wins of blacks, odd, even or any other arbitrary series of 32 wins that pay off even money. If you consider the 32 red wins to be a miracle, then any series of 32 even-money wins is also a miracle. It is only the spectacular effect of a long series of wins of one color that attracts attention and makes it seem remarkable.

On the evening of January 18, 1952, at the Caribe Hilton Casino in San Juan, Puerto Rico, I was thunderstruck to see a woman set a world's record at the Craps table by making 39 consecutive passes. When I came out of my fog, I calculated the lady's chance of making those 39 passes to be 1 in 956,211,843,725. This record still holds today.

When we remember that millions and millions of players rolled the ivories billions and billions of times in hundreds and hundreds of gambling joints in America during the past fifty years, we realize that 39 passes is not as miraculous as it sounds. And I was thunderstruck, not because this world's record was established, but because I was on hand to witness it. The odds against that are many times greater.

Anything may happen to a single individual when gambling, odds or no odds, but don't expect to walk up to a Craps table tomorrow and throw 39 straight passes. The odds are still 956,211,843,724 to 1 that you won't.

CHANCE AND HOW IT WORKS

Chance and how it works is a subject which today's casino personnel and the millions of casino gamblers know little or nothing about. If the average casino gambler knew some of the basic facts of chance, he would save himself many a losing session at the casino tables.

Probability theory supplies mathematical methods for discovering what can be expected to happen when the results depend upon chance. It states, for instance, that each player in a game of chance has an equal chance to win in the long run. If, during a long evening of play at Black Jack or Scarney Baccarat, you never get a decent hand, or when you do get a halfway decent hand someone sitting alongside of you always gets a better one, you may doubt this. But your experience does not contradict the theory of probability because the theory does not pretend to state that you and the other players will get an equal number of good hands in one evening of play. It states that the longer you play the more likely you are to get approximately the same number of good hands.

And be careful that you don't misunderstand that last statement, as many gamblers do. They think that results *must* "even up" in the long run. This is true in one sense, but not in another. Probability theory says, for instance, that when you toss a coin, heads will turn up *about* half the time in the long run. It doesn't say that in a very long run heads and tails *must* come up exactly the *same number* of times.

Coin-tossing experiments have shown that the deviation between the actual numerical results and the expected results sometimes increases in long runs. In a series of 100 tosses you may get 45 heads or 55 heads instead of the expected 50, a deviation of 5 heads from the expectation. In a series of 10,000 tosses the difference between the actual result and the expected result may have increased to 50 over the expected 5,000.

But consider this deviation from the percentage standpoint. In a series of 100 tosses the difference of five heads over or under the expected 50 is 10%. In a series of 10,000 tosses the difference of 50 heads from the expected 5,000 is only 1%. The percentage of difference does tend to decrease in the long run. It is only in this sense that results tend to "even up."

We must also keep in mind just what constitutes a long run or a long series. In one respect it differs for different people. A long run for an occasional gambler may consist of the total number of bets he makes in a lifetime; to the habitual gambler, it may be the number of bets he makes in a week; and to the operator whose casino is patronized by hundreds of players daily, a long run may consist of the total bets made against the house in a single day or night shift.

This means that the casino operator's results tend to conform more closely to the expected results much sooner than that of any individual gambler, because the operator's long run occurs in a much shorter space of time.

WHAT ARE ODDS?

We cannot predict whether heads or tails will be thrown on the next toss of a coin, but since heads can be expected to come half the time, we can say that its chance of appearing is ½, or that it has a probability of ½. With a symmetrical die of six sides, each side has an equal chance with each of the others and we can expect any one side to be thrown an average of once in six times. Its probability is ⅙.

. With two dice, each of the six sides of one die can be combined with each of the six sides of the other to form 6 × 6, or 36, combinations. The chance that any combination of two like numbers, such as two sixes, two fives, etc., will appear is one in 36, or ⅟₃₆.

When an event has a probability of 0 it is an impossible event; when the probability is 1, the event is certain. All other probabilities are expressed by fractions falling between 0 and 1. When the probability is ½, we say the chances are fifty-fifty, or even. A probability of ⅙ is less than an even chance. The fraction is the mathematical way of saying an event has one chance of happening in a total of six possible chances.

We use the fraction when calculating probability problems, but for betting purposes we express the probability differently. We state it in terms of the advantage that the unfavorable chances have over the favorable chances, or in terms of the *odds* against the event's happening. Any specific side of a die has a probability of ⅙, and the odds against that side being thrown are the five chances that some other side will appear against the one chance that the specified side will be thrown. The odds then, are 5 to 1 that the specified side will not appear. When the probability is $\frac{1}{36}$, the odds are 35 to 1. When the probability is $\frac{2}{36}$, the odds are 34 to 2, or 17 to 1.

If I bet $35 to your $1 that a double-ace will not be thrown on the next roll, the betting odds are the same as the true odds. In the long run I can expect to win at the rate of 35 out of every 36 bets, and you can expect to win at the rate of one out of every 36 bets. In the long run neither of us wins or loses but will come out even. Gamblers call such a bet at true odds an *even-up proposition*. In general, odds may be defined as the advantage one bettor or competitor gives to another in proportion to the assumed risk, so that each has an equal chance.

PERCENTAGE AND HOW IT WORKS AGAINST THE PLAYER

The casino operator cannot offer bettors even-up propositions. He cannot pay off at the true or correct odds. As he says: "There is no percentage in that." He must in some way gain an advantage or edge over the player; he must have a better chance to win every single bet. A crooked gambler obtains this by cheating. The honest casino operator obtains it either by levying a direct charge or by extracting a favorable P.C. (percentage) on each wager. He does this last very easily: he simply pays off winners at something less than the correct odds.

Most of the 33 million casino gamblers in America know that the casino operator has the advantage of a favorable percentage over the player. But as most of them can't calculate it, they never know how powerful it actually is, and because it works so smoothly and quietly, they forget most of the time that it is even there.

Here is a simple example that shows how the P.C. operates and why it shouldn't be forgotten. Suppose you sit down at a Roulette table with $38 in your pocket. You purchase 38 one-dollar chips. As we know, a Roulette wheel possesses 36 numbered spaces (1 to 36) and two spaces which possess 0 (zero) and 00 (double zero). The Roulette layout has 38 betting spaces and you are only going to bet the straight numbers which pay off at odds of 35 to 1. You place a $1 bet on number 5. Since the probability is $\frac{1}{38}$, you can expect in the long run to lose 37 bets for each one that you win.

Let's also suppose that the Roulette wheel acts exactly this way in the first 38 spins. You lose the first 37 bets and you are out $37. You have only $1 left. Now you bet that. Number 5 pops up and you win. If the croupier paid off at the correct odds of 37 to 1, he would pay you the $1 you bet plus $37 which you won; you would break even with the $38 you had at the start.

But no casino operator ever does this. In our example, since he pays off at 35 to 1, your win gets you $36. You have $2 less than at the start.

This $2 out of $38 is the house's favorable percentage, the casino's charges for operating the Roulette game. It is what makes the knowledgeable casino operator rich and most gamblers poor.

Now, let's forget probability theory for a moment and look at it another way. Suppose you bet your $38 all at once by placing $1 on each of the 38 numbers on the Roulette layout. You must win one of these bets on the next spin of the wheel because you have the 38 numbers covered. In this situation, spinning the wheel and the Roulette ball is unnecessary. The croupier might just as well scoop up your $38, retain $2 for himself, and hand you $36. You say that only a nitwit would gamble in this fashion. I agree. But, in the long run, this is no different percentagewise from betting a single number 38 times in succession.

Today, even most of the novice and inexperienced casino gamblers are aware that this house P.C. exists, but most of them believe it to be much less than it is. In spite of the fact that the methods for figuring casino game percentages are usually neither complicated nor difficult, very few casino players even know precisely what it is at their favorite casino game. You may even be surprised to learn that most operators don't know either.

The general rule for figuring the percentage is simply this: the operator's favorable percentage (or the player's disadvantage) is the amount the player is short divided by the total amount he would have collected if paid off at the true odds. In the Roulette wheel example above, the player is $2 short, and he would have collected a total of $38 if the croupier had paid off at correct odds. Divide 2 by 38 and you get a percentage of $5\frac{5}{19}\%$ in favor of the Roulette bank. Remember that this $5\frac{5}{19}\%$ is the price you pay on each bet you make. If you make 100 such $1 bets, or one bet of $100, you will end up with a loss of $5.26. But don't make the common mistake of supposing that if you start with $100 and place $1 bets on number 5 all evening, you will lose only this amount. The $5.26 is not your total loss for the evening; it is your average rate of loss. Old Man Percentage is in there grinding away on every bet made. You are losing at the average rate of $2 on every 38 bets of $1 each.

You can start with $100 and place many more than 100 bets of $1 each because you can also bet the money you win. The more bets and the bigger amounts you bet, the more you lose in the long run; and at the end of 1,900 spins of the wheel your average rate of loss will have reduced your average $100 bankroll to zero. The Roulette bank will have earned it all.

Let's carry this further. Suppose you start with $100 and find at the end of the evening that you have made a total of $2,000 worth of action and have finished with the same amount of $100 with which you started. You haven't come out ahead, but you are pleased because the evening's gambling entertainment has cost you nothing—so you think. Actually the

$5\frac{5}{19}\%$ you were bucking cost you $105.26 in winnings because if your winning bets had been paid off at correct odds, you would have walked away from the Roulette table with $205.26 instead of $100.

Now, let's suppose you were playing the bank at Baccarat, in which the house enjoys a 1.19% advantage. On $2,000 worth of action, you would have walked away with $123.80 instead of breaking even. If you were playing Craps and betting the Pass Line and taking the Free Single Point odds behind the line in which the house enjoys .848% on each bet, you would have walked away with $116.96. This should make it obvious that your chances of winning are better when you buck a smaller house percentage than when you buck a bigger one.

I said earlier that the methods for figuring the P.C. are usually not complicated or difficult. Note that word "usually." It all depends on the casino game; sometimes it can be really tough. One example: for over thirty years dozens of America's top mathematicians have tried in vain to calculate the bank's favorable P.C. at the game of Black Jack as it is played in the Nevada casinos. Their writings on the subject indicate clearly why they have failed: they simply don't know enough about the way the game is really played—the problems they work out are never those which are of any practical use to the Black Jack player and are more often wrong than right. They usually suffer from the same handicap when they try to analyze most other casino games.

I take pride in listing here a few of my many difficult mathematical casino accomplishments during the past 40 years. I was the first to calculate all the correct odds on Bank Craps and all other dice games (*Scarne On Dice,* 1945). I was the first to calculate the bank's exact favorable percentage at Black Jack (*Scarne's Complete Guide to Gambling,* 1961). In 1967, I invented Scarney Baccarat, the first new mathematically sound casino game of the past 50 years. In 1968, I invented Scarney Craps. I was the first to rule that the player's cards in the game of Black Jack be dealt face up except for the player's double-down card, and that Black Jack be dealt from a dealing box with four decks of cards. I was the first to rule that an indicator card be inserted some 50 cards from the bottom of the Black Jack four-deck packet to prevent the cutoff cards from coming into play. I invented the four-deck Black Jack shuffle used today in casinos everywhere. My mathematical calculations as published in my books have been the foundation upon which most mathematicians, computer specialists and present-day writers base their analyses—yet, curiously, they never seem to credit the source of their information, pretending to have worked out the calculations for themselves.

CASINO PLAYERS HOT AND COLD

Probability theory states what can be expected to happen in the long run. A casino operator accepts so many more bets than any individual player makes in a single gambling session that it experiences a much longer run, and its wins and losses thus conform much more closely to what probability says it can expect. For the individual player, even an extended series of sessions is still a short run. His winning and losing, therefore, may vary considerably from his long-run expectation; he experiences winning and losing streaks.

A player on a winning streak is said to be *hot;* on a losing streak he is *cold.* I have often seen a player get so hot that no matter what game he plays, or how he places his bets, he continues to win. Such winning streaks sometimes continue for weeks at a time. Since the odds are against the player, however, he experiences more losing than winning streaks, and they last longer.

At Craps, I have seen a player bet the dice to win for an hour or so and win nearly every bet, then turn around, bet the dice to lose and continue to win nearly every bet. I have seen a player run a measly $20 into $56,000 at Roulette over a two-week period. I have seen a Craps player, bucking the house odds for about five hours of play each night, run a $10 bill into $125,000 in a month's time.

Casino operators insure themselves against risk inherent in these hot streaks by putting a minimum and a maximum limit on the size of the wagers they accept. This prevents a hot player from winning too much in too short a space of time. It means that the player who tries to make a big killing when he is hot must play longer and make many more bets. The more bets he makes the less chance he has of walking away with the operator's bankroll because there is more chance that his winning and losing streaks will balance out.

The maximum limit also prevents the progressive-system player from doubling up his bets each time he loses and continuing indefinitely until he finally wins one bet that recoups all his losses plus a profit. As for the player who doubles when he wins, trying for that one big killing, if there was no limit to stop him, and if his capital was large enough, he could eventually bet such huge sums that he might eventually break the bank. The minimum and maximum betting limits are usually so designed that a player who bets the minimum limit at the start can double the size of his previous bet no more than seven times before he is stopped cold by the maximum limit.

The maximum limit also makes it impossible for a big-time gambler to walk into a casino, ask the size of the house bankroll and then bet the full amount. The casino would go broke at once if he won, and if he lost and decided to bet the full amount of the house bankroll again, he would have another shot at closing the casino. Casinos and bookies would all have gone out of business long ago if there were no betting limits.

Casino operators do not operate on the hope that they will win money from the players; their business depends on the fact that their favorable percentage earns them money on every bet made. The greater the volume of bets, the more income they receive. This is why all casino operators prefer long sessions. It is also why the consistent $1 or $2 bettor in Las Vegas, Atlantic City and Puerto Rican casinos is commonly referred to by housemen as an "unpaid shill."

The maximum betting limit and the operator's percentage edge are the two most important reasons why gambling casinos earn fortunes.

GAMBLER'S FALLACY

Many inveterate casino gamblers who are constantly fighting the adverse odds at banking games go broke faster than the house percentage would ordinarily dictate because of a basic misunderstanding about the theory of probability. Their first mistake consists in calling it the "law of averages," and then forgetting that the important word in that phrase is not "law" but "averages." The theory of probability is a mathematical prediction of what may be expected to happen on the average or in the long run, not a law that says that certain things must inevitably happen.

If the color red appears on several successive spins of a Roulette wheel these gamblers bet that black will appear next. They think that black is more likely to turn up than red because they think the "law" says that black and red *must* eventually come up an equal number of times. In a Craps, Black Jack or Baccarat game these players, when losing steadily, insist on sticking it out because they believe the "law" states that the longer they lose the more certain they can be that their luck will change. And if they hit a winning streak, they are afraid to ride with it because they believe the chances of a losing streak's setting in are constantly increasing.

This belief, known as the "doctrine of the Maturity of Chances," has lost fortunes for many gamblers. In spite of the fact that mathematicians have for years called it the "gambler's fallacy," there are still many otherwise well-educated gamblers who argue heatedly in its favor.

They don't, or won't, understand the basic principle that *every chance event is absolutely independent of all preceding or following events.* If you toss a coin and get ten successive heads, it does *not* follow that tails are more likely to come up on the next toss in order to help even things out. The coin doesn't know what happened earlier and couldn't do anything about it in any case. The chance is still 50–50 and is always 50–50 on any single throw, no matter what happened on previous throws.

THE "GUESSER'S DISADVANTAGE"

There is another curious belief held by many educated and uneducated people, including a lot of casino operators who have spent the greater part of their lives at gaming tables and who, of all people, should know better. They say: "The player who does the guessing as to his betting selection has the worst of it. Even when you toss a coin and the chances are fifty-fifty, the guy who cries heads (or tails) is more likely to be wrong and will lose more bets than the guy who keeps his mouth shut and just covers the bet."

This "guesser's disadvantage" theory originated back in the days when the players had no clear notion of why it was that operators of games always showed a profit. They noticed that the operators never expressed any opinion as to the result of the next throw of the dice or turn of the wheel but merely covered the players' bets and let the latter do all the guessing. They jumped to the conclusion that this explained the operator's advantage.

The theory was repeated so often and gained such wide acceptance among gamblers that even today players who know the odds and have some knowledge of the operation of percentage still insist "there is something in it."

If anyone ever tries to give you such an argument, here's the way to stop him. Just say, "Okay, suppose we bet on the toss of a coin and suppose I do all the guessing. And suppose I always guess heads. Are you trying to tell me that the coin is going to land tails oftener than the laws of probability say it can be expected to just because I have a stubborn habit of guessing heads?

"And how does the coin know what I'm guessing? Does it have ears? And suppose it's a Chinese coin, and I make my guesses in English; would the coin be hip to what I am saying or would it have to send out a hurry call for a translator? And even if it did know, how does it manage to make that extra half turn part of the time so it lands tails more often and crosses me up? Maybe it's part jumping bean and part acrobat? Or maybe it's haunted?"

If the guy still wants to argue that his "guessers have the worst of it" theory is right, you should phone the nearest newspaper and tell them you have discovered a freak who believes that a 50¢ piece is so smart it should have the right to vote!

CASINO GAMBLING SYSTEMS

In the gambling casinos where I am a consultant, players often come up to me and say, "Hey, Scarne, give me a system so I can beat this game." They all get the same answer: "If I knew any system that would overcome the house percentage, I would keep it strictly to myself. If you had a surefire winning system you would do the same." There is nothing more futile than the attempt to cook up beating systems that will overcome adverse odds.

The oldest and commonest betting system is the Martingale or "doubling up" system, in which bets are doubled progressively. This probably dates back to the invention of Roulette, but every day of the week some gambler somewhere re-invents it, or some variation of it, and believes he has something new. Over the years hundreds of "surefire" winning systems have been dreamed up, and not one of them is worth the price of yesterday's newspaper.

The reason is simple. When you make a bet at less than the correct odds, which you always do in any casino operation, you are paying the operator a percentage charge for the privilege of making the bet. Your chance of winning has what mathematicians call a "minus expectation." When you use a system you make a series of bets, each of which has a minus expectation. There is no way of adding minuses to get a plus, or adding losses to show a profit.

Add to this the fact that all casino operators limit the size of the player's wagers so that it is impossible to double up bets indefinitely. This and the house percentage make all gambling systems worthless.

The system player believes his system will overcome the operator's favorable edge. He couldn't be more wrong. Systems actually work against the player and for the house because they are all based on a combination or series of bets, and the more bets the system player makes, the more he increases the operator's percentage take.

Casino operators also love system players because they have to bet a specified amount of money, usually more than the average player bets, in order to back up the system. The system demands that the player bet it all, and the gambling operator knows he is going to get it all.

If a casino player with $100 wants merely to double it, the soundest plan is to risk it all in one bet on the "don't pass" line on the Craps table. When he splits his $100 into smaller bets, as he would have to do playing most systems, he merely reduces his chance of doubling his money; the smaller the bets the less chance he has.

CASINO OWNERS AND THEIR PROBLEMS

The bank's favorable percentage at Black Jack, Craps, Roulette, Baccarat, Slot Machines, Keno and casino side games is what enables a casino, when managed properly, to pay its expenses and still make a handsome profit. If it paid winners off at the correct odds, the operation would be gambling with the players—something it avoids like the plague. If it did this it would sometimes win and sometimes lose, and could expect, in the long run, to come out with about the same bankroll it had at the start. After the *nut* (expenses) was deducted, the final figure on the profit-and-loss sheet would have to be written in red ink, a shade of writing fluid no businessman or casino operator likes to use.

The casino operator's percentage take is the price you pay for making use of his gambling facilities. It is a business like any other; and if the operators did not wind up with a yearly net profit, you would not have a casino in which to gamble.

The percentages vary with different bets in each and every casino game and scheme. Players who don't know what percentages they are bucking don't realize that they are often paying much more for the privilege of gambling than they need to. The smart gambler avoids bets and games that have a big percentage going against him.

The average casino gambler, placing all sorts of bets on the Craps layout and bucking various unknown percentages, often bucks such outrageous ones that even when he gets on a lucky streak and should win big, he wins small and eventually ends up a loser. His chance to win is chopped down to less than nothing because he doesn't know what he is doing. Since the bank's percentage at each casino game guarantees that the operators can't lose, because they are not really gambling, you might think that the life of a casino boss is a bed of roses. Nothing could be further from the truth. The headaches encountered by the big-time businessman are minor compared to those that plague the casino bosses. Many of them live on milk diets because the constant tension gives them ulcers.

Casino bosses are always too well aware that the casino's income is entirely dependent on maintaining a steady volume of play. If the tourist season is bad in a resort spot, or if for other reasons the big-time gamblers don't patronize the casino steadily enough for the percentage to pay off the terrific overhead expenses, the casino bosses are suddenly in financial trouble. And they are always apprehensive that an unusually hot streak at the Craps table will play havoc with their casino bankroll.

The greater part of the time, casino bosses act more like players: they are always rooting against some high roller. Most people believe that should a big-time gambler beat the casino for $20,000 or more, the bosses are happy because of the publicity the win generates. They may pay off with a smile, but among themselves they act like a bunch of sore losers which is exactly what most casino operators are: *sore losers.*

Other headaches facing the casino operator are the fights with rival casino owners who often increase their own house's maximum betting limits and player odds to lure the best gamblers; how to handle junket nongamblers; how to protect themselves against crooked employees and professional card and dice cheats; and what to do with the millions of dollars' worth of rubber checks in their possession.

When a big-business conglomerate owns the casino, as most do today, the biggest worry for the executives in charge is the uncertainty of not knowing whether or not their casino manager is honest. In my book, it's a fifty-fifty bet that the casino manager is honest.

The tensions and uncertainties of owning a casino are so great that most owners always wear a glum expression—few if any ever smile, at least when they are working. As a rule, the money they drag down from their investment isn't enough to compensate for the worry and the ulcers they are bound to get.

After studying the present-day casino operations of a number of major hotel casino complexes owned and operated by several big-business conglomerates in Nevada and the Caribbean, I have concluded that any conglomerate lacking previous casino experience has less than a fifty-fifty chance of operating a successful major luxury hotel casino complex in Nevada, Atlantic City or the Caribbean.

Over the past thirty years I have kept a financial record of some 40 major hotel casinos in Las Vegas and the Caribbean, and I regret to report that only ten of the 40 major hotel casino complexes made money for their original owners.

In my capacity as casino consultant and investigator for the Hilton International and various other hotel casino operations, I saved many a would-be doomed hotel casino from bankruptcy by eliminating the casino ripoffs and correcting the casino mismanagement taking place. These successful casino investigations led to the recent formation of Scarne's Casino Consultants, Inc., 4319 Meadowview Avenue, North Bergen, New Jersey 07047, to handle the needs of the rapidly expanding casino industry due to the recent legalization of gambling casinos in many areas of the world. Scarne's Casino Consultants, Inc., is available for casino consultation on all forms of casino operations, casino investigation of possible cheating or inept casino management; it uses its own highly developed and secretive method of screening top-notch casino personnel and supplies highly trained casino security men also trained in the art of spotting casino ripoffs. All these are very specialized and vital services that only John Scarne and his company can provide.

The glossary that follows includes not only the casino gambling argot and technical idioms that appear in the preceding pages but also a great many other argot terms in common use among the gambling fraternity.

Above The earnings of a casino enterprise that are listed in their bookkeeping ledgers.

Ace (1) 1-spot on a die. (2) One dollar. (3) A swell guy. (4) The most valuable card in Black Jack.

Action The betting. "The casino action is good." "The action is slow."

Ada from Decatur; Eighter from Decatur CRAPS: The point number 8.

Agent Player cheat who frequents casinos and works in collusion with casino dealers and employees.

Ahead To be winning. "I'm ahead one hundred dollars."

All Out Pushing the limit to win.

Anchor Man BLACK JACK: A player who sits to the dealer's extreme right and is the last player to play his hand.

Angle (1) An idea. (2) A cheating method.

Animals Professional strong-arm men on a casino syndicate payroll. They keep the casino employees in line and collect players' overdue casino losses.

Ax (The) When a casino operator extracts a cut (charge) from a player's bet, a player may say, "There goes the ax."

Back-Line Odds (To Lay) A Craps player having a bet on the Lose or Don't Pass line lays the odds on the point number. (Most casinos pay the bet off at correct odds.)

Backer Someone behind the scenes who supplies casino gamblers with the required money.

Bang Up To close up a casino or game voluntarily.

Bank (1) A gambling scheme's financier. (2) The casino bankroll. (3) Money used to operate a banking game or gambling establishment.

Bank Craps A form of Craps played in all legal casinos in which all bets are played on a layout against the casino.

Banker In general, anyone who represents the casino, a dealer or croupier.

Bar 6–6 CRAPS: A casino rule that applies to the Don't Pass and Don't Come bets; if the shooter rolls a 6–6 (double 6) on the first roll, the bet is a standoff. Some casinos bar 1–1 (double aces).

Below Unreported earnings or winnings. Also called *Under the Table*.

Best Bet A wager at a casino game with the least amount of P.C. against the player.

Bet Any wager on the outcome of a casino event.

Bet Against the House (1) To bet right at Craps. (2) To buck any casino game.

Bet the Limit To bet the maximum amount permitted at a specific casino game.

Bevels or Beveled Shapes Crooked dice having one or more sides slightly rounded rather than flat so that the dice tend to roll off the rounded surface more often than the flat.

Big Eight A space (usually large) on a Bank Craps layout. A bet placed there indicates that the player is betting an eight will be thrown before a seven.

Big Six BANK CRAPS: Same as a big eight bet, except that a player is betting that a six will be thrown before a seven.

Bingoist BINGO: One who plays Bingo.

Bird Cage Chuck-a-Luck apparatus.

Black Jack (1) A banking casino card game. (2) The highest ranking hand in Black Jack is an ace and a 10-count card.

Blanket Roll CRAPS: A controlled two-dice roll made on a soft surface, usually a blanket.

Block-out Work A method of marking cards in which parts of the design are blocked out with white ink, or some configuration in the design is slightly exaggerated.

Blood Money Money that is hard to get, that one has worked hard to earn.

Bottom Dealer A card cheat who deals from the bottom of the deck while pretending to deal off the top. Also known as a *Base Dealer, Subway Dealer.*

Bowl Wooden bowl-shaped recess which holds the Roulette wheel.

Box Man A casino employee who is in charge of the bank at the dice table.

Box Numbers A betting space on a Money (Open) Craps layout (nearest to the dealer) where each of the possible point numbers (4, 5, 6, 8, 9 and 10) appear within a square or box. Players may bet each or all of these numbers at any time. The same as *Place Bets* in Bank Craps, or *Off Numbers* in Private Craps.

Box Up or Box Them Up CRAPS: To mix up a set of five or six dice so that a player may select a pair from the group.

Boys (The) (1) Inveterate gamblers. (2) Racketeers.

Breaks (The) Good or bad luck, depending on the circumstances.

Brick A crooked die that has been cut so that it is not a true cube.

Buck (1) A marker placed on a Crap betting space to show what point the shooter is trying for. (2) To go against.

Buckaroo The first slot machine manufactured having four reels and paying giant jackpot awards running as high as $5,000.

Bucking the Tiger Playing against the Faro bank.

Bug (1) A steel gimmick placed in the mechanism of a slot machine which prevents certain combinations from hitting. (2) A clip which can be attached to the underside of a card table to hold cards secretly removed from the deck. *To Bug:* To gimmick as above. "The jackpot is bugged."

Buildup The act put on by the operator of a gambling scheme and/or his employees to arouse the player's gambling spirit.

Bum Move (1) A suspicious move. (2) A clumsy or obvious cheating move by a gambling crook.

Bum Rap A false accusation of wrongdoing or crime.

Burn a Card To take a card out of play. BLACK JACK: After the cards have been shuffled and cut, the top card of the deck is burned by placing it face up on the bottom of the deck.

Bust BLACK JACK: A player busts when his total card count exceeds 21. "I lost the last five hands by busting."

Busters CRAPS: A pair of *tops* (misspotted dice). Tops are made in various combinations which make only certain numbers and are called busters because one combination will bust up another combination. "He robbed them by shooting in busters."

Bust-out Man A dice mechanic whose specialty is switching crooked dice (usually *busters*) in and out of the game.

Buy a Number CRAPS: A method of betting the Place Numbers whereby the player pays the house a flat 5% charge for each bet and in return receives the correct odds.

Cackle the Dice To pretend to shake the dice by making them rattle when actually they are held by a special finger grip that prevents them from turning freely in the hand.

Call Bet To make a bet without putting up the money.

Caller BINGO: An employee who calls each Bingo number as it is drawn.

Canoe ROULETTE: A numbered or winning section of a Roulette wheel in which the ball finally comes to a rest after the spin.

Card Counting BLACK JACK: An attempt to keep track of cards as they are played in order to better the chances of winning.

Card Mechanic A person who manipulates cards for cheating purposes.

Card Mob Two or more card cheats working as a team.

Card Sense Said of a card player who has natural cardplaying ability.

Carpet Joint Plush luxury gambling casino. Also *Rug Joint.*

Case the Deck Ability to remember many of the played and exposed cards during the play of a game. "That Black Jack player has been casing the deck and knows that there are two live aces left."

Cases FARO: When three cards of a kind have received action, the remaining card of that group still in the card box and yet to be played is referred to as "cases."

Casino A club whose principal business is gambling.

Casino Manager Person in charge of the casino operation: Craps, Roulette, Black Jack and other gambling games. His word is final in all disputes arising between house employees and players.

Center Bet PRIVATE CRAPS: A wager between the shooter and fader or faders which is placed in the center of the playing surface.

Chance The possibility or probability of your winning a bet you make. The chance of your picking a winner at Roulette is 1 out of 38.

Check Cop An adhesive paste which a cheat places on his palm. When he puts his hand on a stack of checks (chips) or coins, the top one adheres to his palm, and he cops (steals) it.

Checker A casino or Craps game employee who checks junkets to see how many players they bring to the casino or game.

Chill To lose interest.

Chip, Check (1) A token used for betting purposes in place of money. (2) To place chips on a betting layout or to put chips in the pot.

Chippy (1) A sucker. (2) An inexpert player.

Chips (In the) Said of a gambler who has a lot of money.

Chiseler (1) A gambler who tries to pick up another player's bet in a banking game. (2) A gambler who borrows money in a private game and doesn't repay it. (3) A person who would like to be a gambler but lacks the money and class.

Chump An inexperienced gambler. A sucker. Also *Mark, Mooch, Monkey, Pheasant, Bird, Greenie, Rabbit.*

Clean (1) Said of a person who does not have a police record. (2) To win all the money from one or more opponents in a game. The unlucky one is "cleaned" or "taken to the cleaner's."

Clear (In the) (1) Free of debt. (2) Innocent of any wrongdoing.

Clock To count. "I clocked the money bet for the evening."

Cold CRAPS: The dice are said to be cold, when they are not making numbers.

Cold Deck Deck of cards which has secretly been arranged by a card cheat in a certain order for the purpose of switching later for the deck in play. Also called *Cooler; Package.*

Cold Player Player on a losing streak. "He's cold as ice."

Column Bet ROULETTE: A bet on 12 vertical numbers of the layout; a winning unit is paid off at 2 to 1 odds.

Come Bet BANK CRAPS: A bet that the dice will pass (win), the next roll to be considered as a come-out roll.

Come-out Bet CRAPS: A bet on a specific number or on a group of numbers that the number or one of the group will be thrown on the next roll of the dice.

Come-out, Come-out Roll CRAPS: The first throw of the dice or the first throw after a shooter's decision.

Complimentary Play A gambling session indulged in by a casino manager in a rival casino or by a big-time gambler or racketeer as a gesture of friendship toward the casino bosses.

Cooler See *Cold Deck.*

Cop (1) To steal or cheat. (2) A win.

Corker A gambler who is unusual, either good or bad.

Corner Bet See *Square Bet.*

Count Room Room or office in which casino receipts are counted at the end of each gambling session.

Coup French word for "bet," used in the United States by Baccarat and Chemin de Fer players.

Cover (1) To accept a wager. (2) To place a bet on a gambling layout.

Coverall BINGO: A winning position on a Bingo card in which all 24 numbers have been called and covered.

Covered Square BINGO: The center square in the N column of a Bingo card. It has no number and is considered a free play.

Cowboy A reckless and fast gambler.

Crap CRAPS: A losing throw by the shooter on his first come-out roll of the dice.

Crap Out CRAPS: To roll a 2, 3, or 12 on the first roll.

Craps The most popular and biggest-betting private and banking dice game in the world.

Craps Dealer A Craps-table employee who collects and pays off winning and losing bets for the house.

Craps Hustler A player who gets the best of it by placing Craps bets at a private dice game at less than correct odds.

Credit Manager The casino employee who assesses your bankroll as you gamble. He may extend credit up to $50,000 or more—or refuse to give you any credit at all.

Crimp (1) To bend one or more cards in the deck in such a way that the cheat or his confederate can cut the deck at a certain place, or so that a player will unknowingly cut at the place desired by the cheat. (2) The bend itself.

Crossroader A card cheat who travels over the country seeking card games in which he can ply his trade.

Croupier A casino employee who deals the game and collects and pays off winning and losing bets at Roulette, Baccarat, Chemin de Fer and other games with French antecedents.

Crumb Bun A gambling chiseler.

Cup A leather receptacle used for shaking dice.

Cushion (1) Money in the bank. (2) Reserve bankroll.

Cut (1) To divide the pack into two or more packets and then reassemble them in a different order. (2) A house charge, taken by the dealer, croupier or houseman, such as 5%

of the money wagered by players at Baccarat or Open Craps.

Cut-Edge Dice Crooked dice with some edges cut at a 60-degree angle and others at a 45-degree angle. They tend to fall in the direction of the 60-degree cut more often than the 45-degree cut.

Cut-out Card Markings To make these, a minute area of ink on the back design is chemically bleached or scraped with a knife, adding a white area that wasn't there originally.

Daub A paste or fluid used in marking cards during play.

Dead Card A card which has already been played, or one that cannot be used in play.

Dealer A general term for the casino employee the players bet against. Almost anyone who represents the house in a game is called a dealer: croupiers, stickmen, bankers, etc., are all dealers.

Dean (The) A smart gambler who can calculate odds and percentages. Also called *The Professor*.

Desperado A gambler who bets big with the casino and cannot pay off when he loses.

Deuce (1) A die with two spots. (2) Any 2-spot card. (3) Two dollars.

Dice Are Off (The) Said of dice that are not true.

Dice Degenerate Compulsive Craps player who can't control his urge to gamble.

Dice Mob A group of dice cheats who operate crooked dice games.

"Do" Bettor CRAPS: A player who bets the Pass Line or Come, thus betting that the dice will pass or win.

"Don't" Bettor CRAPS: A player who bets the Don't Pass Line or the Don't Come, thus betting that the dice will not pass, will not win.

Don't Come Bet CRAPS: A bet which is made after the shooter has come out on a point. The player is betting that the dice will lose, and as far as his bet is concerned the next roll is considered the *Come-out*.

Don't Pass Line A betting space on the Bank Craps layout. Money placed there is a bet that the dice will lose.

Double Down BLACK JACK: A player may double the amount of his original wager on his first two cards; however, if he doubles down he can draw only one card.

Double-Five or Fives A doctored die having two fives, the extra 5 spot taking the place of the 2 spot.

Doubling Up Doubling the size of a previous bet on the next wager. Many betting systems are based on this principle.

Down Card A card that is dealt face down.

Down CRAPS: To call off all place bets.

Drop Box A removable, locked cashbox located under a Roulette, Craps or Black Jack table or casino side game. The money paid by players for chips is dropped into the box through a slot in the table top.

Drowned Said of a heavy loser. "I'm drowned."

Dry Broke.

Ear A bent corner put on a playing card to identify or locate it. "He put the ear on the aces."

Easy Way CRAPS: To make a point number (4, 6, 8 or 10) any way but the hardway.

Edge An advantage.

Edge Work or Edge Markings A deck of cards marked with a slight bevel or "belly" drawn on certain points of each card between the design and the edge of the card. A bevel mark high up marks an ace, lower down a king, etc.

Eighter from Decatur CRAPS: The point eight.

Electric Dice Crooked dice loaded with steel slugs and used over an electric magnet hidden in or under a counter or dice table.

End A share. "What's my end?"

English The simultaneous sliding and spinning action of the dice that is characteristic of most controlled shots.

Even Roll See *Blanket Roll*.

Even-up, Even-up Proposition (1) A bet or proposition that gives each player an equal chance to win. (2) A bet at correct odds. (3) A 50–50 bet.

Exit To get out of the game.

Eye-in-the-Sky A casino employee who sits above the mirrored ceiling of a casino. The mirror is one-way, allowing him to see the play going on below him. A knowledgeable gambler himself, the Eye-in-the-Sky is quick to spot any monkey business.

Face Card A king, queen or jack in a deck of cards.

Fade PRIVATE CRAPS: To cover part or all of the shooter's center bet.

Fader PRIVATE CRAPS: A bettor who has made a fading bet.

Fairbank To make a cheating move in favor of the player to entice him to continuing playing or increase the size of his bet.

False Cut A cut which leaves the deck or part of the deck in its original position.

Fast Company Seasoned or smart gamblers.

Fever The gambling habit. "She has the fever, she can't stay away from that Roulette table."

Field Bet BANK CRAPS: A bet that one of the group of seven numbers on the *Field* will appear on the next roll.

Fill Slip A slip of paper signed by a casino pit boss and given to the casino cashier stating that a certain number of additional chips are required at the Craps, Roulette or Black Jack table.

First Flop Dice Heavily loaded dice used with a slick cup. So called because the loads are so heavy that a skilled dice cheat can throw five of a kind. Also called *Dead Number* dice.

Fish (1) A gambling sucker with money. (2) A two-dollar bill.

Flat Bet CRAPS: A side bet made among players in a private game that the shooter will or will not win. Similar to center bets made between shooters and faders.

Flat Passers Crooked dice which have the 6–1 sides cut down on one die and the 3–4 sides cut down on the other so that 4, 5, 9 and 10 appear more often.

Flats Crooked dice which have been shaved so that they are slightly brick-shaped. Also called *Bricks*.

Floating Game An illegal gambling game which is shifted from place to place in order to avoid police raids.

Floorman The floorwalker in a gambling house whose duties are to spot and correct irregularities.

Flush-Spotted Dice Dice whose spots are flush with the surface rather than countersunk as with most dice.

Free Bet BANK CRAPS: A bet which permits a player who has made a previous bet on the Pass or Don't Pass line, or the Come and Don't Come to take the correct point odds equal to the amount he previously bet.

Free Double-Odds Bet Same as *Free Bet,* except that right or wrong bettors with line bets can take or lay double the amount riding on the line. Found in most legalized casinos.

Freeze Out (To) To force a player out of the game.

Freeze-Out Proposition Wager, usually a long series of bets between a hustler and a gambler, in which the total sum to be wagered and the betting conditions are mutually agreed upon before the action begins.

Frets The metal partitions that separate each of the 38 numbered sections of a Roulette wheel.

Frisk To search a person.

Frisk Room An anteroom in an illegal casino where players are searched immediately before entering the actual gambling room in order to minimize the chances of a holdup.

Front Line Same as *Pass Line.*

Front Line Odds Taking the odds on the point number. Some casinos permit a player free action on this bet. See *Free Bet.*

Front Man A person, usually without a police record, who is the apparent owner of a gambling operation. "He's fronting for the Cleveland boys."

Front Money (1) Money that has been won. (2) Money used to make an impression on possible suckers.

Full Table A crowded table. BLACK JACK, DICE: Table at which no seat is available or there is no more room.

G-Note $1,000 bill.

Gaff, G or Gimmick Any secret device or method that accomplishes or aids in cheating.

Gaffed Dice Doctored or crooked dice.

Gag Bet See *Hardway Bet.*

Gambling Junket A group of supposedly qualified gamblers solicited to travel to a gambling casino for the sole purpose of gambling.

Get Behind It To back up a crooked gambling move.

Get Out To regain one's losses.

Get Your Feet Wet An invitation to a spectator to get into the game.

Go for It To be taken in by a crooked gambling scheme.

Go for the Money To cheat.

Go South with It (1) To put money in one's pocket either legitimately or illegitimately. (2) To remove a card or cards from the deck secretly. "He went south with a couple of aces."

Good Man (1) A player with a large amount of money. (2) A skilled cheater. (3) A good gambling-scheme operator or employee.

Good Thing A good bet.

Gorilla A strong-arm or muscle man.

Grand or G $1,000.

Graveyard Shift The early-morning shift of a gambling establishment.

Grifter A fast talker, a con man.

Half a Yard $50.

Hand-Mucker or Holdout Man A card cheat who specializes in palming cards.

Handle The total amount of money that repeatedly changes hands at the casino tables before it is actually won or lost.

Hardway Bet CRAPS: The numbers 4, 6, 8 or 10 thrown with two duplicate numbers such as two deuces, two threes, etc. Also called *Gag Bet.*

Head-to-Head Betting Betting of one player against the dealer. "He played the Black Jack dealer head to head."

Heart Courage. "He has plenty of heart; he bets them up."

Heavy A big-time racketeer.

High Belly Strippers A deck of cards doctored so that cards with high numerical values can be controlled.

High Roller Big-time bettor.

Hit (1) BLACK JACK: To draw another card. (2) To win money.

Hit It (1) BLACK JACK: To ask the dealer for another card. (2) CRAPS:

To make the point or any desired number.

Hit the Boards CRAPS: Term used by the stickman when he requests the shooter to throw the dice against the dice-table rail.

Hits CRAPS: A pair of crooked misspotted dice that will not throw seven and will always make or hit certain point numbers.

Hold Check A postdated check.

Hold Count A mental countdown once used by slot-machine rhythm players to beat the slot machines before the variator was developed.

Hold-out Artist A gambler or cheat who, when calculating the score or dividing the amount of winnings with his partner or partners, says that his winnings are less than they are and pockets the difference.

Hold-out Man A card cheat who specializes in palming, holding out of play and reintroducing valuable cards into a game by means of palming.

Hole Card BLACK JACK: The face-down card dealt to the dealer.

Hooked (1) To be on a losing streak. (2) To lose money. "I'm hooked."

Hop A secret sleight-of-hand move made after the cut which replaces the cards in their original position. Also called *Shift*.

Hot Said of a player on a winning streak. "The dice are making passes; they're hot."

Hot Player Player on a winning streak. "He's hot."

House (The) The operators of a gambling game or games.

House Limit The standard limit bet a casino will allow. $1,000 in Las Vegas and Atlantic City.

House Numbers ROULETTE: Zero and Double Zero.

House Percentage The portion the casino expects to win of all the money that is bet at the tables, including casino side games.

Humps See *Strippers*.

Hunch Players Players who know little or nothing about the game on which they are wagering and who bet on impulse.

Hush Money A bribe paid to keep someone from talking.

Hustle A practice frowned on by the casino, whereby a dealer subtly or otherwise tries to get a tip from a player.

Ice The money paid to police or gambling officials to overlook the violation of casino rules. So called because it takes the heat off. Also called *Fix Money*.

Inside Man An employee in any gambling scheme who handles the bookkeeping or gambling finances.

Inside Work Any gaff—*Loads*, for example—placed inside a die or pair of dice.

Insurance Bet (1) CRAPS: Two or more wagers made at a Craps table in an attempt to insure one or the other. (2) BLACK JACK: A bet that a dealer does not hold a natural when he has an ace showing.

Jackpot Light-up Board A large electric sign that hangs in a slot-machine parlor or gambling establishment and is connected to the slot machines. It lights up and a chime rings whenever a jackpot is hit.

John Scarne Games, Inc. Holders of copyright on Scarney Baccarat.

Jonah (1) A superstitious player or casino operator who tries to control his luck with phrases or gestures. (2) One whose presence is thought to bring bad luck.

Juice What a casino employee who is favored by the casino bosses is said to have. "Juice got him his manager's job."

Juice Joint A crooked dice or Roulette game in which the cheating is done by concealed electromagnets in the table, and the Roulette ball or the dice are gaffed with a steel slug.

Junket See *Gambling Junket*.

Junketeer An organizer of a gambling junket.

Junketors Gamblers who make up a gambling junket.

Kangaroo A pimp.

Kids Gunmen.

Ladder Man A casino employee who sits on an elevated stand overlooking a Bank Craps, Money Craps, Baccarat or Chemin de Fer table and whose duty it is to correct dealer's errors and to spot cheats.

Last Turn The last three undealt cards in Faro or Faro Bank.

Lay or Lay It CRAPS: To bet a greater amount against a lesser amount. "I'm laying two to one behind the line on the point 10."

Lay the Odds CRAPS: To bet that a point, box or place number (4, 5, 6, 8, 9, 10) will not be thrown before a seven. The right bettor who bets that a point, box or place number *will* be thrown before a seven is *Taking the Odds*.

Layout A diagram with spaces designated for different casino bets. The players place their money on the spaces to signify what bets they are making.

Legal Tie, Standoff or Push BLACK JACK, BACCARAT OR CHEMIN DER FER: When the banker's card count is the same as the player's.

Legit Game An honest game.

Legit Guy A person who has no underworld connections. This does not necessarily imply that he is an honest man.

Let It Ride To leave the original bet and the winnings of the various bet on the gaming table and wager them again.

Liberty Bell The first slot machine, invented in San Francisco in 1895, by Charles Fey, a 29-year-old mechanic and the first slot-machine operator in America.

Line Bet ROULETTE: A bet on six numbers in two rows of three numbers each running across the layout. The payoff is at 5 to 1 odds.

Line Work On doctored cards, additional small spots, curlicues or lines added to the back design of playing cards so that they can be read from the back by the cheat.

Little Joe or Little Joe from Kokomo CRAPS: The point four.

Live Card BLACK JACK: A hidden card in the opponent's hand or in the remaining part of the undealt or unplayed part of the deck. A card that is not dead because it has not yet been played.

Live One A player with money.

Load A weight placed within a die.

Loads Loaded dice. See also *Inside Work*.

Looking for Action Said of a gambler who is trying to find a game.

Lookout A gambling-house employee who sees that everything runs smoothly and is on the constant alert for crookedness by both player and casino personnel.

Low Belly Strippers A crooked deck of cards in which the edges of the high cards are concave rather than straight, making it possible for the cheat to cut to a low or high card at will.

Lugger A person who transports players to an illegal casino game. Not to be confused with a *Steerer*.

Luminous Readers Marked cards that can be read only through tinted glasses.

Main CRAPS: An old term for point number from the English game of Two-Dice Hazard.

Map A check. "Don't take that guy's map; he's a paperhanger."

Mark Sucker.

Marker (1) An IOU. (2) A numbered chip used at casino games to keep track of money owed the bank by the player during the game. "His marker's on the Roulette rim for a thousand." (3) A buck or coin placed on a numbered space of a layout to indicate the player's bet.

Martingale System ROULETTE: A progressive system long used in Monte Carlo and other European casinos; now used in many other games.

Mechanic A skilled gambling cheat who resorts to sleight of hand to accomplish his crooked work.

Mechanical Games Casino gambling games which lack the element of skill. Craps, Baccarat, Roulette, Keno, Slot Machines and casino side games.

Mechanic's Grip A method of holding a deck of cards (in either the left or right hand) with three fingers curled around the long edge of the deck and the index finger at the narrow upper edge away from the body.

Memphis Dominoes Dice.

Miss CRAPS: (1) A miss-out. (2) To miss or miss it; to make a miss-out.

Miss a Pass CRAPS: To fail to make a point number. "The shooter missed his pass."

Miss-out CRAPS: A losing Craps decision for the shooter (and the other players who are betting with the shooter) obtained on the come-out when a crap is thrown and after the come-out when a seven is throw instead of the shooter's point number.

Misses (1) Crooked dice that are gaffed to make more sevens than point numbers. (2) Crooked dice that are gaffed to make more miss-outs than passes.

Monicker Underworld nickname.

Monkey A sucker.

Move Sleight of hand. "That's when he made the move."

Multiple Slot Machines Modern slot machines which accept from one to eight coins and pay off winners in multiple fashion.

Nailed (1) Caught cheating. "He was nailed red-handed switching the deck." (2) Arrested.

Natural (1) BLACK JACK: A high combination of two cards such as a ten spot and an ace. (2) CRAPS: A winning decision (7 or 11) on the first roll.

New York Craps A form of *Bank Craps* played mostly in the eastern states in which the player must pay a 5% charge for betting the box or off numbers.

No Dice A dice roll that does not count.

Nut A casino or gambling enterprise's overhead expenses. "The nut's too high."

Nutman A gambling hustler.

Odds Correct odds are the ratio of the unfavorable chances to the favorable chances. See also *Payoff Odds*.

Off-Number Bet CRAPS: A bet made at house odds that the shooter will or will not throw a specified number other than his point (any of the numbers 4, 5, 6, 8, 9 and 10) before throwing seven.

Off Numbers PRIVATE CRAPS: All the numbers 4, 5, 6, 8, 9 and 10 except the point number the shooter is trying to make.

Off the Board After a point number is made the player calls off all his riding place or box bets.

Old Bill A word or hand signal (open palm) which means, "Is there another card cheat in the game?"

On the Cuff Bet A free bet for the player.

One-Armed Bandit Slot machine.

One Big One Gambler's term for $1,000.

One-Roll Action or Come-Out Bet CRAPS: A bet that the shooter does or does not throw (1) a certain number any way; (2) a certain number a certain way; or (3) any one of a group of numbers on the next roll.

One-Roll Bet CRAPS: A bet which is decided on the next roll of the dice.

One-Way Cards Cards whose backs bear pictures or designs that are not symmetrical top to bottom.

One-Way Tops and Bottoms See *Percentage Tops and Bottoms*.

Open Craps A banking dice game in which side bets among the players are permitted only on the point number. Also called *Money Craps*.

Open Up (1) To start a game. (2) To give information. "He's a rat; he opened up to the law."

Operator's Bell Slot machine manufactured by Herbert Stephen Mills in 1907. Nicknamed "the Iron Case."

Out in Front To be ahead money.

Outside Work Anything done to gaff dice on their surfaces.

Pad Payroll. "Everybody's on the pad, including the cop on the beat."

Paint (1) A picture card. (2) BLACK JACK: A king, queen, jack or ten spot. "There are six paints left in the deck."

Palette A wooden palette with a long thin handle, used by Baccarat and Chemin de Fer dealers to move the cash and chips around.

Paper (1) Marked cards. "I laid down paper in the Black Jack game." (2) A check or other negotiable document.

Paperhanger A passer of bad checks. See *Map*.

Pass CRAPS: A winning decision for the Craps shooter obtained on the come-out by throwing a 7 or 11 or repeating the point before throwing a 7.

Pass Line CRAPS: A space on the Craps layout. Money placed in this space is a bet that the shooter will pass.

Passers Crooked dice which are so gaffed that they tend to make more passes than fair dice.

Pay Line The center line in the window of a slot machine on which the pay-off symbols appear.

Payoff (1) The collection of a bet. (2) Any final event.

Payoff Olds The casino odds at which a bet is paid off. Usually less than the correct odds.

Peek To glimpse the top card of a deck secretly.

Pencil (The) The privilege of signing checks which the casino pays. "He has the power of the pencil."

Percentage (P.C.) An advantage obtained by offering less than the true odds or by the use of crooked dice or controlled shots. Also *Edge*.

Percentage Dice Crooked dice which over a period of time supply a percentage in the cheater's favor.

Percentage or P.C. Game A casino banking game in which a favorable advantage is obtained through offering less than correct odds.

Percentage Tops and Bottoms A pair of gaffed dice, one of which is mis-spotted. One number, usually the deuce or five, appears on the die twice.

Perfects Dice that are true cubes to a tolerance of 1/5,000 of an inch.

Philadelphia Layout The first Bank Craps layout to give the players an opportunity to bet the dice to win *and* lose.

Philistines Loan sharks.

Piece See under *Point*.

Pit The area enclosed by the gambling tables, barred to the public.

Pit Boss, Supervisor or Inspector ROULETTE and BLACK JACK: A casino employee who supervises several gaming tables. He stands in the pit ring, watches the games, writes cash-out and fill slips, corrects errors made by croupiers or players and watches for cheating.

Place Bet BANK CRAPS: A right or wrong bet placed on one or more of the numbers 4, 5, 6, 8, 9, 10.

Play The betting. Same as *Action*.

Point (1) Any number or a total in a gambling game on which a wager can be placed. (2) CRAPS: The numbers 4, 5, 6, 8, 9 and 10 are possible point numbers. (3) Also called *Piece* in this sense: A share or percentage of a gambling enterprise or play. "He's got five points in the casino." "I've got a piece of his action."

Point Bet CRAPS: A bet at odds that the shooter's point will or will not be made.

Press It To increase a wager after winning a bet.

Private Game Any game which has no houseman or banker and in which no charge is extracted for the privilege of playing.

Professor See *Dean*.

Progressive Slot Machine A slot machine in which the top jackpot increases in a predetermined ratio to the number of coins played into the machine.

Proposition Bet (1) Any bet made at Black Jack or any other game that is not covered by the rules. (2) A bet to settle any difference of opinion between two or more persons.

Proposition Cheat A crooked gambler whose policy is never to give his opponent a break. He gaffs or angles his proposition bets so that they are surefire and give him a 100% edge, or as close to that as possible.

Proposition Hustler A better who offers betting propositions which appear at first glance to be fair or to favor his opponent, but which actually give the hustler a big advantage.

Pull Down To take down or pocket all or part of a wager just won.

Punter BACCARAT OR CHEMIN DE FER: The player or shooter.

Put the Horns On To try to influence one's luck by changing position at a table, carrying a rabbit's foot or using any other superstitious device.

Quarter Bet See *Square Bet*.

Readers Marked cards.

Ready Up To get ready to make a crooked move.

Renege To refuse to honor a lost wager or debt; to welsh.

Result Player A gambler who tells you how you should have made your bet or play after a decision has been rendered.

Rhythm System A means of beating the slot machines without using mechanical gimmicks.

Rig To gaff or make crooked. "The game is rigged."

Right Bettor, Right Player, Rightie CRAPS: A player who bets the dice to win.

Rip In CRAPS: To switch dice into a game.

Roll (1) To roll dice or a Roulette ball. (2) To rob a person while he is drunk or asleep.

Rough It Up To bet heavily, thus livening the tempo of the game.

Rug Joint A lavishly decorated casino having top-grade gaming equipment. See *Carpet Joint* and *Sawdust Joint*.

Sand To edge-mark cards with sandpaper.

Sawdust Joint Unpretentious gambling casino.

Scarney Baccarat A casino banking card game invention of the author which combines the principles of Baccarat and Black Jack.

Score a Big Touch To fleece a player or players for a large amount of money.

Screen Out To cover up or misdirect attention away from a crooked gambling move.

Second Dealer A cheat who deals the second card from the deck when he appears to be dealing the top card.

Send It In To make big bets, or many bets, usually against the bank. "When he's on a winning streak, he sends it in." See also *Zing It In*.

Shading A method of marking cards. The backs of cards are delicately shaded with a dilute solution of marking ink which is the same color as the ink already printed on the backs.

Shift the Cut To return secretly the halves of a cut deck to their original position.

Shill A casino employee whose job it is to attract the customers to a table. When enough people are playing to make for a lively game, the shill or shills leave. Shills are used predominantly at Baccarat in Nevada casinos.

Shimmy Chemin de Fer.

Shimmy Table Table at which Chemin de Fer is played.

Shoe or Sabot A card-dealing box used to deal Chemin de Fer and Baccarat.

Shooter In any dice game, the player who throws the dice.

Side Game A minor banking game in a large casino.

Silver Tongue A high-class member of a mob. A good talker, often a lawyer.

Six-Ace Flats Crooked dice which give a favorable percentage to a wrong bettor.

Skimming Secretly taking money from the gross handle of a casino or other gambling operation to avoid taxes.

Sleeper (1) Money or a bet left on the table or gambling layout which belongs to a player who has forgotten about it; not to be confused with (2) A horse which suddenly wakes up and runs a surprisingly strong race.

Slick Dice Cup A cup which is gaffed with a polished inner surface.

Slicker A gambler who cannot be trusted.

Slot A slot machine.

Smart Bettor Seasoned gambler who knows odds and percentages.

Snake Eyes CRAPS: A one spot showing on both dice.

Soft Player (1) An inexperienced gambler. (2) A player who can't stand to win big money.

Soft 17 BLACK JACK: A count of 17 which includes an ace.

Spell A series of winning or losing decisions. "The dice had a hot spell."

Split Bet ROULETTE: A bet on two adjacent numbers. Each winning unit is paid off at 17 to 1 odds.

Splitting Pairs BLACK JACK: To separate two cards of the same numerical value and consider each card as the first card of a new hand.

Spooning A method of cheating a slot machine by inserting a spoon-shaped device through the payout opening into the payout mechanism.

Spot Card Any card ranked from ace to ten.

Square Bet ROULETTE: A bet on four spaces of the layout. Each winning unit is paid off at 8 to 1 odds. Also called *Corner Bet, Quarter Bet*.

Square, On the Square (1) Honest. "He's a square guy." "The joint is on the square." (2) *To square:* To satisfy a complaint. "We squared the beef by paying him off."

Stacked Deck A deck which has been secretly prearranged.

Stand BLACK JACK: To refuse to draw another card.

Standoff (1) No decision, a tie, cancellation of a bet. (2) BLACK JACK: So called when player and dealer have the same count of 21 or less. (3) CRAPS: A two-ace standoff means that the wrong bettor does not win when two aces appear on the first roll.

Steer Game Crooked game into which the marks are steered.

Steer Joint A crooked gambling house.

Steerer An individual who secretly works for a crooked gambling establishment and persuades the customers to patronize it.

Stick (1) A Craps stick used by the stickman to push the dice around the table. (2) An employee of the house who bets house money and pretends to be a player in order to attract business or stimulate the action, Also known as a *Shill.*

Stickman Craps dealer who pushes the dice from player to player and calls out the numbers thrown.

Stiff A nonplayer.

Storm An apparent upset in the law of averages.

Straight Bet ROULETTE: A bet on one number. Each winning unit is paid off at 35 to 1 odds.

Streak A run of good or bad luck.

Street Bet ROULETTE: A bet on three numbers running vertically across the layout. A winning unit is paid off at 11 to 1 odds.

Strippers A deck of cards whose edges have been trimmed, making some cards either narrower or shorter than others. *Combination Strippers:* A deck trimmed so that certain desired combinations (such as an ace or ten) can be stripped out of the shuffled deck and brought to the top. *Belly Strippers or Humps:* A deck in which cards are trimmed narrow, others cut so that they are narrower at the ends only, leaving a belly in the middle. When the low cards belly out, it is a deck of *Low Belly Strippers,* and the chump who, in cutting, grasps the deck at the middle of the long sides will always cut to a low card. *High Belly Strippers* are trimmed in the opposite manner.

Strong Work Crooked cards marked with heavy lines.

Sucker Bet A bet that supplies the operator or hustler with a high percentage.

Take (1) The receipts of a casino or a casino game. (2) To accept a bribe. (3) To cheat. "We took him for all he had."

Take the Odds To accept the larger figure in an odds to 1 figure. "I'll take 2 to 1 on the underdog." See also under *Lay the Odds.*

Tear-up (The) A method of blowing off a suspicious mark. The cheat pretends not to accept the mark's gambling loss and tears up his check. Actually he switches in a dummy check, destroys it and then cashes the original before the sucker stops payment.

Telegraph To give away unconsciously the fact that a cheating move is about to be made, usually by some clumsy preparatory action or by a change in attitude.

Ten Count Cards BLACK JACK: Ten, jack, queen and king.

Ten-Stop Machine A gaffed slot machine that has 20 symbols on each of its reels but is gaffed so that only 10 of them can appear on its payline.

There's Work Down Crooked cards or dice or some gimmick is being used to cheat.

Top (1) The gross handle of a casino or casino game. "Take the expenses off the top." (2) The officials who supply protection. "The okay came right down from the top."

Tops and Bottoms Gaffed dice which bear only three different numbers on each die. Also called *Tops, Busters, Ts* or *Misspots.*

Touch (1) A loan. (2) To borrow money. (3) A score.

Trim To fleece, gyp, clip, beat, etc.

Trims Crooked cards gaffed by trimming some cards one way and the others another way.

Twenty-One (1) The game of Black Jack. (2) The highest hand at Black Jack when made with two cards.

Two-Number Bet CRAPS: A private game Craps bet that one of two specified numbers will or will not be thrown before a seven.

Two-Roll Bet CRAPS: A private game Craps bet which is decided within the next two rolls.

Unpaid Shill Casino operator's term for describing a consistent small-money bettor.

Vigorish, Viggerish or Vig The percentage taken by a casino-game operator. It may be either overt or hidden by the mechanics or mathematics of the game.

Wave (1) To bend the edge of a card during play for identification purposes. (2) The bend itself.

Way Off Very imperfect. "The Roulette wheel is way off."

Wheel Roller ROULETTE: The croupier who spins the wheel and deals the game.

Whip Shot A controlled dice shot in which the two dice are spun from the hand and strike the table surface with a flat spinning motion so that the controlled numbers are on top when the dice stop.

Wood Hangers-on, nonplayers, gamblers without money. Also called *Deadwood.*

Work (1) Crooked cards, or dice. (2) The gaff itself.

Working Points A small share (percentage) of a casino enterprise bought in order to secure a job with the casino enterprise. "That floorman has six working points in the casino."

Wrong Bettor, Wrong Player, Wrongie CRAPS: A player who bets the dice to lose.

X (The) The control of all the gambling in town. "The Irish combination has the X on the town."

Yard $100.

Zing It In To bet heavily, particularly to parlay one's winnings.

INDEX

Ace-deuce bar, 137
"African dominoes," 136
Agents
  cheating by, 42
  steer joints and, 60
Aladdin Hotel Casino, 129, 310
American Airlines, 56
American Hotel Casino, Puerto Rico, 56
American Hoyle, 72, 198
American Magazine, 59
American Mathematics Society, 113
Arnold, Gen. H. H. ("Hap"), 59
Atlantic City casinos, 27, 43, 59
  Black Jack in, 63
  boring type of gambling in, 47
  gambling history and, 42–48
  hotel requirements for, 45
  possible bankruptcies in, 46
  privately owned, 44
  rip-offs in, 29
  Roulette in, 229
  unfavorable rules for, 46–47

Baccara, 72, 257
Baccarat, 27, 43, 46, 48
  biggest loss in, 257
  crooked dealing shoes in, 270
  earning power of, 62
  house percentage in, 267, 327
  Las Vegas style, 263–64
  maximum betting at, 47
  Scarne's rules for, 264
  side bets in, 21
  table in, 264
Baccarat à Deux Tableaux, 271–72
Baccarat-Chemin de Fer, 27, 29, 256–63
  advice to players in, 267
  cheating at, 268–70
  house percentage in, 23
  percentages against players in, 265–67
Baccarat-en-Banque, 256, 271–72
Backgammon, 132, 184
Bagatelle, 254
Baker, Con, 34, 173
Baldwin, Roger R., 113–14
Bally Manufacturing Co., 235

Bank Craps, 31, 40, 43, 57, 130–87
  see also Dice; Private Craps
  ace-deuce standoff in, 154
  bets in, 151–64
  biggest loss in, 133–35
  Big Six and Big Eight in, 155–56
  Come and Don't Come bets in, 154
  Come-out bets in, 159–62
  defined, 135
  dice tables in, 149–50
  Don't Pass line, 152
  double side dealer layouts in, 153
  earning power of, 62
  field bets in, 156–58
  gambling sensibly at, 168–69
  hardway bets in, 158–59
  Hazard and, 298
  high rollers in, 134
  house percentage in, 23, 134, 151, 154,
    157–61, 163, 168, 197
  Las Vegas style, 148–50, 153
  loser line in, 154
  Miami bets in, 161
  Monte and, 303–04
  one-roll action in, 159–62
  Philadelphia layout in, 137
  place or box number bets in, 162–64
  record $400,000 win at, 132–33
  right and wrong way system in, 195–96
  Santurce bets in, 161
  Scarne's system in, 196–97
  Scarney layout in, 151
  "unfinished hand" in, 133–35
  win line in, 152
Banker and Broker, 73
Barbouth, 27, 301–02
Barbudey, 301
Barn, The (Lodi, N.J.), 32–33, 53, 169
Batista, Fulgencio, 68
Batisti, Analito, 68, 268
Beach Club (Palm Beach), 38–39
Beat the Banker, 299
Beat the Dealer, 299
Beat the Dealer (Thorp), 19–20, 69, 111–
    112, 114–17, 296
Beat the Shaker, 27, 299–300